MY HERO ACADEMIA Vol.25

Tomura Shigaraki: Origin

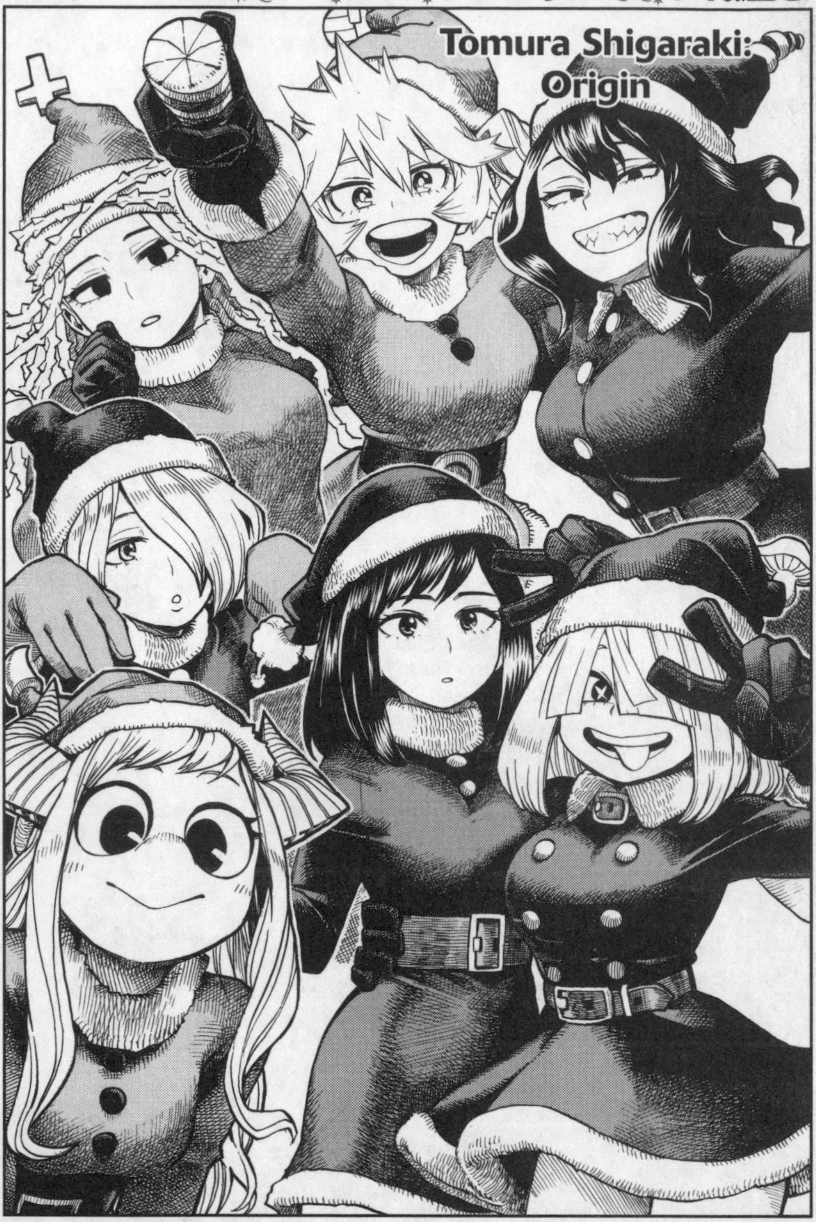

KOHEI HORIKOSHI

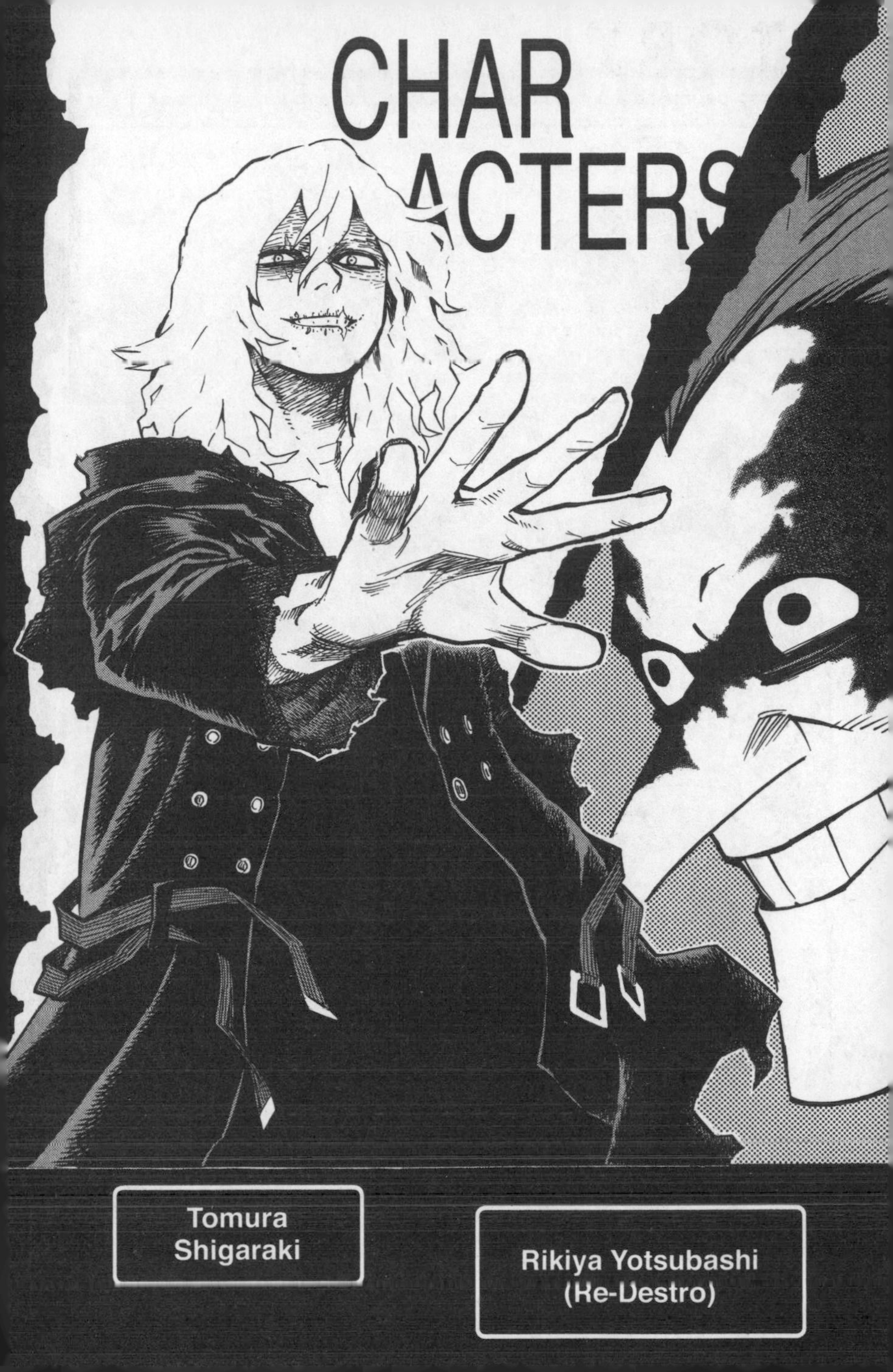
CHARACTERS
Tomura Shigaraki
Rikiya Yotsubashi (Re-Destro)

STORY

One day, people began manifesting special abilities that came to be known as "Quirks," and before long, the world was full of superpowered humans. But with the advent of these exceptional individuals came an increase in crime, and governments alone were unable to deal with the situation. At the same time, others emerged to oppose the spread of evil! As if straight from the comic books, these heroes keep the peace and are even officially authorized to fight crime. Our story begins when a certain Quirkless boy and lifelong hero fan meets the world's number one hero, starting him on his path to becoming the greatest hero ever!

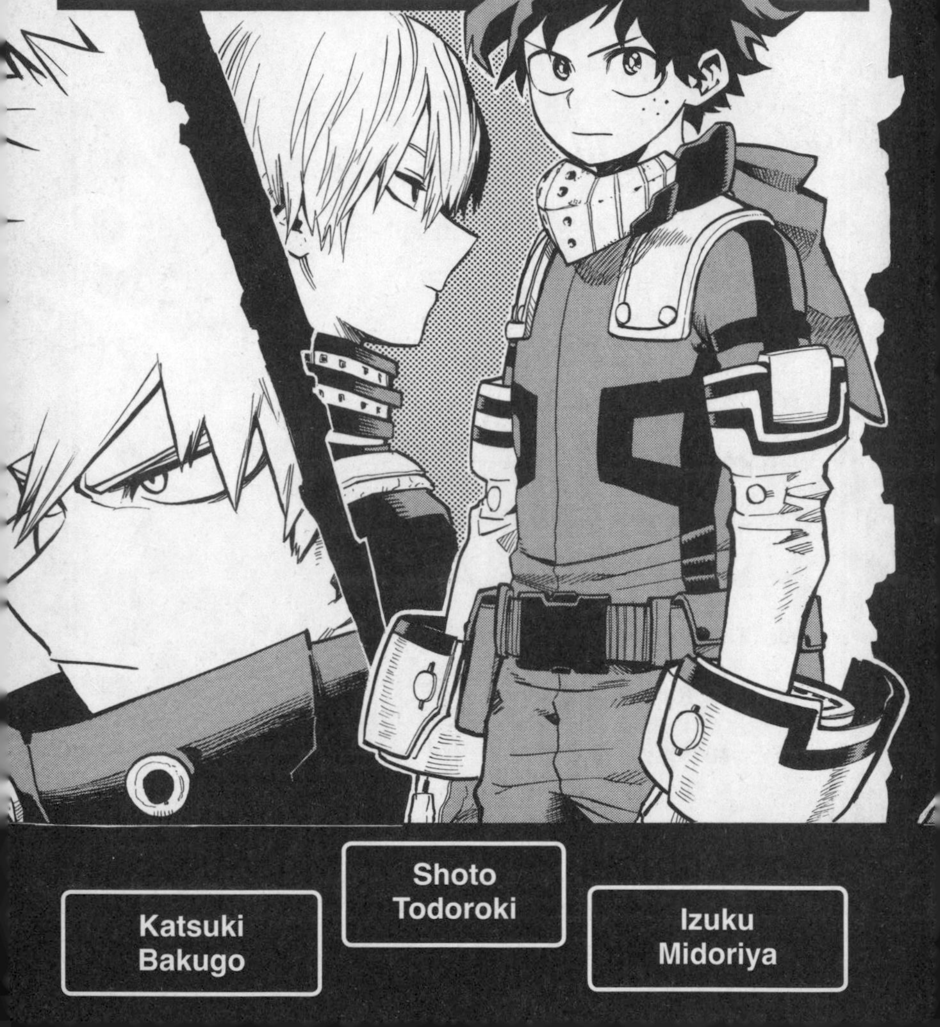
Shoto Todoroki
Katsuki Bakugo
Izuku Midoriya

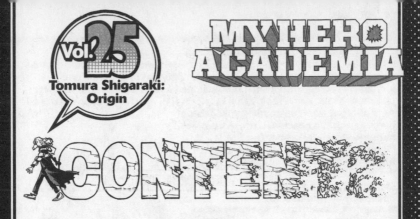

Vol. 25
Tomura Shigaraki: Origin

MY HERO ACADEMIA

CONTENTS

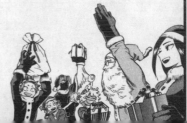

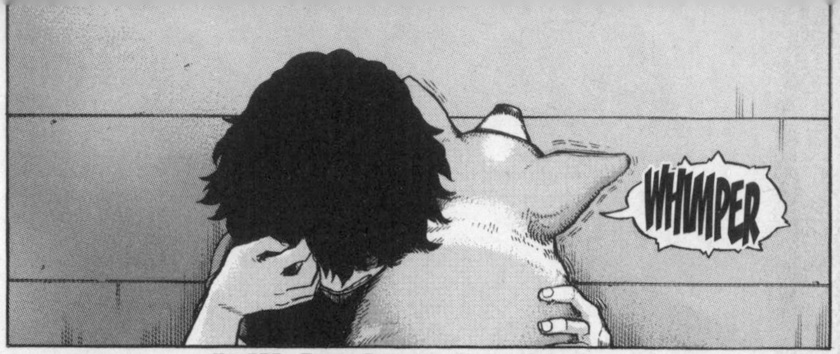
WHIMPER

No. 236 - Tenko Shimura: Origin, Part 2

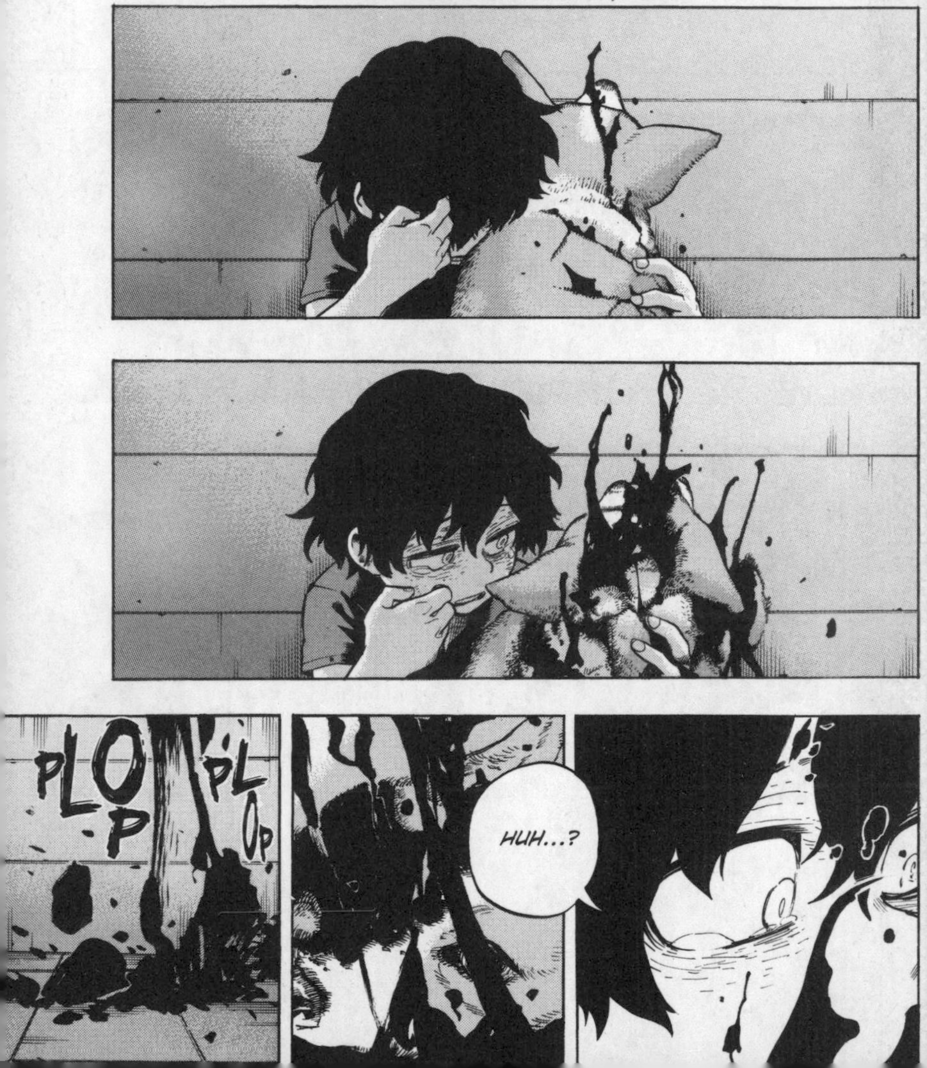
HUH...?
PLOP
PLOP

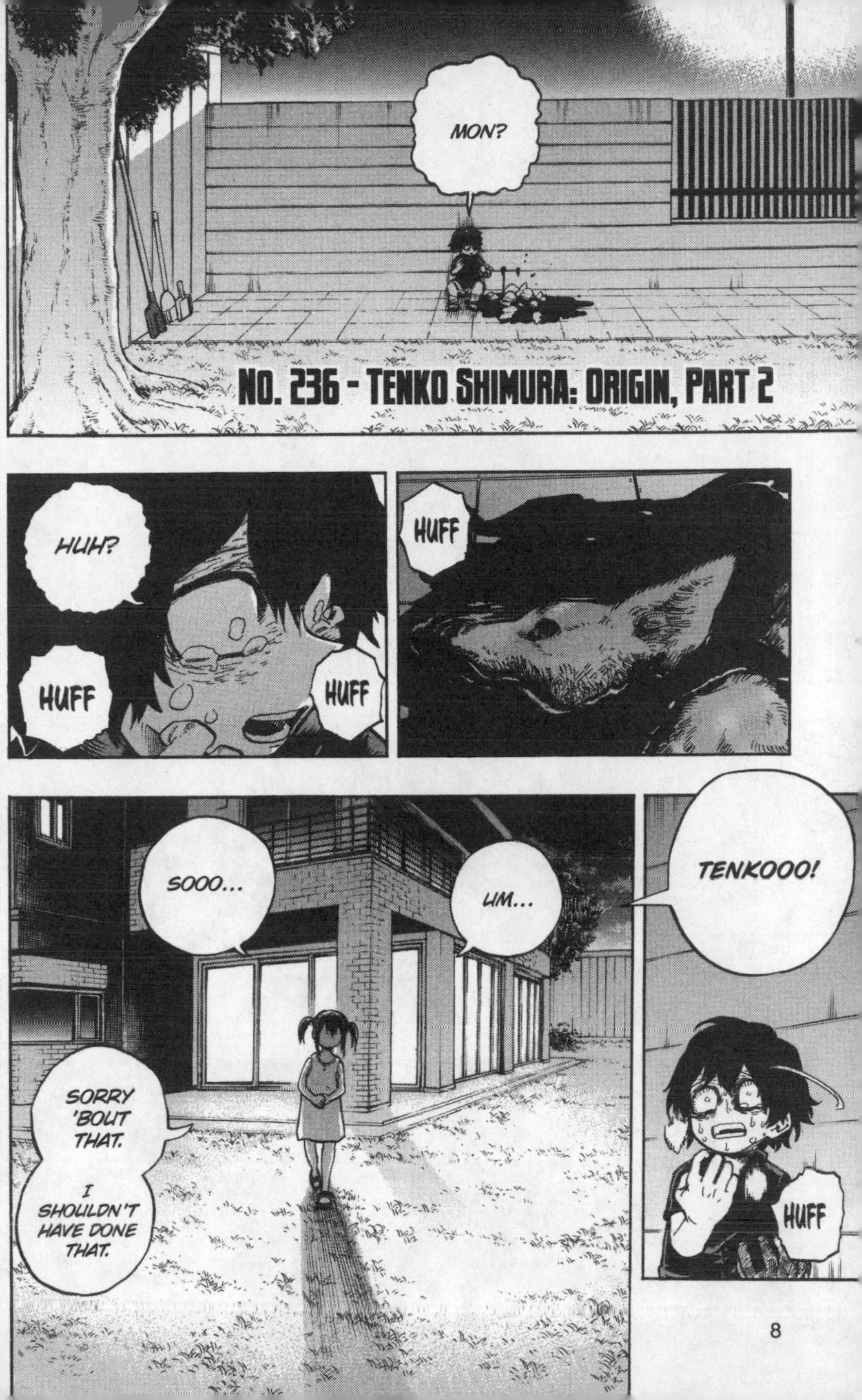
MON?
NO. 236 - TENKO SHIMURA: ORIGIN, PART 2
HUFF
HUH?
HUFF
HUFF
TENKOOO!
HUFF
UM...
SOOO...
SORRY 'BOUT THAT.
I SHOULDN'T HAVE DONE THAT.

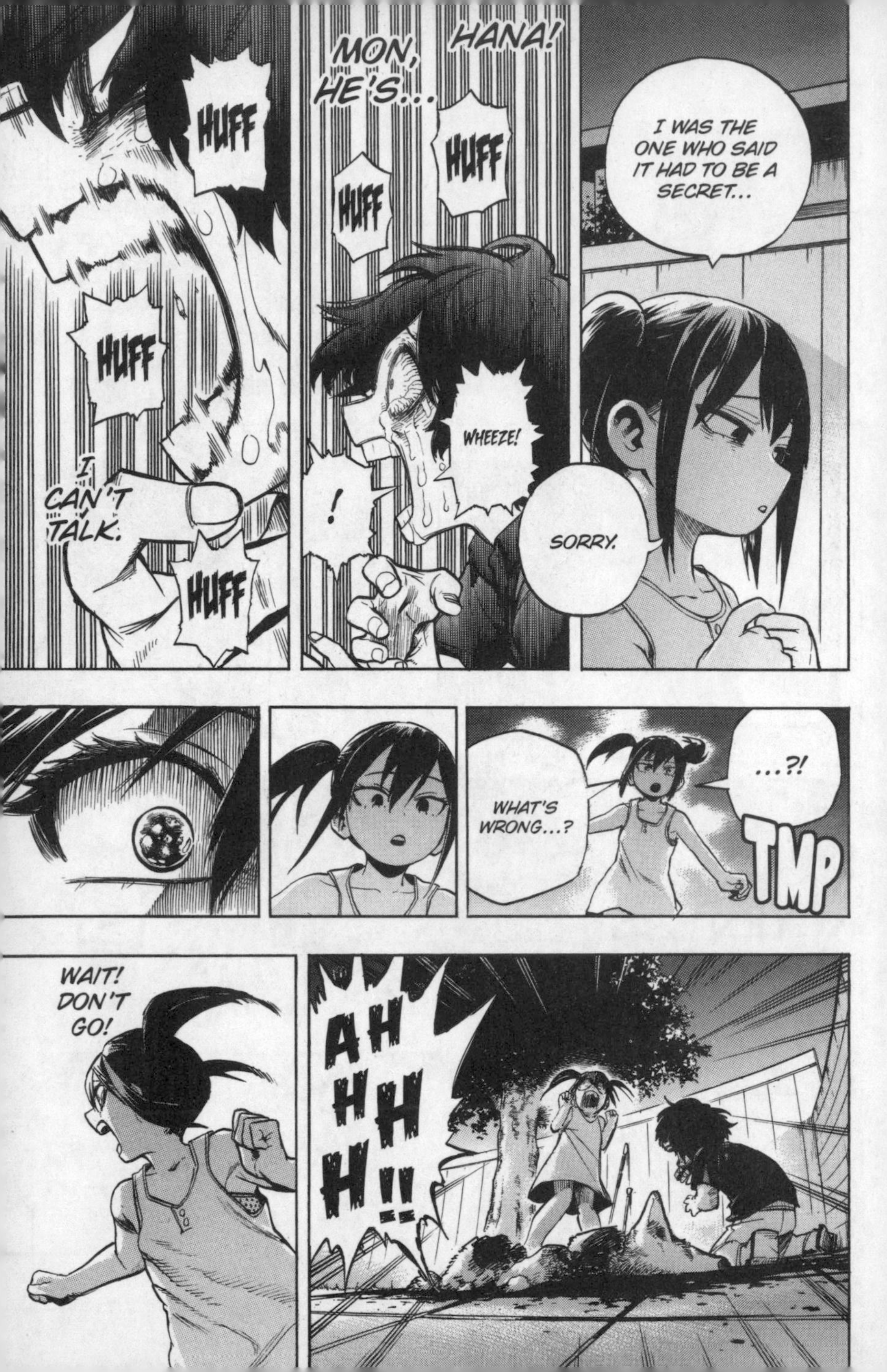
I WAS THE ONE WHO SAID IT HAD TO BE A SECRET...
SORRY.
HANA!
MON, HE'S...
HUFF
HUFF
WHEEZE!
!
HUFF
HUFF
I CAN'T TALK.
HUFF
...?!
TMP
WHAT'S WRONG...?
AHHHH!!
WAIT! DON'T GO!

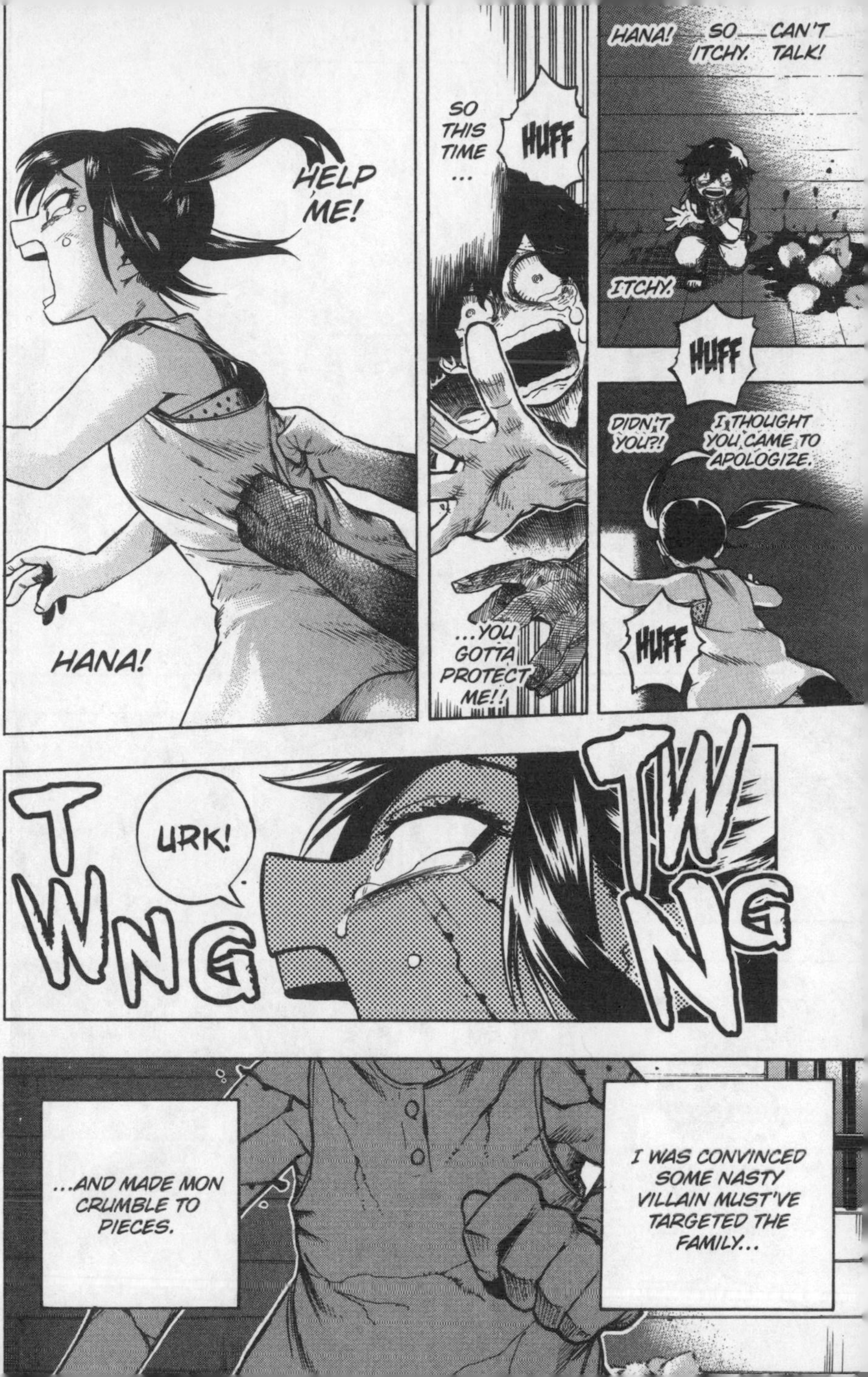
CAN'T TALK!
SO— ITCHY.
HANA!
ITCHY.
HUFF
I THOUGHT YOU CAME TO APOLOGIZE.
DIDN'T YOU?!
HUFF
SO THIS TIME...
HUFF
...YOU GOTTA PROTECT ME!!
HELP ME!
HANA!
TWNG
URK!
TWNG
I WAS CONVINCED SOME NASTY VILLAIN MUST'VE TARGETED THE FAMILY...
...AND MADE MON CRUMBLE TO PIECES.

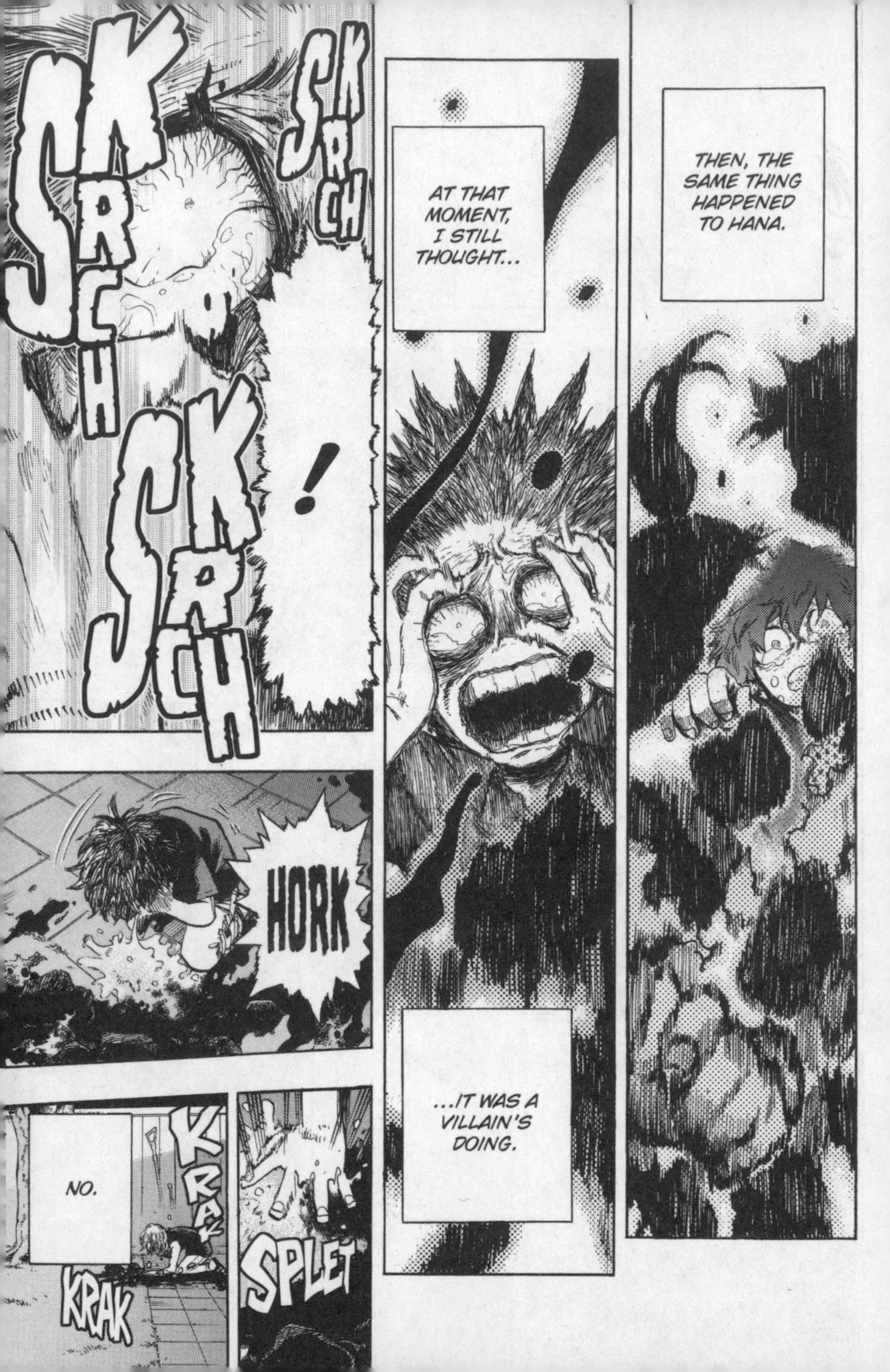
THEN, THE SAME THING HAPPENED TO HANA.
AT THAT MOMENT, I STILL THOUGHT...
...IT WAS A VILLAIN'S DOING.
SKRCH
SKRCH
SKRCH
!
HORK
SPLET
KRAK
NO.
KRAK

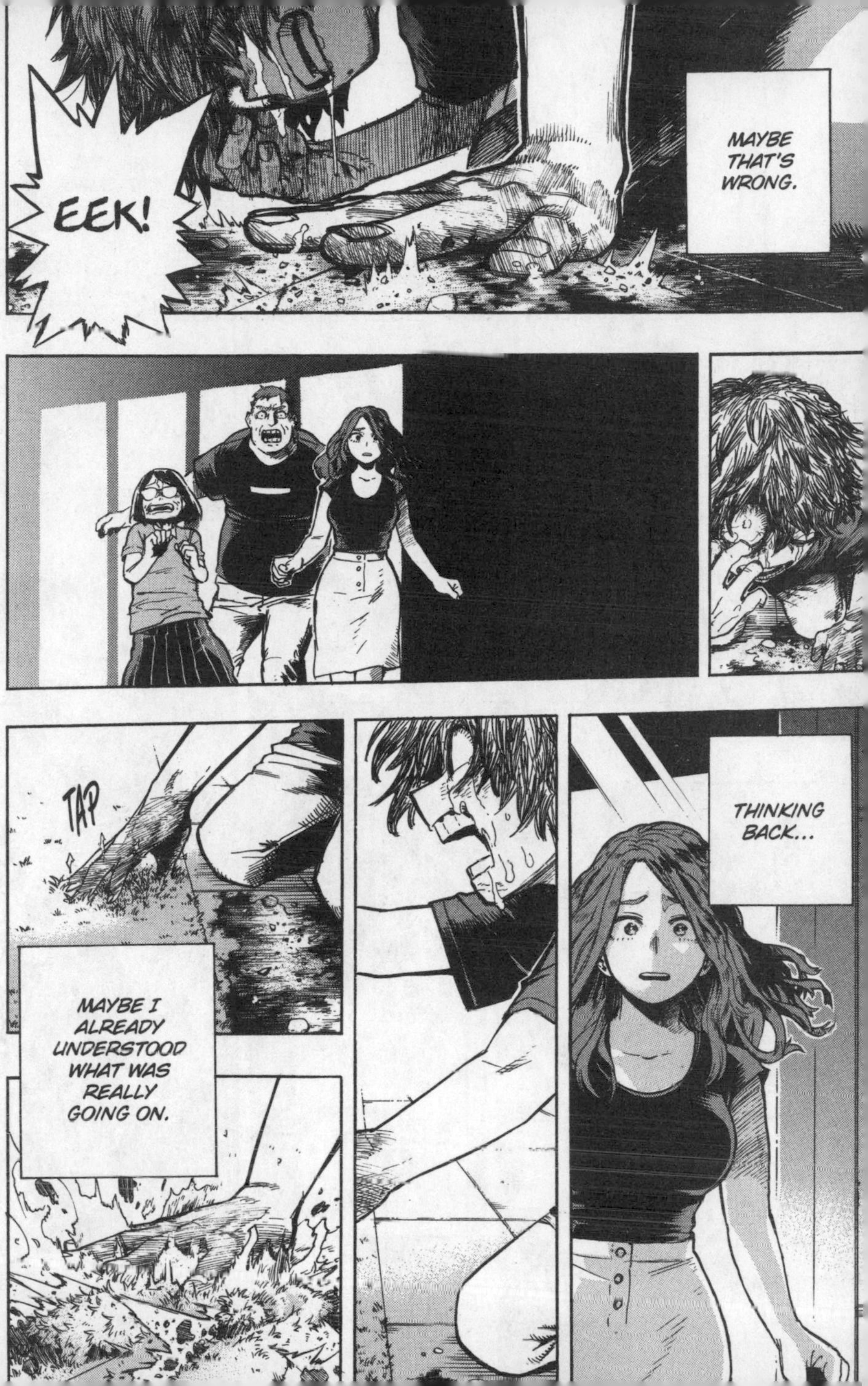
MAYBE THAT'S WRONG.
EEK!
THINKING BACK...
TAP
MAYBE I ALREADY UNDERSTOOD WHAT WAS REALLY GOING ON.

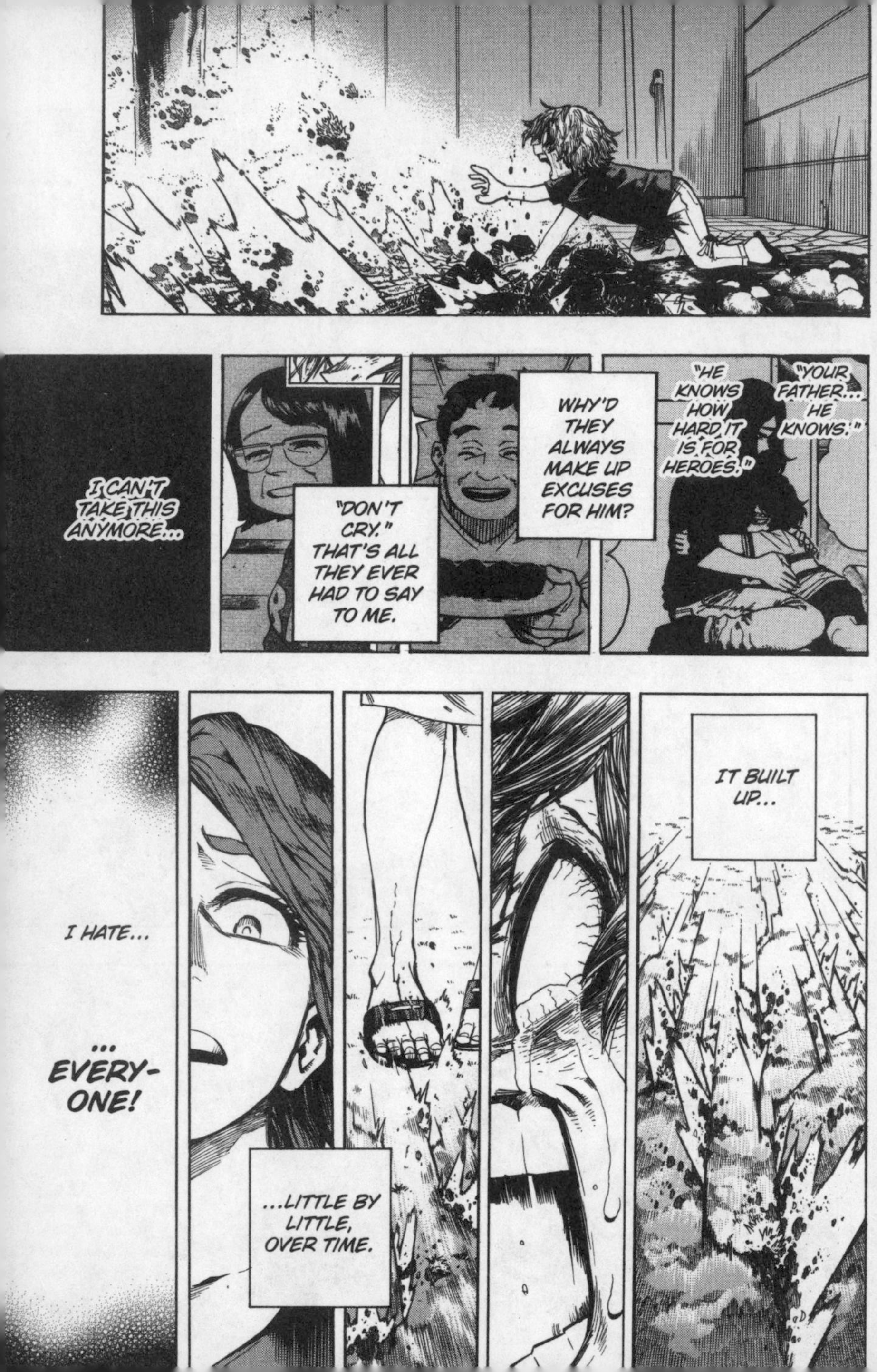
"YOUR FATHER... HE KNOWS."
"HE KNOWS HOW HARD IT IS FOR HEROES."
WHY'D THEY ALWAYS MAKE UP EXCUSES FOR HIM?
"DON'T CRY." THAT'S ALL THEY EVER HAD TO SAY TO ME.
I CAN'T TAKE THIS ANYMORE...
IT BUILT UP...
...LITTLE BY LITTLE, OVER TIME.
I HATE...
...EVERY-ONE!

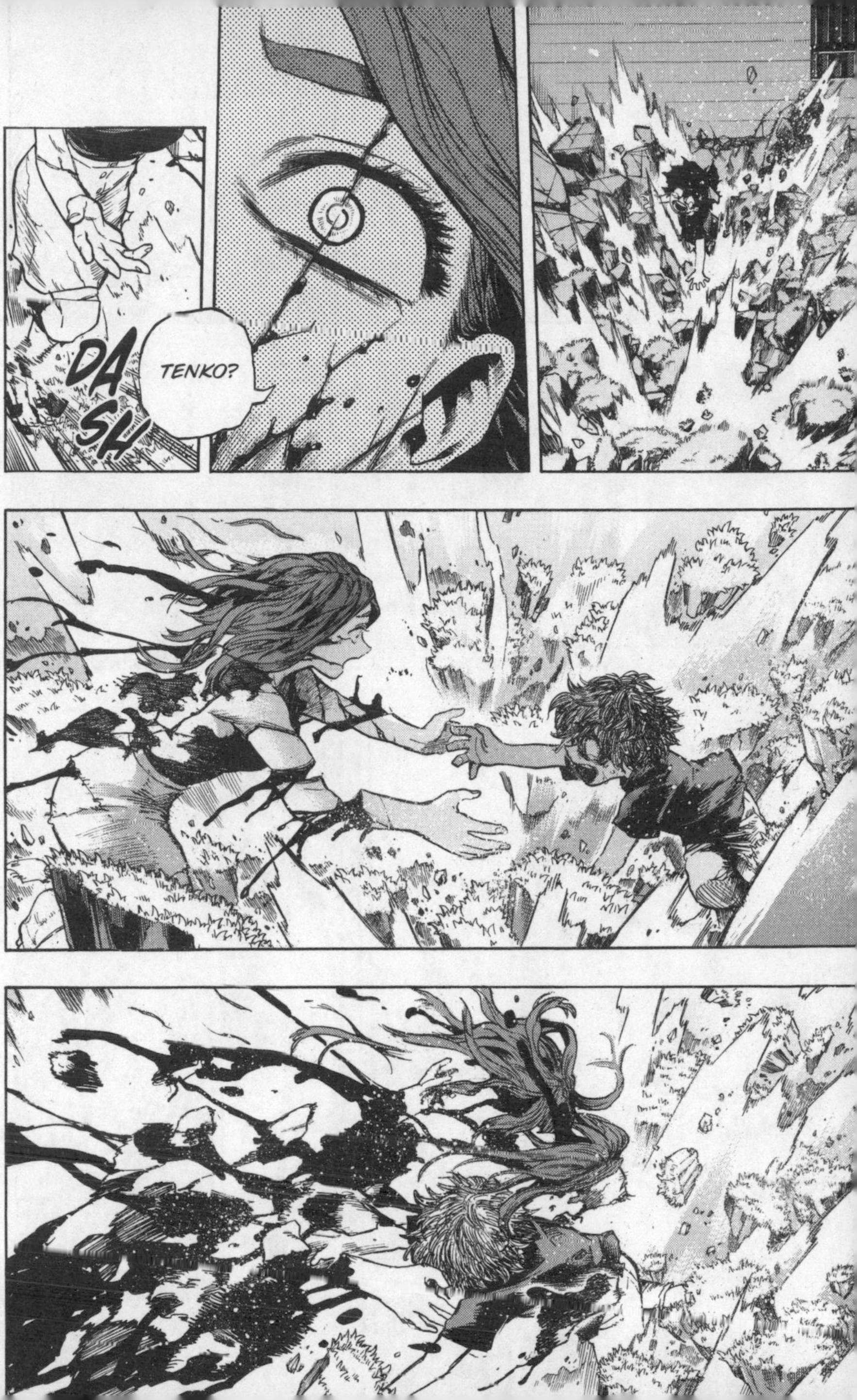
TENKO?
DASH

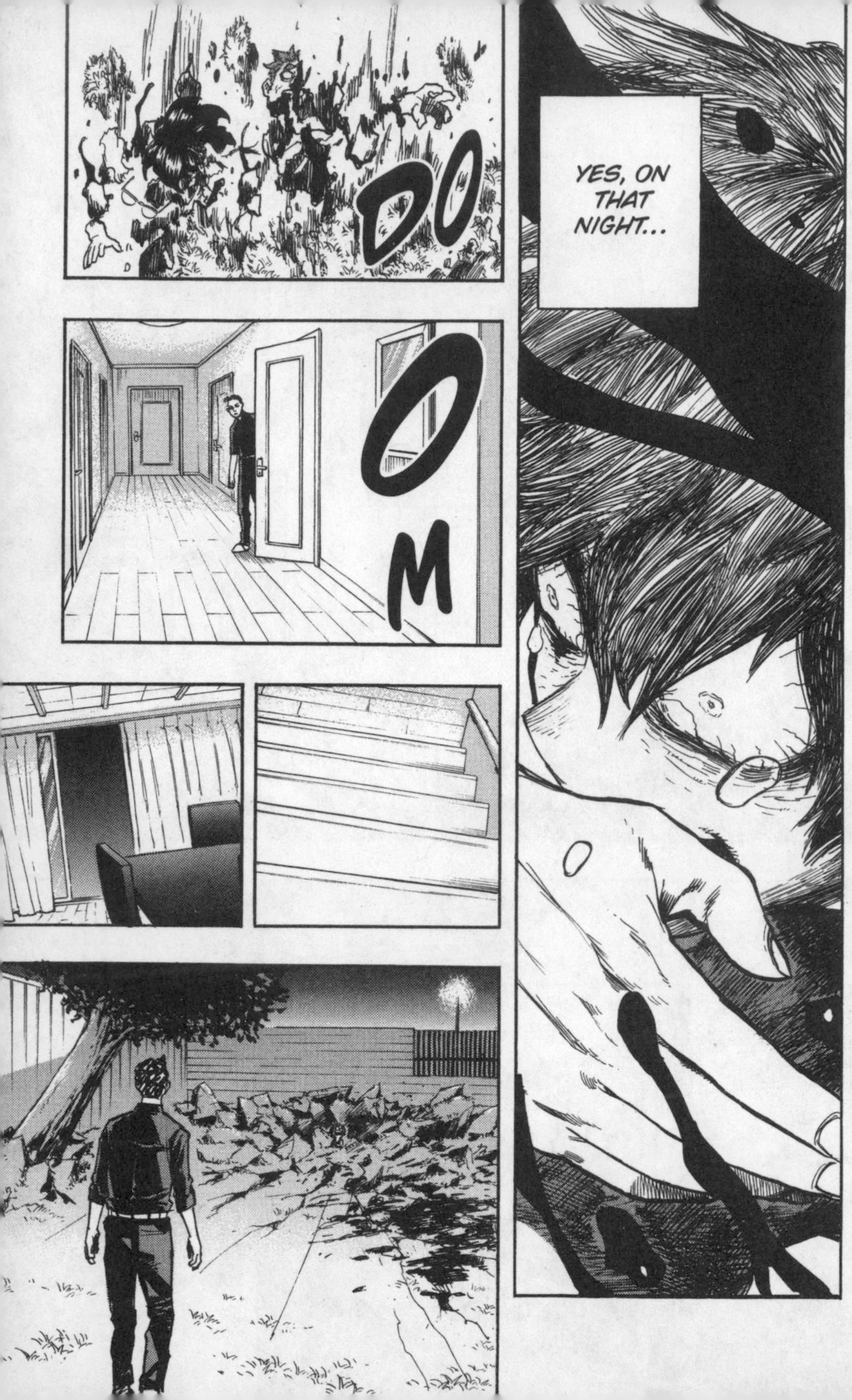
YES, ON THAT NIGHT...
DO
O
M

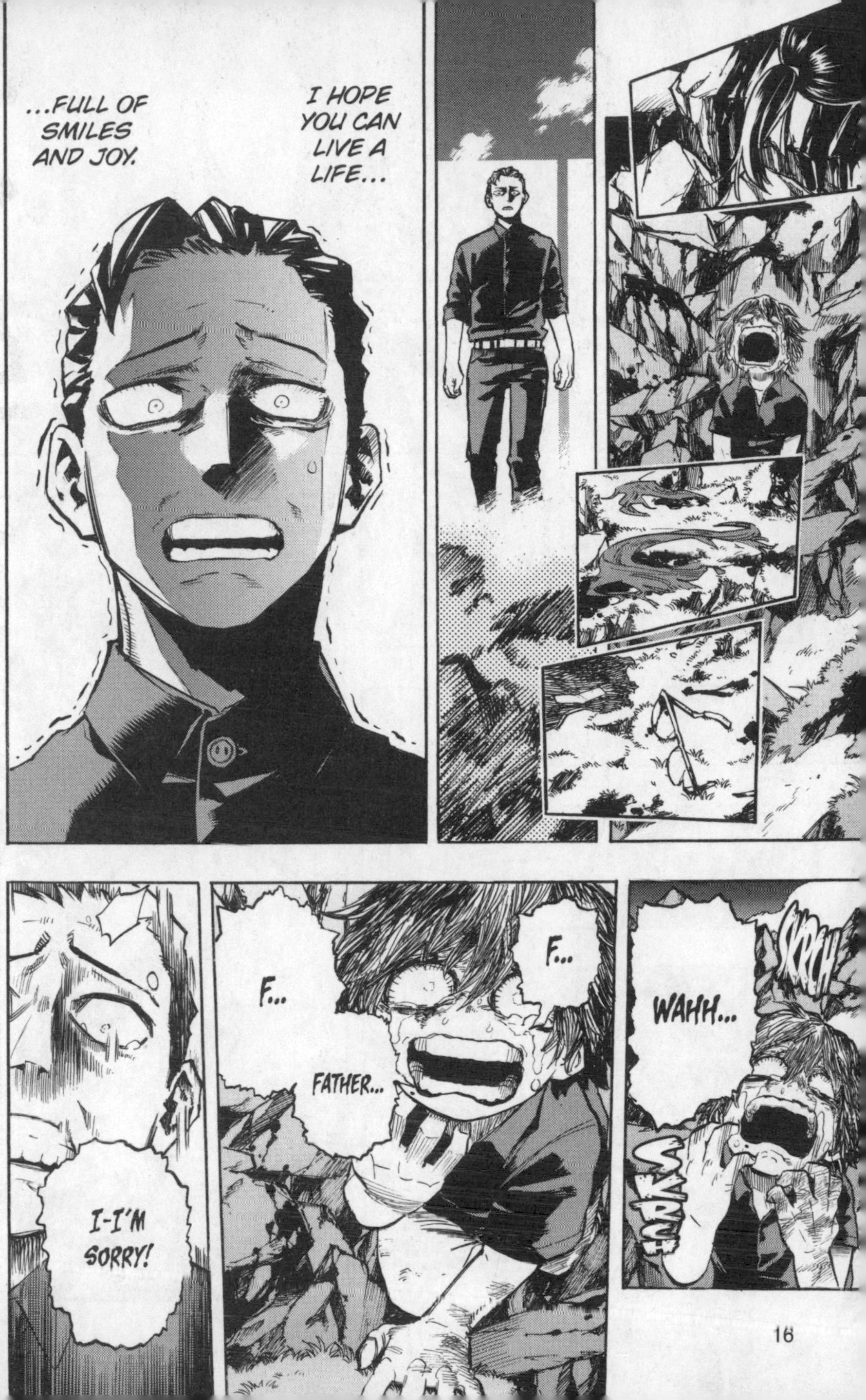
I HOPE YOU CAN LIVE A LIFE...
...FULL OF SMILES AND JOY.
SKRCH
WAHH...
SKRCH
F...
F...
FATHER...
I-I'M SORRY!

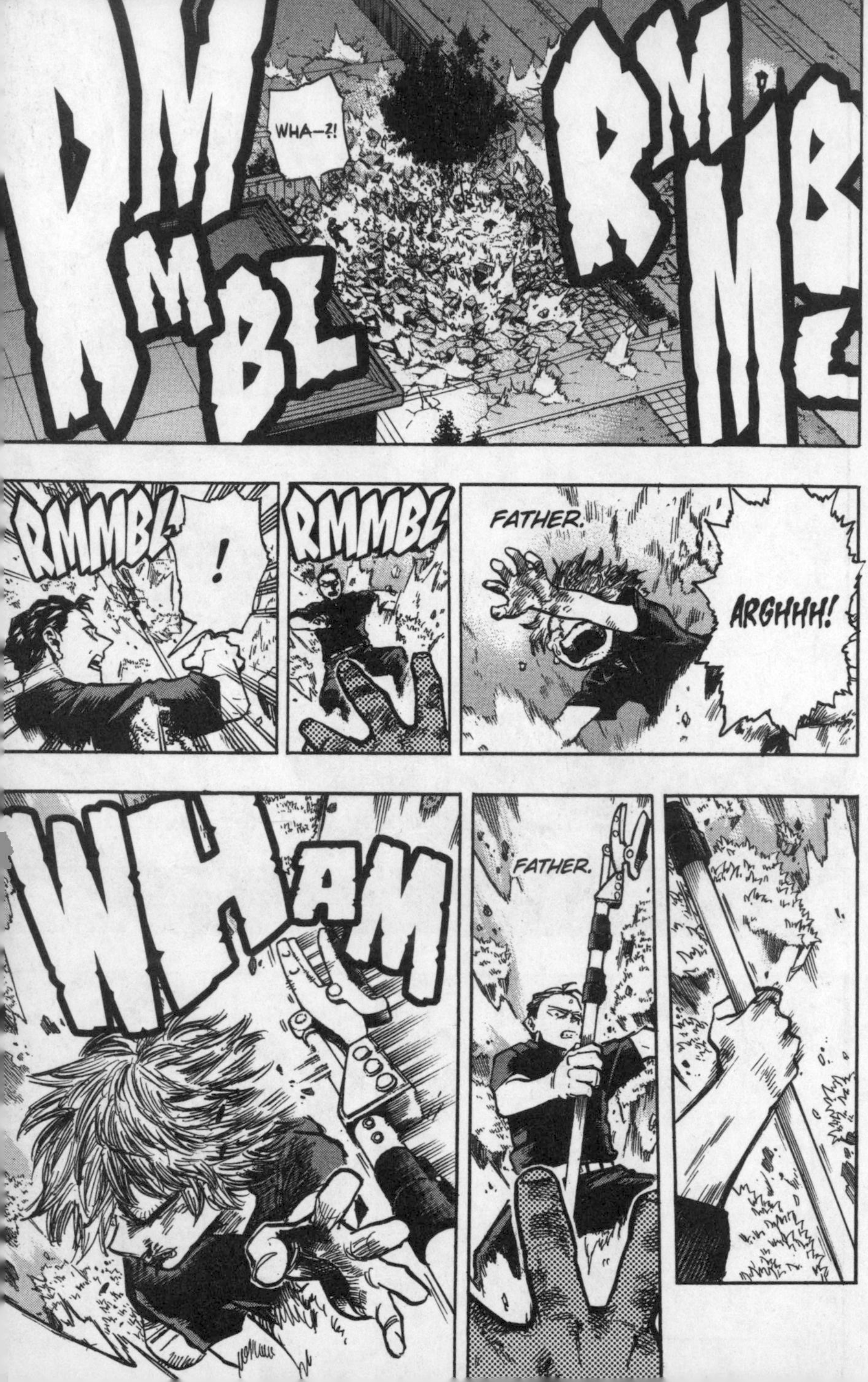
WHA—?!
FATHER.
ARGHHH!
RMMBL
RMMBL
!
FATHER.
WHAM

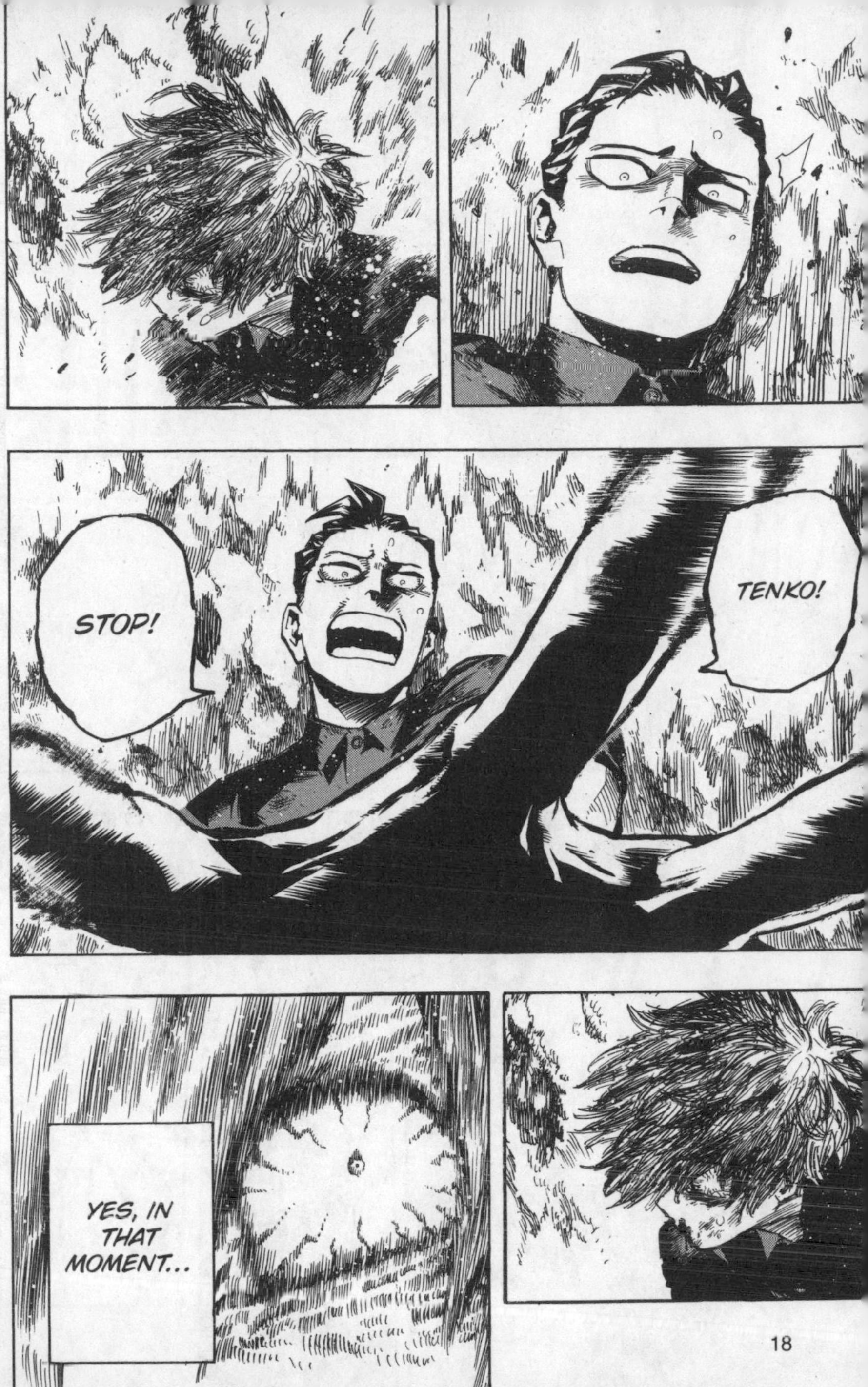
TENKO!
STOP!
YES, IN THAT MOMENT...

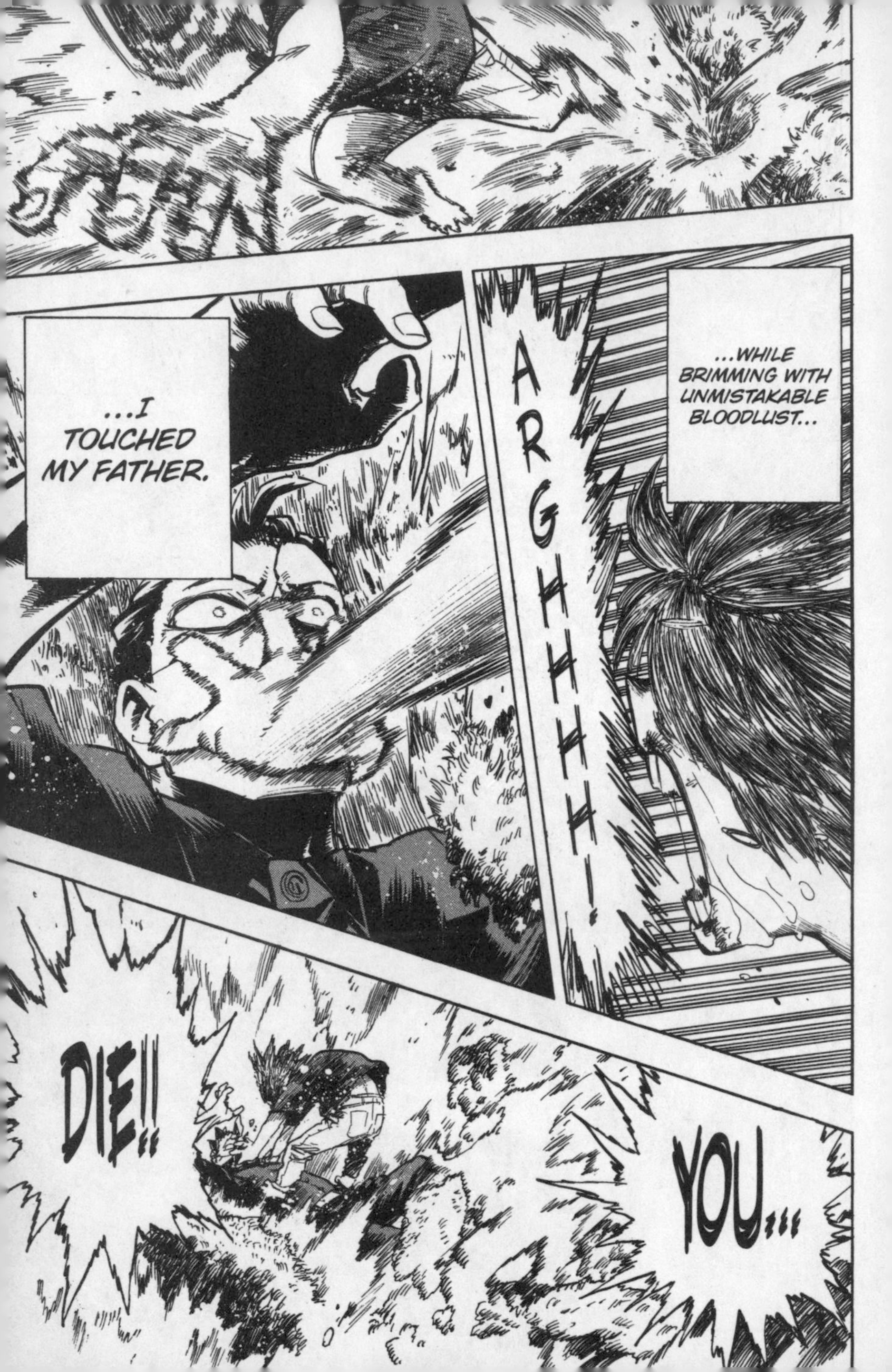

...WHILE BRIMMING WITH UNMISTAKABLE BLOODLUST...
ARGHHHH!
...I TOUCHED MY FATHER.
YOU...
DIE!!

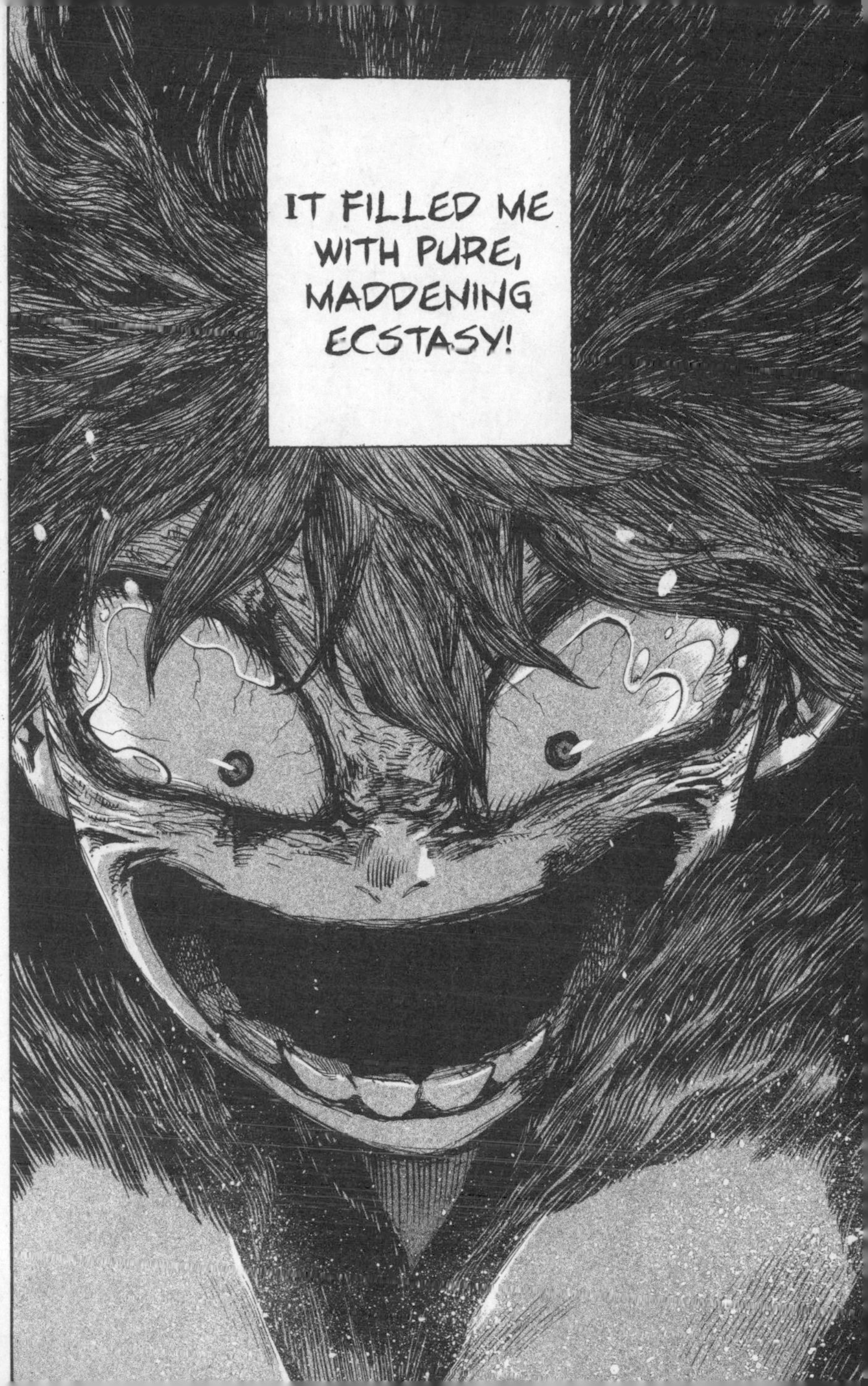
IT FILLED ME WITH PURE, MADDENING ECSTASY!

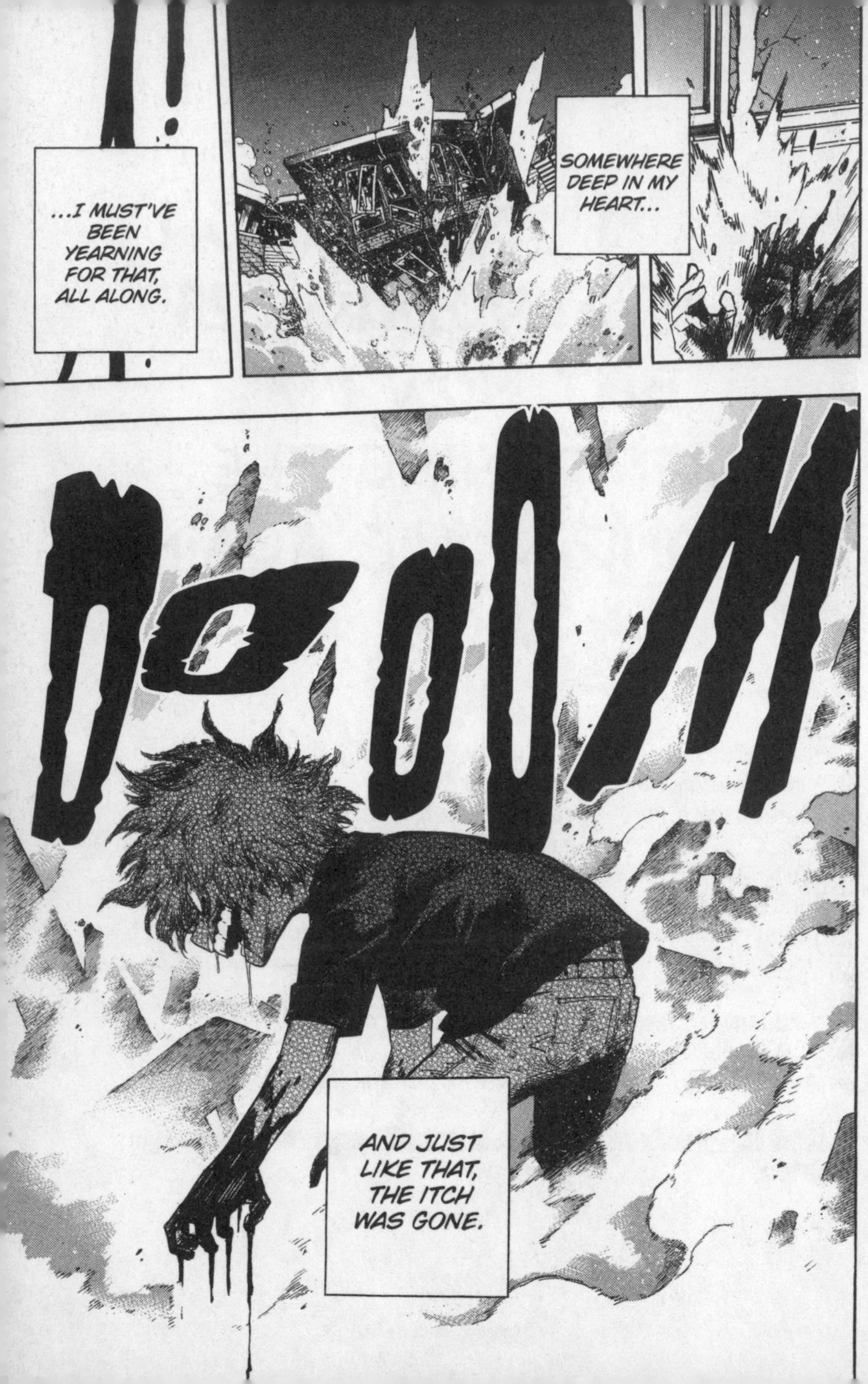
SOMEWHERE DEEP IN MY HEART...
...I MUST'VE BEEN YEARNING FOR THAT, ALL ALONG.
DOOOM
AND JUST LIKE THAT, THE ITCH WAS GONE.

THE "I TOUCHED ON THIS IN VOLUME 23 BUT NOW I'M MENTIONING THE SECOND MOVIE AGAIN" PAGE!

If I had a container where I was depositing all my gratefulness, it'd be overflowing and filling up the entire room at this point. I haven't seen the movie yet myself, but I'm excited as heck about it. This one fits into the timeline of the manga and takes place around the events of this very volume. Shocking, right? I think it'll still be fun for those who don't read the manga, but I bet if you see it after reading this far in the story, you'll find yourself nodding knowingly about various things that pop up.

And Hawks hasn't shown up in the anime yet, either.

All that aside, let's get rolling with volume 25!

Oh? It's already rolling? This is actually page 22? Whaddaya know!

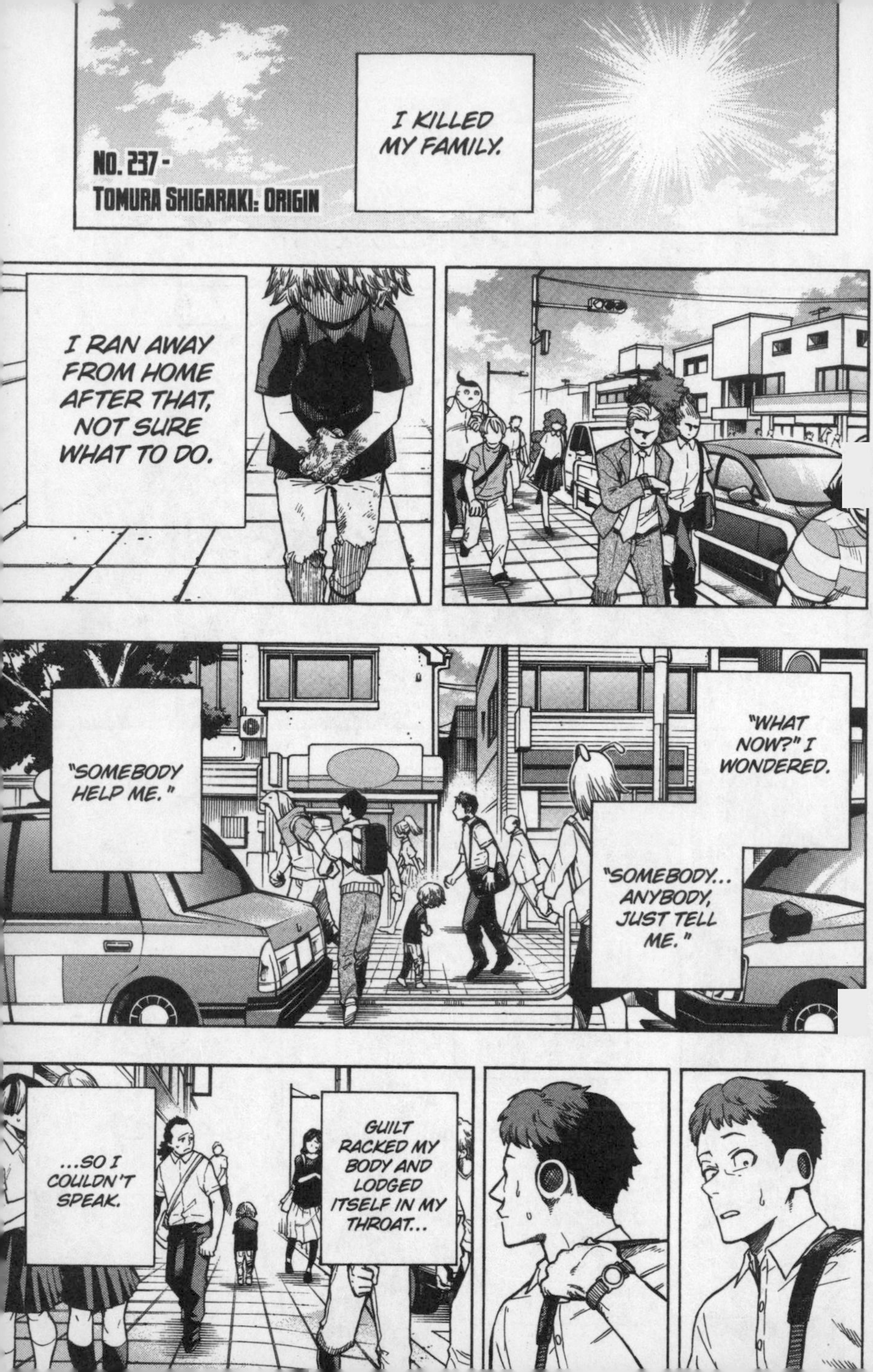
I KILLED MY FAMILY.
NO. 237 - TOMURA SHIGARAKI: ORIGIN
I RAN AWAY FROM HOME AFTER THAT, NOT SURE WHAT TO DO.
"WHAT NOW?" I WONDERED.
"SOMEBODY... ANYBODY, JUST TELL ME."
"SOMEBODY HELP ME."
GUILT RACKED MY BODY AND LODGED ITSELF IN MY THROAT...
...SO I COULDN'T SPEAK.

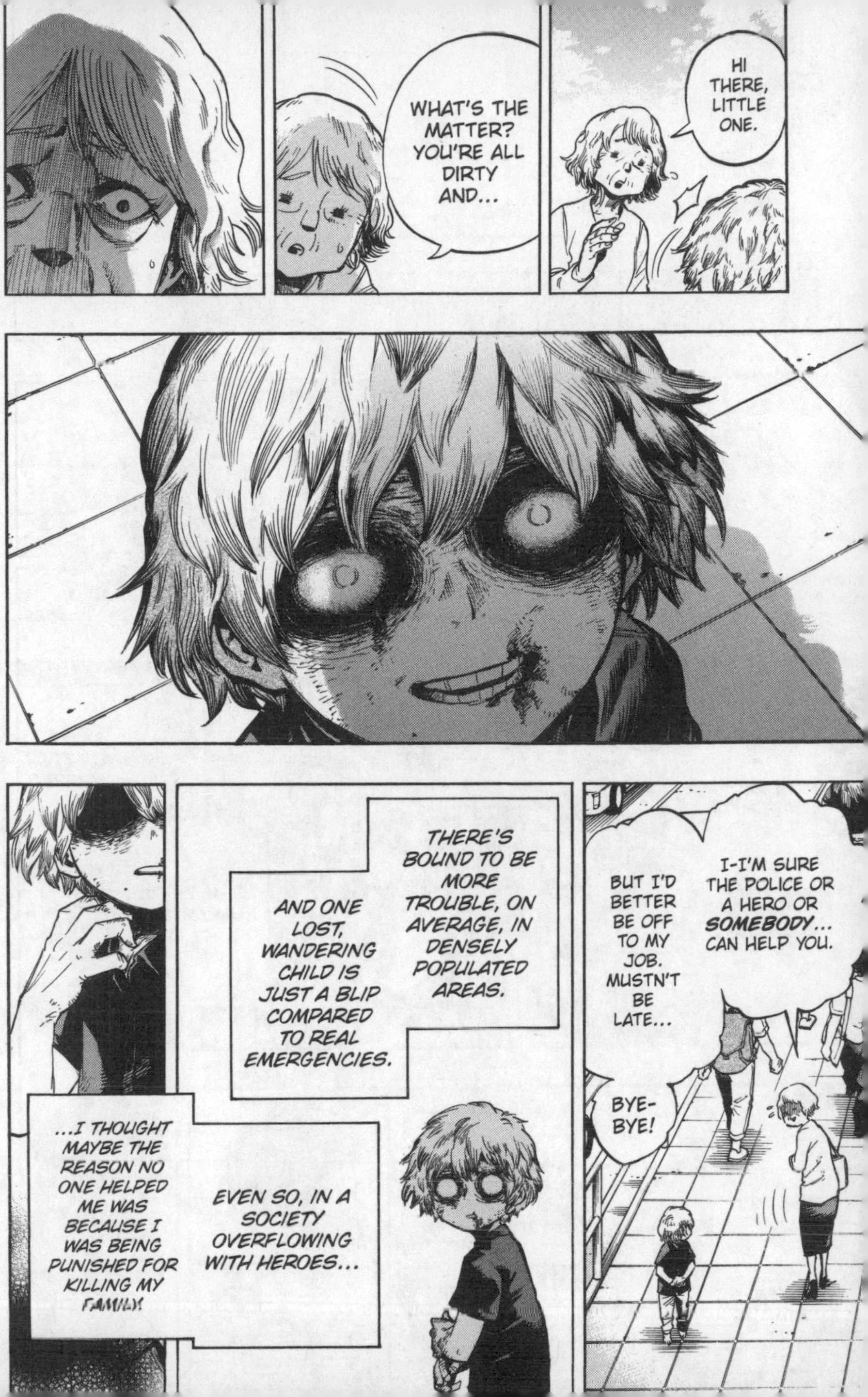
HI THERE, LITTLE ONE.
WHAT'S THE MATTER? YOU'RE ALL DIRTY AND...
I-I'M SURE THE POLICE OR A HERO OR ***SOMEBODY***... CAN HELP YOU.
BUT I'D BETTER BE OFF TO MY JOB. MUSTN'T BE LATE...
BYE-BYE!
THERE'S BOUND TO BE MORE TROUBLE, ON AVERAGE, IN DENSELY POPULATED AREAS.
AND ONE LOST, WANDERING CHILD IS JUST A BLIP COMPARED TO REAL EMERGENCIES.
EVEN SO, IN A SOCIETY OVERFLOWING WITH HEROES...
...I THOUGHT MAYBE THE REASON NO ONE HELPED ME WAS BECAUSE I WAS BEING PUNISHED FOR KILLING MY FAMILY.

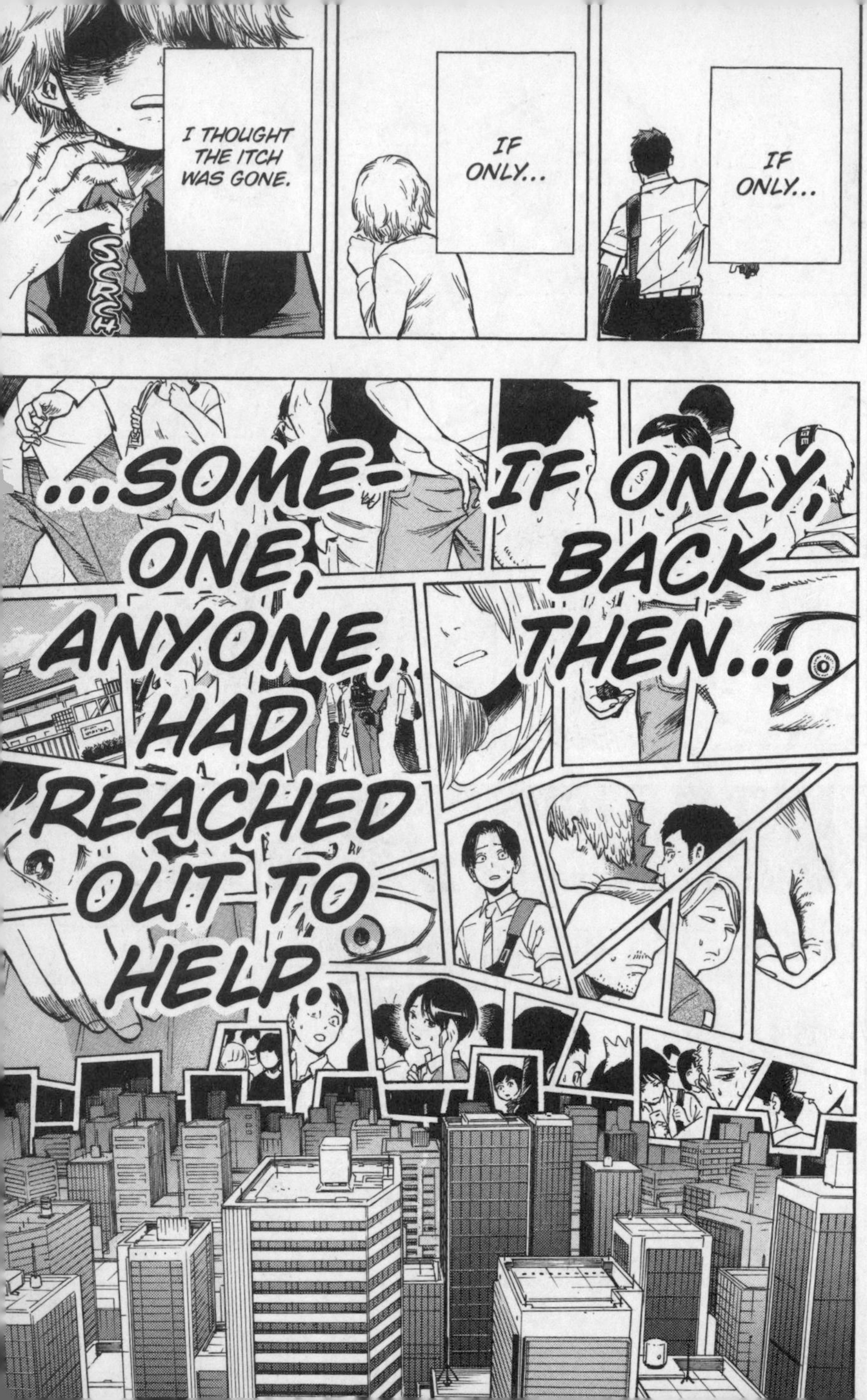
IF ONLY...
IF ONLY...
I THOUGHT THE ITCH WAS GONE.
SCRCH
IF ONLY, BACK THEN...
...SOME-ONE, ANYONE, HAD REACHED OUT TO HELP.

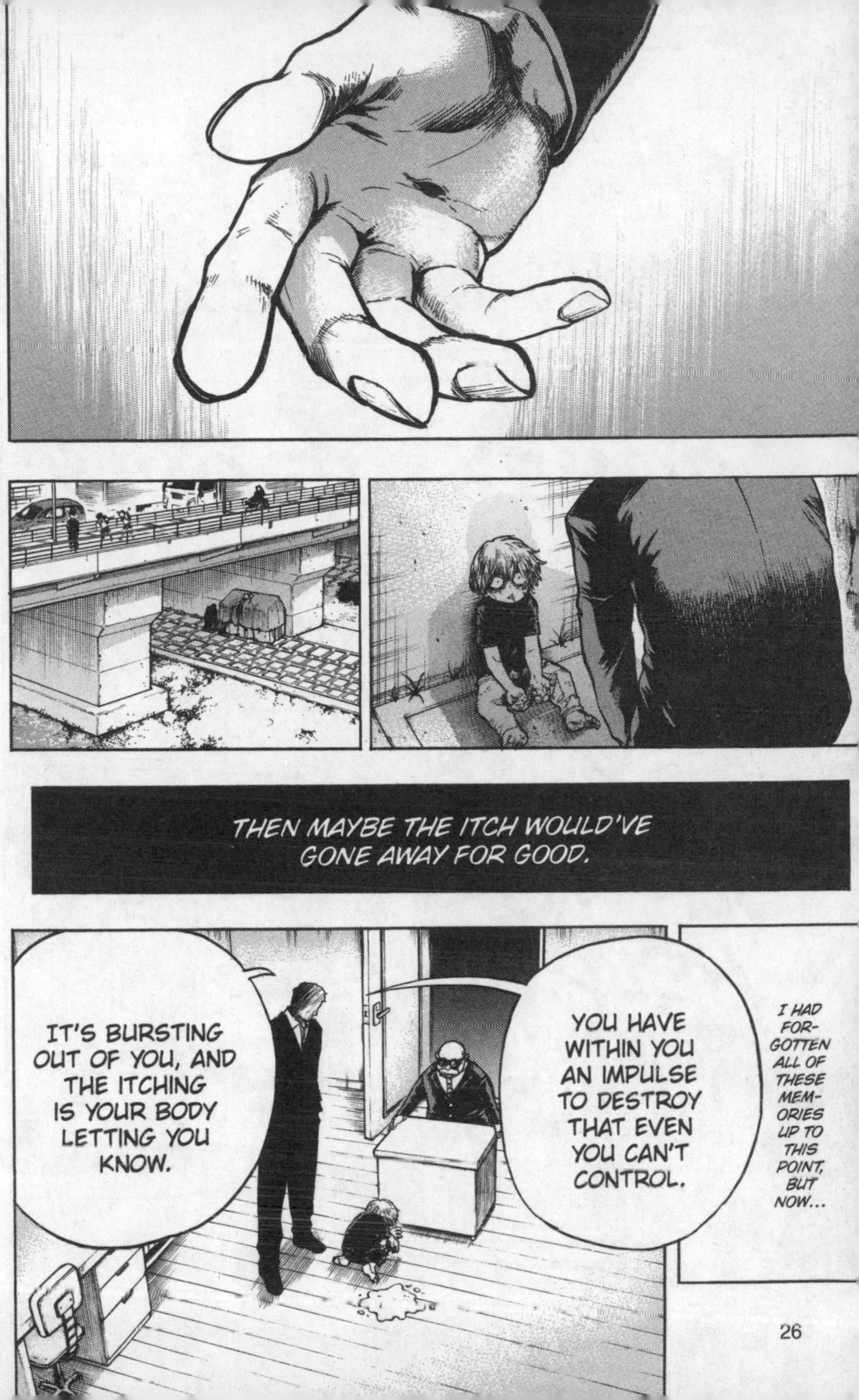
THEN MAYBE THE ITCH WOULD'VE GONE AWAY FOR GOOD.
I HAD FOR-GOTTEN ALL OF THESE MEM-ORIES UP TO THIS POINT, BUT NOW...
YOU HAVE WITHIN YOU AN IMPULSE TO DESTROY THAT EVEN YOU CAN'T CONTROL.
IT'S BURSTING OUT OF YOU, AND THE ITCHING IS YOUR BODY LETTING YOU KNOW.

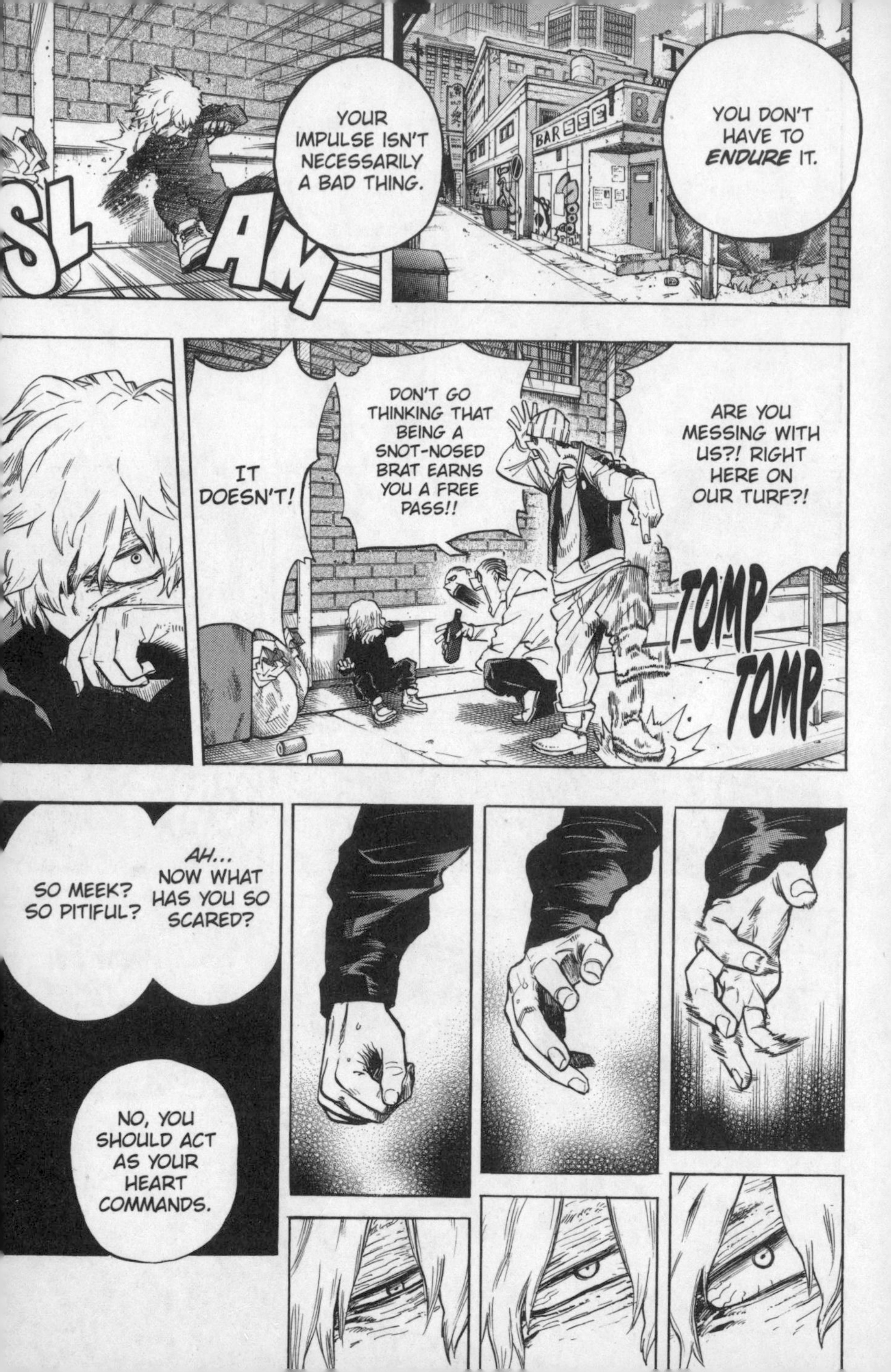
YOU DON'T HAVE TO *ENDURE* IT.
YOUR IMPULSE ISN'T NECESSARILY A BAD THING.
SLAM
ARE YOU MESSING WITH US?! RIGHT HERE ON OUR TURF?!
DON'T GO THINKING THAT BEING A SNOT-NOSED BRAT EARNS YOU A FREE PASS!!
IT DOESN'T!
TOMP TOMP
AH... NOW WHAT HAS YOU SO SCARED?
SO MEEK? SO PITIFUL?
NO, YOU SHOULD ACT AS YOUR HEART COMMANDS.

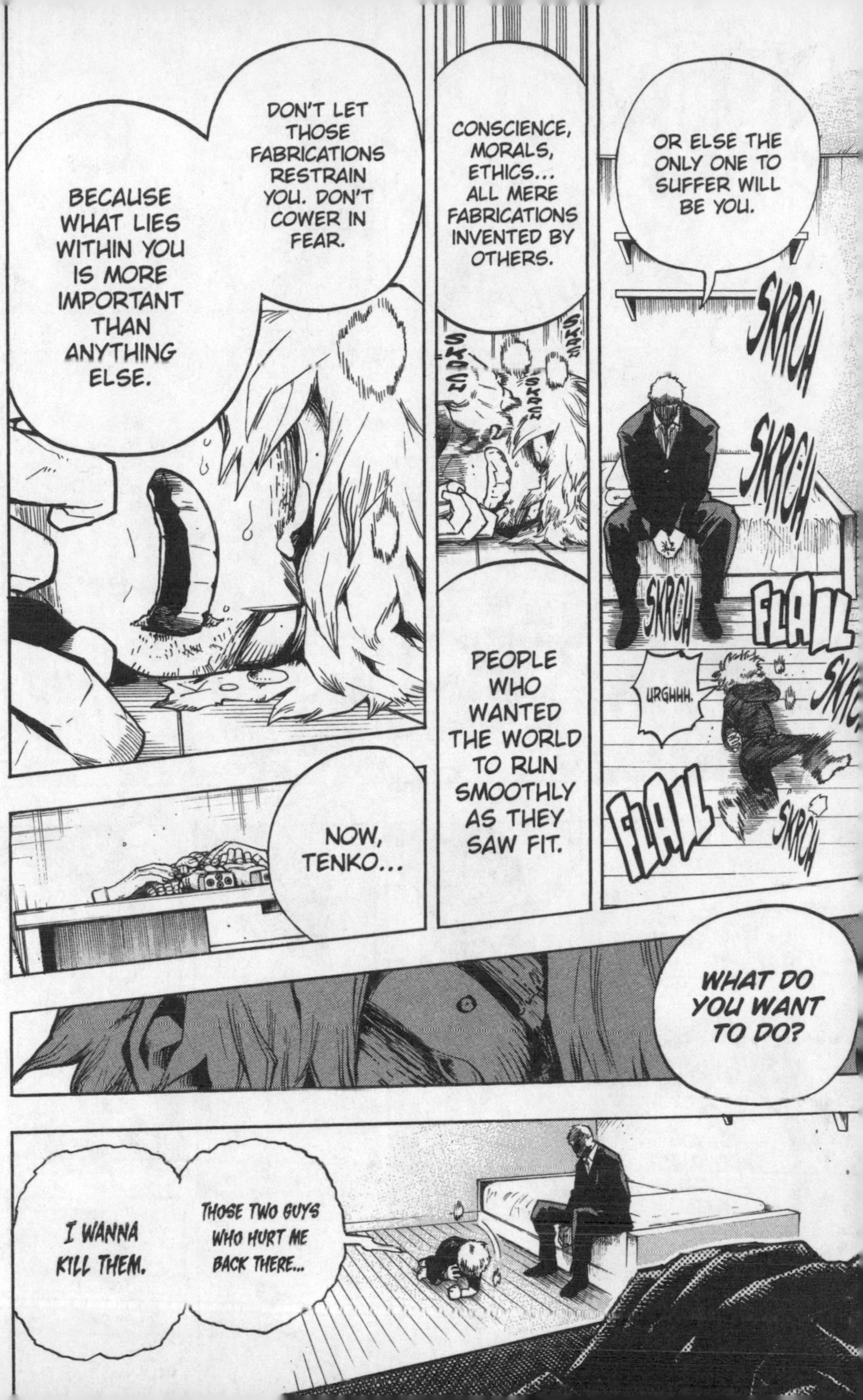
OR ELSE THE ONLY ONE TO SUFFER WILL BE YOU.
SKRCH
SKRCH
SKRCH
FLAIL
SKRCH
URGHHH.
FLAIL
SKRCH
CONSCIENCE, MORALS, ETHICS... ALL MERE FABRICATIONS INVENTED BY OTHERS.
SKRCH
SKRCH
SKRCH
PEOPLE WHO WANTED THE WORLD TO RUN SMOOTHLY AS THEY SAW FIT.
DON'T LET THOSE FABRICATIONS RESTRAIN YOU. DON'T COWER IN FEAR.
BECAUSE WHAT LIES WITHIN YOU IS MORE IMPORTANT THAN ANYTHING ELSE.
NOW, TENKO...
WHAT DO YOU WANT TO DO?
THOSE TWO GUYS WHO HURT ME BACK THERE...
I WANNA KILL THEM.

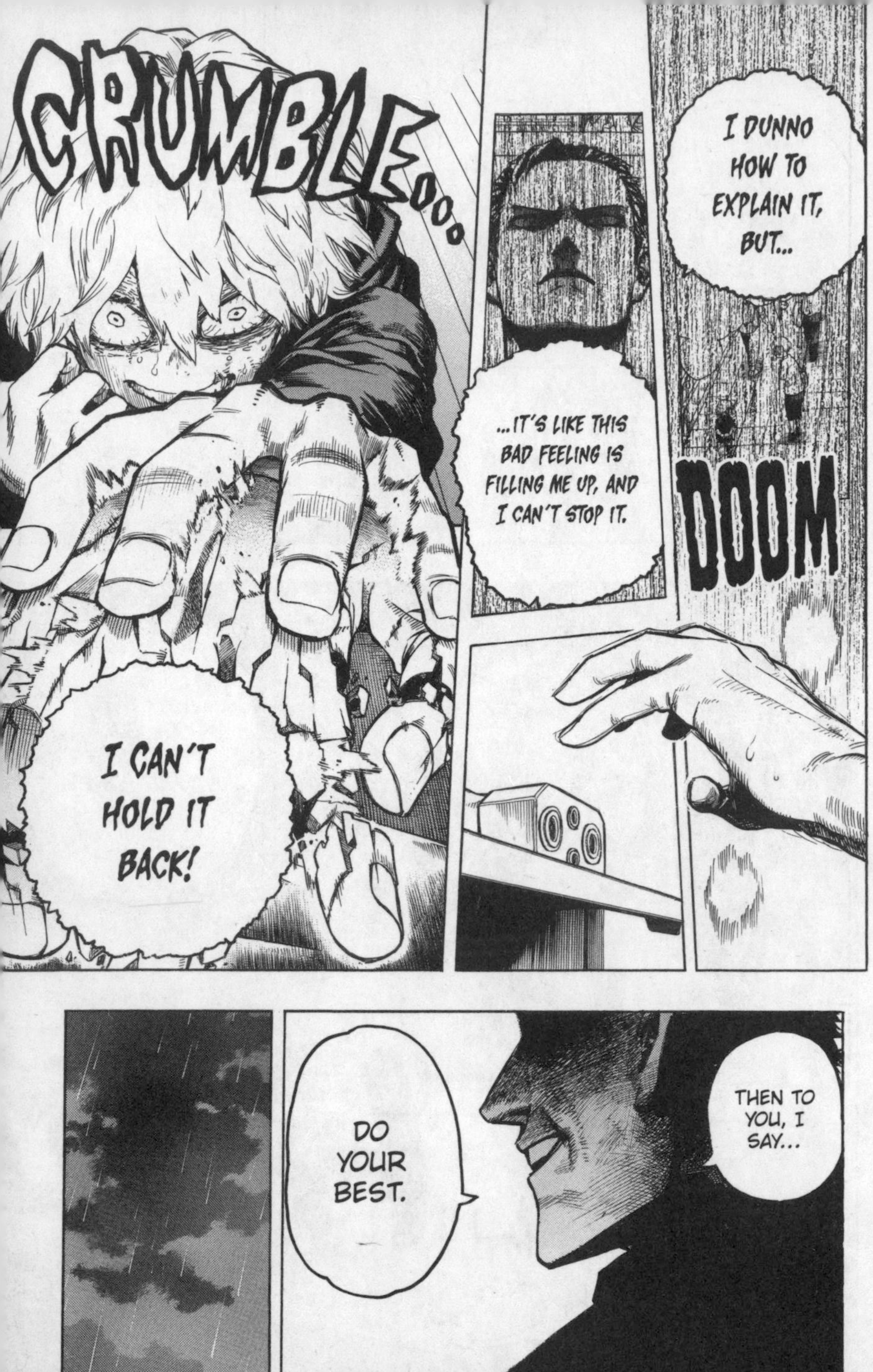
I DUNNO HOW TO EXPLAIN IT, BUT...
DOOM
...IT'S LIKE THIS BAD FEELING IS FILLING ME UP, AND I CAN'T STOP IT.
CRUMBLE
I CAN'T HOLD IT BACK!
THEN TO YOU, I SAY...
DO YOUR BEST.

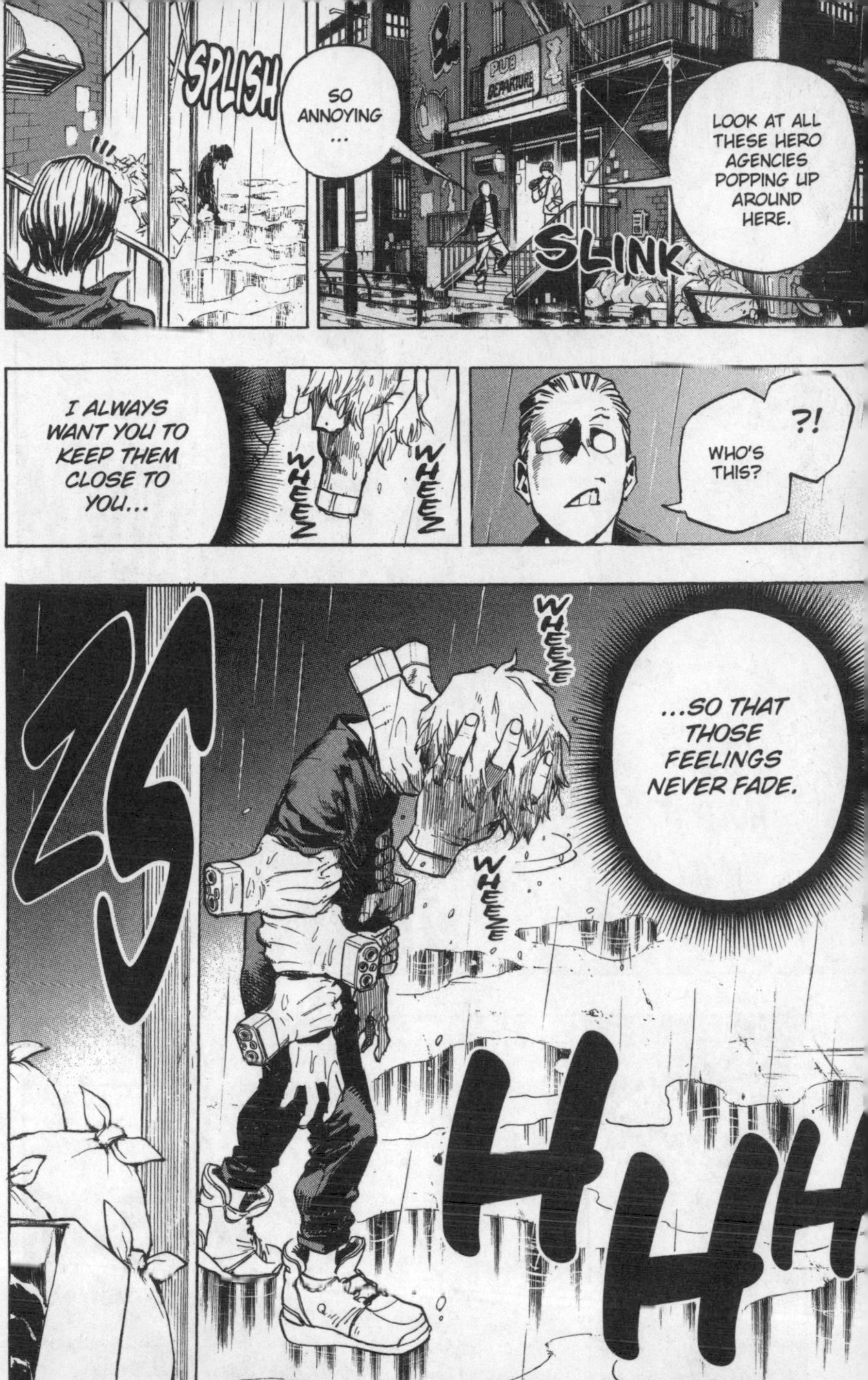
LOOK AT ALL THESE HERO AGENCIES POPPING UP AROUND HERE.
PUB
DEPARTURE
SO ANNOYING ...
SLINK
SPLISH
?!
WHO'S THIS?
WHEEZE
WHEEZE
I ALWAYS WANT YOU TO KEEP THEM CLOSE TO YOU...
WHEEZE
...SO THAT THOSE FEELINGS NEVER FADE.
WHEEZE
ZS
HHH

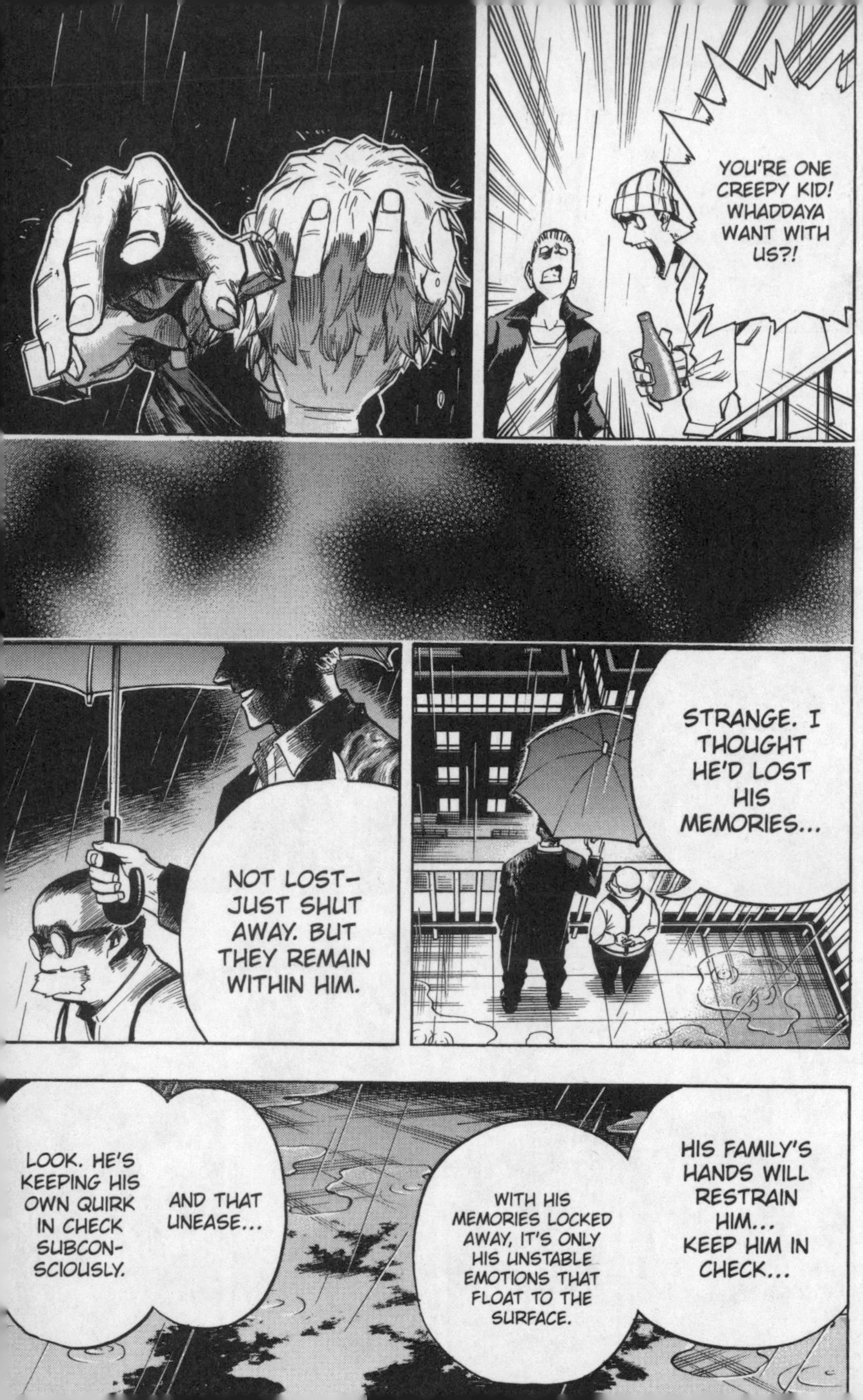
YOU'RE ONE CREEPY KID! WHADDAYA WANT WITH US?!
STRANGE. I THOUGHT HE'D LOST HIS MEMORIES...
NOT LOST-JUST SHUT AWAY. BUT THEY REMAIN WITHIN HIM.
HIS FAMILY'S HANDS WILL RESTRAIN HIM... KEEP HIM IN CHECK...
WITH HIS MEMORIES LOCKED AWAY, IT'S ONLY HIS UNSTABLE EMOTIONS THAT FLOAT TO THE SURFACE.
AND THAT UNEASE...
LOOK. HE'S KEEPING HIS OWN QUIRK IN CHECK SUBCONSCIOUSLY.

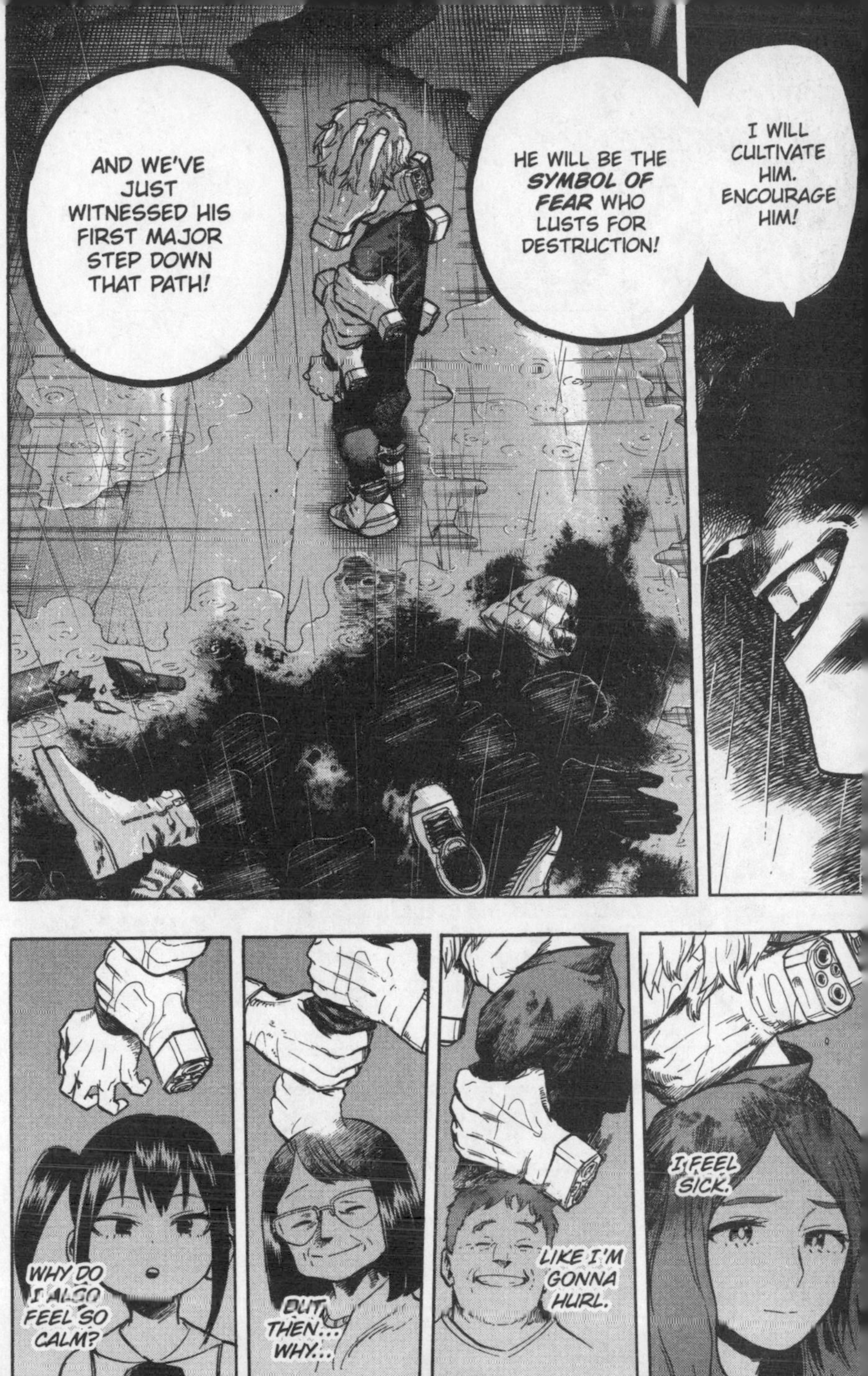
I WILL CULTIVATE HIM. ENCOURAGE HIM!
HE WILL BE THE SYMBOL OF FEAR WHO LUSTS FOR DESTRUCTION!
AND WE'VE JUST WITNESSED HIS FIRST MAJOR STEP DOWN THAT PATH!
I FEEL SICK.
LIKE I'M GONNA HURL.
BUT THEN... WHY...
WHY DO I ALSO FEEL SO CALM?

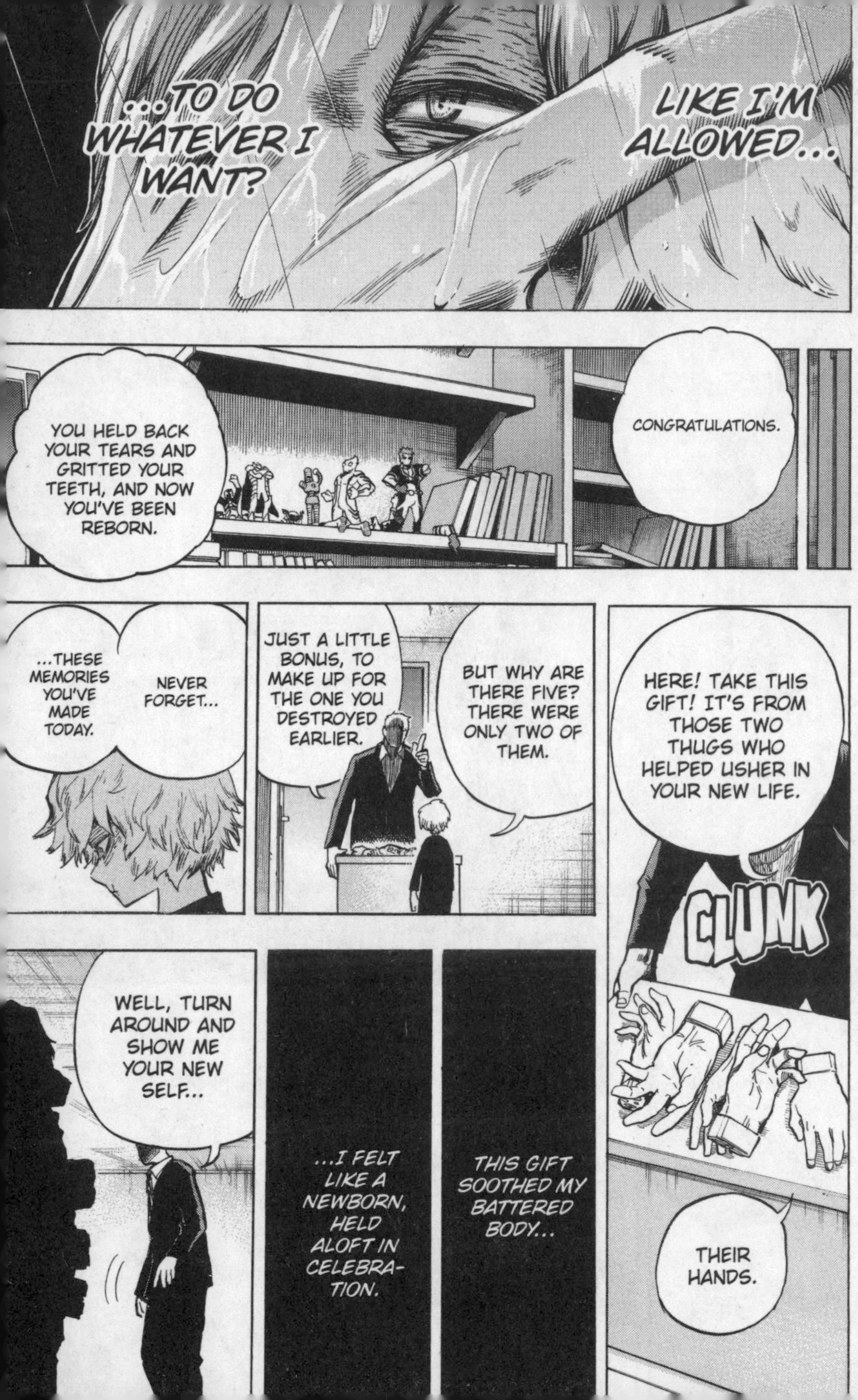
LIKE I'M ALLOWED...
...TO DO WHATEVER I WANT?
CONGRATULATIONS.
YOU HELD BACK YOUR TEARS AND GRITTED YOUR TEETH, AND NOW YOU'VE BEEN REBORN.
HERE! TAKE THIS GIFT! IT'S FROM THOSE TWO THUGS WHO HELPED USHER IN YOUR NEW LIFE.
CLUNK
THEIR HANDS.
BUT WHY ARE THERE FIVE? THERE WERE ONLY TWO OF THEM.
JUST A LITTLE BONUS, TO MAKE UP FOR THE ONE YOU DESTROYED EARLIER.
NEVER FORGET...
...THESE MEMORIES YOU'VE MADE TODAY.
THIS GIFT SOOTHED MY BATTERED BODY...
...I FELT LIKE A NEWBORN, HELD ALOFT IN CELEBRA- TION.
WELL, TURN AROUND AND SHOW ME YOUR NEW SELF...

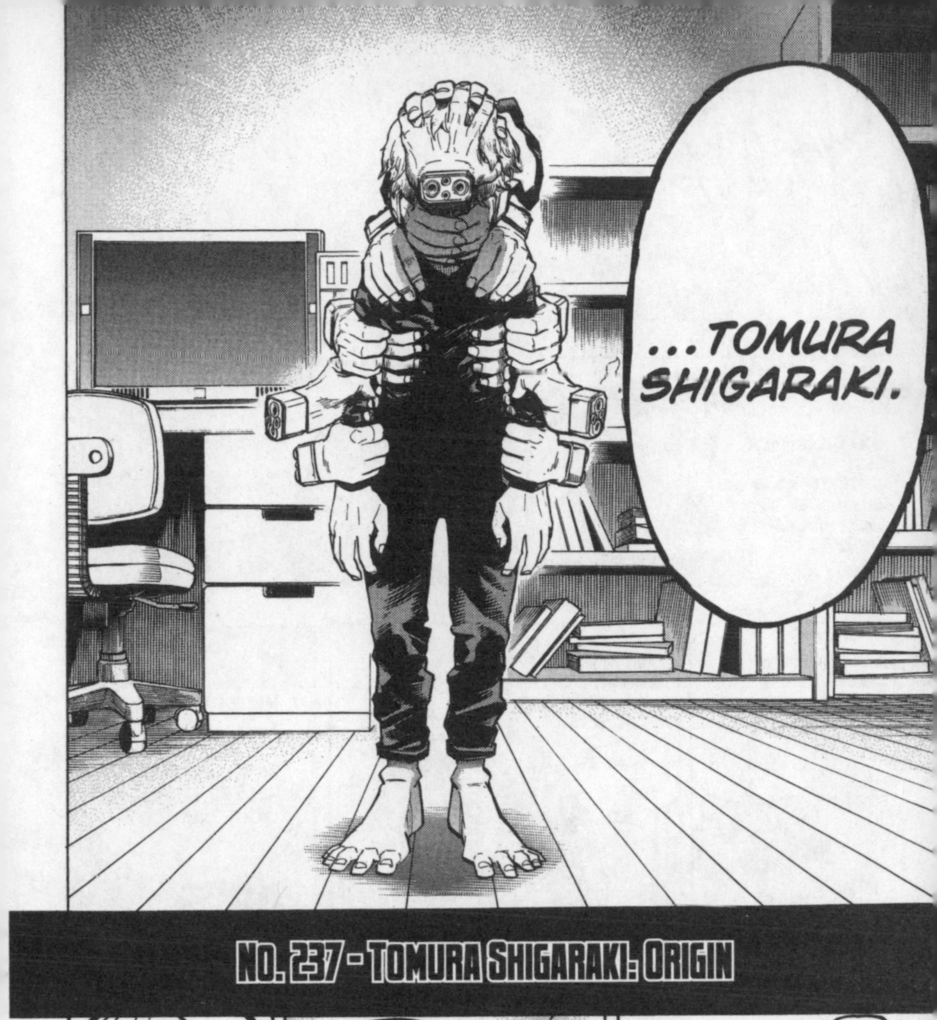
...TOMURA SHIGARAKI.

No. 237 - Tomura Shigaraki: Origin

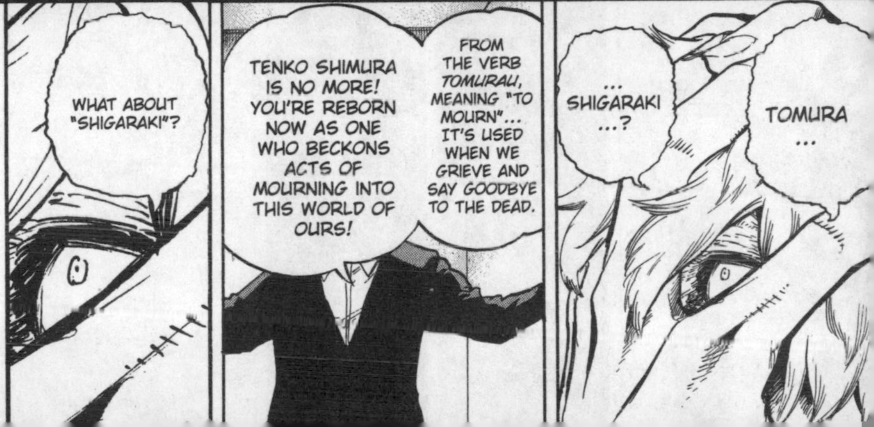
TOMURA ...
... SHIGARAKI ...?
FROM THE VERB *TOMURAU*, MEANING "TO MOURN"... IT'S USED WHEN WE GRIEVE AND SAY GOODBYE TO THE DEAD.
TENKO SHIMURA IS NO MORE! YOU'RE REBORN NOW AS ONE WHO BECKONS ACTS OF MOURNING INTO THIS WORLD OF OURS!
WHAT ABOUT "SHIGARAKI"?

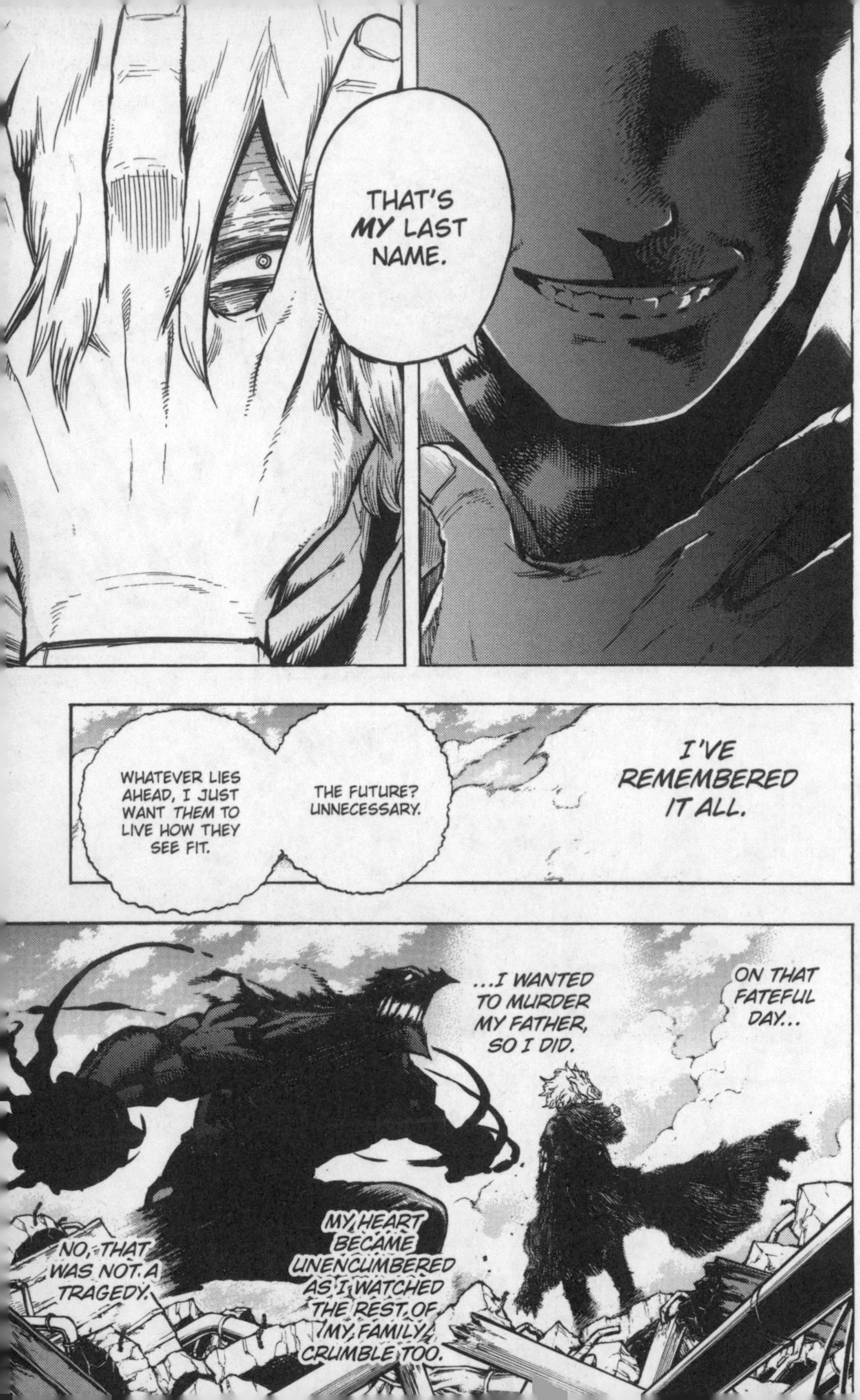
THAT'S MY LAST NAME.
I'VE REMEMBERED IT ALL.
THE FUTURE? UNNECESSARY.
WHATEVER LIES AHEAD, I JUST WANT THEM TO LIVE HOW THEY SEE FIT.
ON THAT FATEFUL DAY...
...I WANTED TO MURDER MY FATHER, SO I DID.
MY HEART BECAME UNENCUMBERED AS I WATCHED THE REST OF MY FAMILY CRUMBLE TOO.
NO, THAT WAS NOT A TRAGEDY.

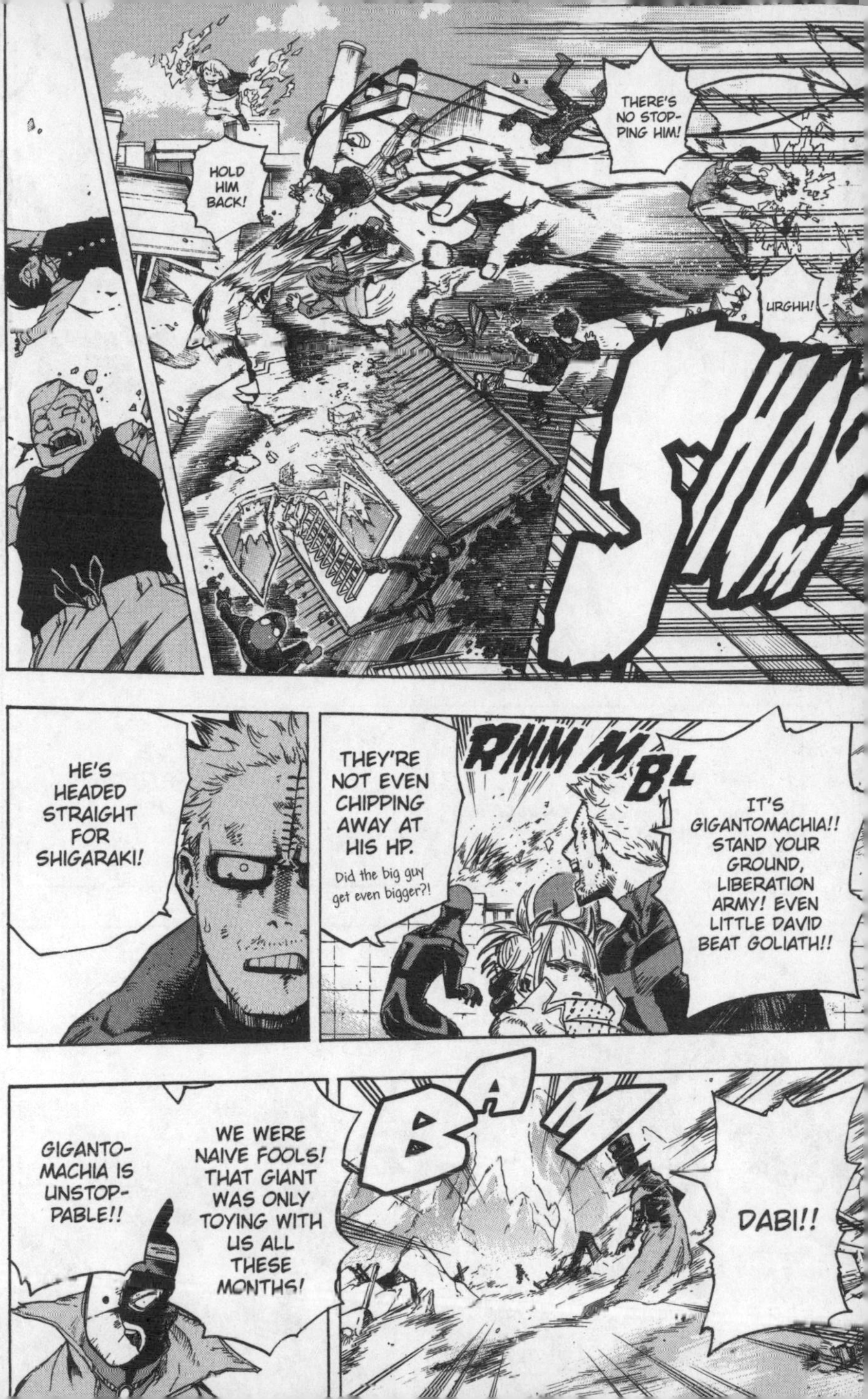

THERE'S NO STOP-PING HIM!
HOLD HIM BACK!
URGHH!
RMM MBL
IT'S GIGANTOMACHIA!! STAND YOUR GROUND, LIBERATION ARMY! EVEN LITTLE DAVID BEAT GOLIATH!!
THEY'RE NOT EVEN CHIPPING AWAY AT HIS HP.
Did the big guy get even bigger?!
HE'S HEADED STRAIGHT FOR SHIGARAKI!
BAM
DABI!!
WE WERE NAIVE FOOLS! THAT GIANT WAS ONLY TOYING WITH US ALL THESE MONTHS!
GIGANTO-MACHIA IS UNSTOP-PABLE!!

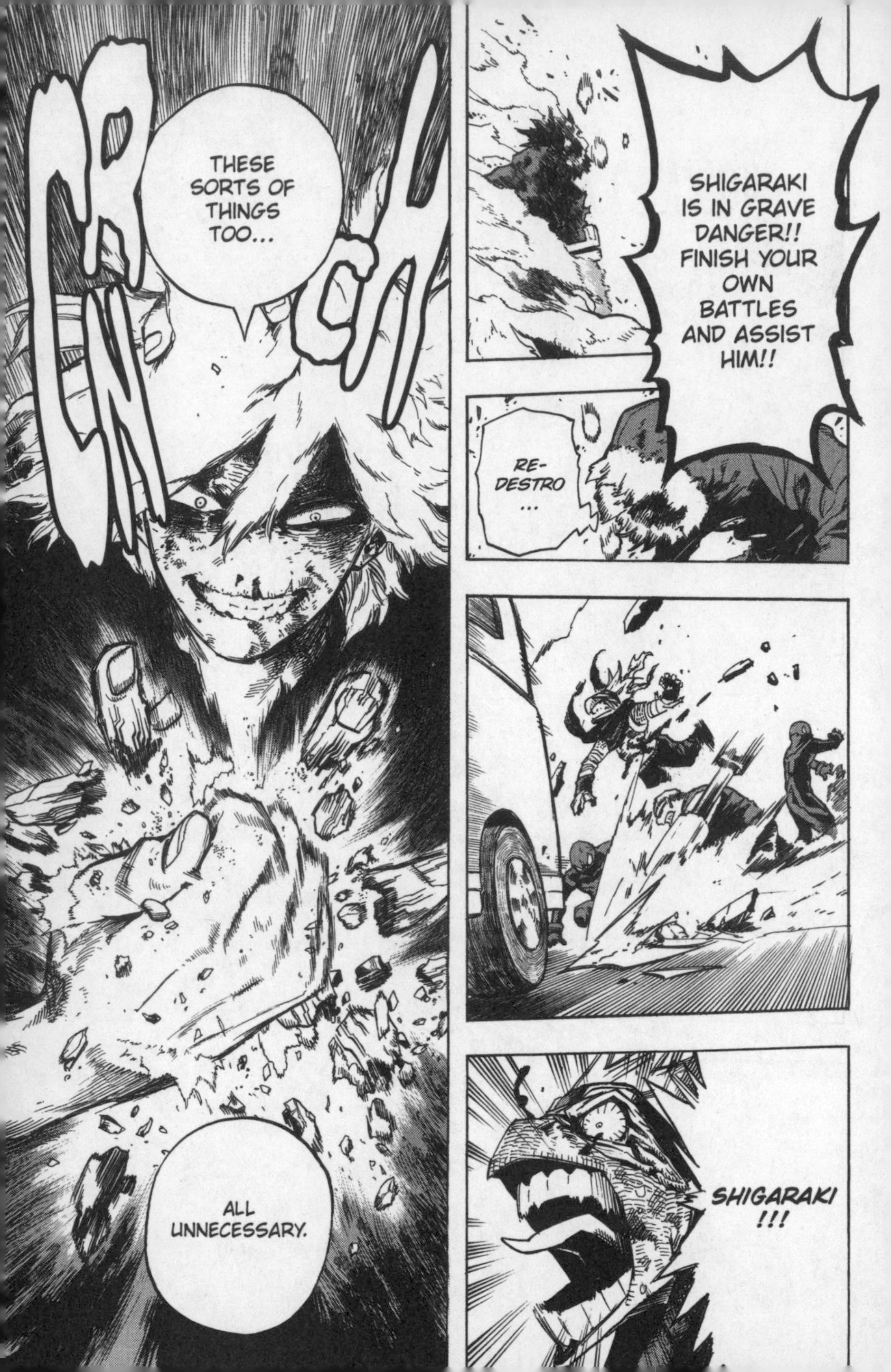
SHIGARAKI IS IN GRAVE DANGER!! FINISH YOUR OWN BATTLES AND ASSIST HIM!!
RE-DESTRO ...
SHIGARAKI !!!
THESE SORTS OF THINGS TOO...
ALL UNNECESSARY.

Family

KOTARO SHIMURA (32)

BUSINESS STYLE

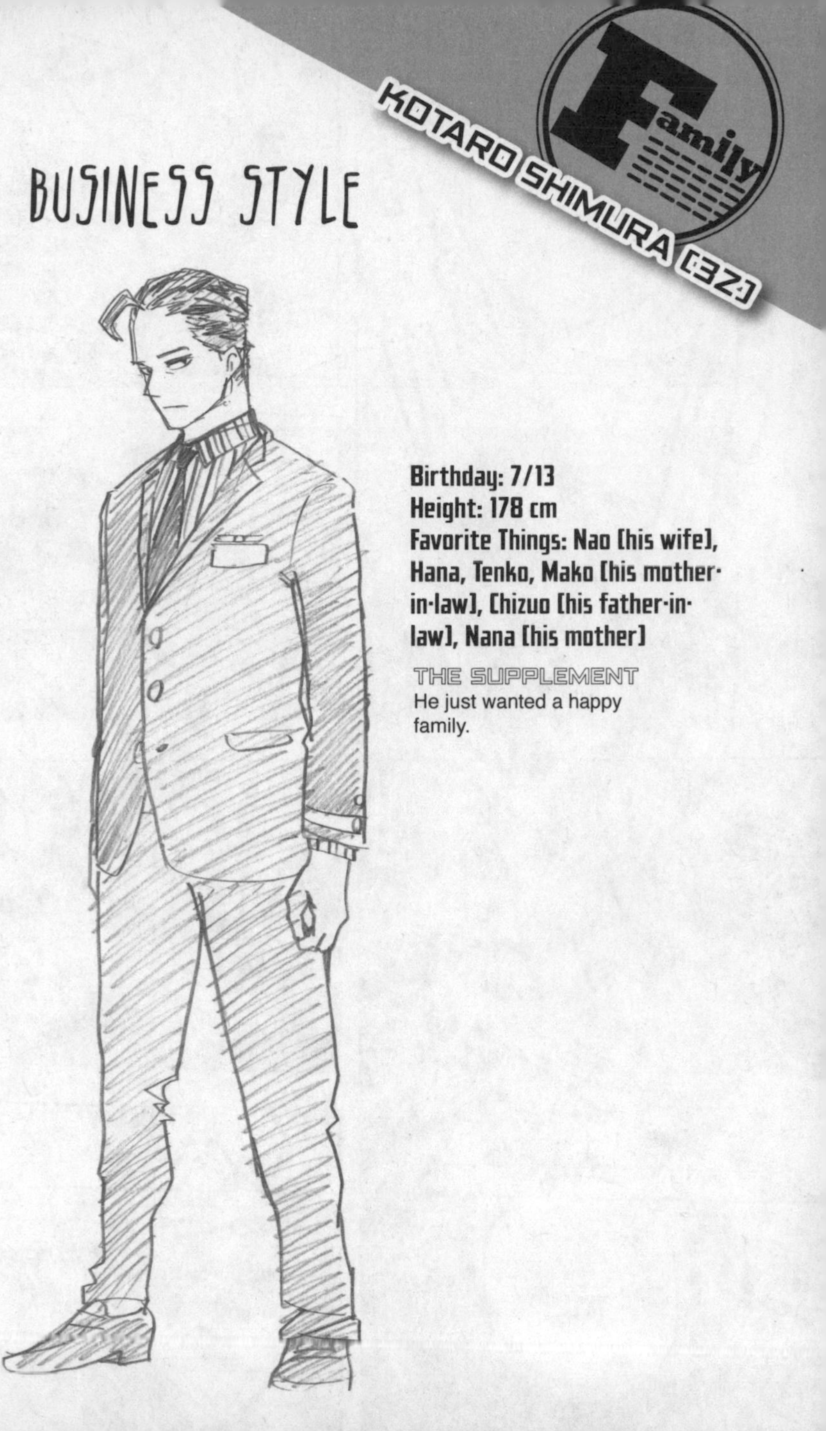

Birthday: 7/13
Height: 178 cm
Favorite Things: Nao (his wife), Hana, Tenko, Mako (his mother-in-law), Chizuo (his father-in-law), Nana (his mother)

THE SUPPLEMENT

He just wanted a happy family.

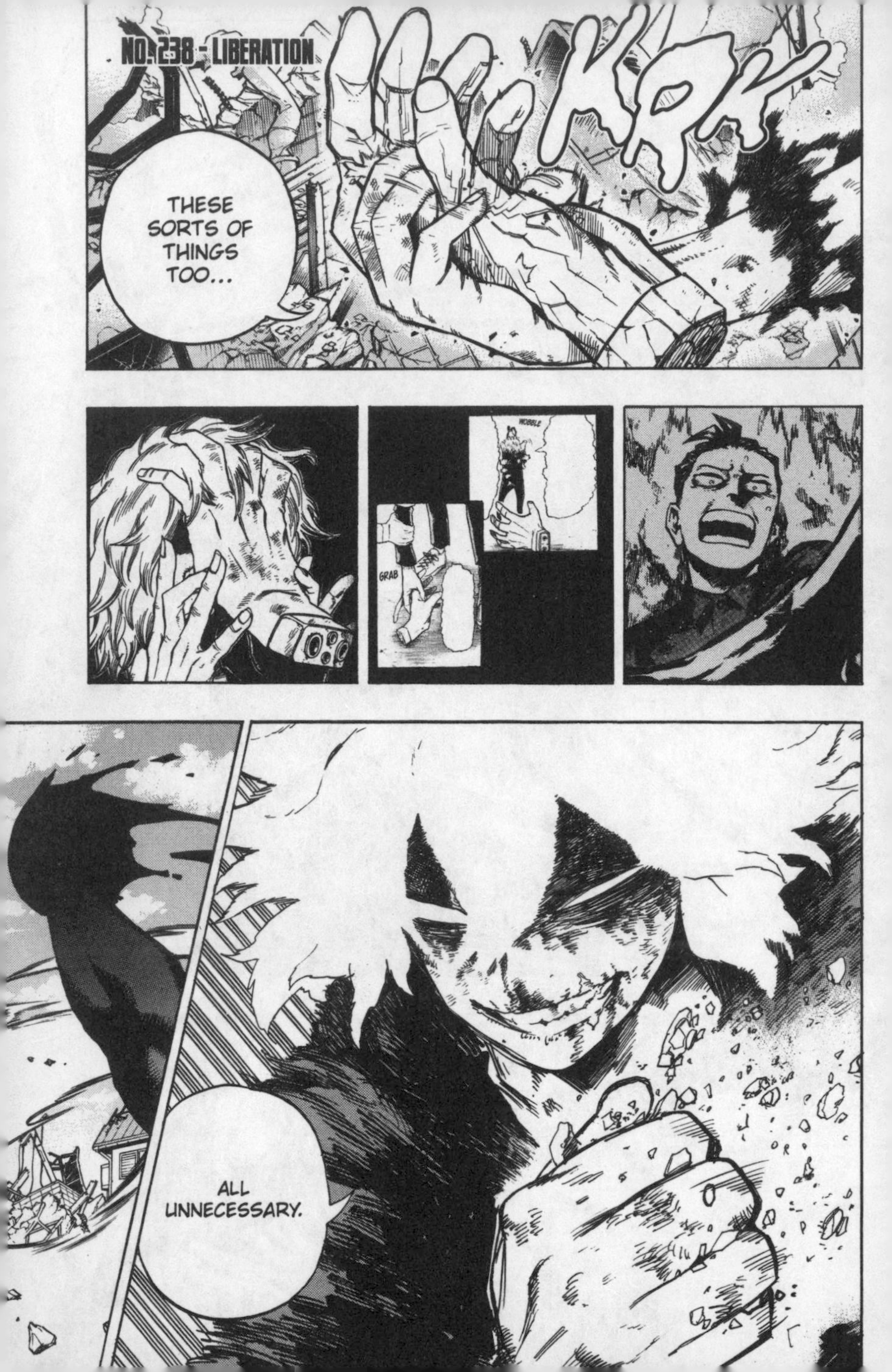
NO. 238 - LIBERATION
KRK
THESE SORTS OF THINGS TOO...
WOBBLE
GRAB
ALL UNNECESSARY.

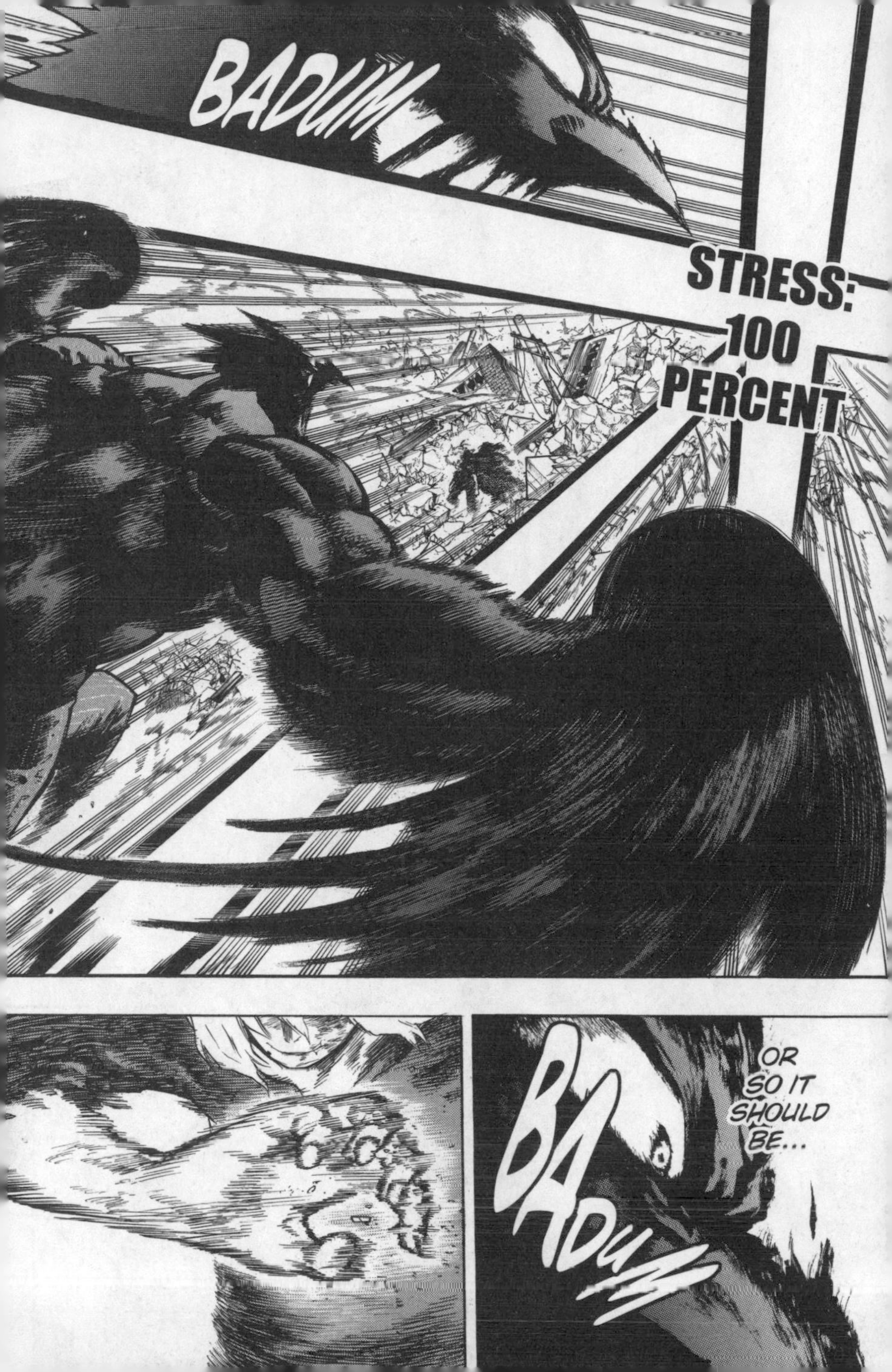
BADUM
STRESS: 100 PERCENT
BADUM
OR SO IT SHOULD BE...

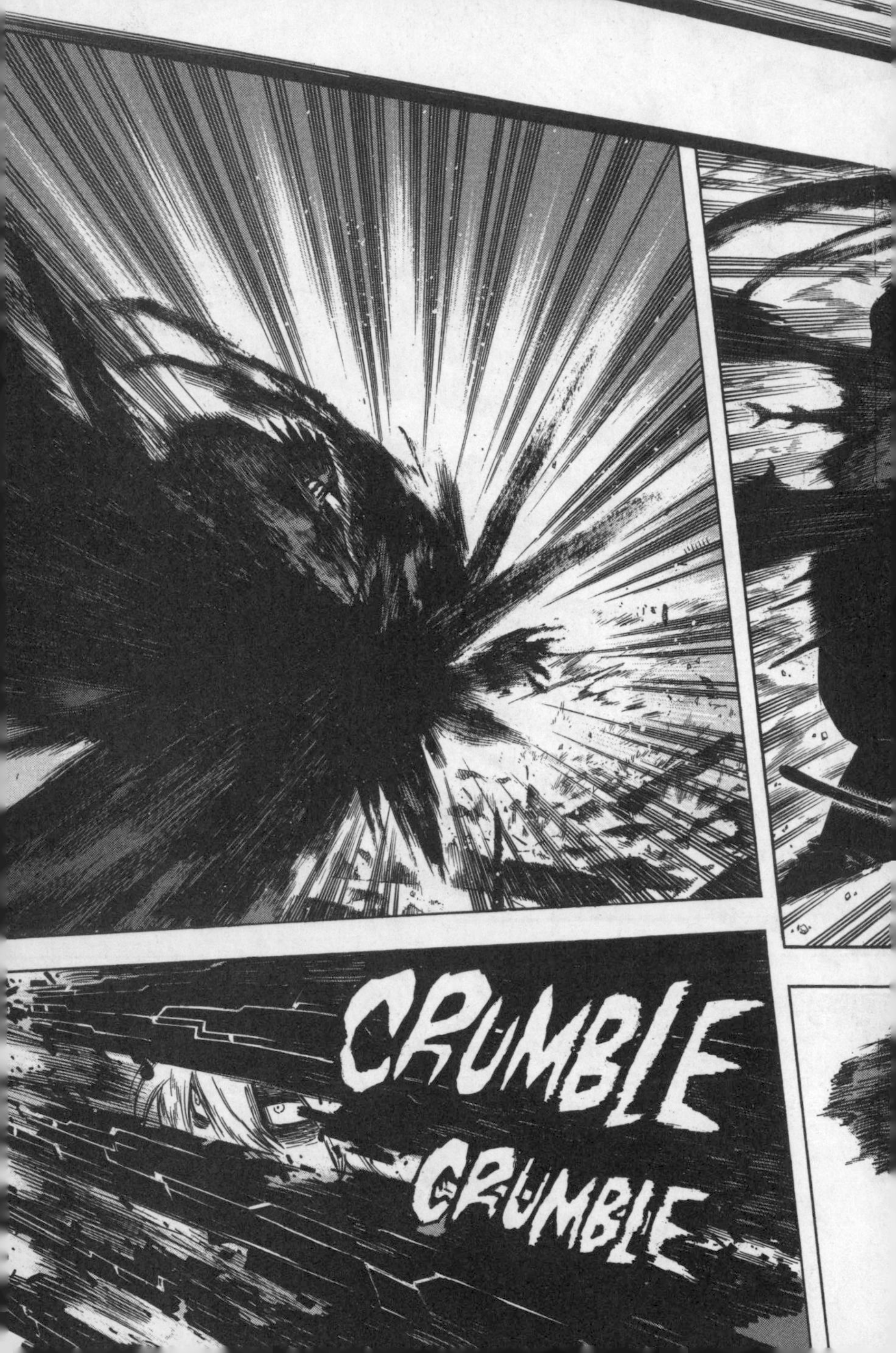
CRUMBLE
CRUMBLE

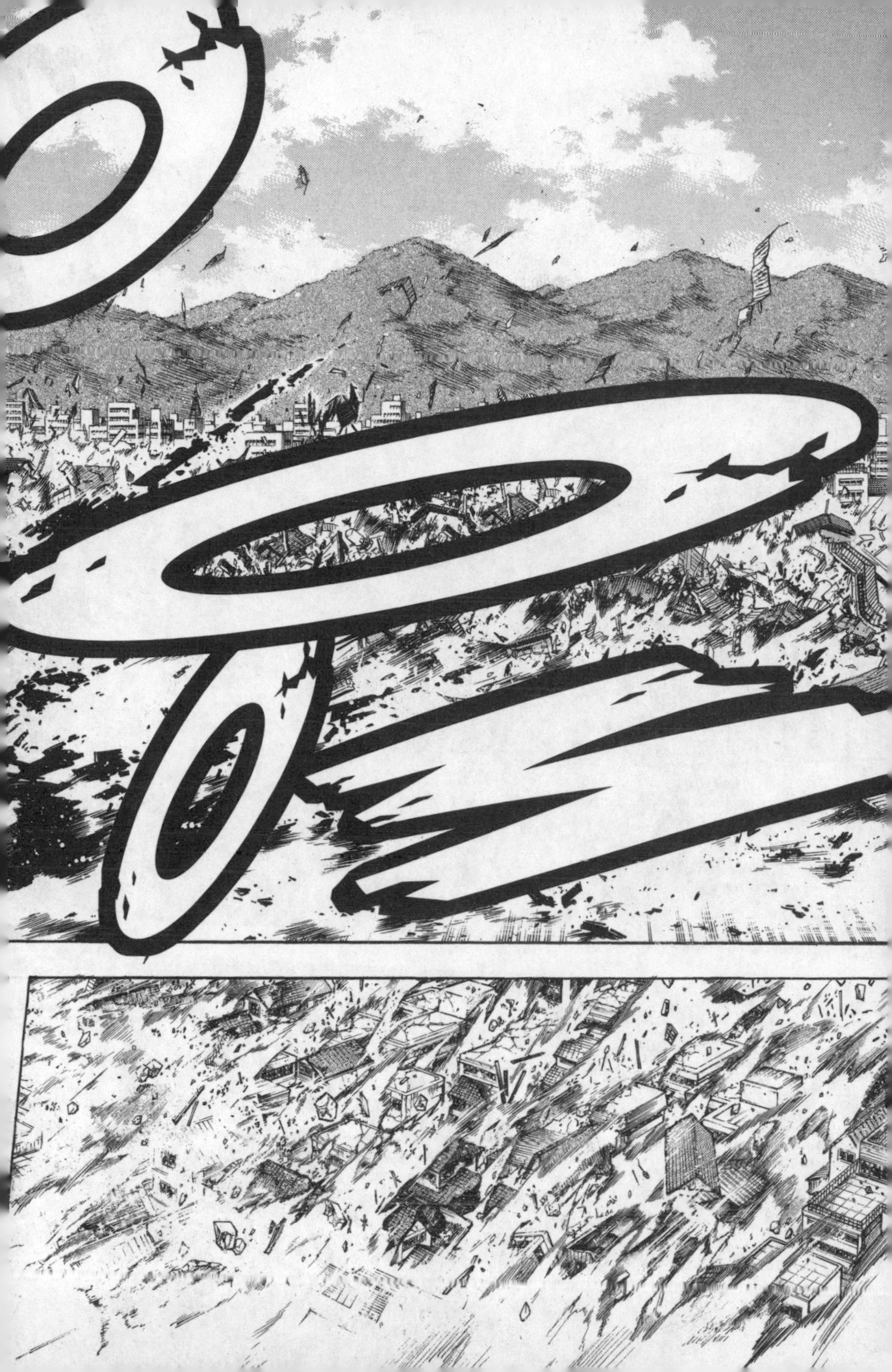

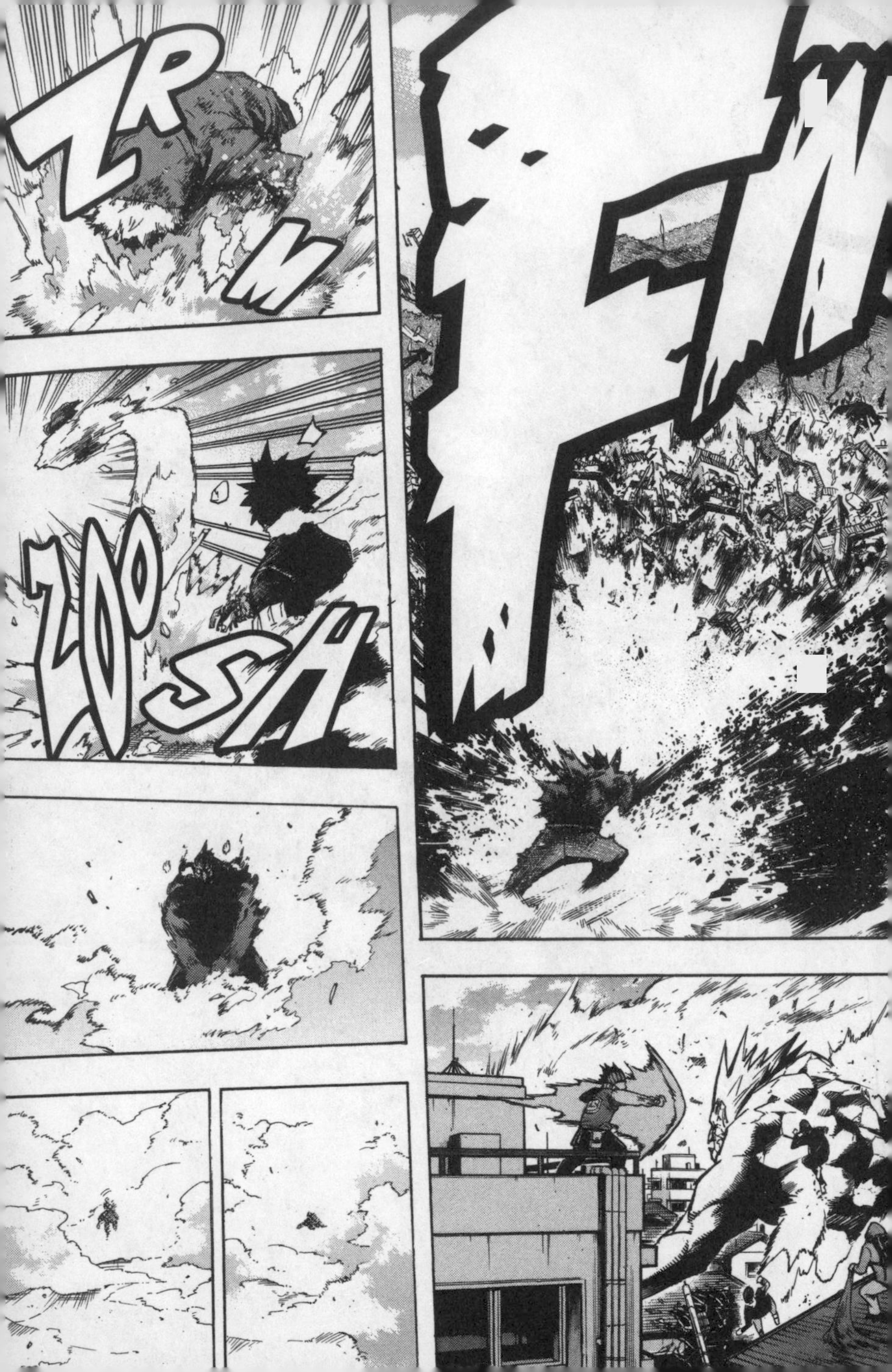
ZRM
ZOOSH

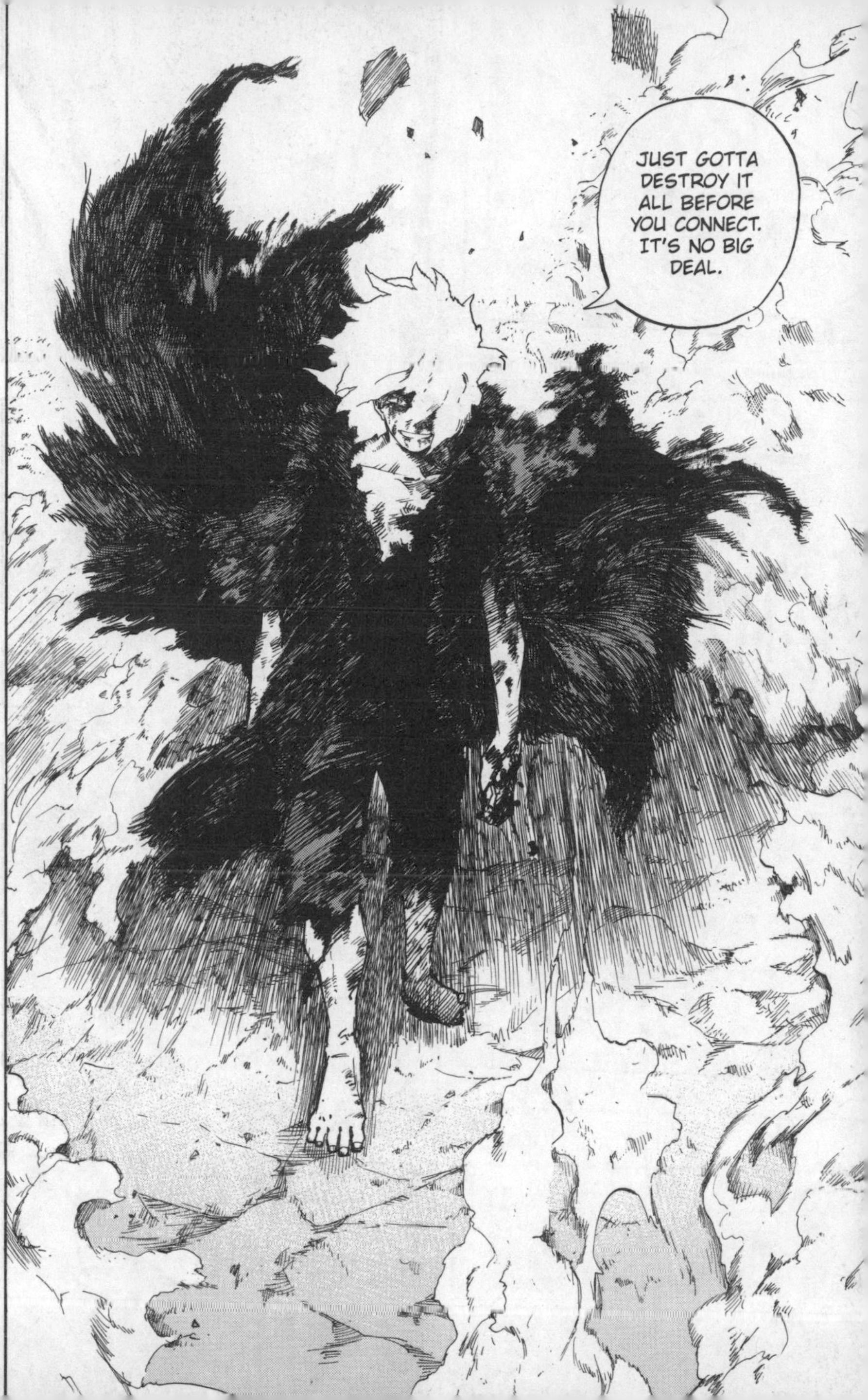
JUST GOTTA DESTROY IT ALL BEFORE YOU CONNECT. IT'S NO BIG DEAL.

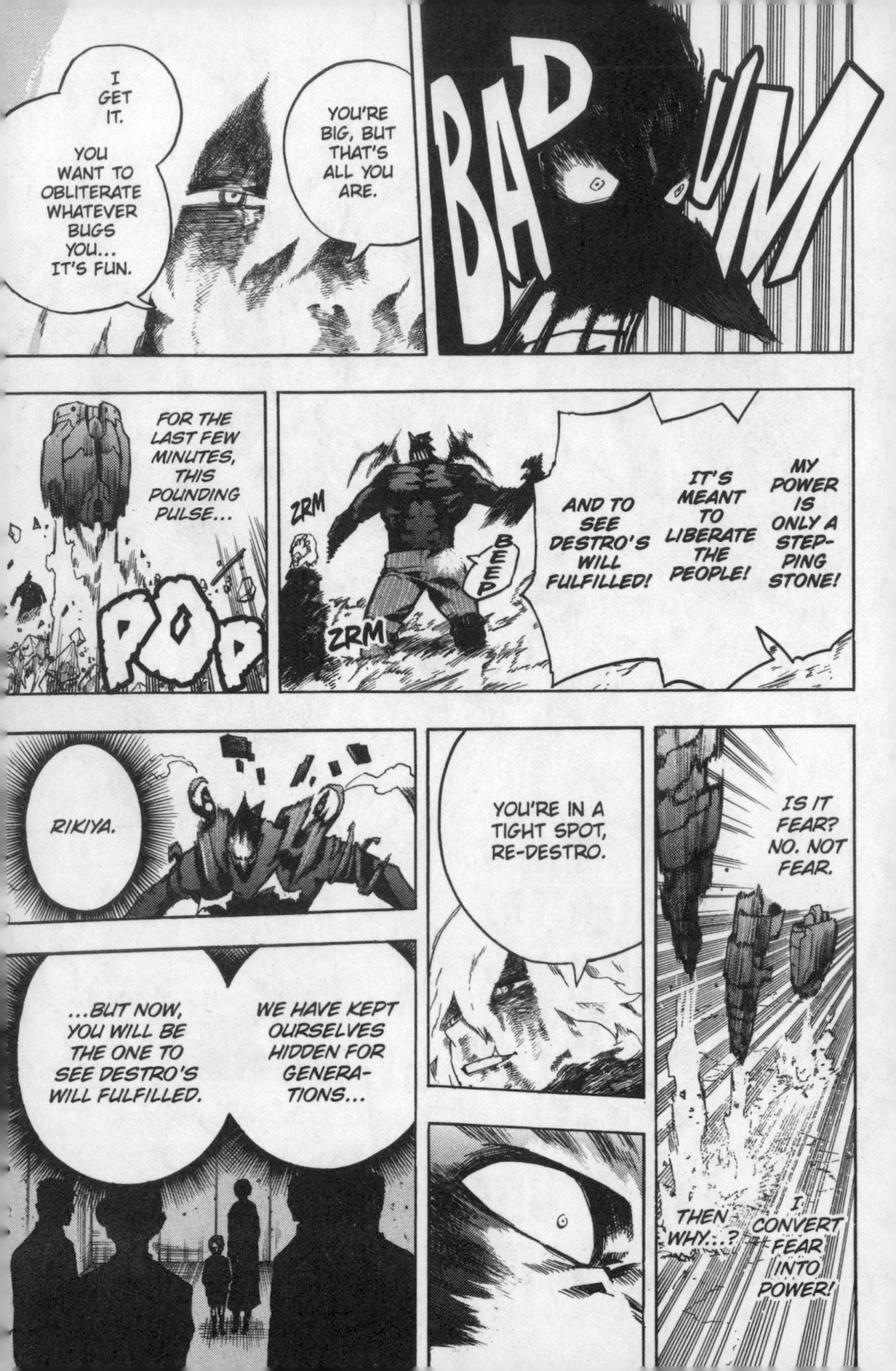
BADUM
YOU'RE BIG, BUT THAT'S ALL YOU ARE.
I GET IT. YOU WANT TO OBLITERATE WHATEVER BUGS YOU... IT'S FUN.
MY POWER IS ONLY A STEP-PING STONE!
IT'S MEANT TO LIBERATE THE PEOPLE!
AND TO SEE DESTRO'S WILL FULFILLED!
ZRM
BEEP
ZRM
FOR THE LAST FEW MINUTES, THIS POUNDING PULSE...
POP
IS IT FEAR? NO. NOT FEAR.
YOU'RE IN A TIGHT SPOT, RE-DESTRO.
THEN WHY...?
I CONVERT FEAR INTO POWER!
RIKIYA.
WE HAVE KEPT OURSELVES HIDDEN FOR GENERA-TIONS...
...BUT NOW, YOU WILL BE THE ONE TO SEE DESTRO'S WILL FULFILLED.

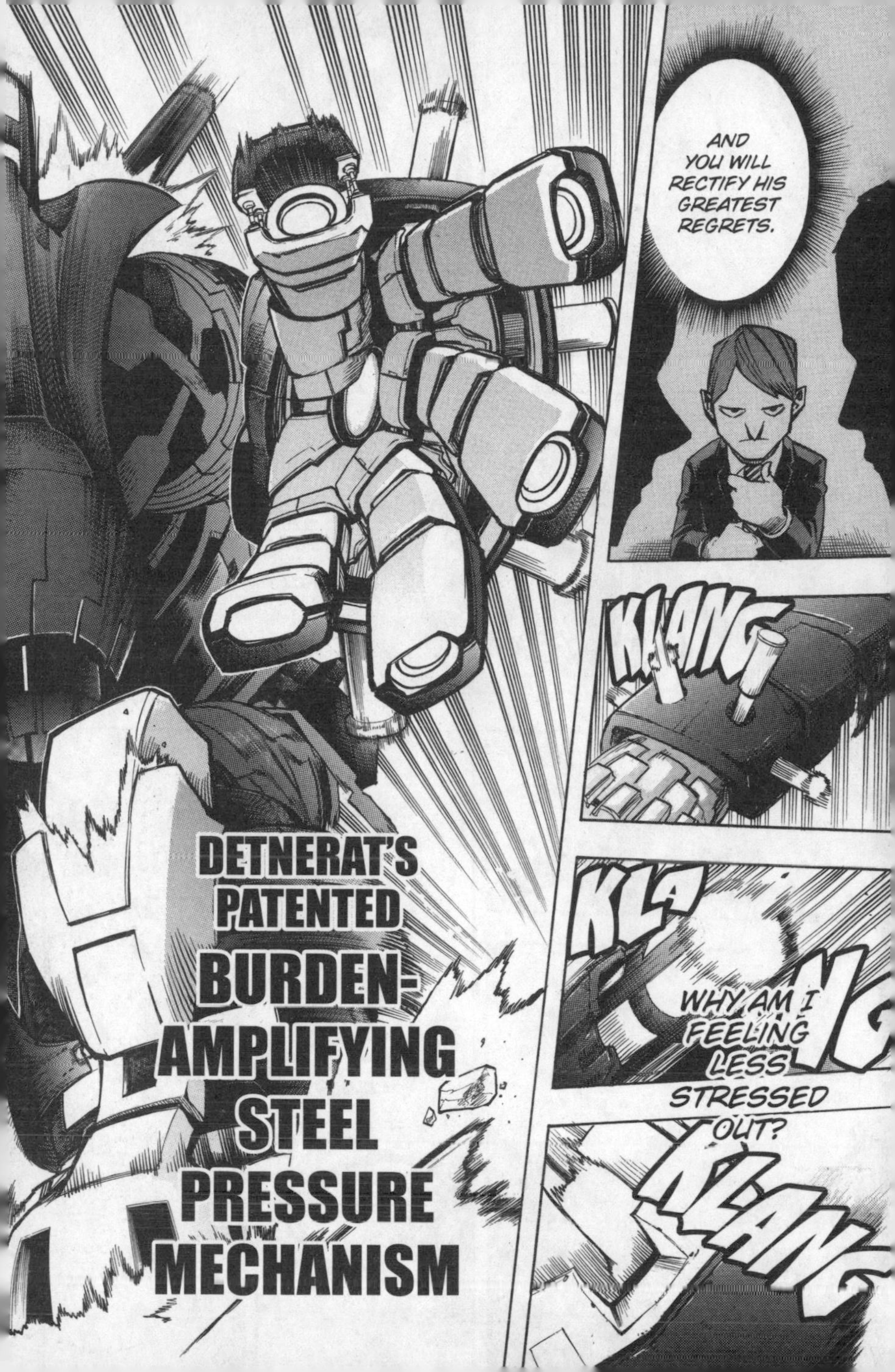
AND YOU WILL RECTIFY HIS GREATEST REGRETS.
KLANG
KLA
NG
WHY AM I FEELING LESS STRESSED OUT?
KLANG
DETNERAT'S PATENTED BURDEN-AMPLIFYING STEEL PRESSURE MECHANISM

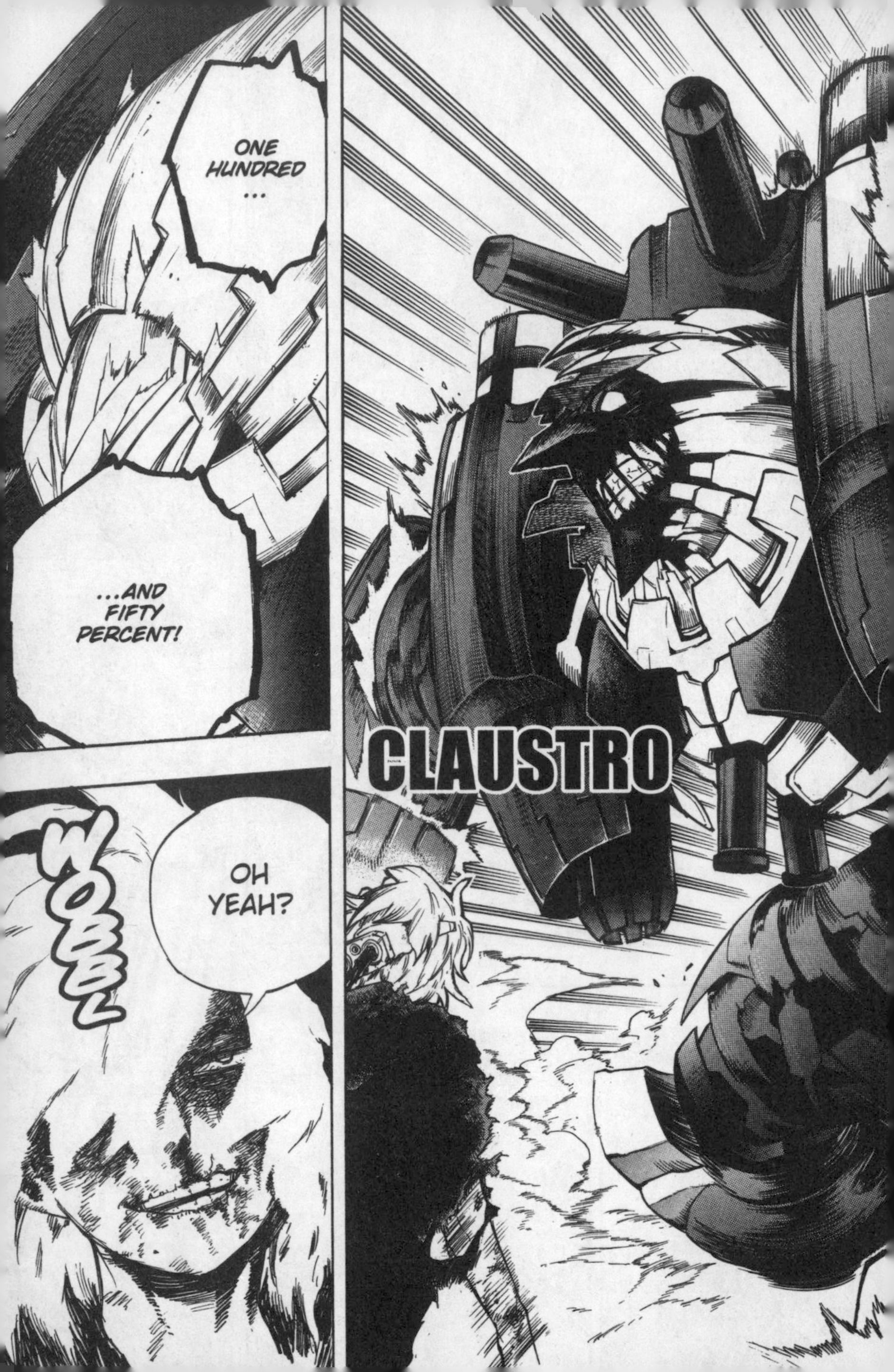

CLAUSTRO
ONE HUNDRED ...
...AND FIFTY PERCENT!
OH YEAH?
WOBBL

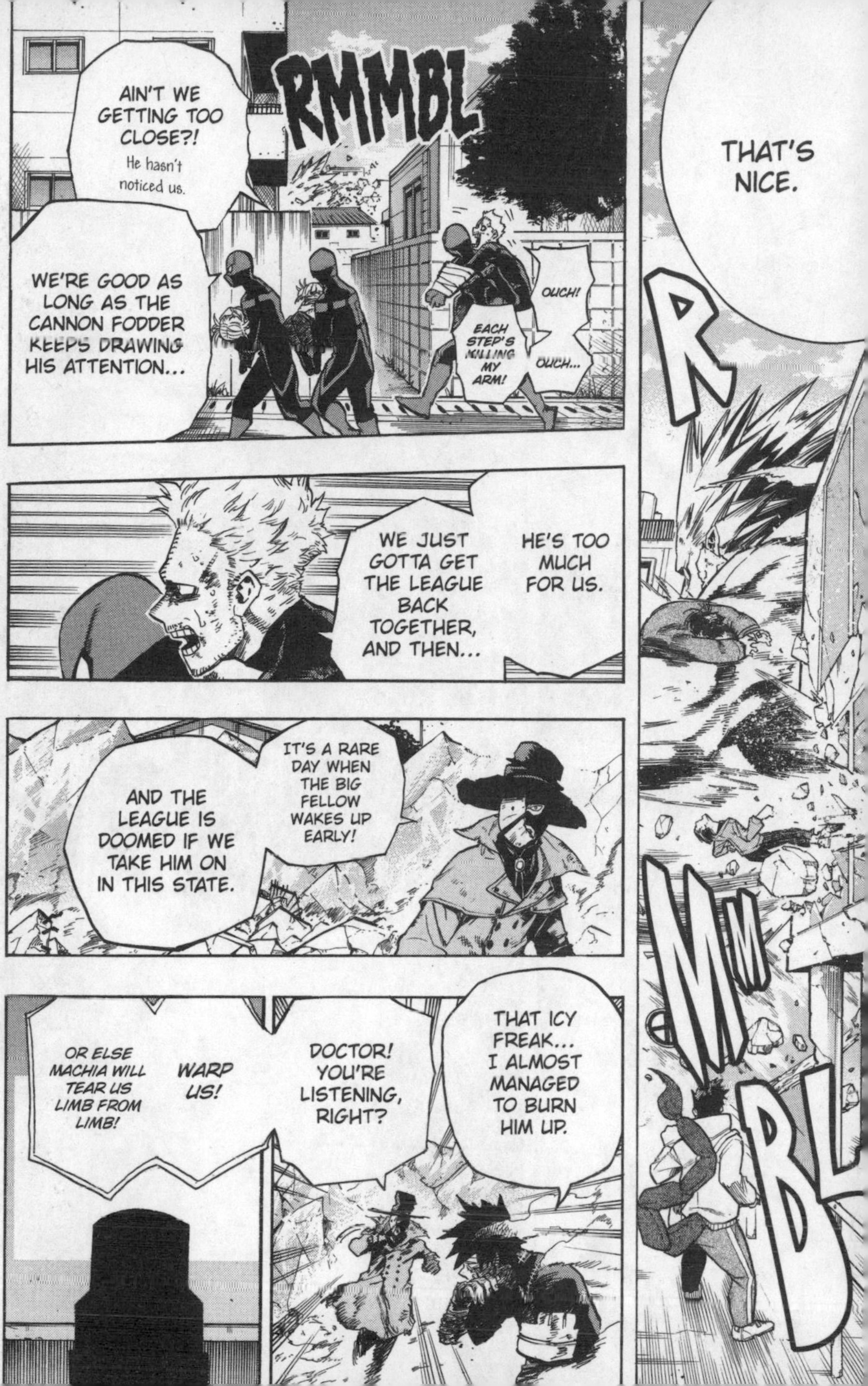

THAT'S NICE.
R
MM
BL
RMMBL
OUCH!
EACH STEP'S KILLING MY ARM!
OUCH...
AIN'T WE GETTING TOO CLOSE?!
He hasn't noticed us.
WE'RE GOOD AS LONG AS THE CANNON FODDER KEEPS DRAWING HIS ATTENTION...
HE'S TOO MUCH FOR US.
WE JUST GOTTA GET THE LEAGUE BACK TOGETHER, AND THEN...
IT'S A RARE DAY WHEN THE BIG FELLOW WAKES UP EARLY!
AND THE LEAGUE IS DOOMED IF WE TAKE HIM ON IN THIS STATE.
THAT ICY FREAK... I ALMOST MANAGED TO BURN HIM UP.
DOCTOR! YOU'RE LISTENING, RIGHT?
WARP US!
OR ELSE MACHIA WILL TEAR US LIMB FROM LIMB!

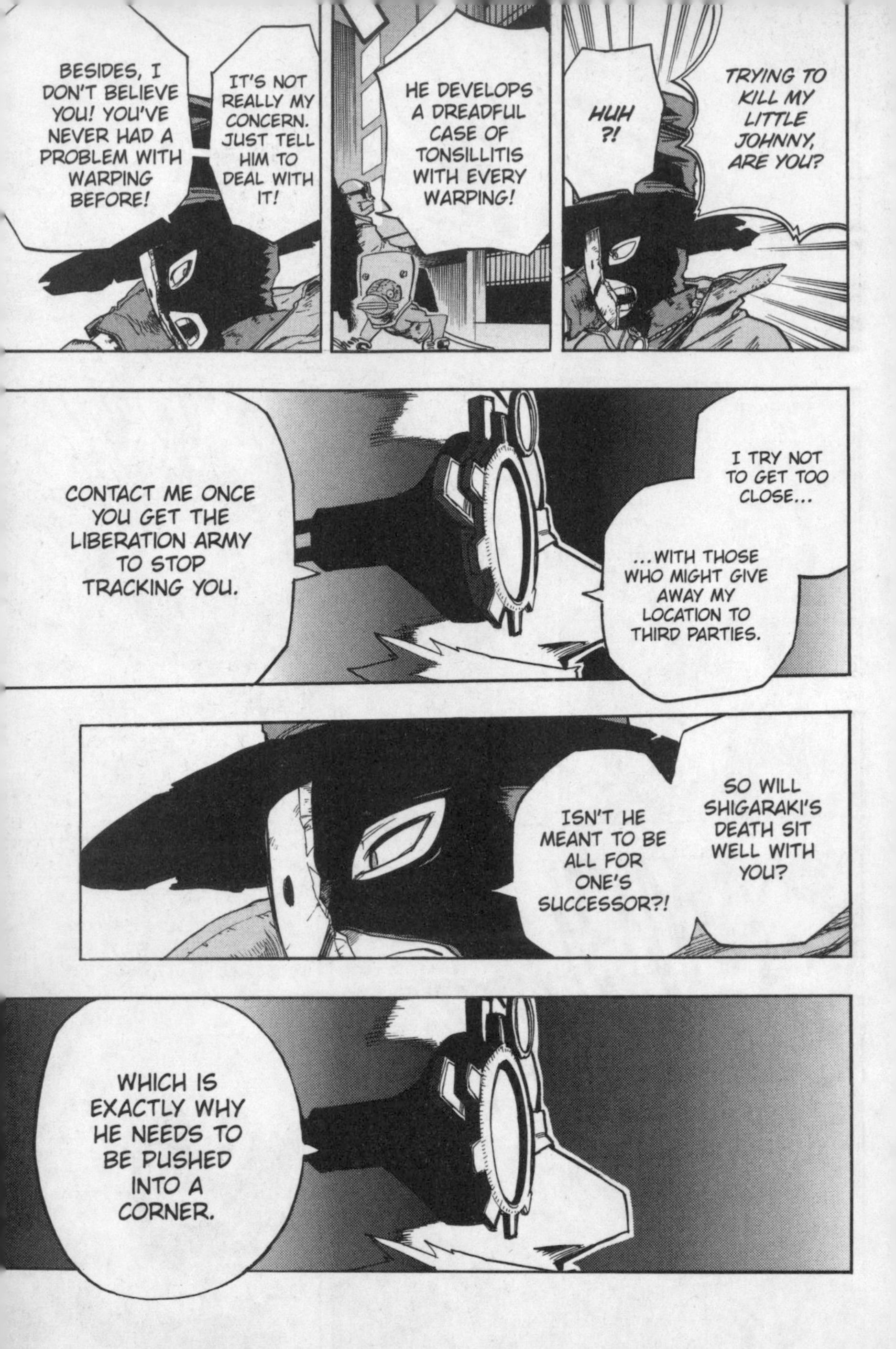
TRYING TO KILL MY LITTLE JOHNNY, ARE YOU?
HUH ?!
HE DEVELOPS A DREADFUL CASE OF TONSILLITIS WITH EVERY WARPING!
IT'S NOT REALLY MY CONCERN. JUST TELL HIM TO DEAL WITH IT!
BESIDES, I DON'T BELIEVE YOU! YOU'VE NEVER HAD A PROBLEM WITH WARPING BEFORE!
I TRY NOT TO GET TOO CLOSE...
...WITH THOSE WHO MIGHT GIVE AWAY MY LOCATION TO THIRD PARTIES.
CONTACT ME ONCE YOU GET THE LIBERATION ARMY TO STOP TRACKING YOU.
SO WILL SHIGARAKI'S DEATH SIT WELL WITH YOU?
ISN'T HE MEANT TO BE ALL FOR ONE'S SUCCESSOR?!
WHICH IS EXACTLY WHY HE NEEDS TO BE PUSHED INTO A CORNER.

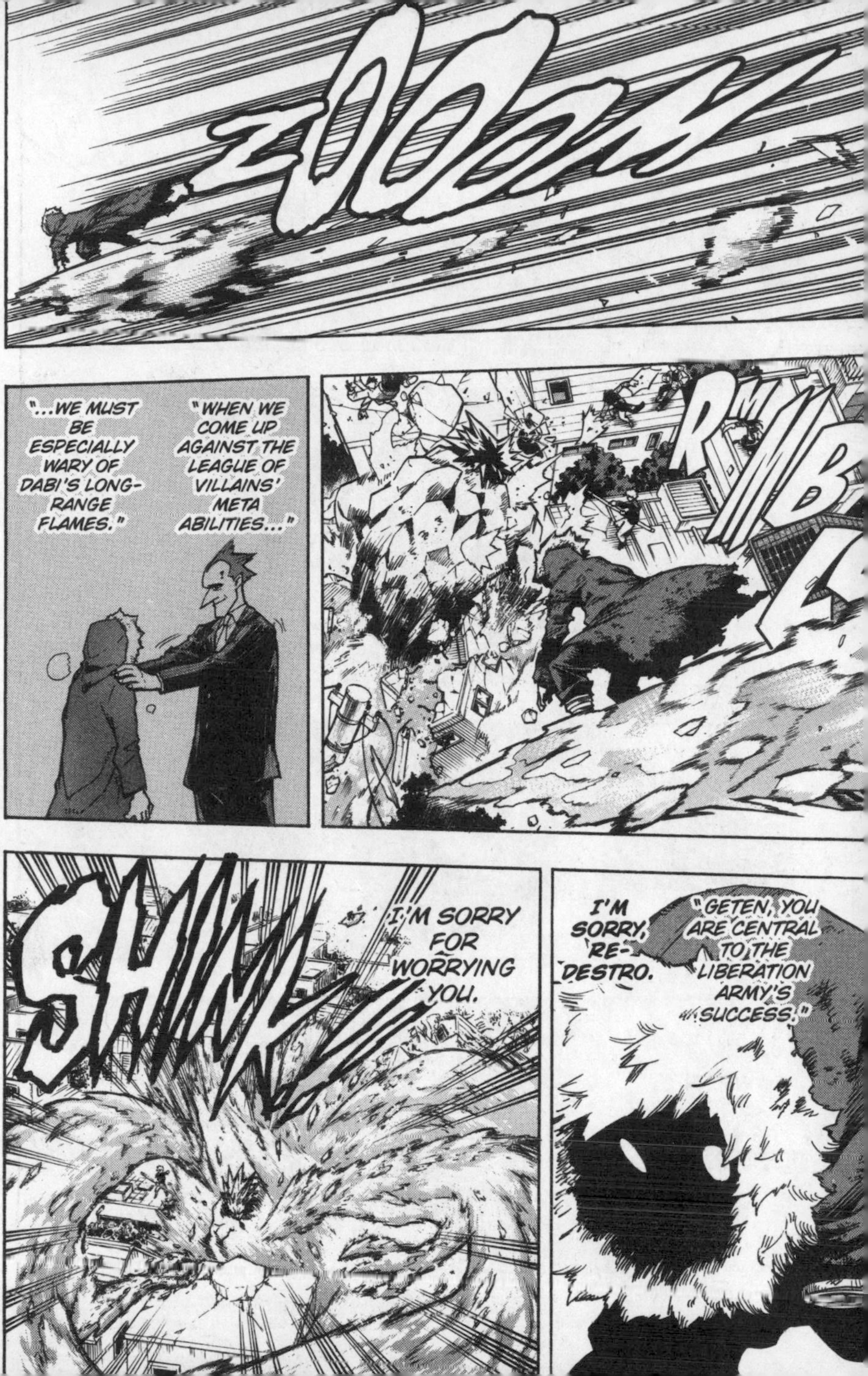
"WHEN WE COME UP AGAINST THE LEAGUE OF VILLAINS' META ABILITIES..."
"...WE MUST BE ESPECIALLY WARY OF DABI'S LONG-RANGE FLAMES."
"GETEN, YOU ARE CENTRAL TO THE LIBERATION ARMY'S SUCCESS."
I'M SORRY, RE-DESTRO.
I'M SORRY FOR WORRYING YOU.

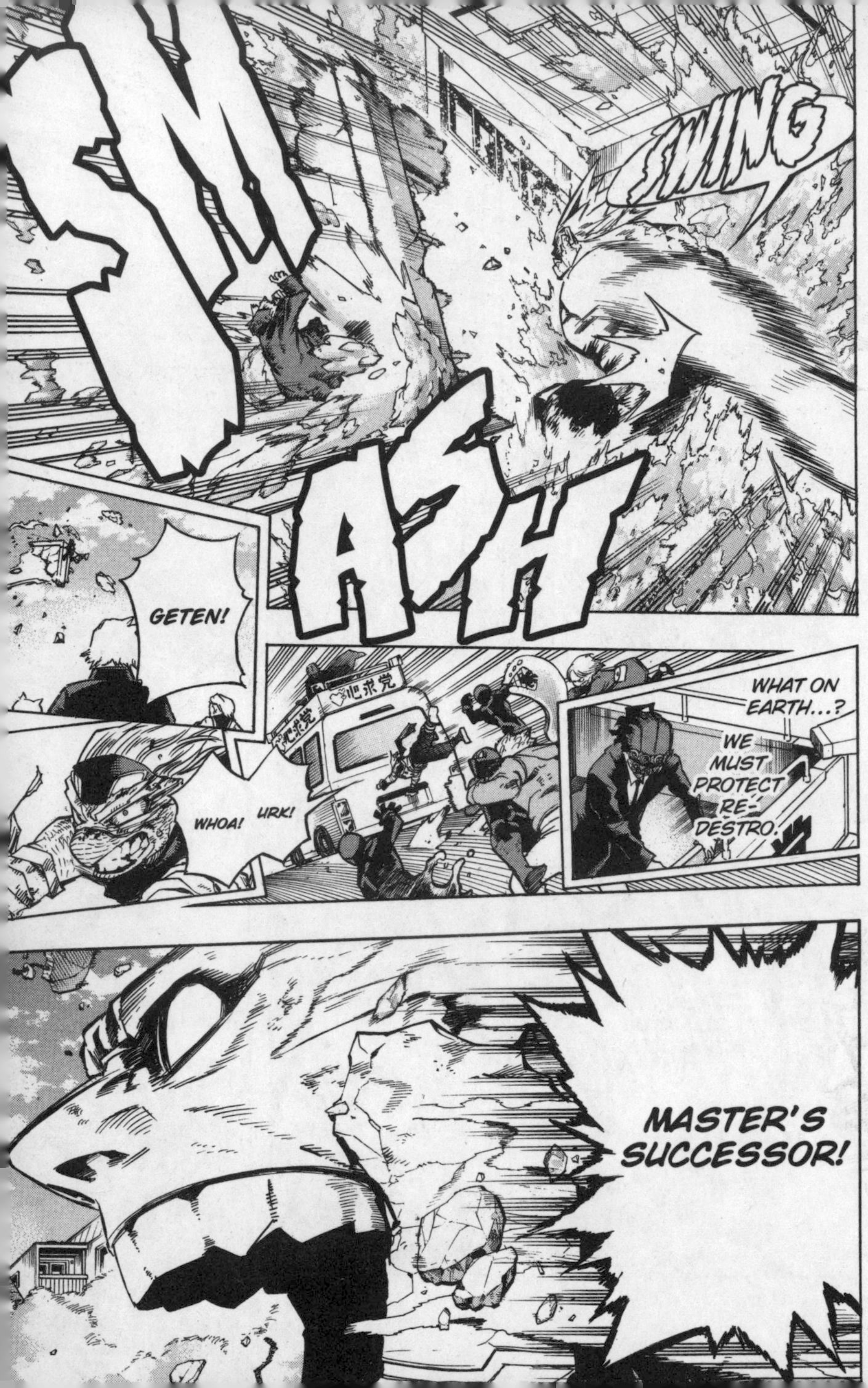
SHWING
SMASH
WHAT ON EARTH...?
WE MUST PROTECT RE-DESTRO.
GETEN!
URK!
WHOA!
MASTER'S SUCCESSOR!

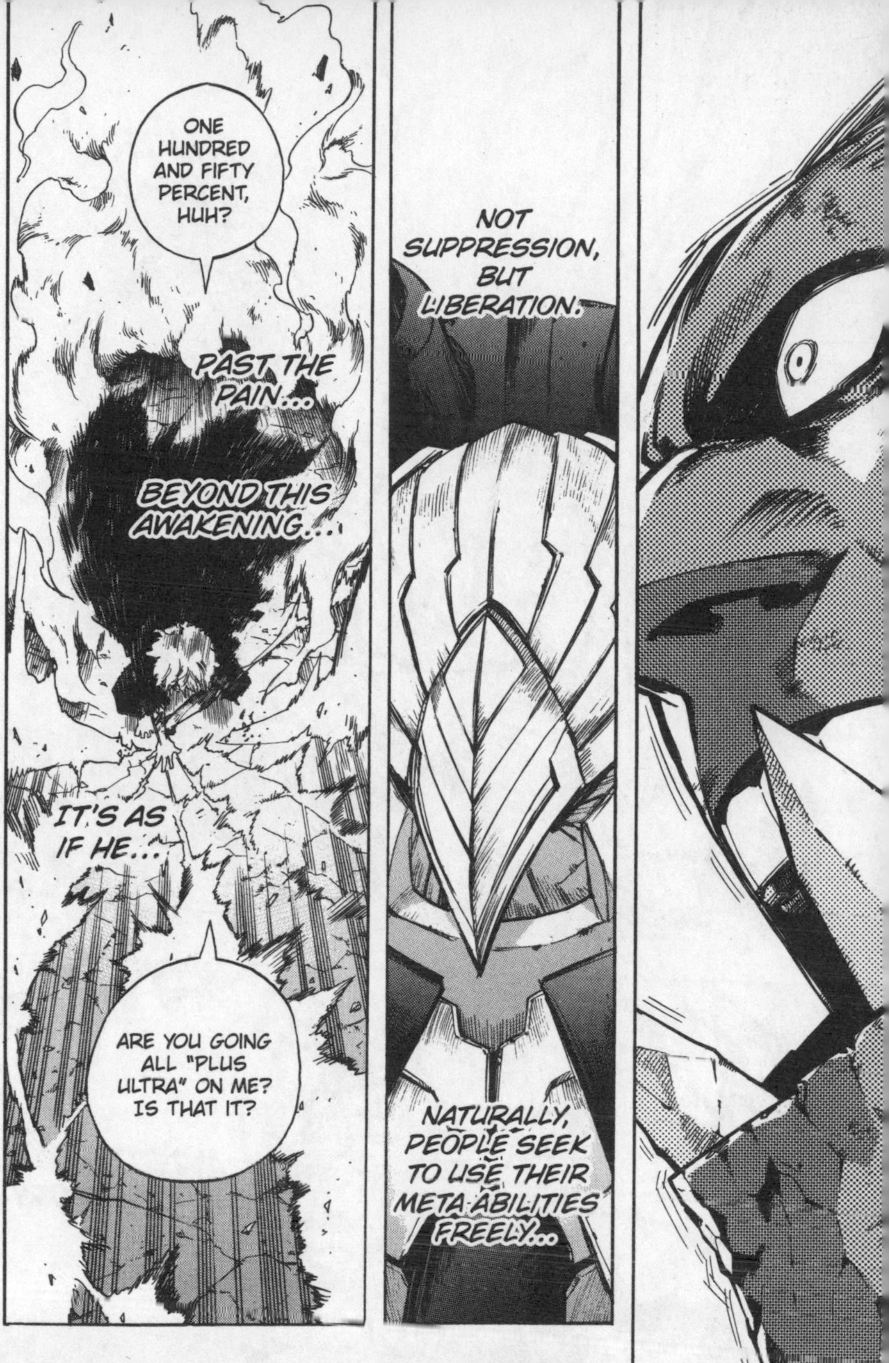
NOT SUPPRESSION, BUT LIBERATION.
NATURALLY, PEOPLE SEEK TO USE THEIR META ABILITIES FREELY...
ONE HUNDRED AND FIFTY PERCENT, HUH?
PAST THE PAIN...
BEYOND THIS AWAKENING...
IT'S AS IF HE...
ARE YOU GOING ALL "PLUS ULTRA" ON ME? IS THAT IT?

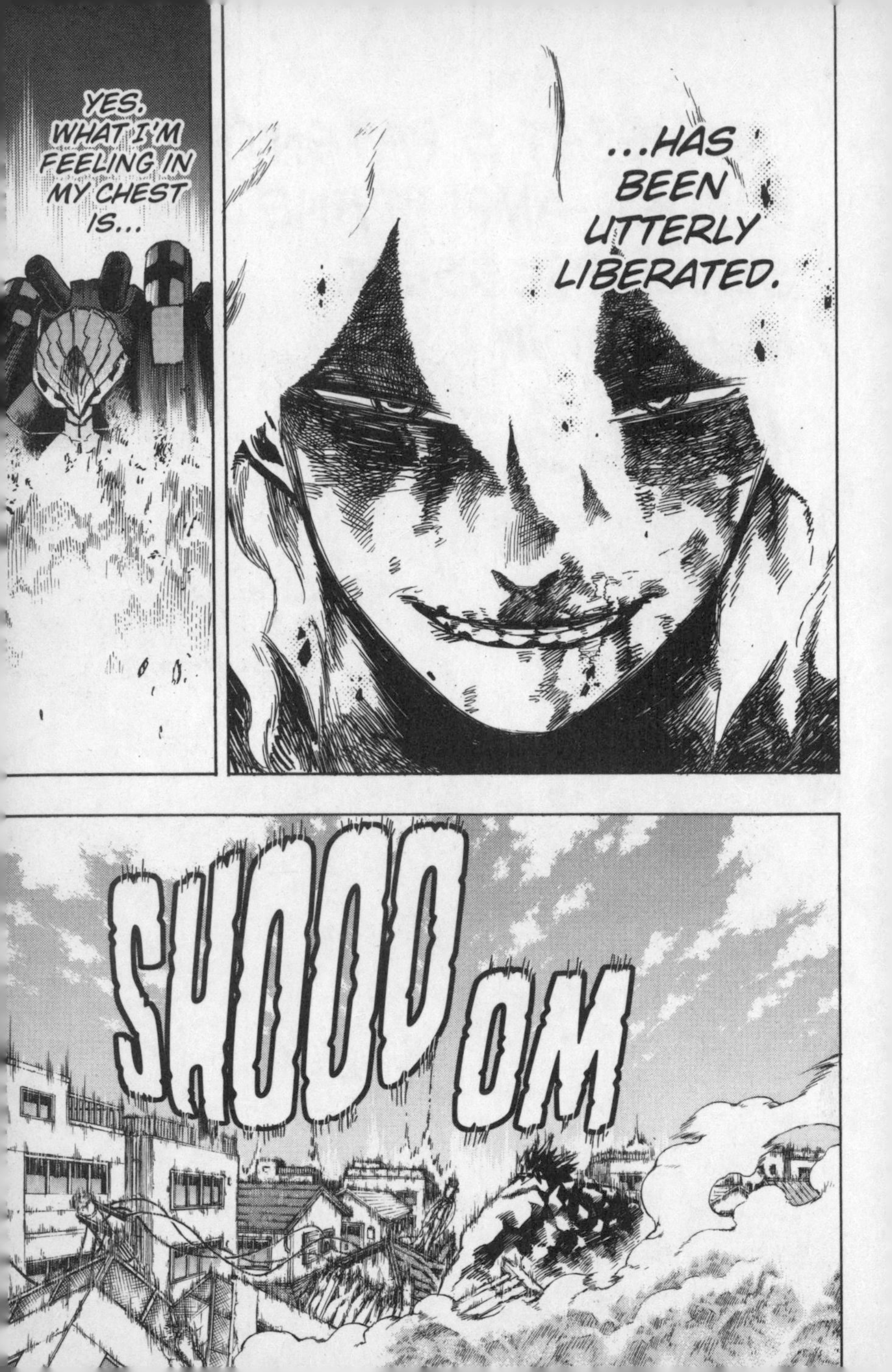
...HAS BEEN UTTERLY LIBERATED.
YES. WHAT I'M FEELING IN MY CHEST IS...
SHOOOOM

DETNERAT'S PATENTED BURDEN-AMPLIFYING STEEL PRESSURE MECHANISM

CLAUSTRO

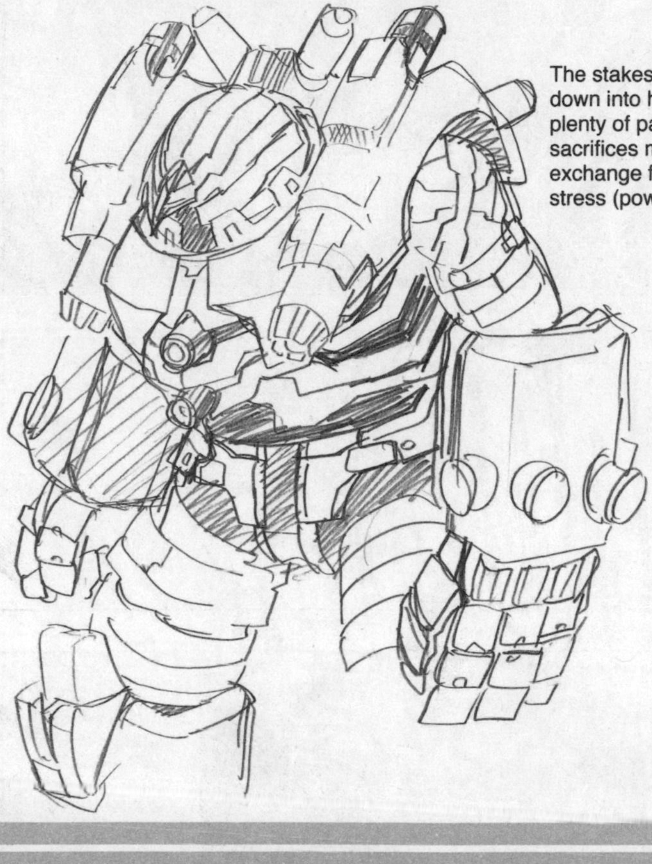

The stakes that clamp down into his body cause plenty of pain. This suit sacrifices mobility in exchange for explosive stress (power).

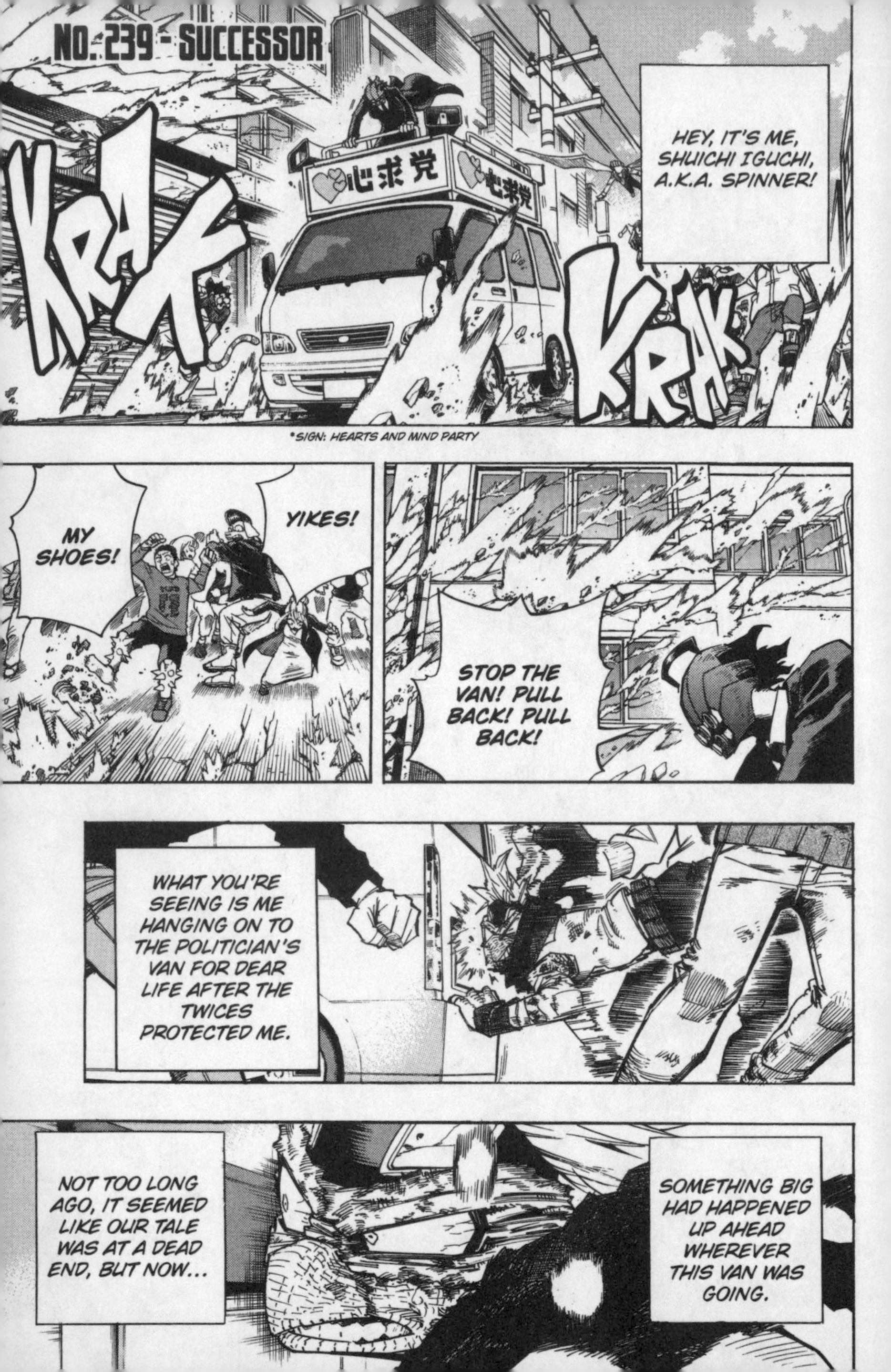
NO. 239 - SUCCESSOR
HEY, IT'S ME, SHUICHI IGUCHI, A.K.A. SPINNER!
KRAK
KRAK
心求党
*SIGN: HEARTS AND MIND PARTY
STOP THE VAN! PULL BACK! PULL BACK!
YIKES!
MY SHOES!
WHAT YOU'RE SEEING IS ME HANGING ON TO THE POLITICIAN'S VAN FOR DEAR LIFE AFTER THE TWICES PROTECTED ME.
SOMETHING BIG HAD HAPPENED UP AHEAD WHEREVER THIS VAN WAS GOING.
NOT TOO LONG AGO, IT SEEMED LIKE OUR TALE WAS AT A DEAD END, BUT NOW...

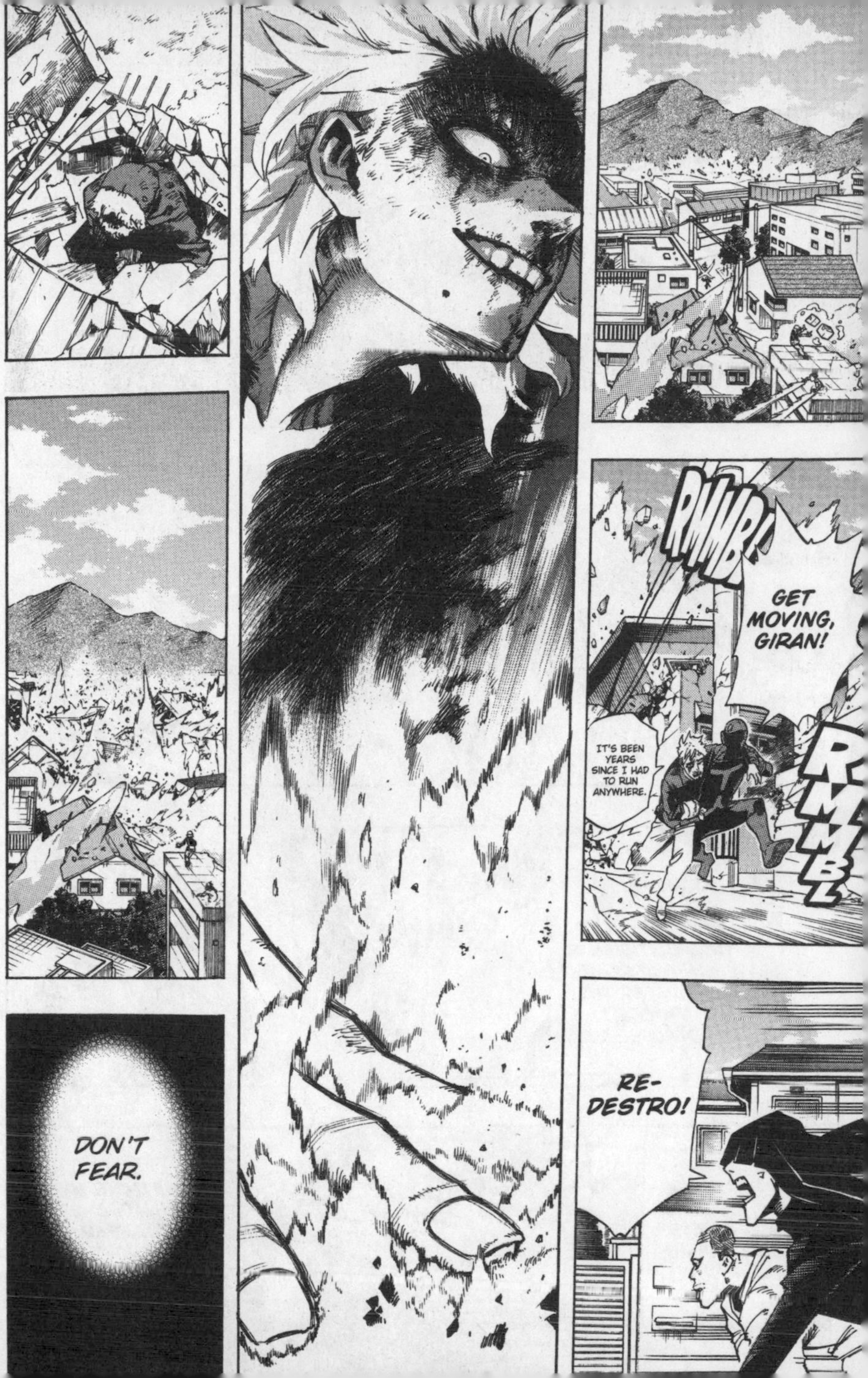
RMMB!
GET MOVING, GIRAN!
IT'S BEEN YEARS SINCE I HAD TO RUN ANYWHERE.
RMMBL
RE-DESTRO!
DON'T FEAR.

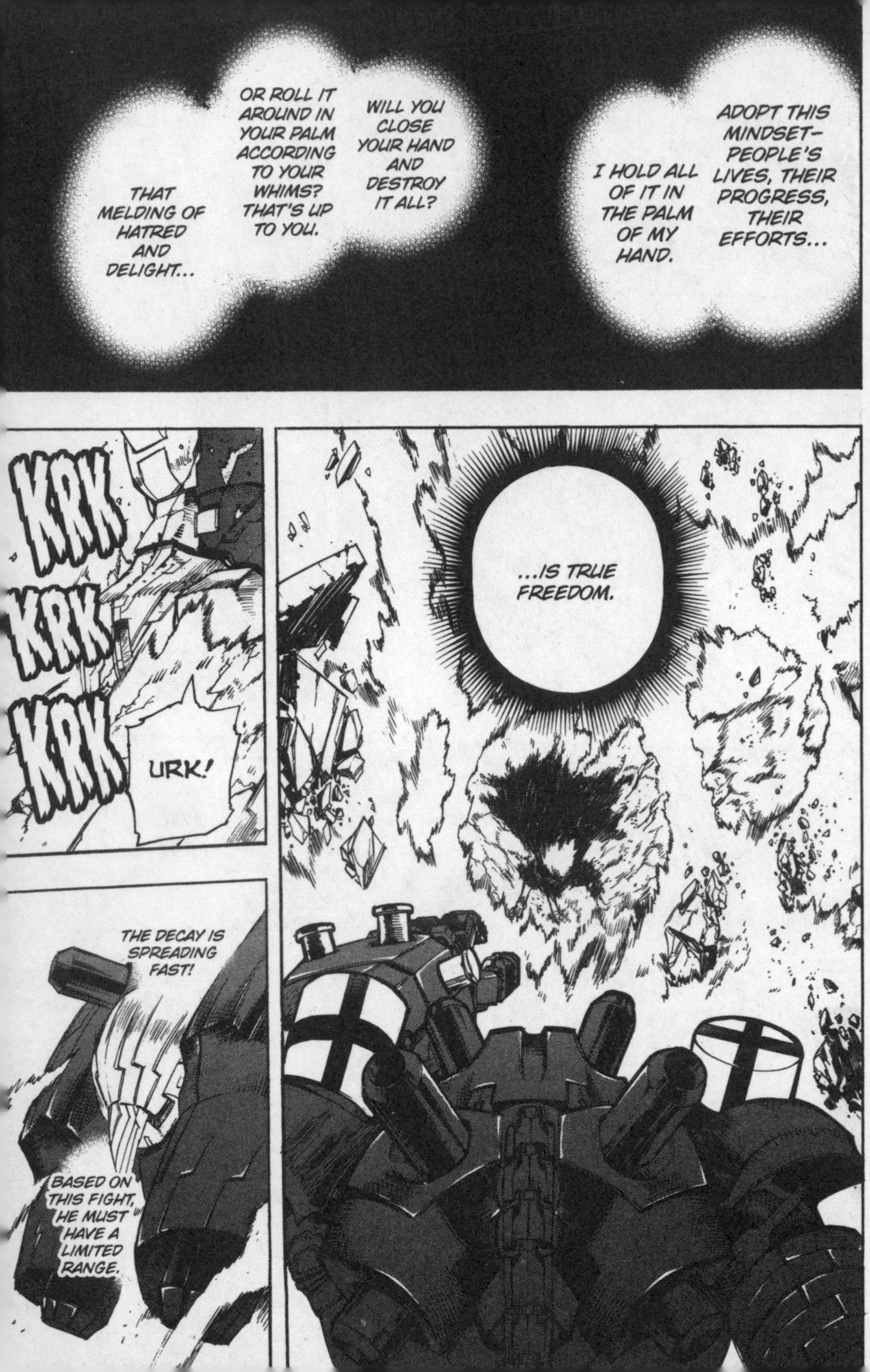
ADOPT THIS MINDSET— PEOPLE'S LIVES, THEIR PROGRESS, THEIR EFFORTS...
I HOLD ALL OF IT IN THE PALM OF MY HAND.
WILL YOU CLOSE YOUR HAND AND DESTROY IT ALL?
OR ROLL IT AROUND IN YOUR PALM ACCORDING TO YOUR WHIMS? THAT'S UP TO YOU.
THAT MELDING OF HATRED AND DELIGHT...
...IS TRUE FREEDOM.
KRK
KRK
KRK
URK!
THE DECAY IS SPREADING FAST!
BASED ON THIS FIGHT, HE MUST HAVE A LIMITED RANGE.

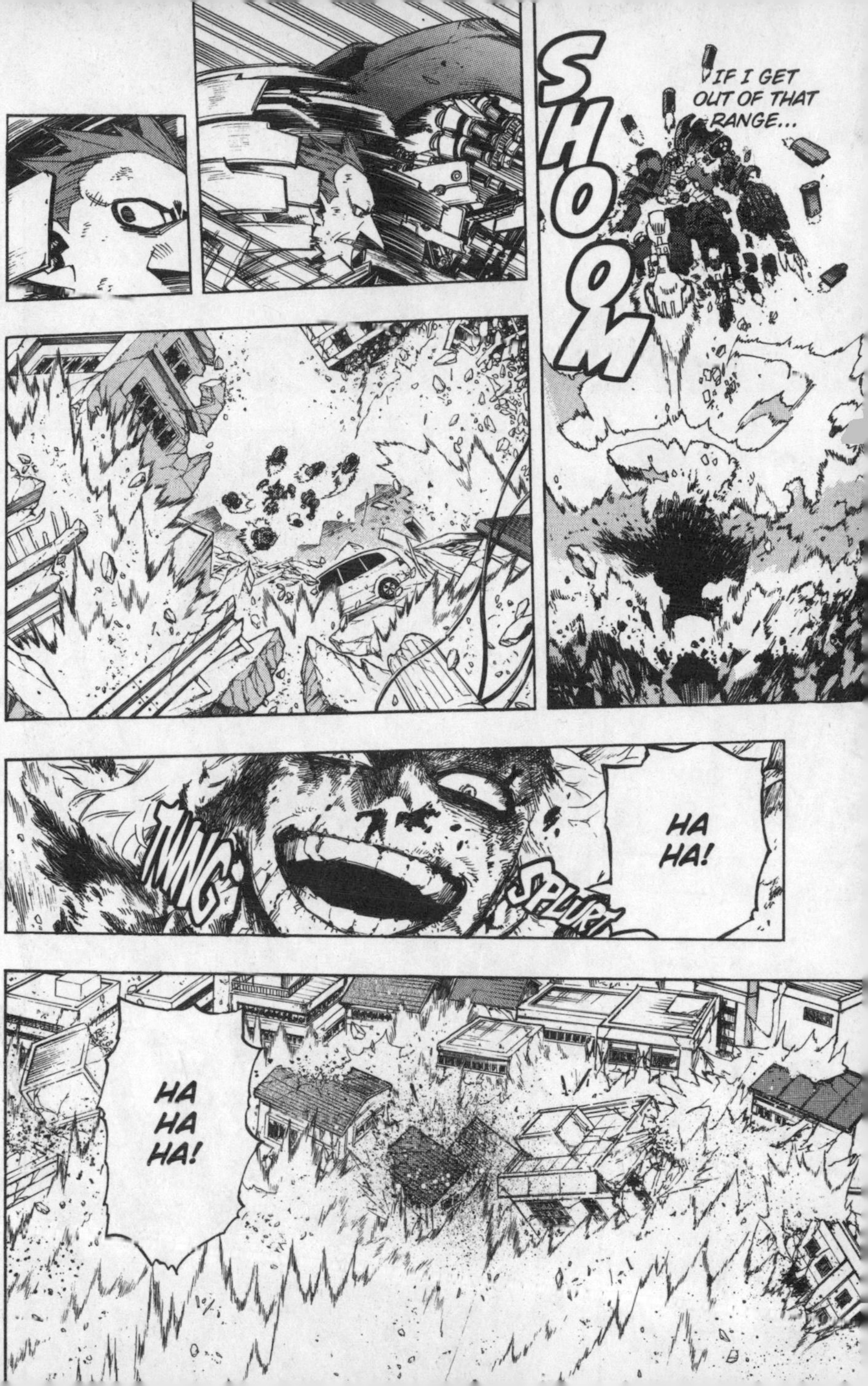
SHOOM
IF I GET OUT OF THAT RANGE...
HA HA!
SPLURT
TWNG
HA HA HA!

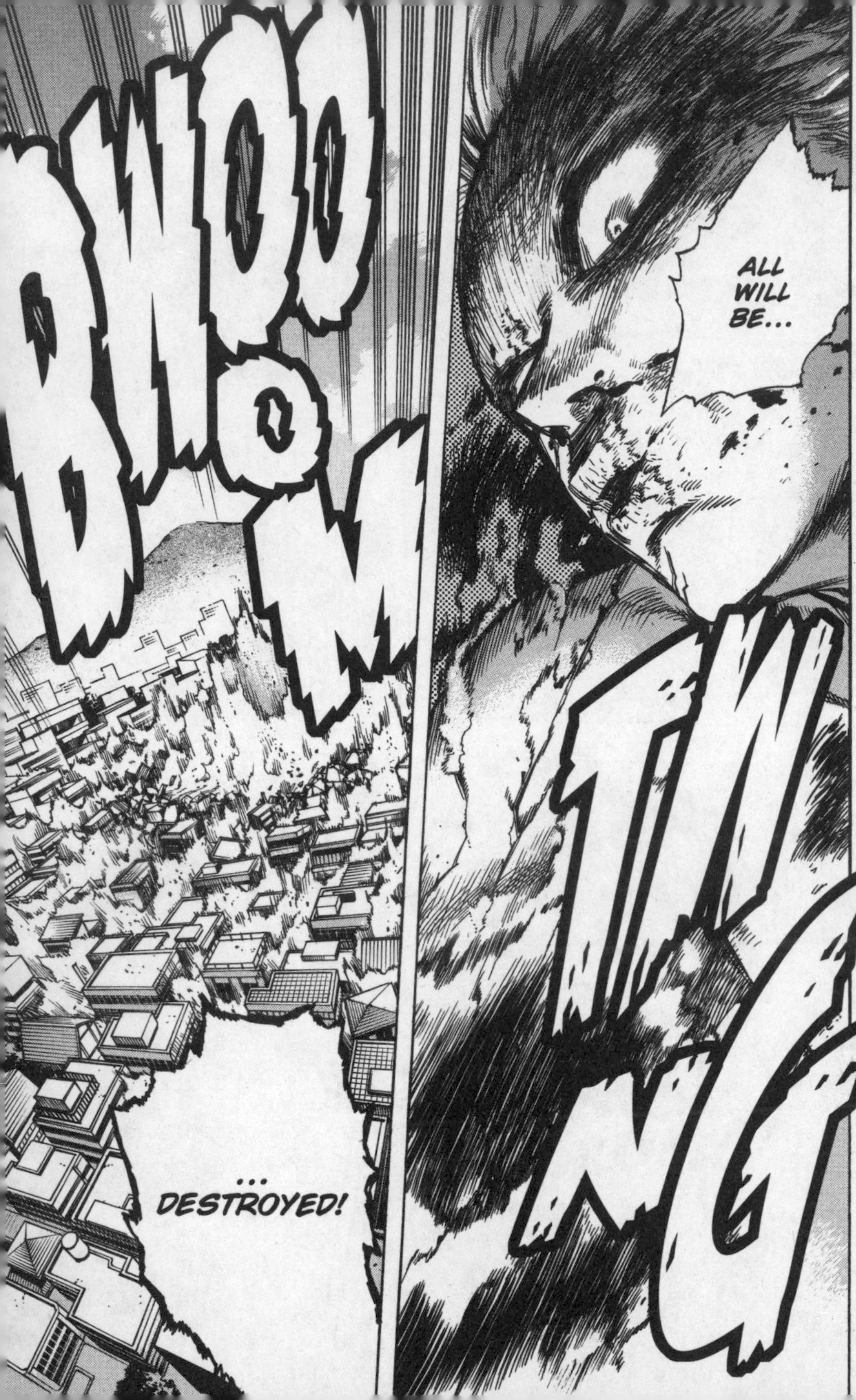
ALL WILL BE...
...DESTROYED!

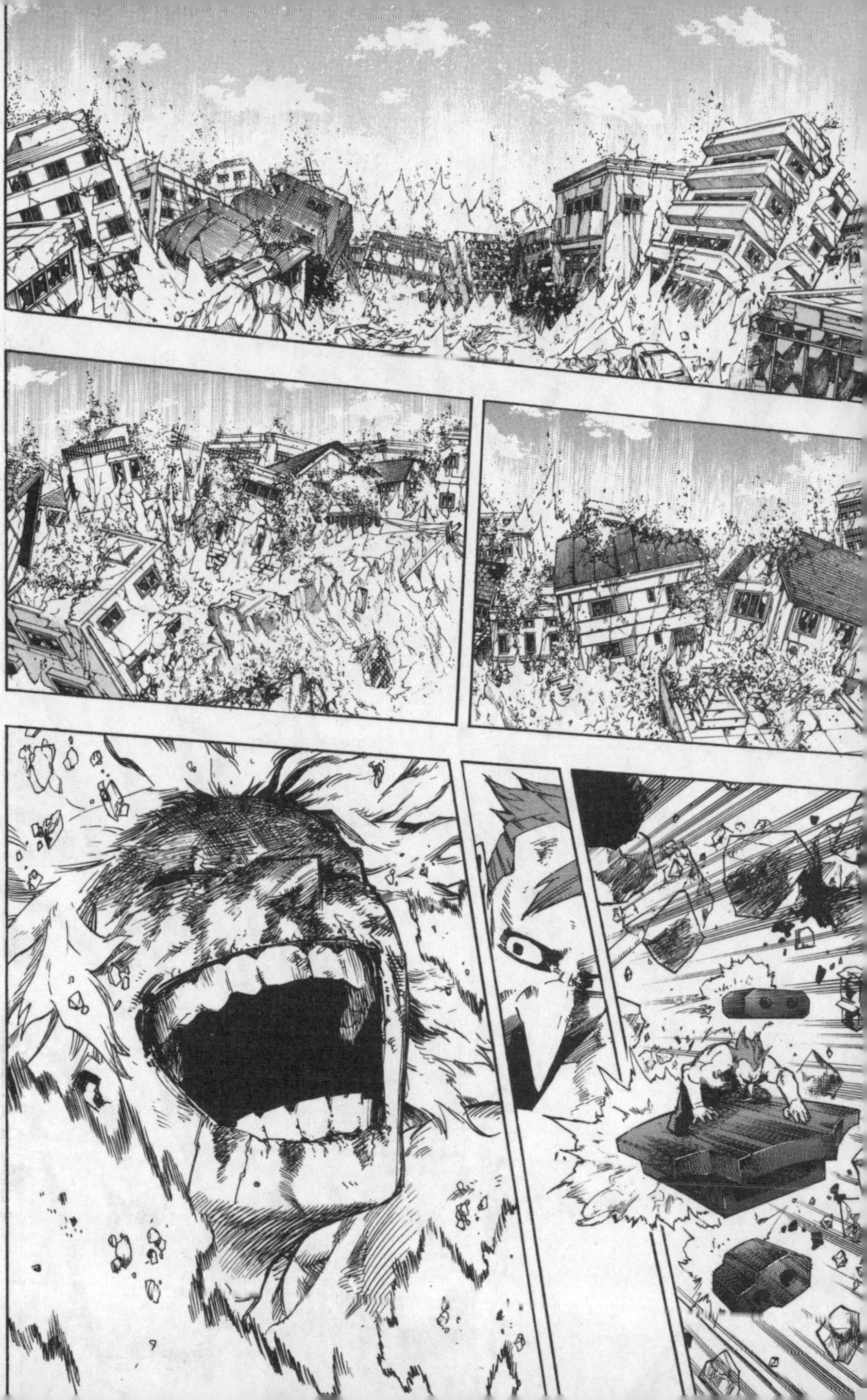

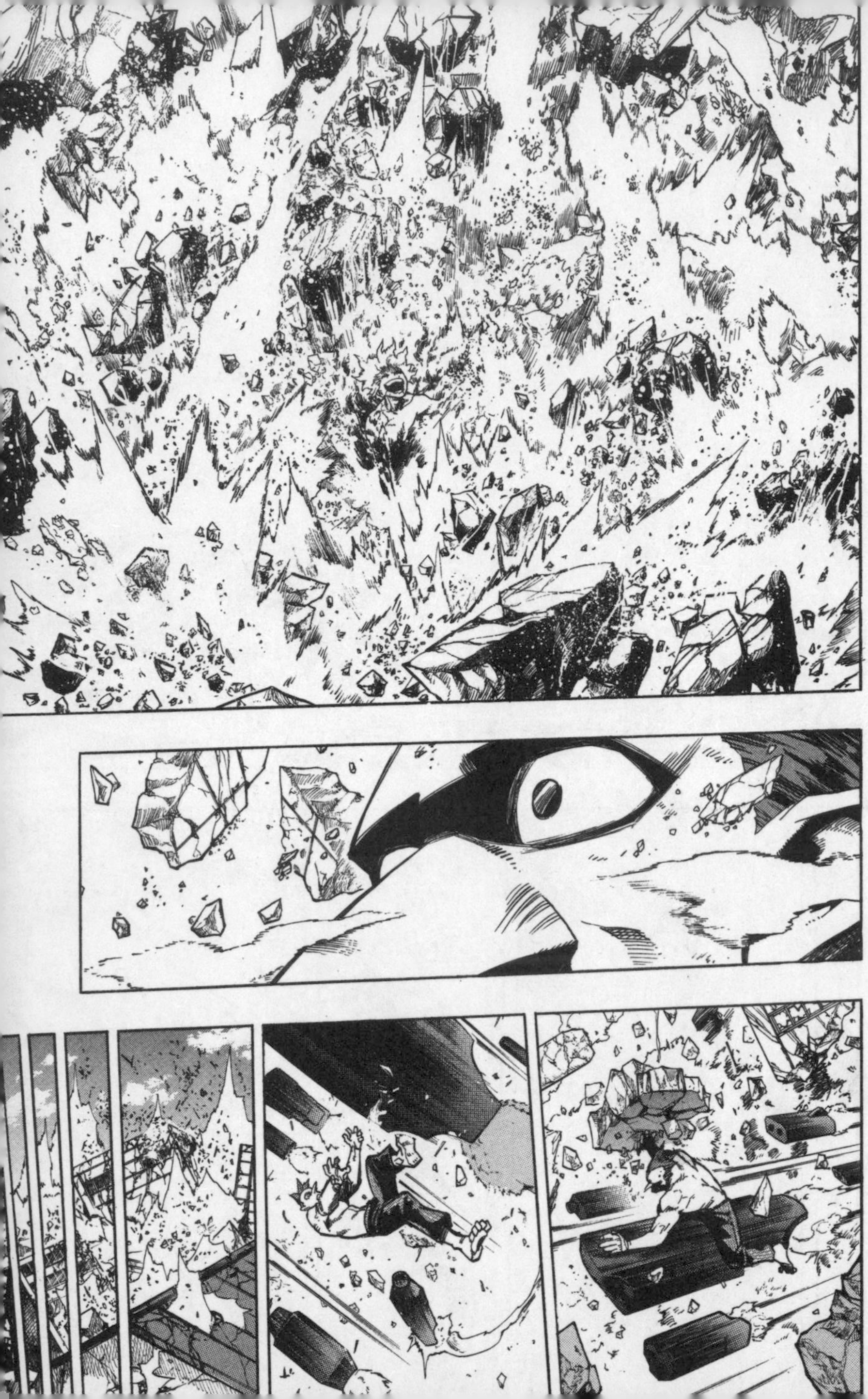

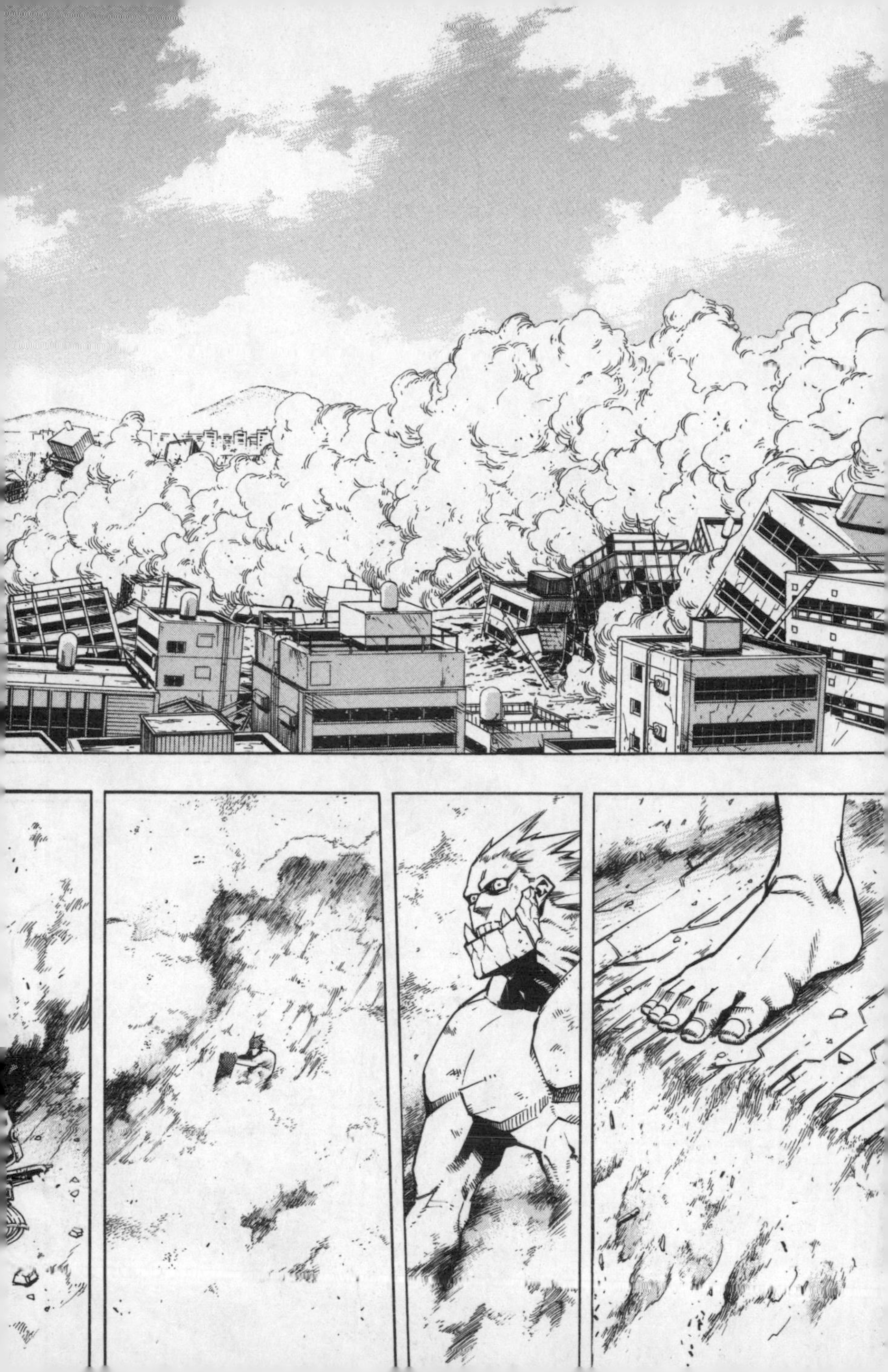

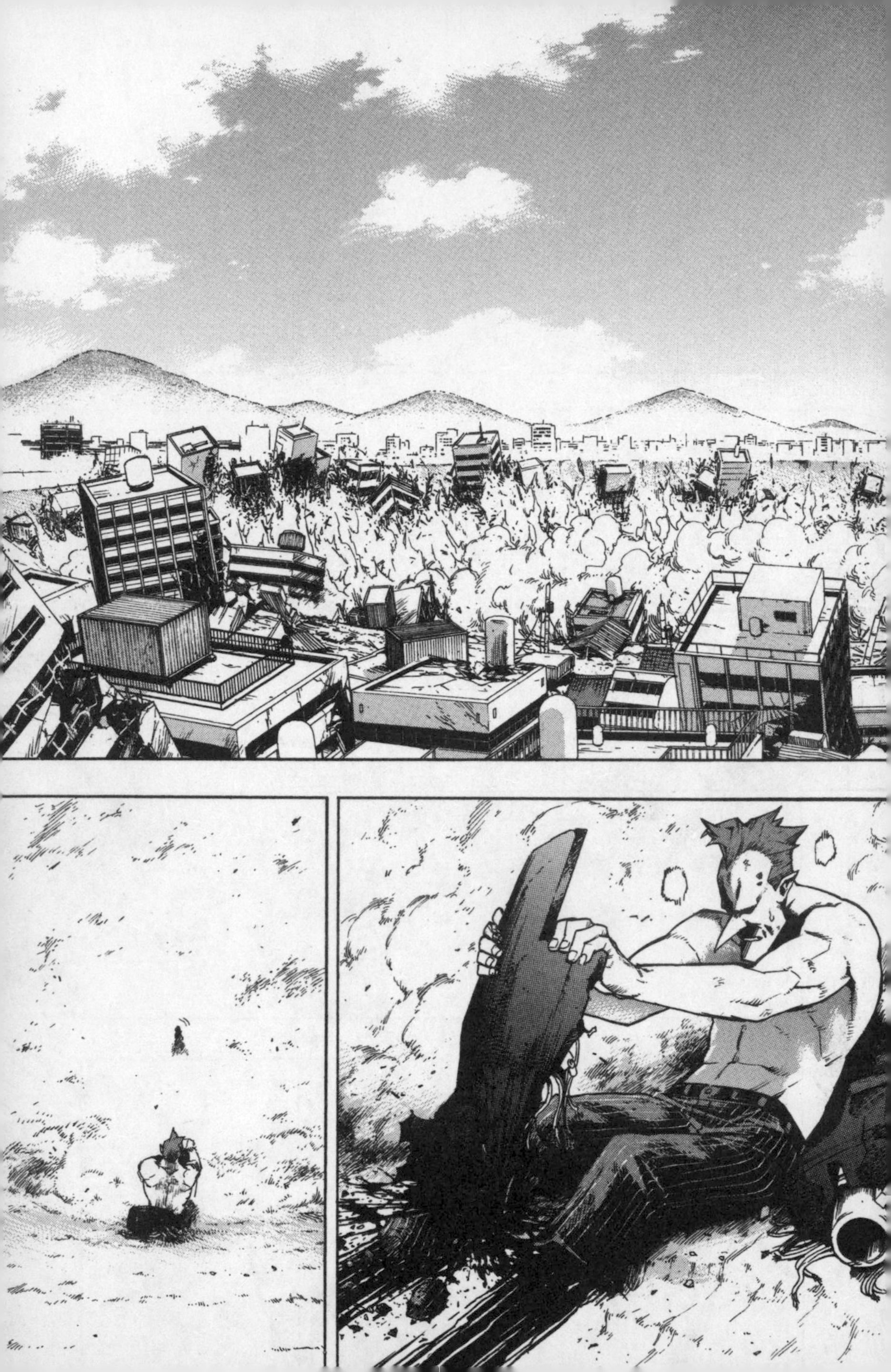

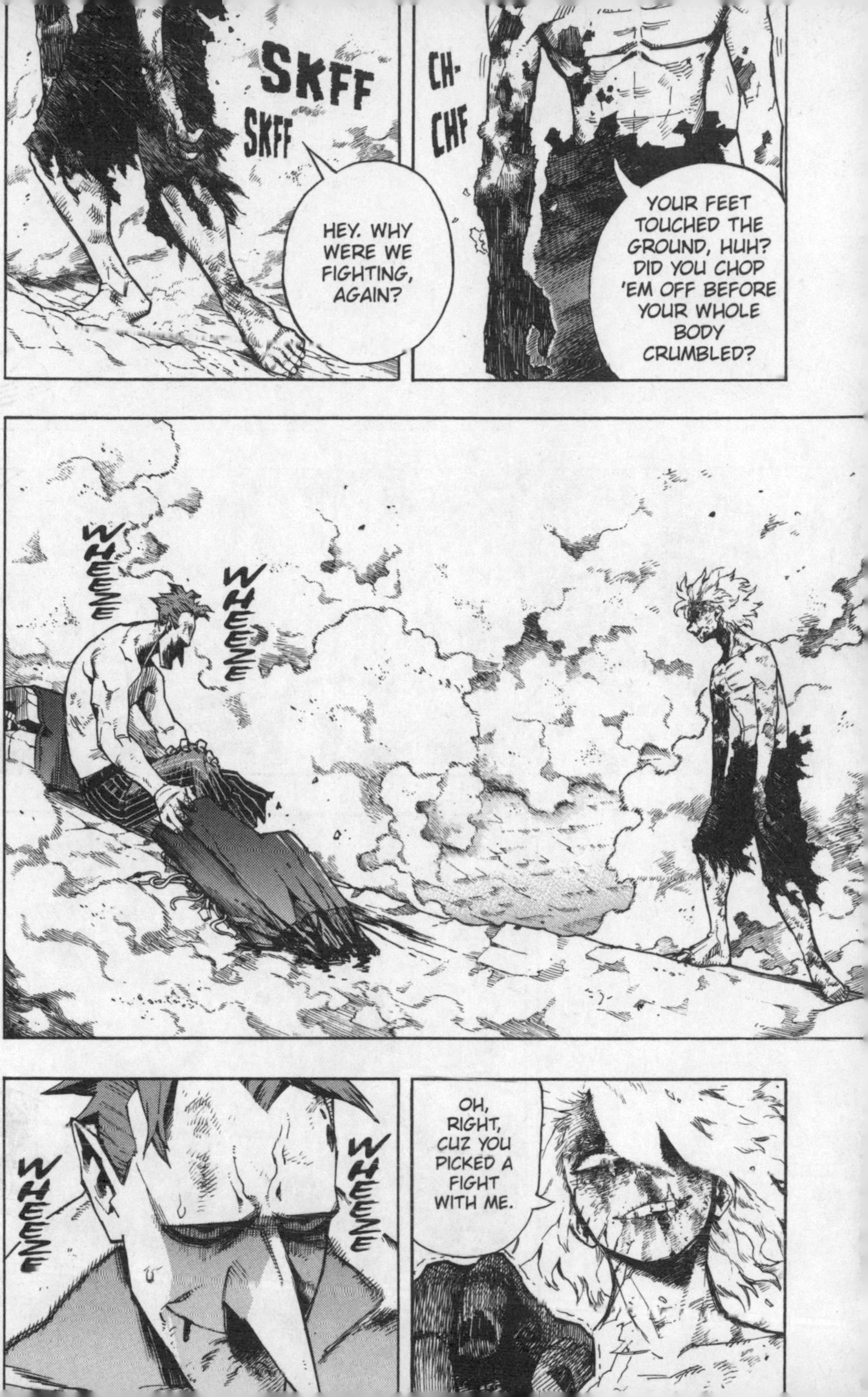
CH-
CHF
YOUR FEET TOUCHED THE GROUND, HUH? DID YOU CHOP 'EM OFF BEFORE YOUR WHOLE BODY CRUMBLED?
SKFF
SKFF
HEY. WHY WERE WE FIGHTING, AGAIN?
WHEEZE
WHEEZE
OH, RIGHT, CUZ YOU PICKED A FIGHT WITH ME.
WHEEZE
WHEEZE

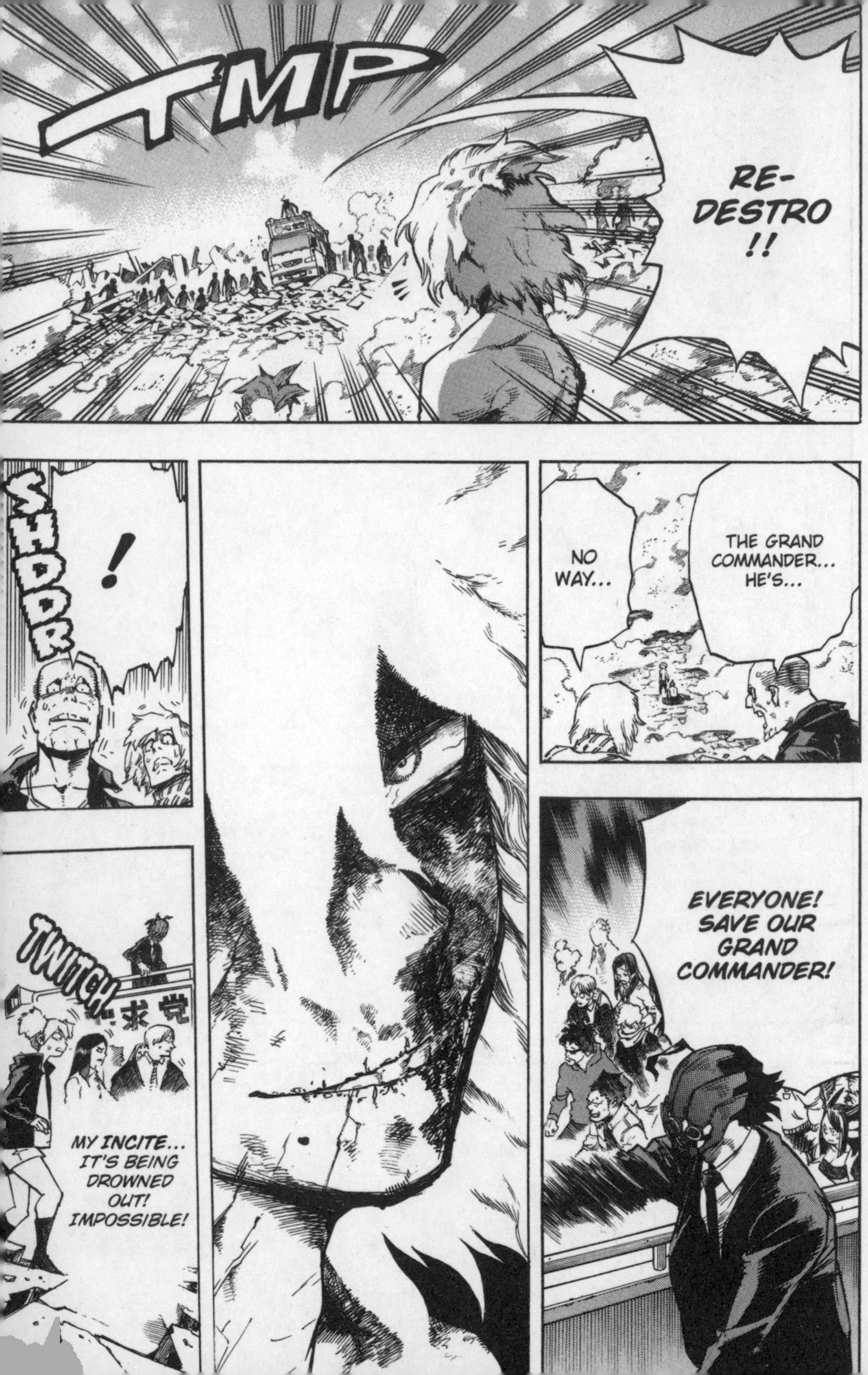
TMP
RE-DESTRO!!
THE GRAND COMMANDER... HE'S...
NO WAY...
EVERYONE! SAVE OUR GRAND COMMANDER!
SHDDR
!
TWITCH
求党
MY INCITE... IT'S BEING DROWNED OUT! IMPOSSIBLE!

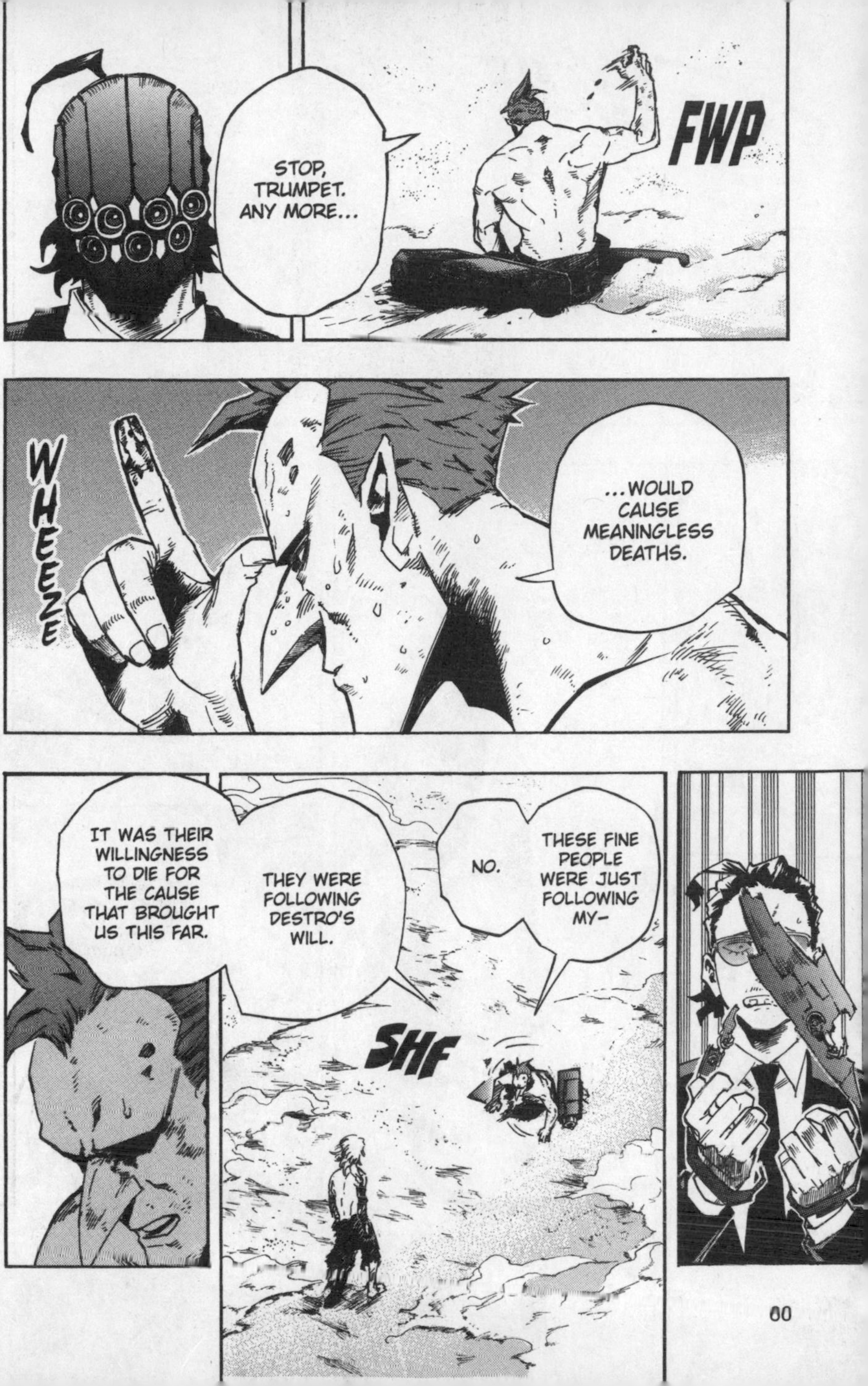
FWP
STOP, TRUMPET. ANY MORE...
...WOULD CAUSE MEANINGLESS DEATHS.
WHEEZE
THESE FINE PEOPLE WERE JUST FOLLOWING MY–
NO.
THEY WERE FOLLOWING DESTRO'S WILL.
IT WAS THEIR WILLINGNESS TO DIE FOR THE CAUSE THAT BROUGHT US THIS FAR.
SHF

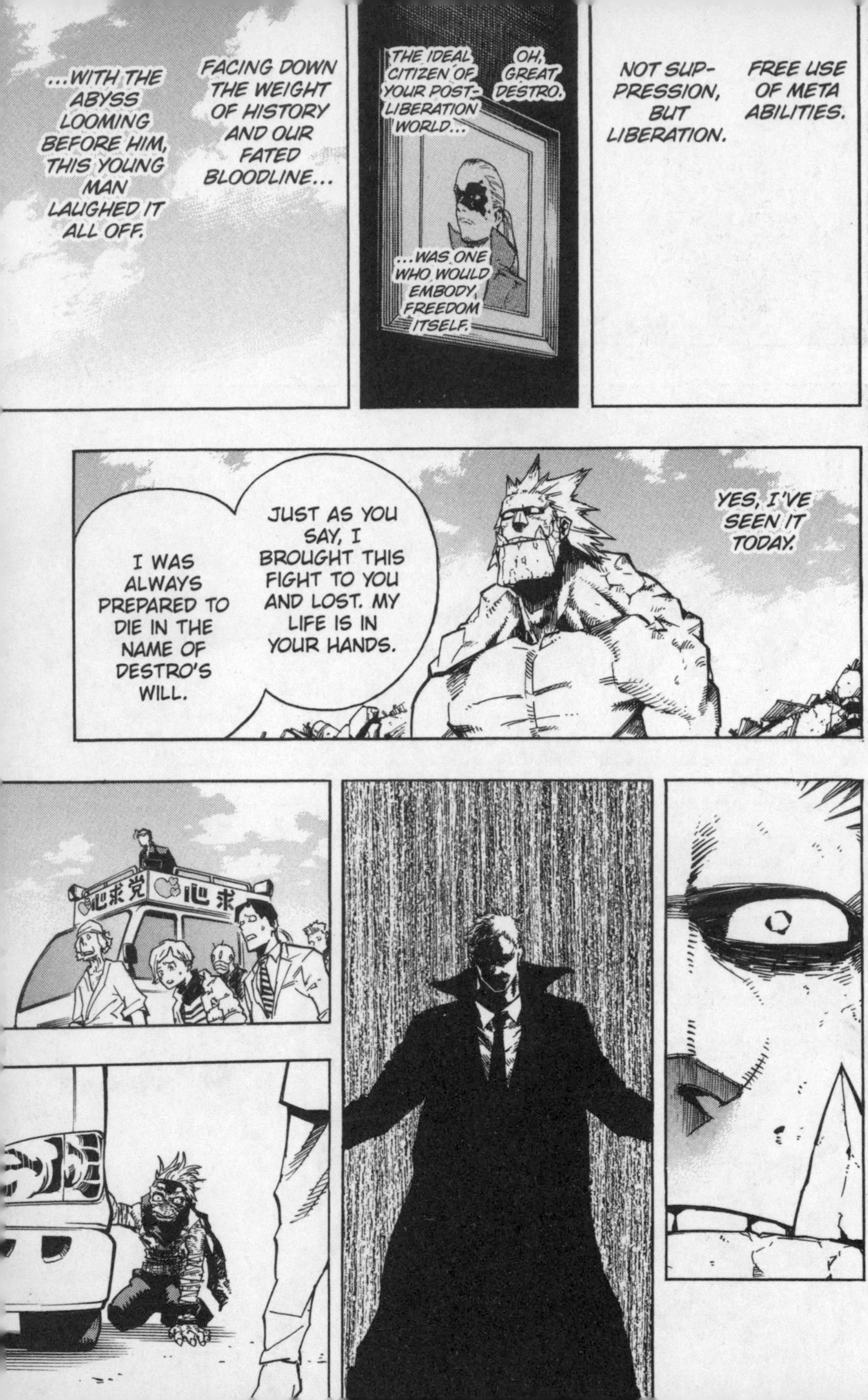
FREE USE OF META ABILITIES.
NOT SUP-PRESSION, BUT LIBERATION.
OH, GREAT DESTRO.
THE IDEAL CITIZEN OF YOUR POST-LIBERATION WORLD...
...WAS ONE WHO WOULD EMBODY FREEDOM ITSELF.
FACING DOWN THE WEIGHT OF HISTORY AND OUR FATED BLOODLINE...
...WITH THE ABYSS LOOMING BEFORE HIM, THIS YOUNG MAN LAUGHED IT ALL OFF.
YES, I'VE SEEN IT TODAY.
JUST AS YOU SAY, I BROUGHT THIS FIGHT TO YOU AND LOST. MY LIFE IS IN YOUR HANDS.
I WAS ALWAYS PREPARED TO DIE IN THE NAME OF DESTRO'S WILL.
心求党
心求

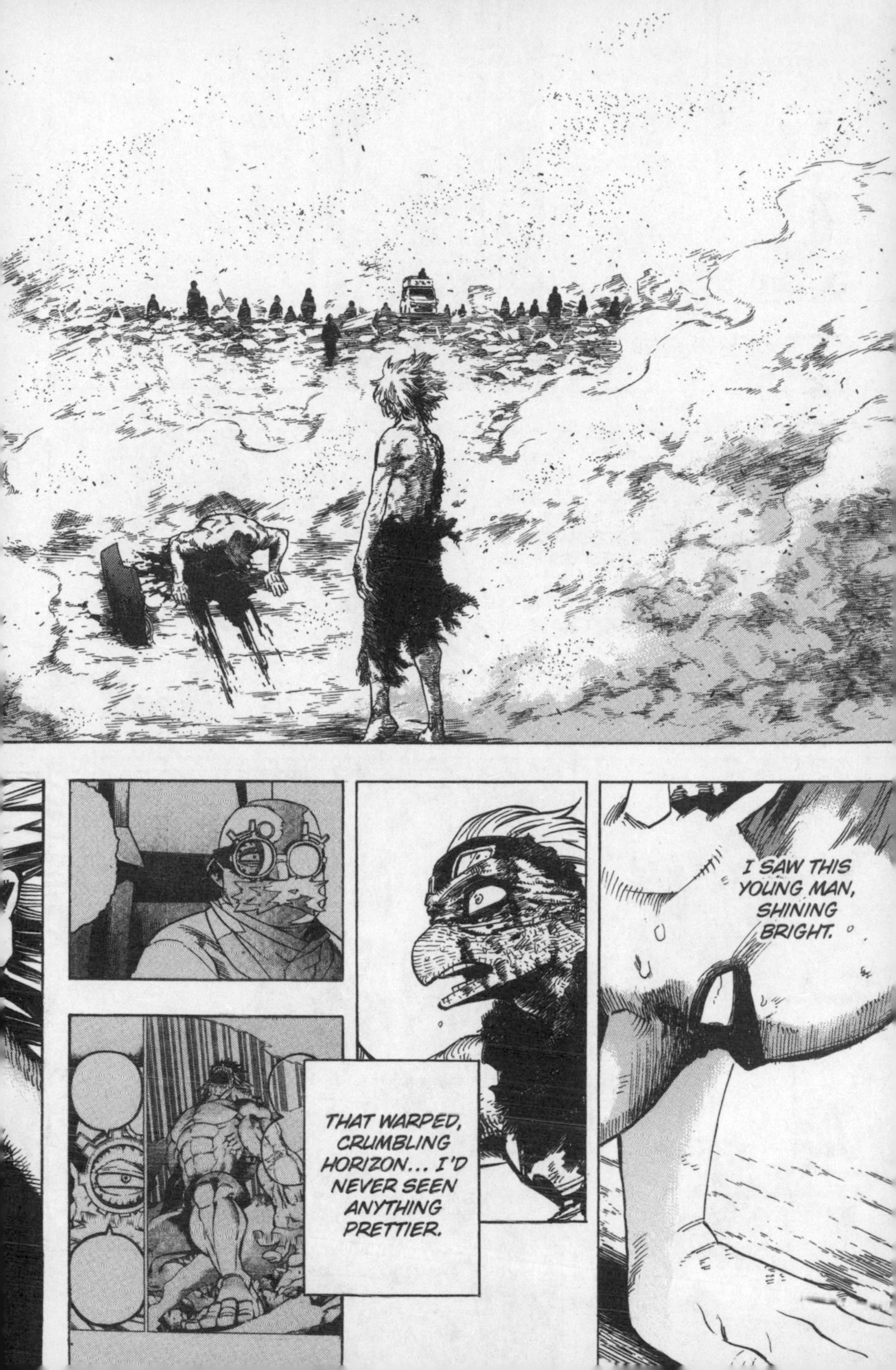
I SAW THIS YOUNG MAN, SHINING BRIGHT.
THAT WARPED, CRUMBLING HORIZON… I'D NEVER SEEN ANYTHING PRETTIER.

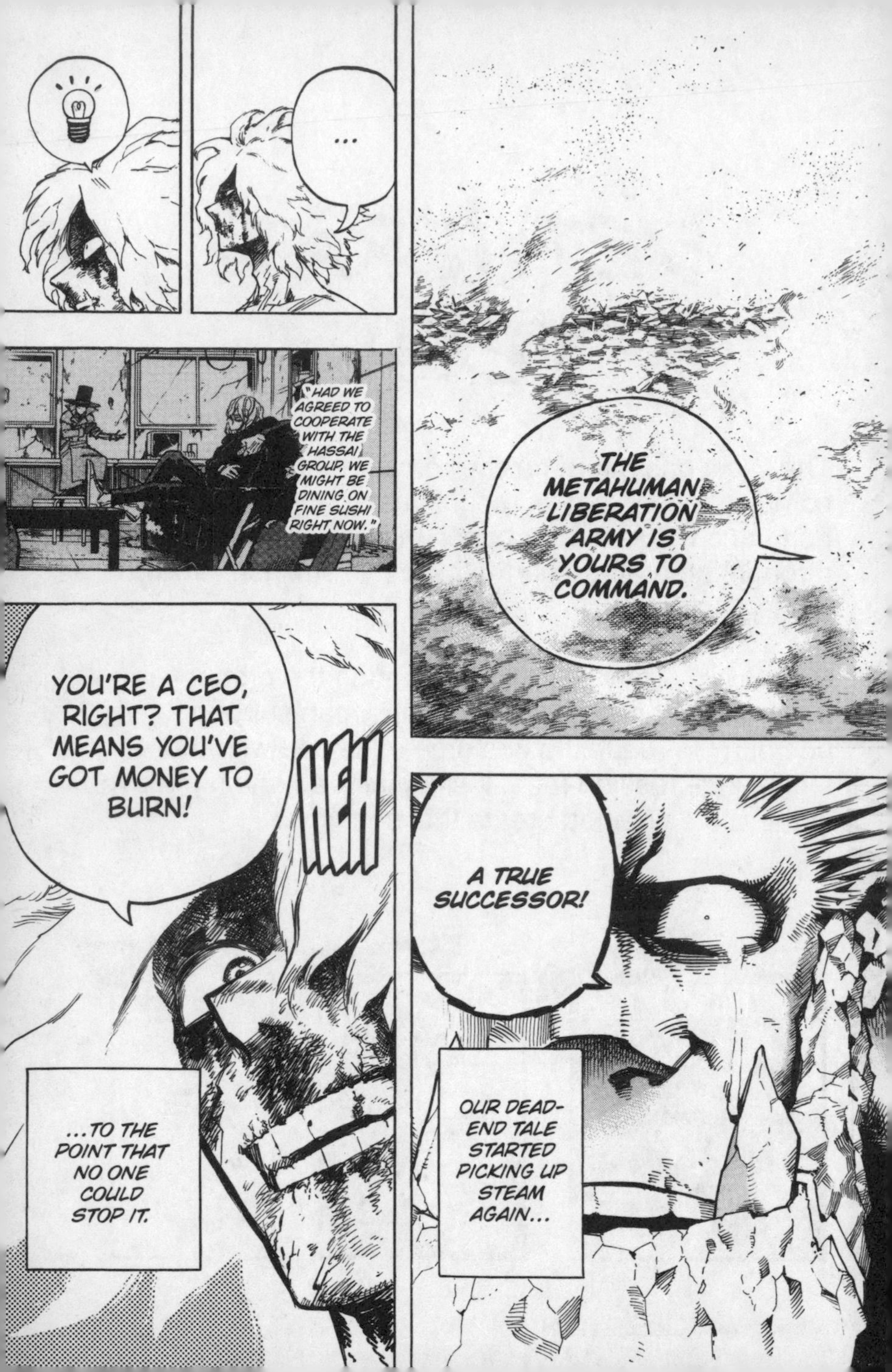
THE METAHUMAN LIBERATION ARMY IS YOURS TO COMMAND.
A TRUE SUCCESSOR!
OUR DEAD-END TALE STARTED PICKING UP STEAM AGAIN...
...
"HAD WE AGREED TO COOPERATE WITH THE HASSAI GROUP, WE MIGHT BE DINING ON FINE SUSHI RIGHT NOW."
YOU'RE A CEO, RIGHT? THAT MEANS YOU'VE GOT MONEY TO BURN!
HEH
...TO THE POINT THAT NO ONE COULD STOP IT.

DETNERAT TECH

The West has been making remarkable strides in compact technology in recent years, and Detnerat's gone and plagiarized a bunch of it. They haven't gone through the proper channels, so this stuff isn't known to the public.

Meanwhile, Endeavor did go through the proper channels when he went to an American support company to request a costume equipped with the latest compression tech. Incidentally, a certain girl over in the States helped create that costume.

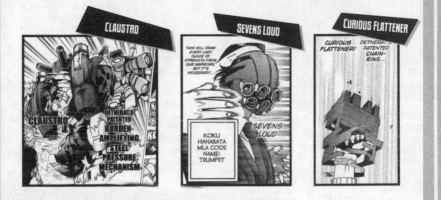

CURIOUS FLATTENER

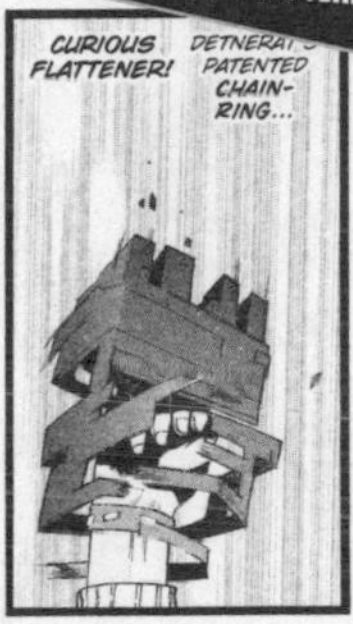
DETNERAT'
PATENTED CHAIN-RING...
CURIOUS FLATTENER!

SEVENS LOUD

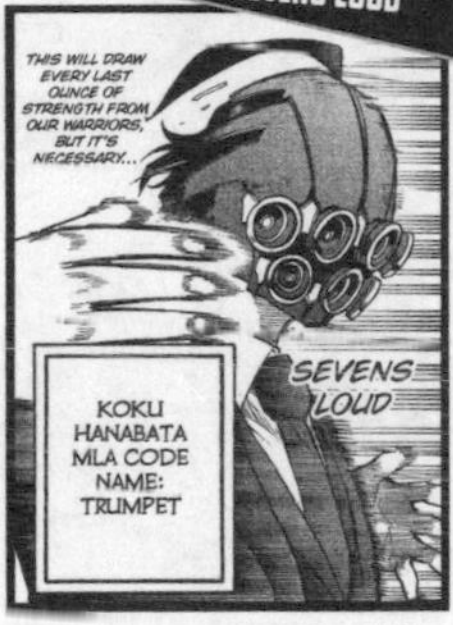
THIS WILL DRAW EVERY LAST OUNCE OF STRENGTH FROM OUR WARRIORS, BUT IT'S NECESSARY...
SEVENS LOUD
KOKU HANABATA MLA CODE NAME: TRUMPET

CLAUSTRO

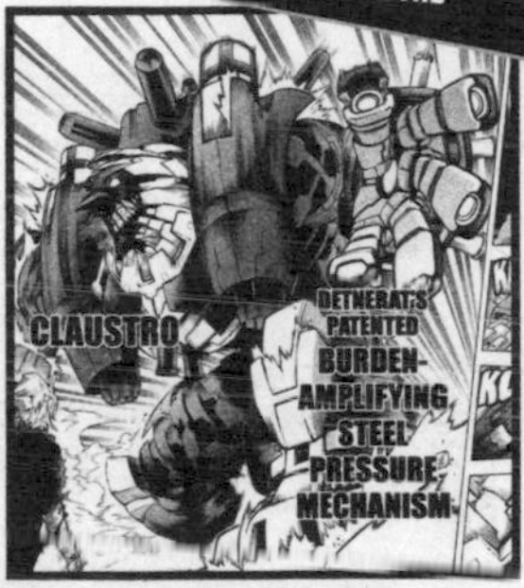
DETNERAT'S PATENTED BURDEN-AMPLIFYING STEEL PRESSURE MECHANISM
CLAUSTRO

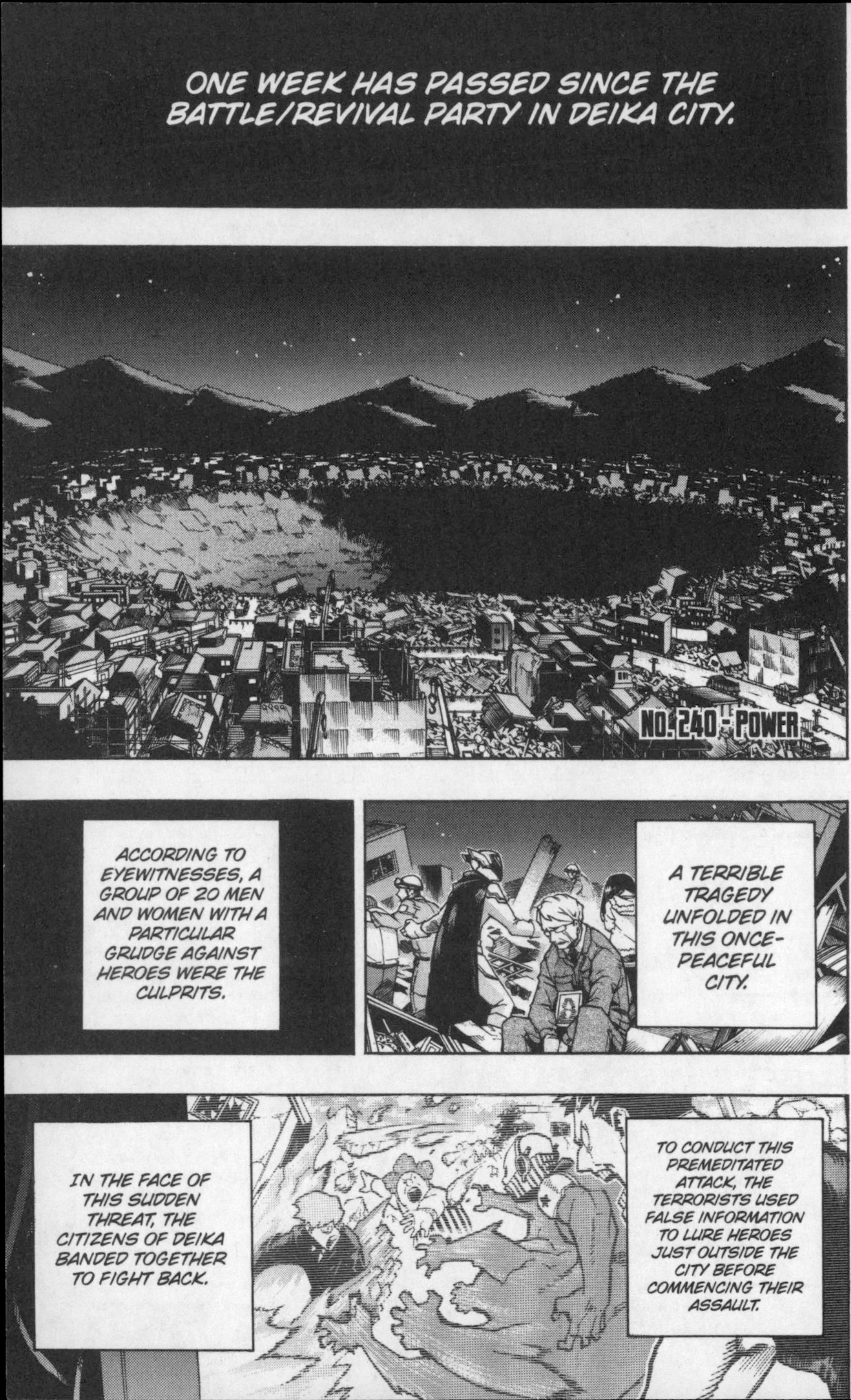
ONE WEEK HAS PASSED SINCE THE BATTLE/REVIVAL PARTY IN DEIKA CITY.
NO. 240 - POWER
A TERRIBLE TRAGEDY UNFOLDED IN THIS ONCE-PEACEFUL CITY.
ACCORDING TO EYEWITNESSES, A GROUP OF 20 MEN AND WOMEN WITH A PARTICULAR GRUDGE AGAINST HEROES WERE THE CULPRITS.
TO CONDUCT THIS PREMEDITATED ATTACK, THE TERRORISTS USED FALSE INFORMATION TO LURE HEROES JUST OUTSIDE THE CITY BEFORE COMMENCING THEIR ASSAULT.
IN THE FACE OF THIS SUDDEN THREAT, THE CITIZENS OF DEIKA BANDED TOGETHER TO FIGHT BACK.

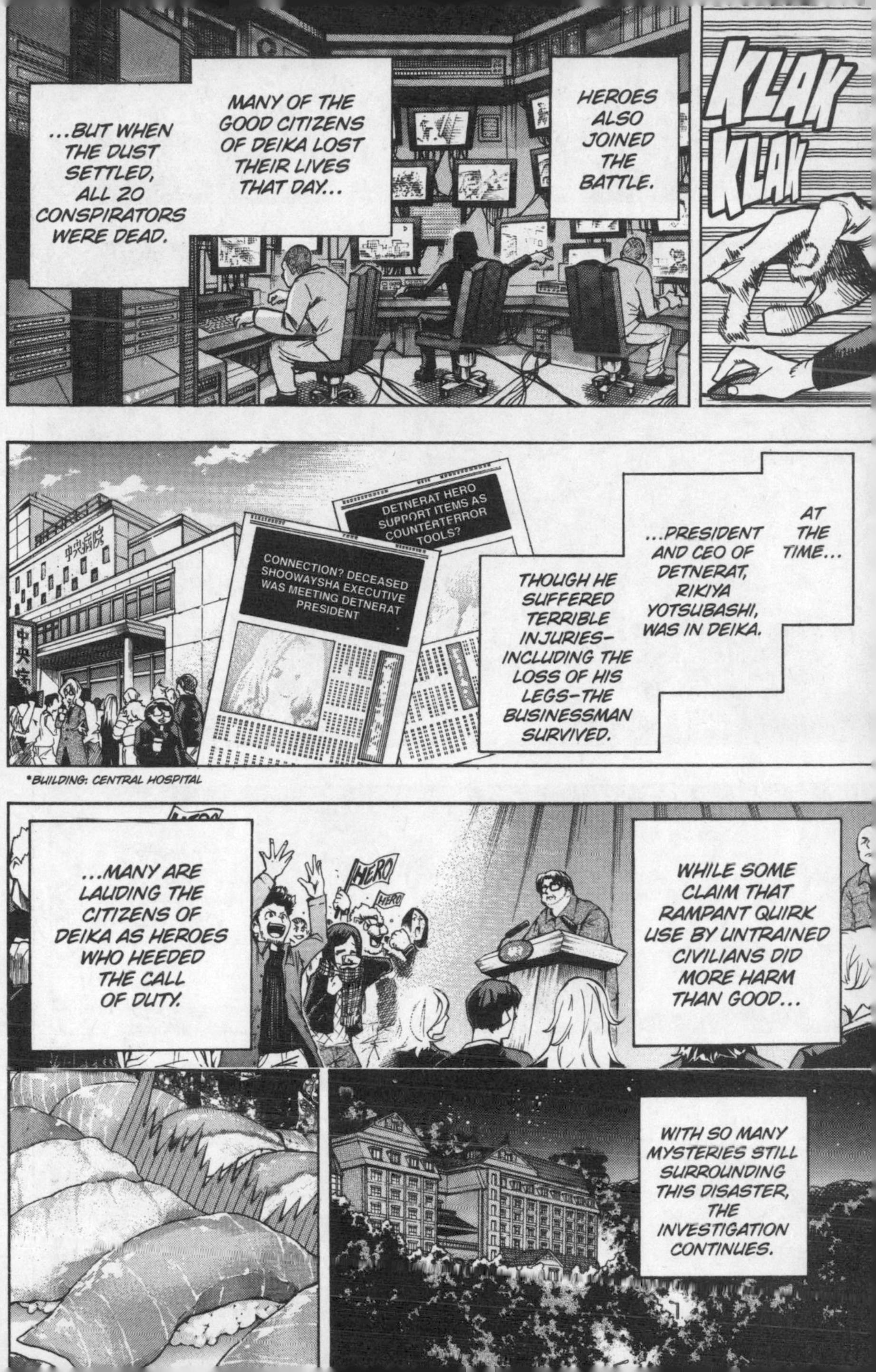
KLAK
KLAK
HEROES ALSO JOINED THE BATTLE.
MANY OF THE GOOD CITIZENS OF DEIKA LOST THEIR LIVES THAT DAY...
...BUT WHEN THE DUST SETTLED, ALL 20 CONSPIRATORS WERE DEAD.
AT THE TIME...
...PRESIDENT AND CEO OF DETNERAT, RIKIYA YOTSUBASHI, WAS IN DEIKA.
THOUGH HE SUFFERED TERRIBLE INJURIES—INCLUDING THE LOSS OF HIS LEGS—THE BUSINESSMAN SURVIVED.
DETNERAT HERO SUPPORT ITEMS AS COUNTERTERROR TOOLS?
CONNECTION? DECEASED SHOOWAYSHA EXECUTIVE WAS MEETING DETNERAT PRESIDENT
中央病院
*BUILDING: CENTRAL HOSPITAL
WHILE SOME CLAIM THAT RAMPANT QUIRK USE BY UNTRAINED CIVILIANS DID MORE HARM THAN GOOD...
...MANY ARE LAUDING THE CITIZENS OF DEIKA AS HEROES WHO HEEDED THE CALL OF DUTY.
HERO
HERO
WITH SO MANY MYSTERIES STILL SURROUNDING THIS DISASTER, THE INVESTIGATION CONTINUES.

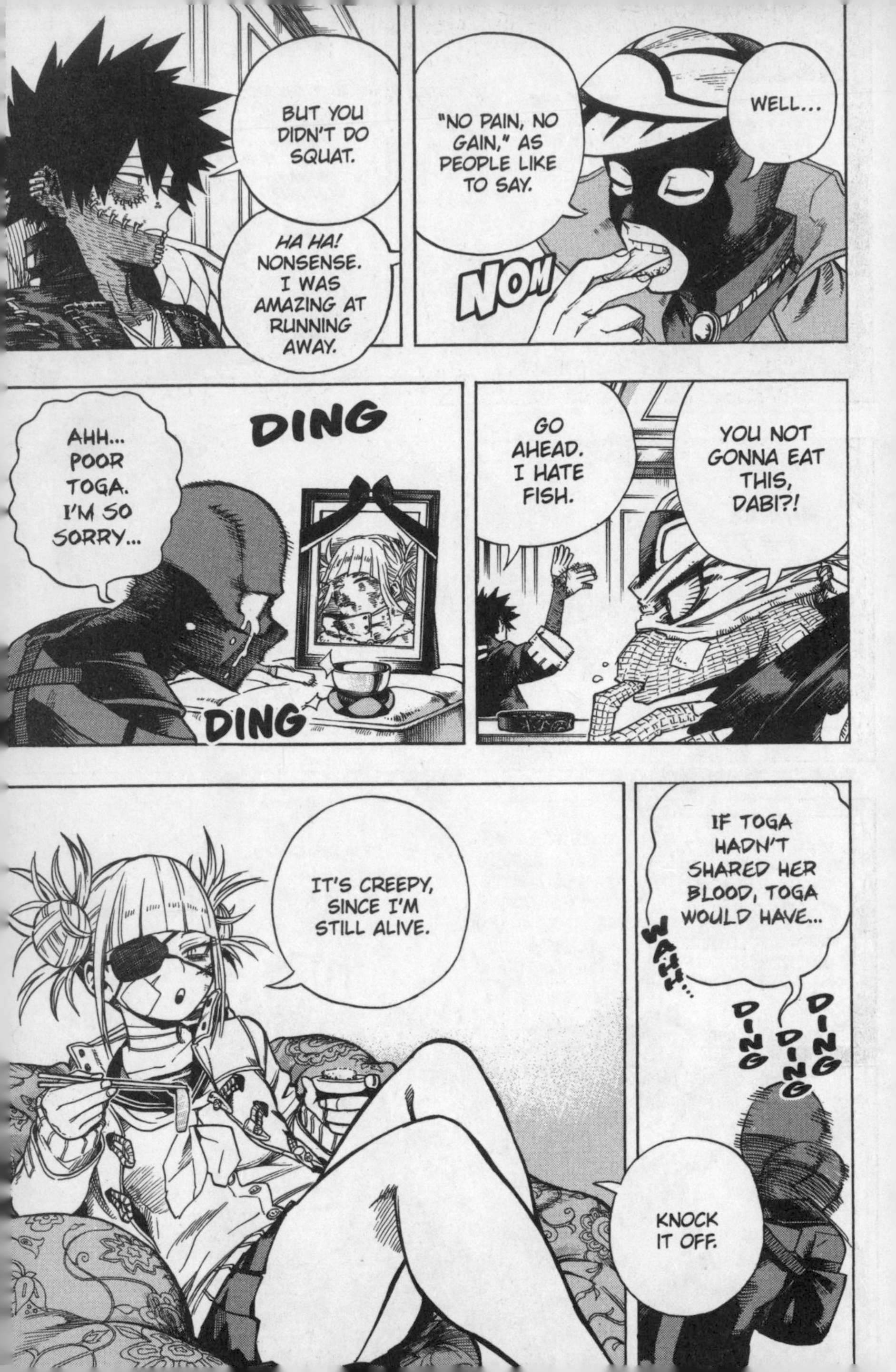
WELL...
"NO PAIN, NO GAIN," AS PEOPLE LIKE TO SAY.
NOM
BUT YOU DIDN'T DO SQUAT.
HA HA! NONSENSE. I WAS AMAZING AT RUNNING AWAY.
YOU NOT GONNA EAT THIS, DABI?!
GO AHEAD. I HATE FISH.
DING
AHH... POOR TOGA. I'M SO SORRY...
DING
IF TOGA HADN'T SHARED HER BLOOD, TOGA WOULD HAVE...
DING DING DING
WAHH...
KNOCK IT OFF.
IT'S CREEPY, SINCE I'M STILL ALIVE.

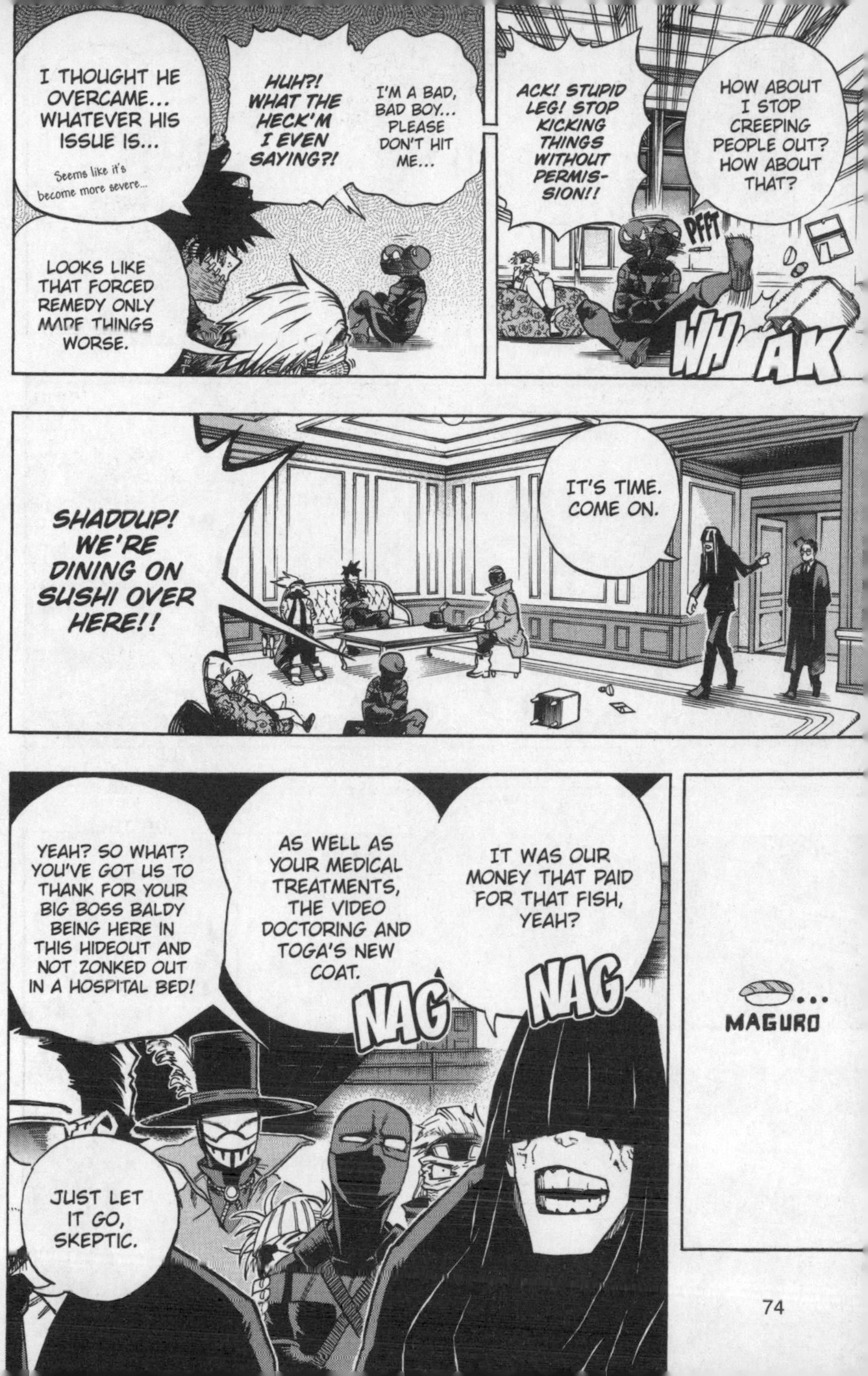
HOW ABOUT I STOP CREEPING PEOPLE OUT? HOW ABOUT THAT?
ACK! STUPID LEG! STOP KICKING THINGS WITHOUT PERMIS-SION!!
PFFT
WHAK
I'M A BAD, BAD BOY... PLEASE DON'T HIT ME...
HUH?! WHAT THE HECK'M I EVEN SAYING?!
I THOUGHT HE OVERCAME... WHATEVER HIS ISSUE IS...
Seems like it's become more severe...
LOOKS LIKE THAT FORCED REMEDY ONLY MADE THINGS WORSE.
IT'S TIME. COME ON.
SHADDUP! WE'RE DINING ON SUSHI OVER HERE!!
...
MAGURO
IT WAS OUR MONEY THAT PAID FOR THAT FISH, YEAH?
AS WELL AS YOUR MEDICAL TREATMENTS, THE VIDEO DOCTORING AND TOGA'S NEW COAT.
NAG
NAG
YEAH? SO WHAT? YOU'VE GOT US TO THANK FOR YOUR BIG BOSS BALDY BEING HERE IN THIS HIDEOUT AND NOT ZONKED OUT IN A HOSPITAL BED!
JUST LET IT GO, SKEPTIC.

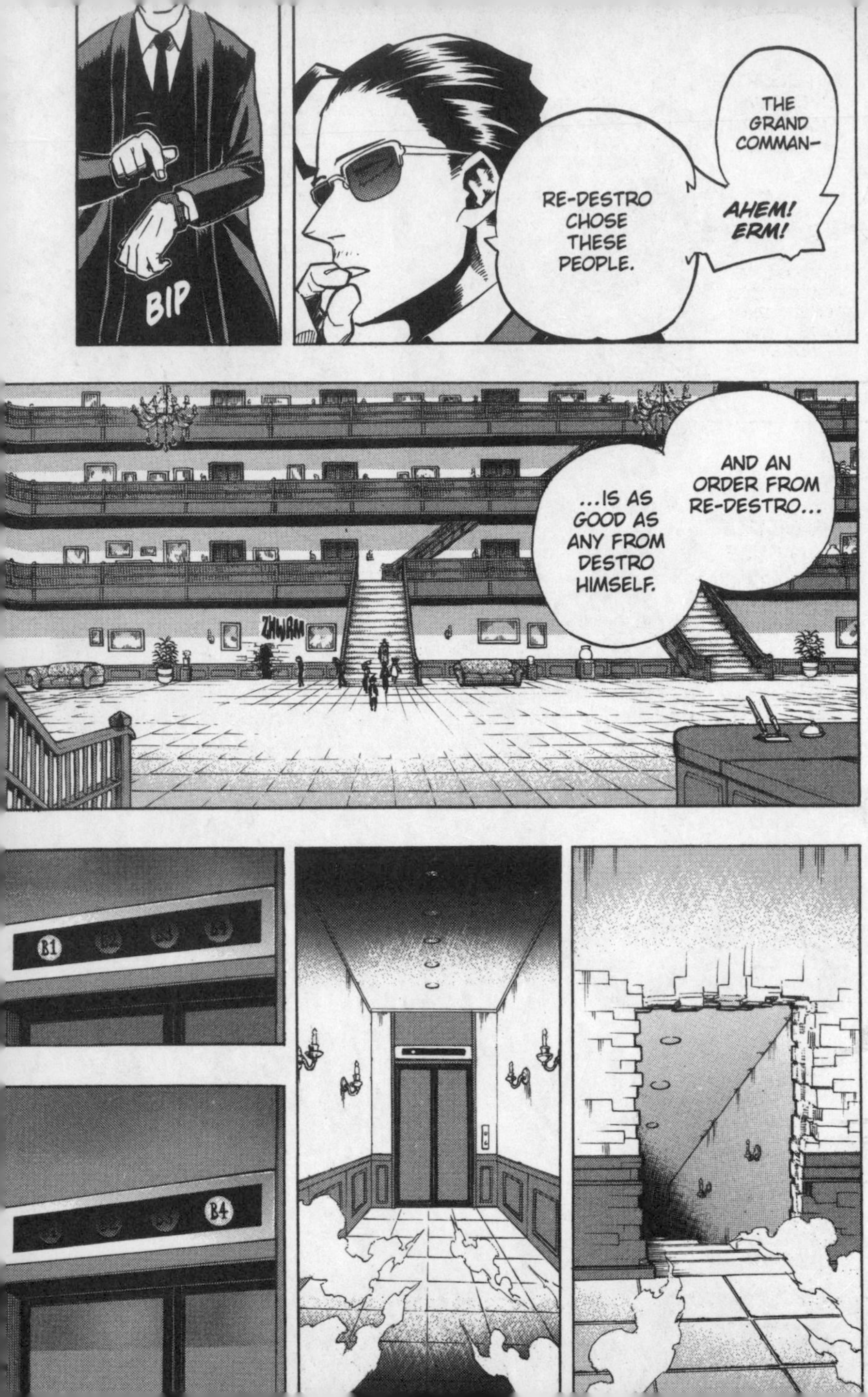
THE GRAND COMMAN—
AHEM! ERM!
RE-DESTRO CHOSE THESE PEOPLE.
BIP
AND AN ORDER FROM RE-DESTRO...
...IS AS GOOD AS ANY FROM DESTRO HIMSELF.
ZHWRM
B1
B4

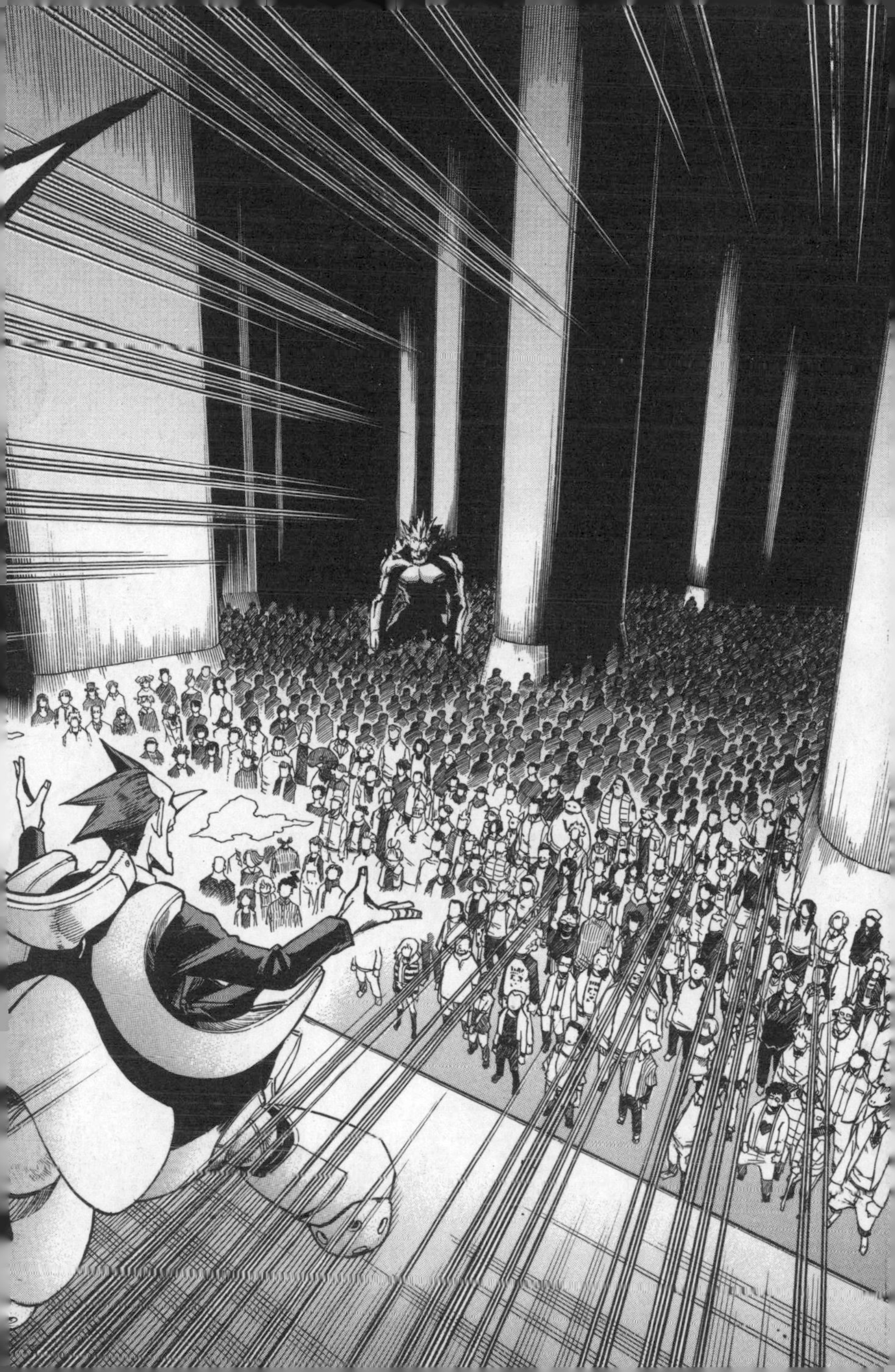

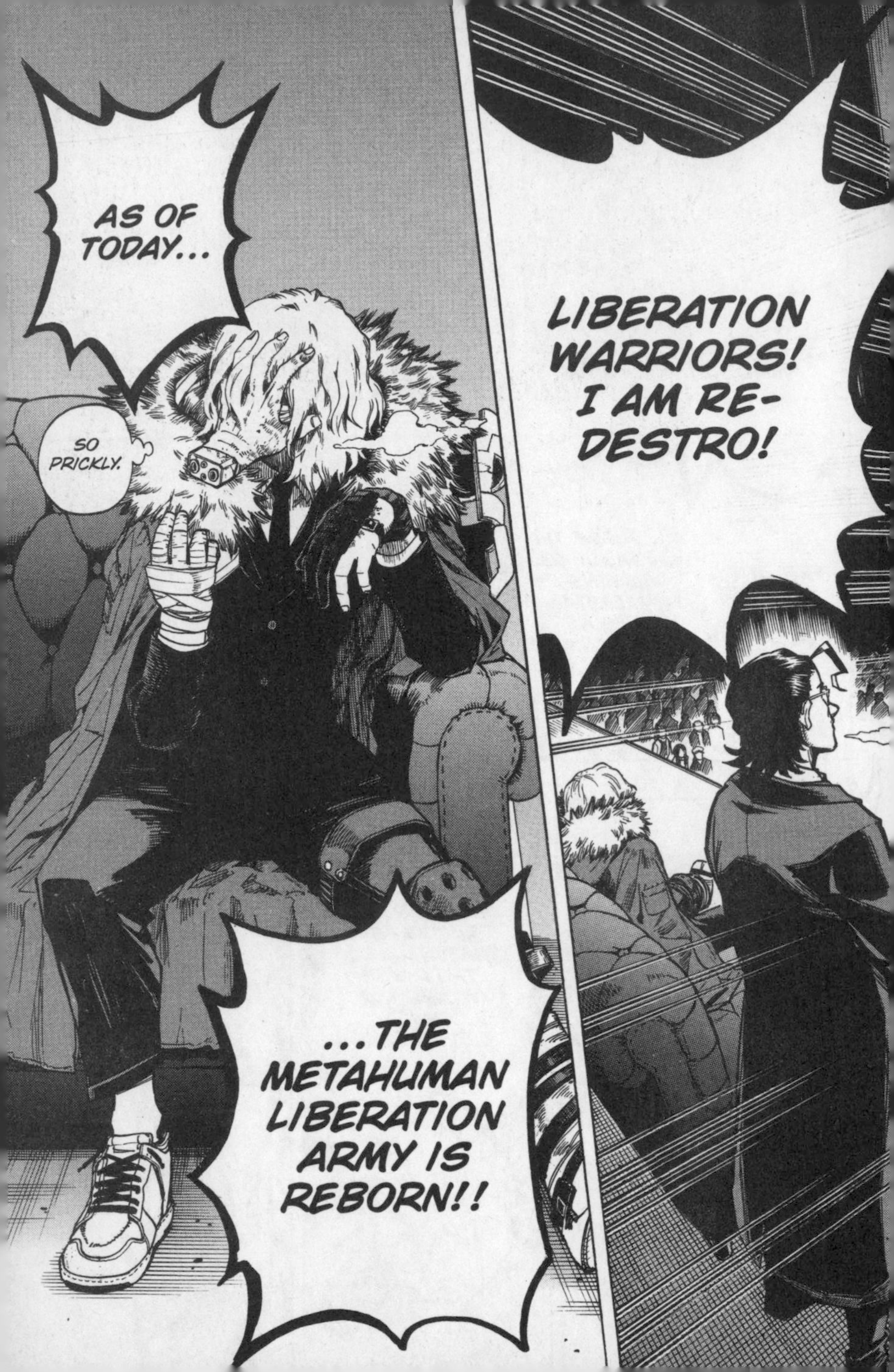
LIBERATION WARRIORS! I AM RE-DESTRO!
AS OF TODAY...
SO PRICKLY.
...THE METAHUMAN LIBERATION ARMY IS REBORN!!

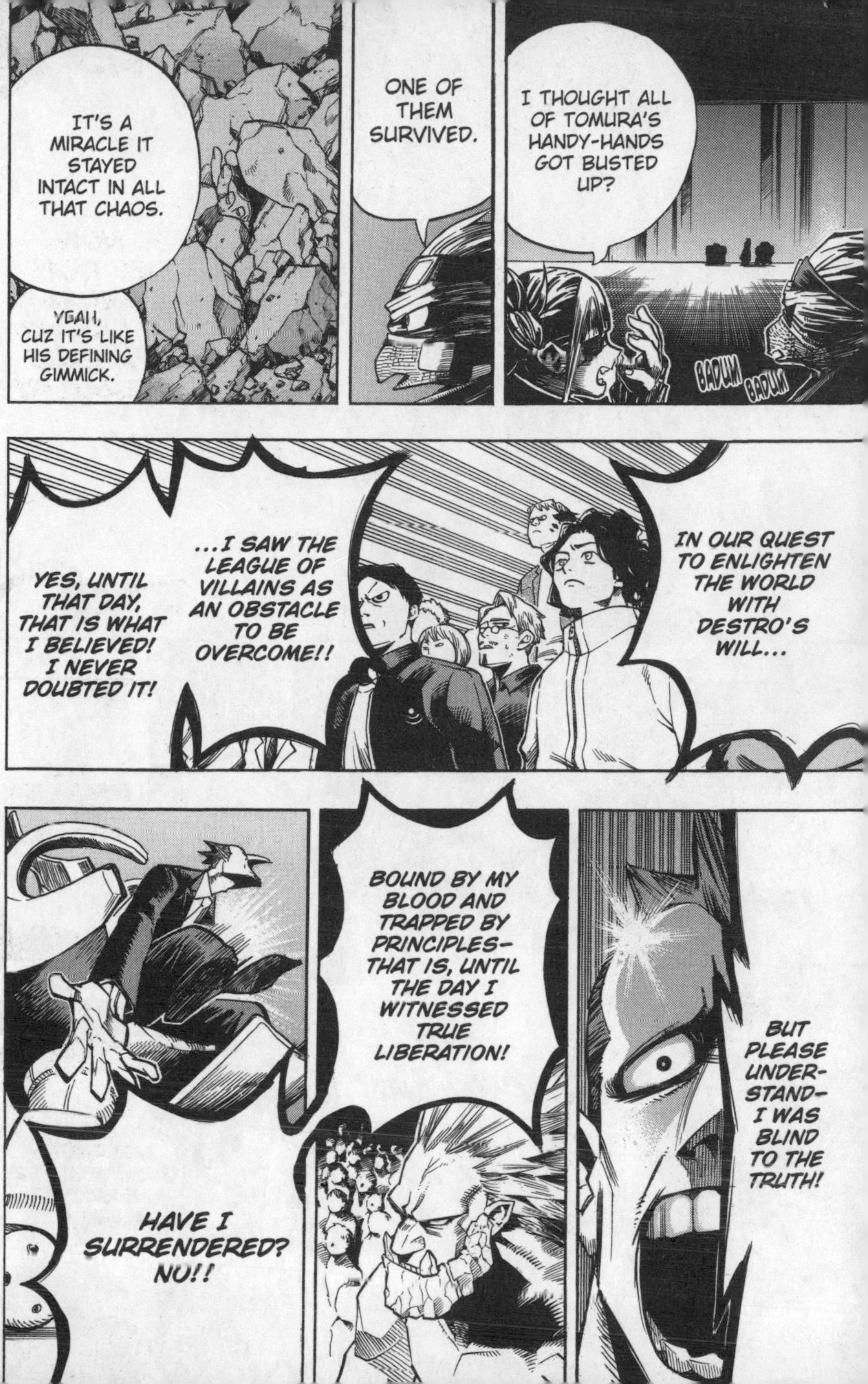
I THOUGHT ALL OF TOMURA'S HANDY-HANDS GOT BUSTED UP?
BADUM BADUM
ONE OF THEM SURVIVED.
IT'S A MIRACLE IT STAYED INTACT IN ALL THAT CHAOS.
YEAH, CUZ IT'S LIKE HIS DEFINING GIMMICK.
IN OUR QUEST TO ENLIGHTEN THE WORLD WITH DESTRO'S WILL...
...I SAW THE LEAGUE OF VILLAINS AS AN OBSTACLE TO BE OVERCOME!!
YES, UNTIL THAT DAY, THAT IS WHAT I BELIEVED! I NEVER DOUBTED IT!
BUT PLEASE UNDERSTAND- I WAS BLIND TO THE TRUTH!
BOUND BY MY BLOOD AND TRAPPED BY PRINCIPLES- THAT IS, UNTIL THE DAY I WITNESSED TRUE LIBERATION!
HAVE I SURRENDERED? NO!!

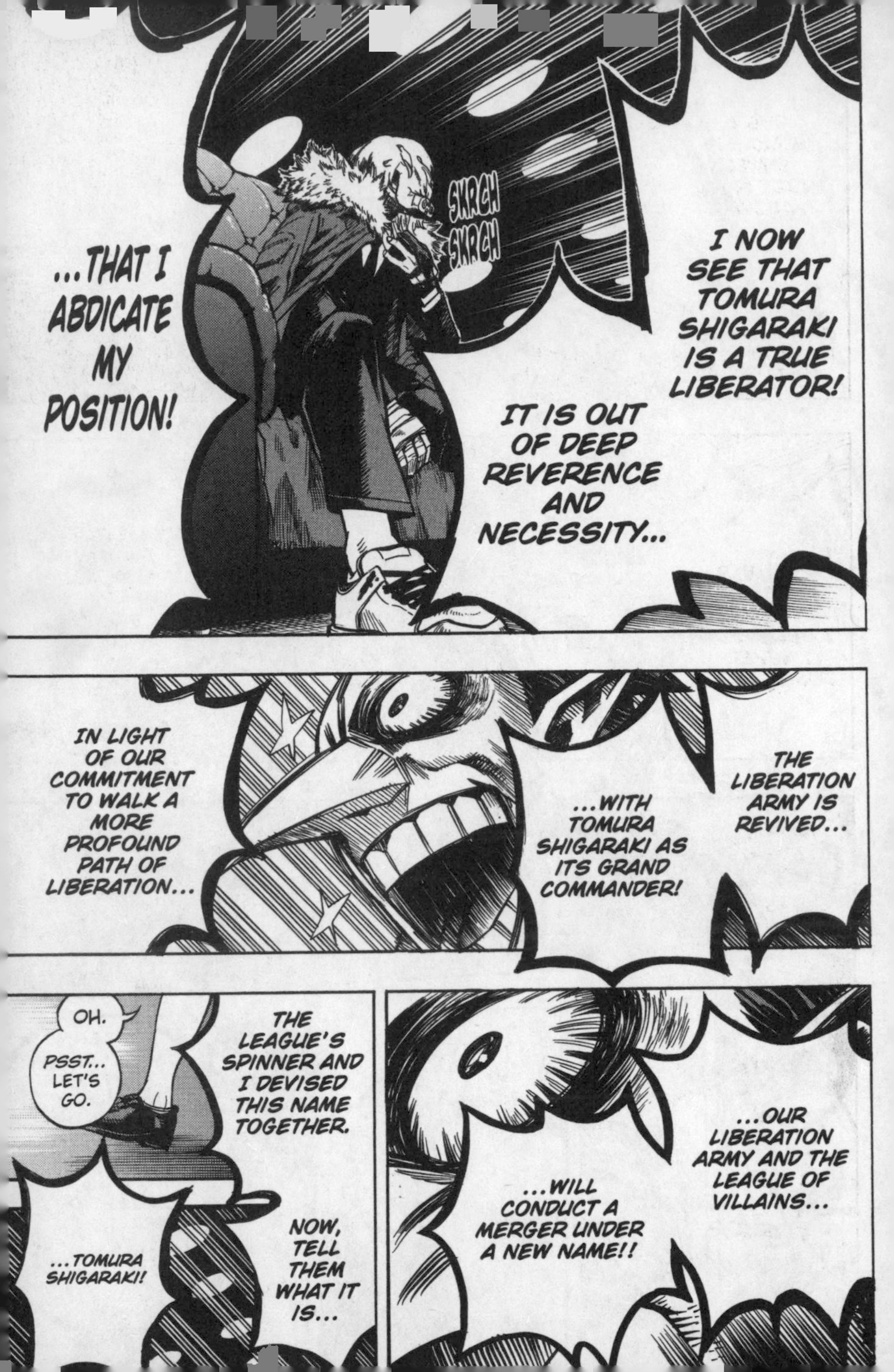
I NOW SEE THAT TOMURA SHIGARAKI IS A TRUE LIBERATOR!
IT IS OUT OF DEEP REVERENCE AND NECESSITY...
SKRCH SKRCH
...THAT I ABDICATE MY POSITION!
THE LIBERATION ARMY IS REVIVED...
...WITH TOMURA SHIGARAKI AS ITS GRAND COMMANDER!
IN LIGHT OF OUR COMMITMENT TO WALK A MORE PROFOUND PATH OF LIBERATION...
...OUR LIBERATION ARMY AND THE LEAGUE OF VILLAINS...
...WILL CONDUCT A MERGER UNDER A NEW NAME!!
THE LEAGUE'S SPINNER AND I DEVISED THIS NAME TOGETHER.
OH.
PSST... LET'S GO.
NOW, TELL THEM WHAT IT IS...
...TOMURA SHIGARAKI!

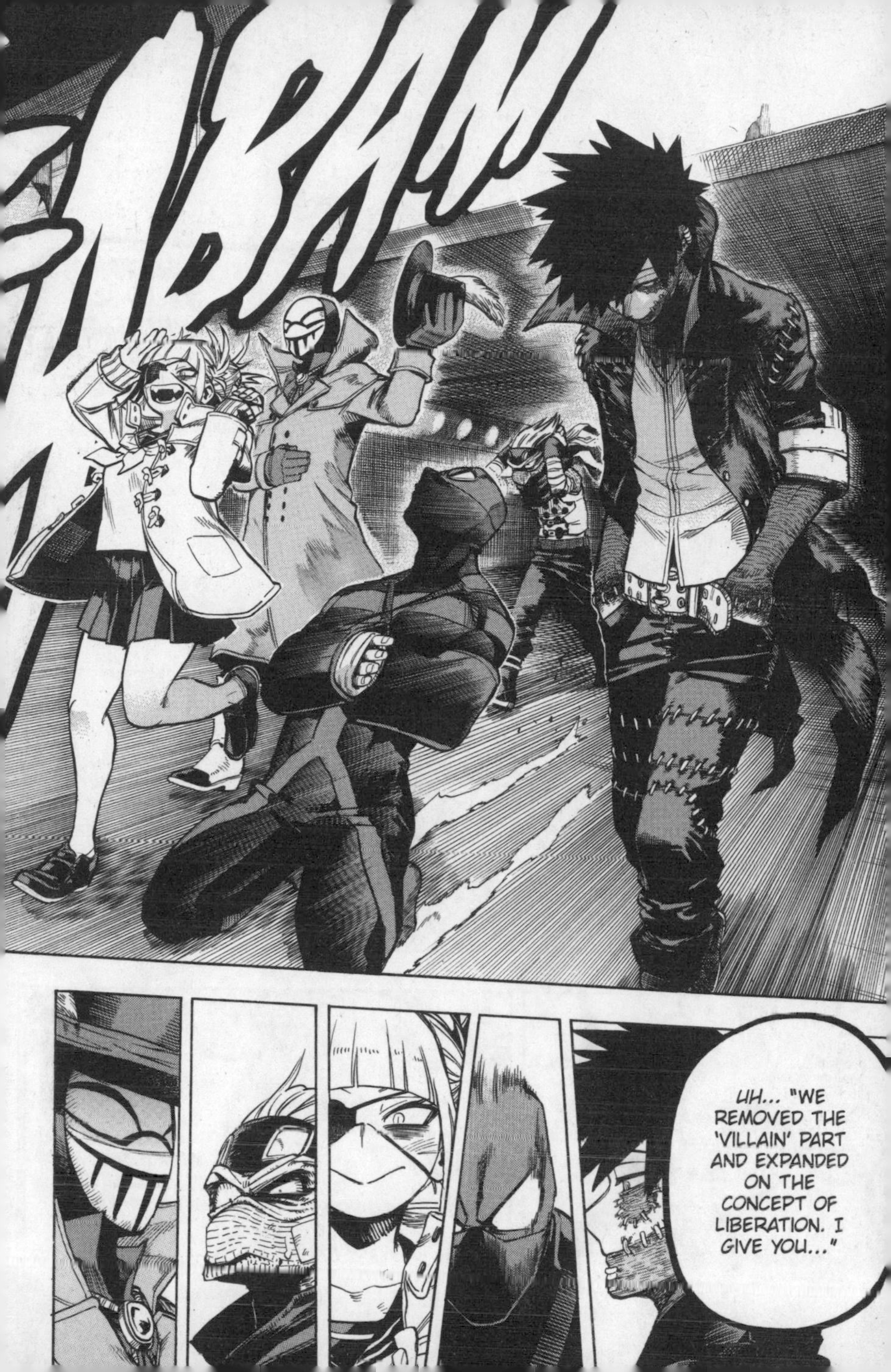
UH... "WE REMOVED THE 'VILLAIN' PART AND EXPANDED ON THE CONCEPT OF LIBERATION. I GIVE YOU..."

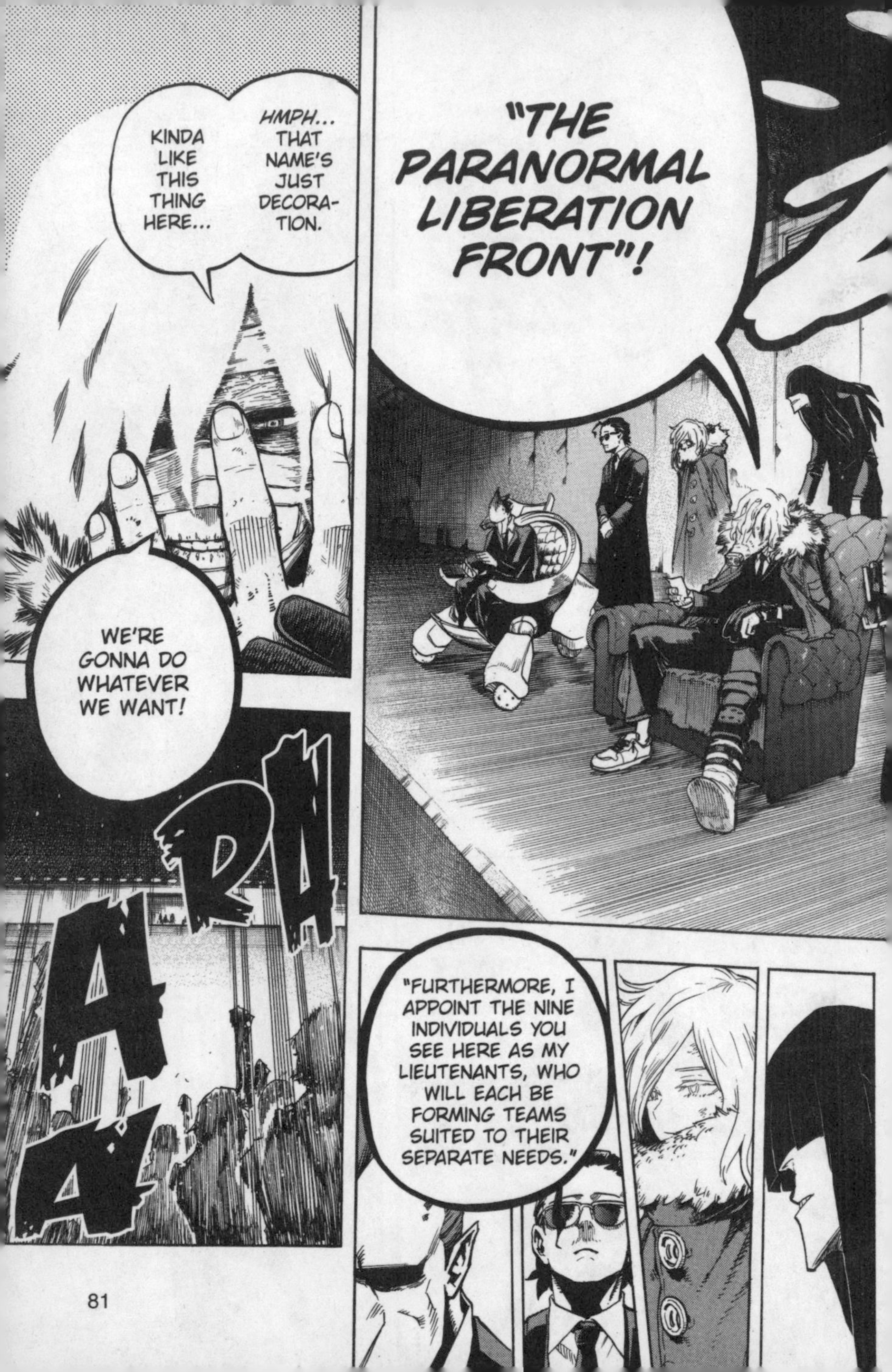
"THE PARANORMAL LIBERATION FRONT"!
HMPH... THAT NAME'S JUST DECORA-TION.
KINDA LIKE THIS THING HERE...
WE'RE GONNA DO WHATEVER WE WANT!
RAAA
"FURTHERMORE, I APPOINT THE NINE INDIVIDUALS YOU SEE HERE AS MY LIEUTENANTS, WHO WILL EACH BE FORMING TEAMS SUITED TO THEIR SEPARATE NEEDS."

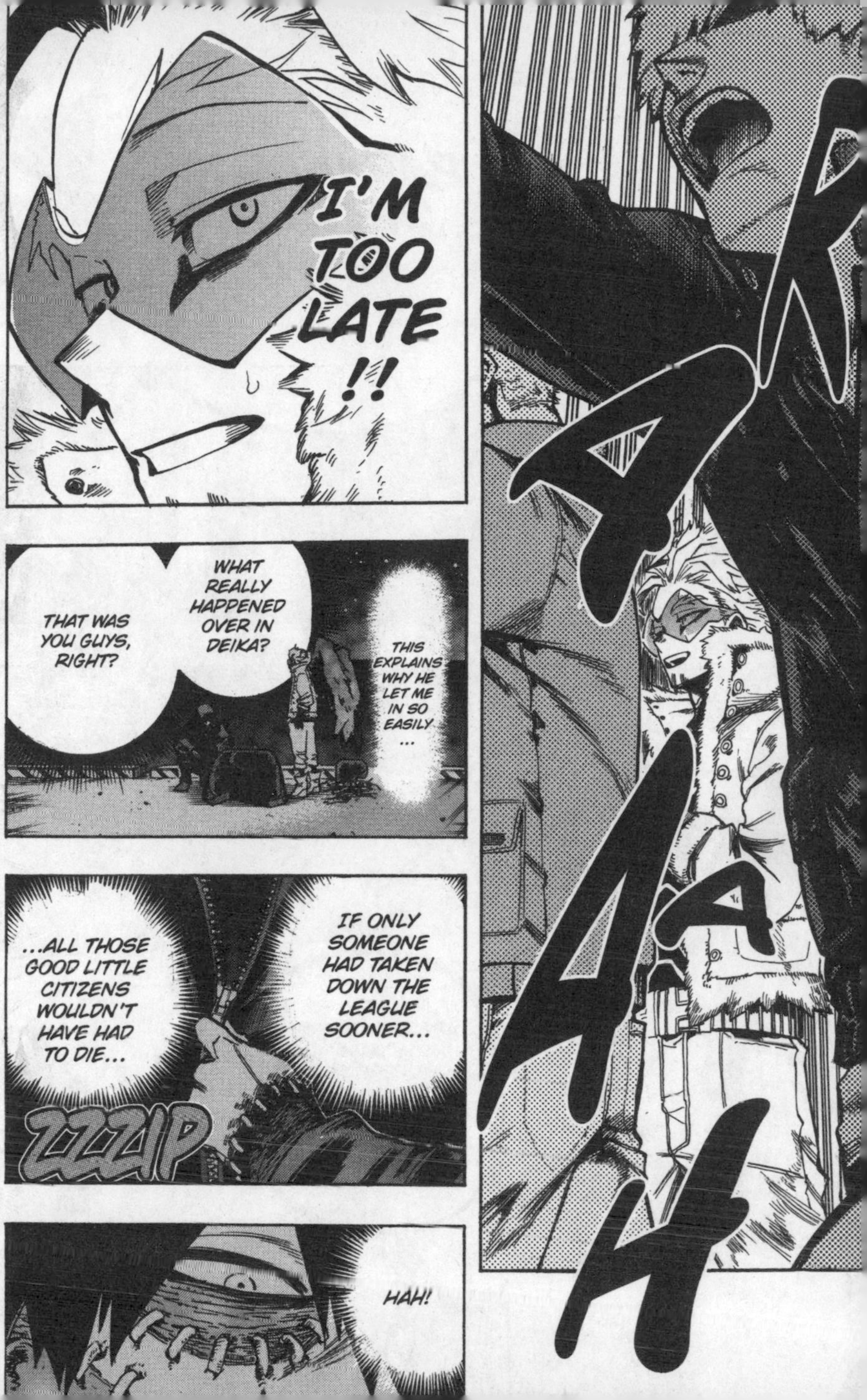
AAAAH
I'M TOO LATE!!
THIS EXPLAINS WHY HE LET ME IN SO EASILY...
WHAT REALLY HAPPENED OVER IN DEIKA?
THAT WAS YOU GUYS, RIGHT?
IF ONLY SOMEONE HAD TAKEN DOWN THE LEAGUE SOONER...
...ALL THOSE GOOD LITTLE CITIZENS WOULDN'T HAVE HAD TO DIE...
ZZZIP
HAH!

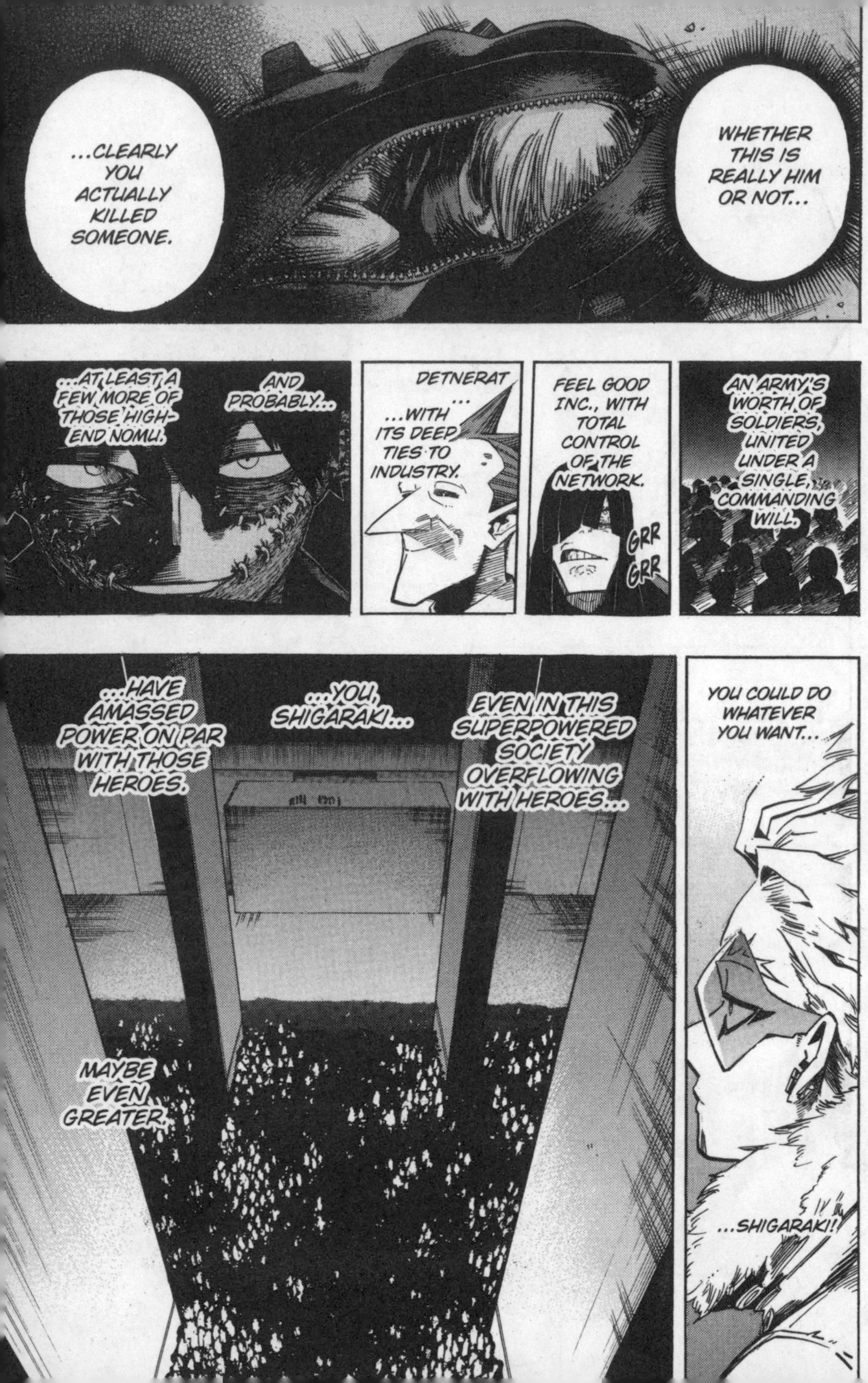
WHETHER THIS IS REALLY HIM OR NOT...
...CLEARLY YOU ACTUALLY KILLED SOMEONE.
AN ARMY'S WORTH OF SOLDIERS, UNITED UNDER A SINGLE, COMMANDING WILL.
FEEL GOOD INC., WITH TOTAL CONTROL OF THE NETWORK.
GRR GRR
DETNERAT...
...WITH ITS DEEP TIES TO INDUSTRY.
AND PROBABLY...
...AT LEAST A FEW MORE OF THOSE HIGH-END NOMU.
YOU COULD DO WHATEVER YOU WANT...
...SHIGARAKI!
EVEN IN THIS SUPERPOWERED SOCIETY OVERFLOWING WITH HEROES...
...YOU, SHIGARAKI...
...HAVE AMASSED POWER ON PAR WITH THOSE HEROES.
MAYBE EVEN GREATER.

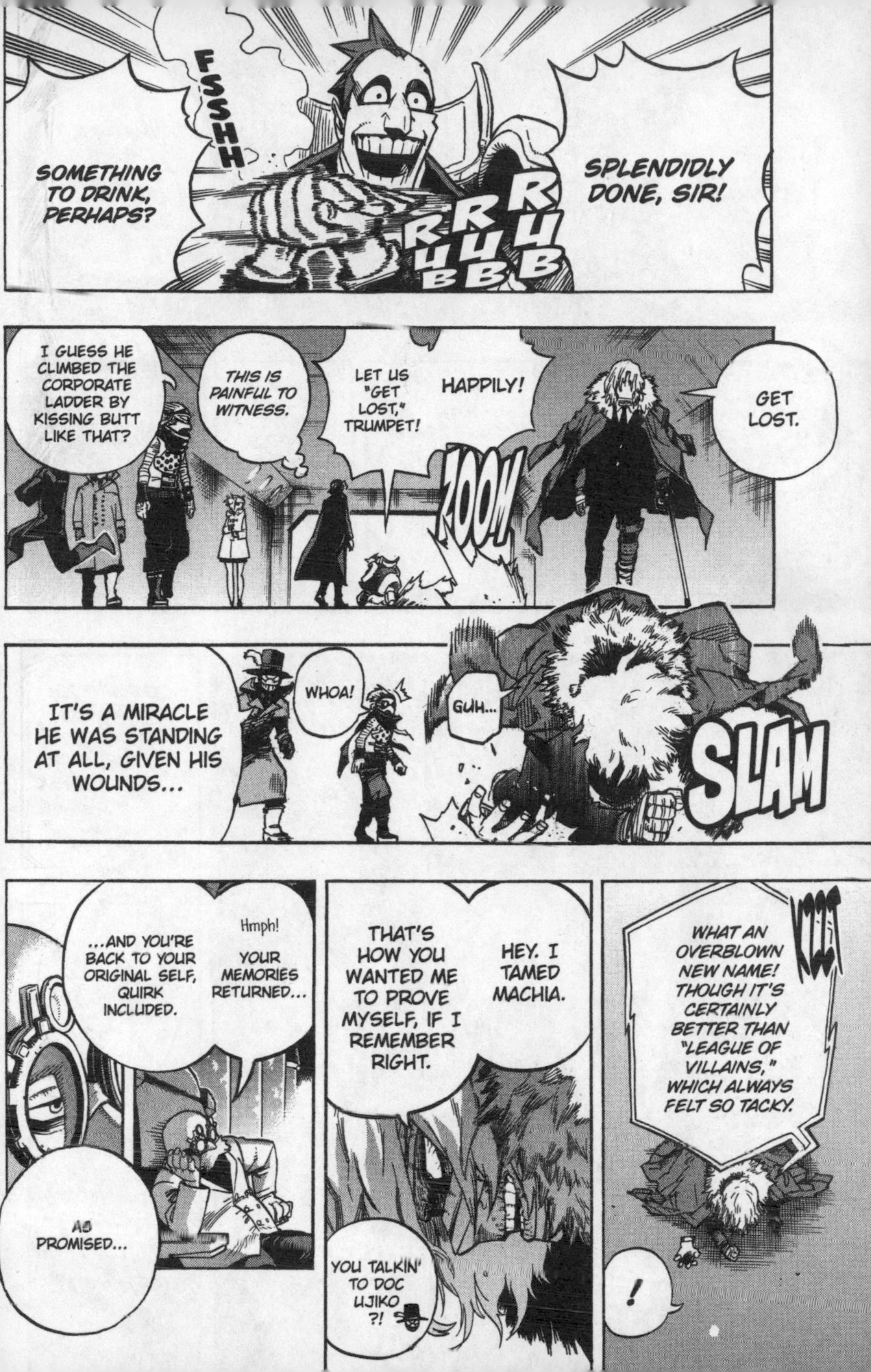
SPLENDIDLY DONE, SIR!
RUB RUB RUB
FSSHH
SOMETHING TO DRINK, PERHAPS?
GET LOST.
ZOOM
HAPPILY!
LET US "GET LOST," TRUMPET!
THIS IS PAINFUL TO WITNESS.
I GUESS HE CLIMBED THE CORPORATE LADDER BY KISSING BUTT LIKE THAT?
SLAM
GUH...
WHOA!
IT'S A MIRACLE HE WAS STANDING AT ALL, GIVEN HIS WOUNDS...
WHAT AN OVERBLOWN NEW NAME! THOUGH IT'S CERTAINLY BETTER THAN "LEAGUE OF VILLAINS," WHICH ALWAYS FELT SO TACKY.
!
HEY. I TAMED MACHIA.
THAT'S HOW YOU WANTED ME TO PROVE MYSELF, IF I REMEMBER RIGHT.
YOU TALKIN' TO DOC UJIKO ?!
Hmph!
YOUR MEMORIES RETURNED...
...AND YOU'RE BACK TO YOUR ORIGINAL SELF, QUIRK INCLUDED.
AS PROMISED...

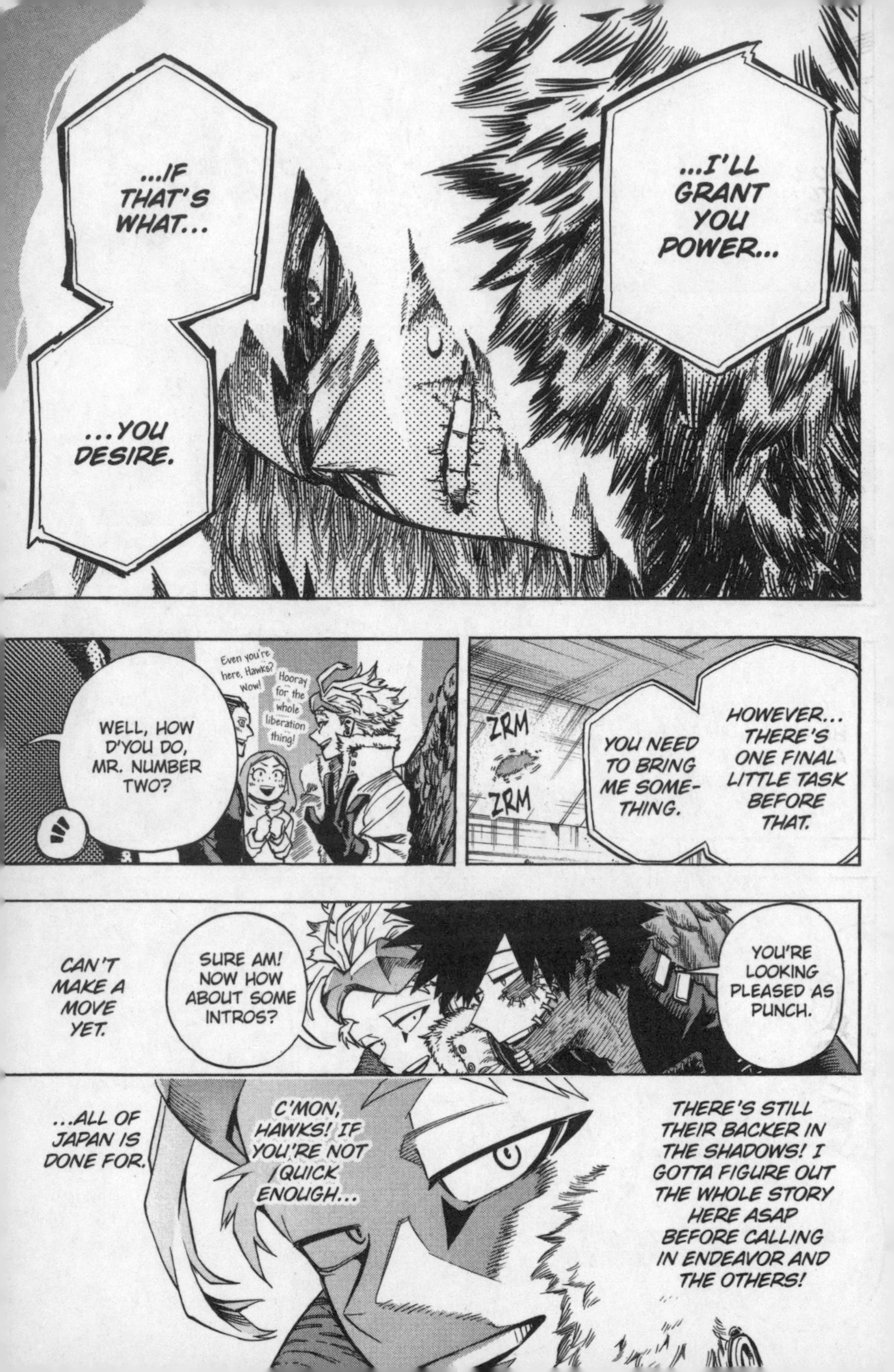
...I'LL GRANT YOU POWER...
...IF THAT'S WHAT...
...YOU DESIRE.
HOWEVER... THERE'S ONE FINAL LITTLE TASK BEFORE THAT.
YOU NEED TO BRING ME SOME-THING.
ZRM
ZRM
Even you're here, Hawks? Wow!
Hooray for the whole liberation thing!
WELL, HOW D'YOU DO, MR. NUMBER TWO?
YOU'RE LOOKING PLEASED AS PUNCH.
SURE AM! NOW HOW ABOUT SOME INTROS?
CAN'T MAKE A MOVE YET.
THERE'S STILL THEIR BACKER IN THE SHADOWS! I GOTTA FIGURE OUT THE WHOLE STORY HERE ASAP BEFORE CALLING IN ENDEAVOR AND THE OTHERS!
C'MON, HAWKS! IF YOU'RE NOT QUICK ENOUGH...
...ALL OF JAPAN IS DONE FOR.

THE NEW LOOK

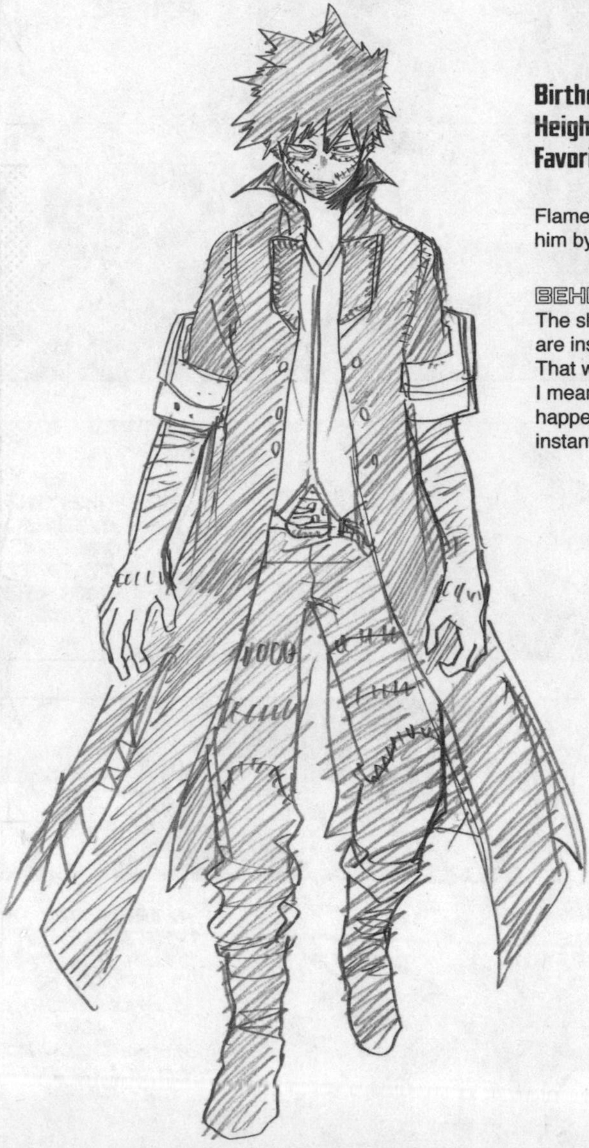

Birthday: 1/18
Height: 176 cm
Favorite Thing: ???

Flame-retardant clothes, made for him by Detnerat.

BEHIND THE SCENES

The sleeve-cuff decorations are inspired by gas burners. That was *my* inspiration, I mean. Not Dabi's. It happened when I was making instant noodles one day.

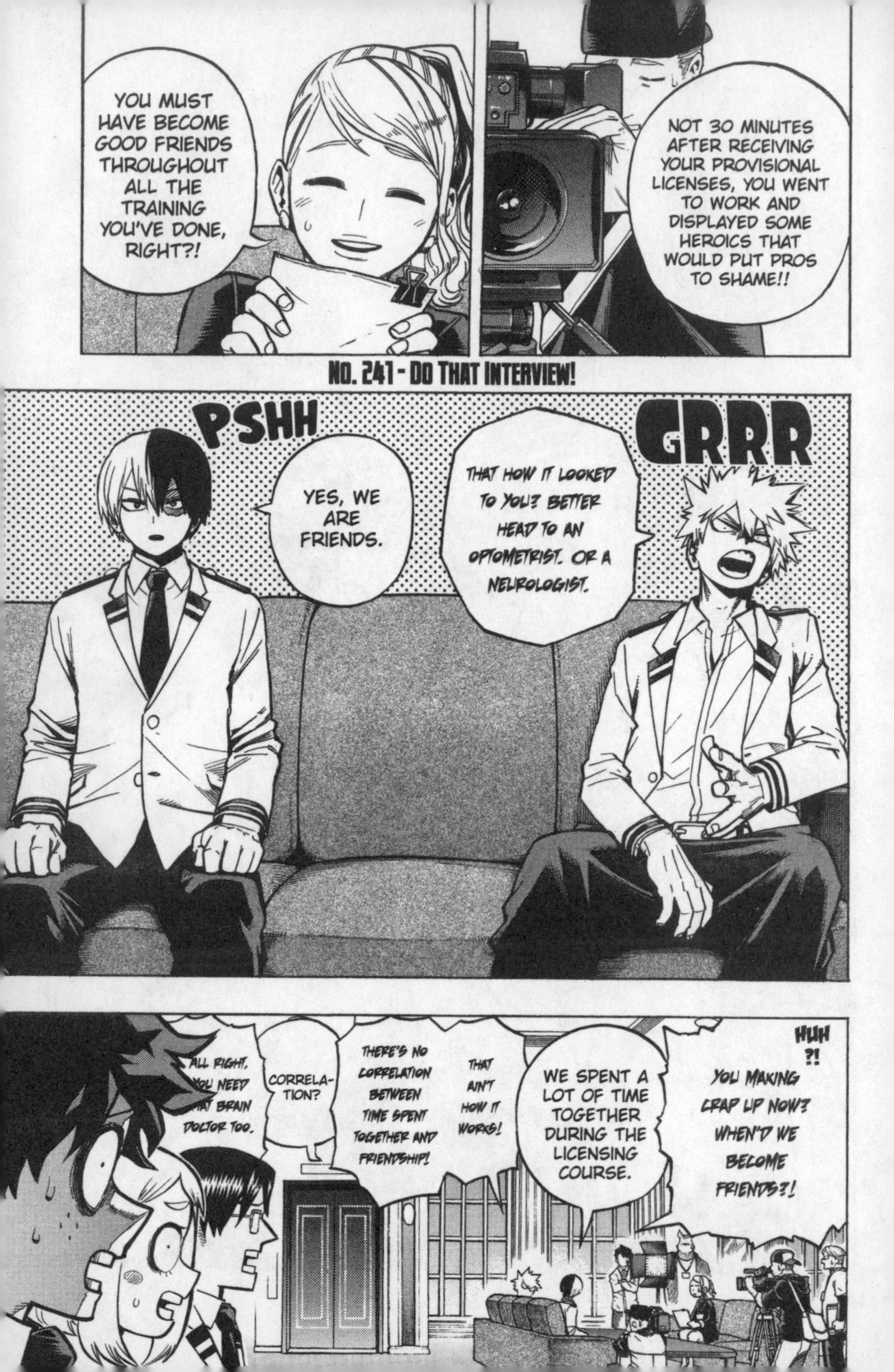
NOT 30 MINUTES AFTER RECEIVING YOUR PROVISIONAL LICENSES, YOU WENT TO WORK AND DISPLAYED SOME HEROICS THAT WOULD PUT PROS TO SHAME!!
YOU MUST HAVE BECOME GOOD FRIENDS THROUGHOUT ALL THE TRAINING YOU'VE DONE, RIGHT?!
NO. 241 - DO THAT INTERVIEW!
GRRR
THAT HOW IT LOOKED TO YOU? BETTER HEAD TO AN OPTOMETRIST. OR A NEUROLOGIST.
PSHH
YES, WE ARE FRIENDS.
HUH ?!
YOU MAKING CRAP UP NOW? WHEN'D WE BECOME FRIENDS?!
WE SPENT A LOT OF TIME TOGETHER DURING THE LICENSING COURSE.
THAT AIN'T HOW IT WORKS!
THERE'S NO CORRELATION BETWEEN TIME SPENT TOGETHER AND FRIENDSHIP!
CORRELA-TION?
ALL RIGHT, YOU NEED THAT BRAIN DOCTOR TOO.

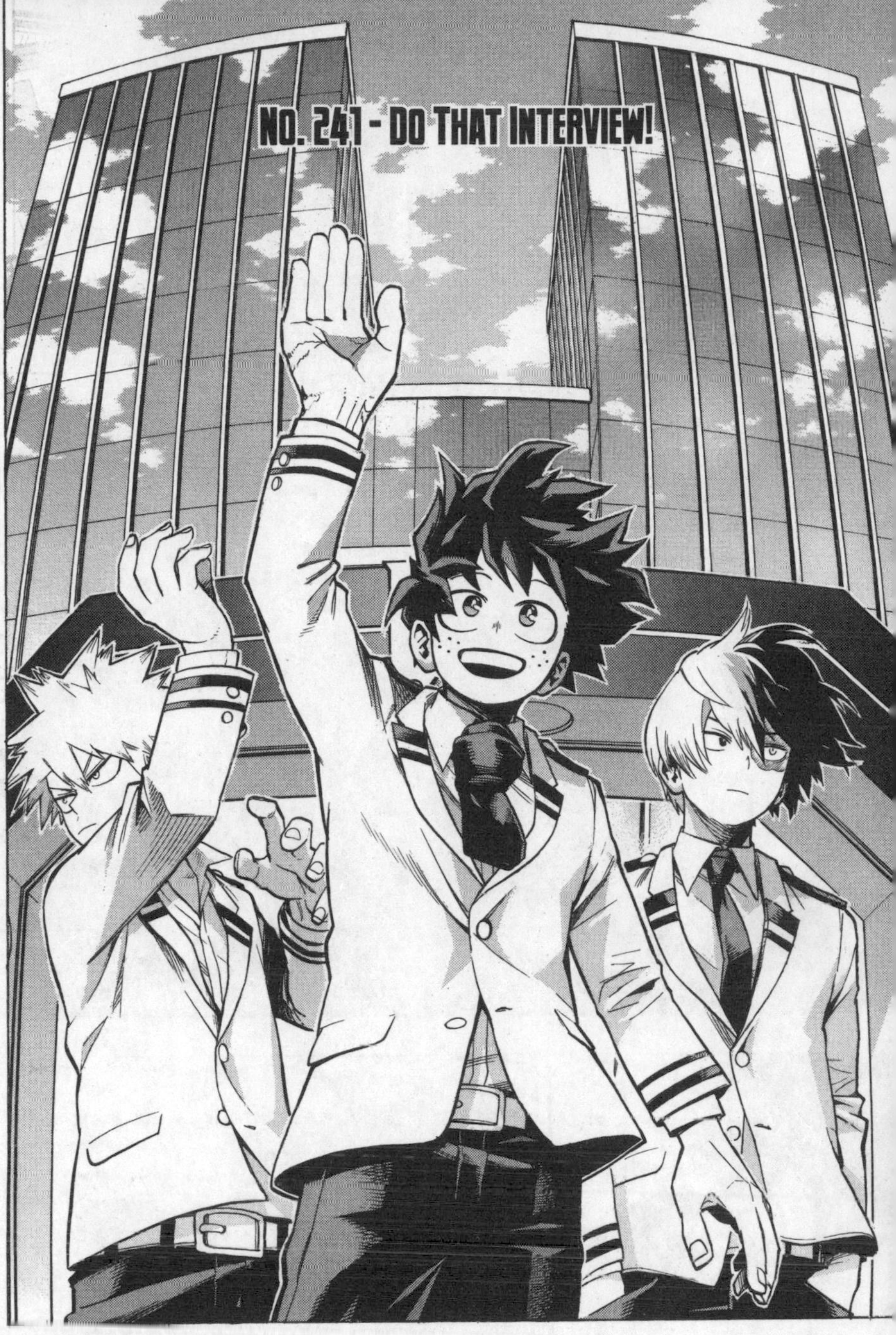
No. 241 - Do That Interview!

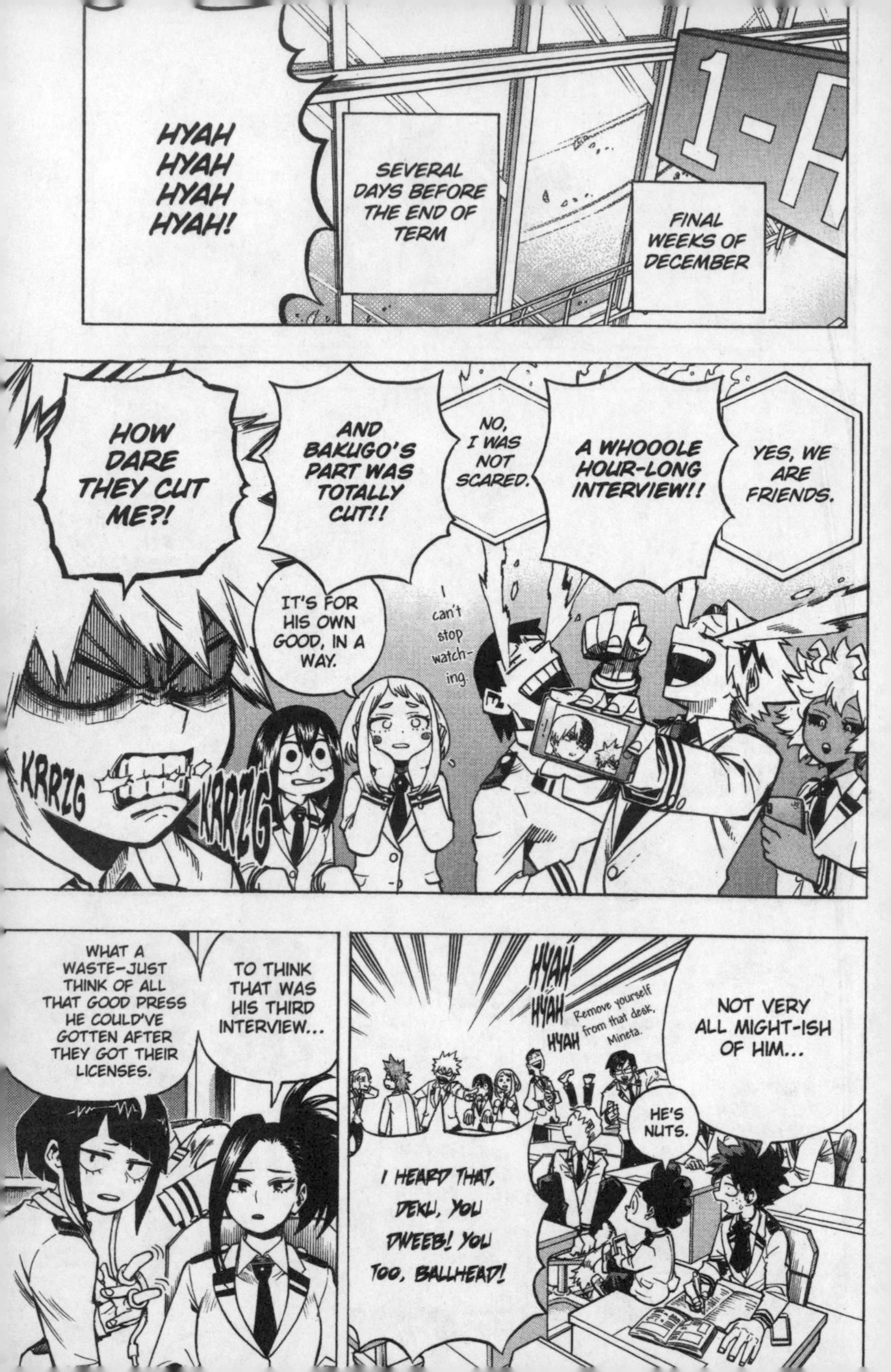
1-A
FINAL WEEKS OF DECEMBER
SEVERAL DAYS BEFORE THE END OF TERM
HYAH HYAH HYAH HYAH!
YES, WE ARE FRIENDS.
A WHOOOLE HOUR-LONG INTERVIEW!!
NO, I WAS NOT SCARED.
AND BAKUGO'S PART WAS TOTALLY CUT!!
HOW DARE THEY CUT ME?!
I can't stop watch-ing.
IT'S FOR HIS OWN GOOD, IN A WAY.
KRRZG
KRRZG
NOT VERY ALL MIGHT-ISH OF HIM...
HYAH HYAH HYAH
Remove yourself from that desk, Mineta.
HE'S NUTS.
I HEARD THAT, DEKU, YOU DWEEB! YOU TOO, BALLHEAD!
TO THINK THAT WAS HIS THIRD INTERVIEW...
WHAT A WASTE—JUST THINK OF ALL THAT GOOD PRESS HE COULD'VE GOTTEN AFTER THEY GOT THEIR LICENSES.

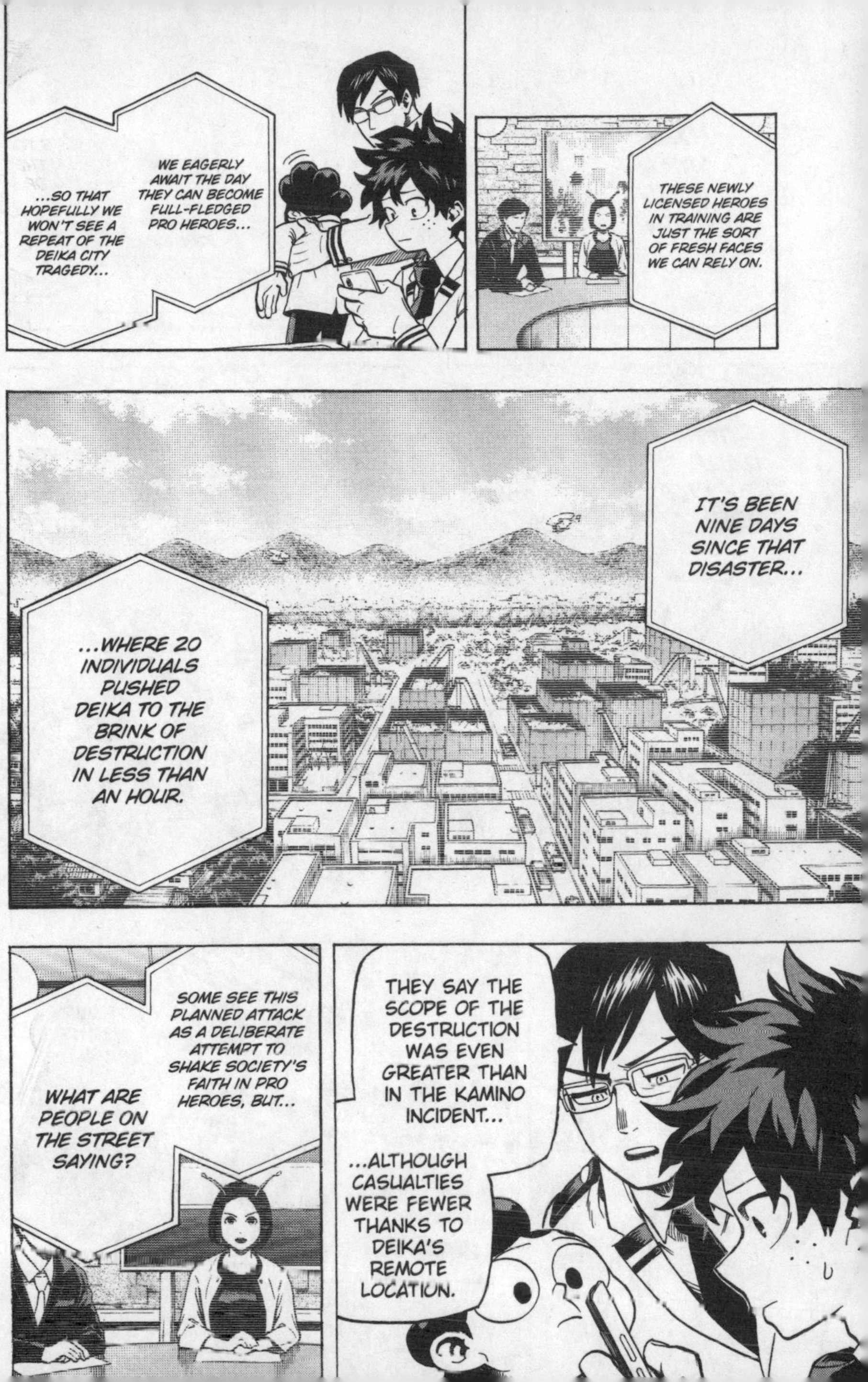
THESE NEWLY LICENSED HEROES IN TRAINING ARE JUST THE SORT OF FRESH FACES WE CAN RELY ON.
WE EAGERLY AWAIT THE DAY THEY CAN BECOME FULL-FLEDGED PRO HEROES...
...SO THAT HOPEFULLY WE WON'T SEE A REPEAT OF THE DEIKA CITY TRAGEDY...
IT'S BEEN NINE DAYS SINCE THAT DISASTER...
...WHERE 20 INDIVIDUALS PUSHED DEIKA TO THE BRINK OF DESTRUCTION IN LESS THAN AN HOUR.
THEY SAY THE SCOPE OF THE DESTRUCTION WAS EVEN GREATER THAN IN THE KAMINO INCIDENT...
...ALTHOUGH CASUALTIES WERE FEWER THANKS TO DEIKA'S REMOTE LOCATION.
SOME SEE THIS PLANNED ATTACK AS A DELIBERATE ATTEMPT TO SHAKE SOCIETY'S FAITH IN PRO HEROES, BUT...
WHAT ARE PEOPLE ON THE STREET SAYING?

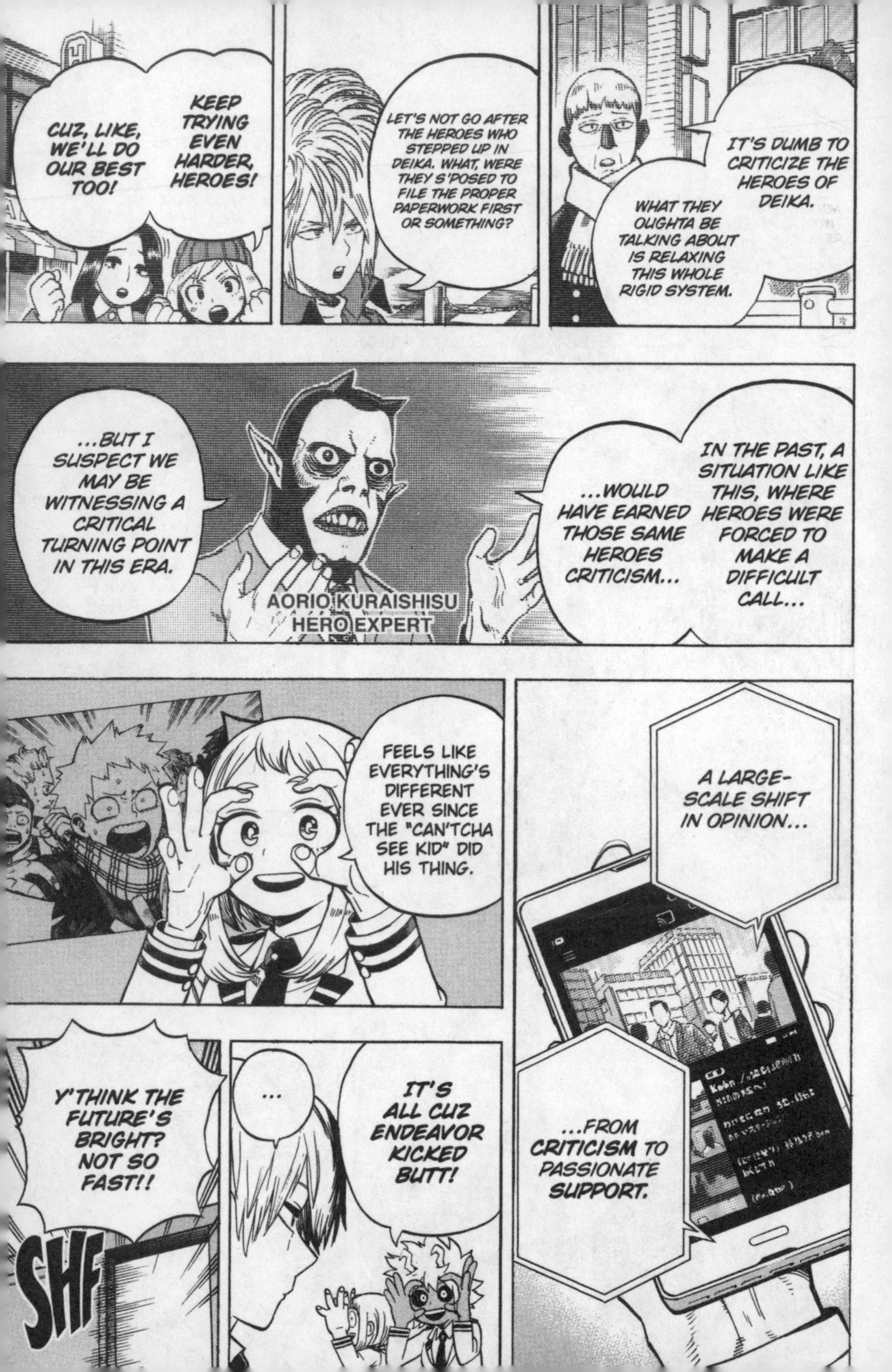
IT'S DUMB TO CRITICIZE THE HEROES OF DEIKA.
WHAT THEY OUGHTA BE TALKING ABOUT IS RELAXING THIS WHOLE RIGID SYSTEM.
LET'S NOT GO AFTER THE HEROES WHO STEPPED UP IN DEIKA. WHAT, WERE THEY S'POSED TO FILE THE PROPER PAPERWORK FIRST OR SOMETHING?
KEEP TRYING EVEN HARDER, HEROES!
CUZ, LIKE, WE'LL DO OUR BEST TOO!
IN THE PAST, A SITUATION LIKE THIS, WHERE HEROES WERE FORCED TO MAKE A DIFFICULT CALL...
...WOULD HAVE EARNED THOSE SAME HEROES CRITICISM...
AORIO KURAISHISU
HERO EXPERT
...BUT I SUSPECT WE MAY BE WITNESSING A CRITICAL TURNING POINT IN THIS ERA.
A LARGE-SCALE SHIFT IN OPINION...
...FROM CRITICISM TO PASSIONATE SUPPORT.
FEELS LIKE EVERYTHING'S DIFFERENT EVER SINCE THE "CAN'TCHA SEE KID" DID HIS THING.
IT'S ALL CUZ ENDEAVOR KICKED BUTT!
...
Y'THINK THE FUTURE'S BRIGHT? NOT SO FAST!!
SHF

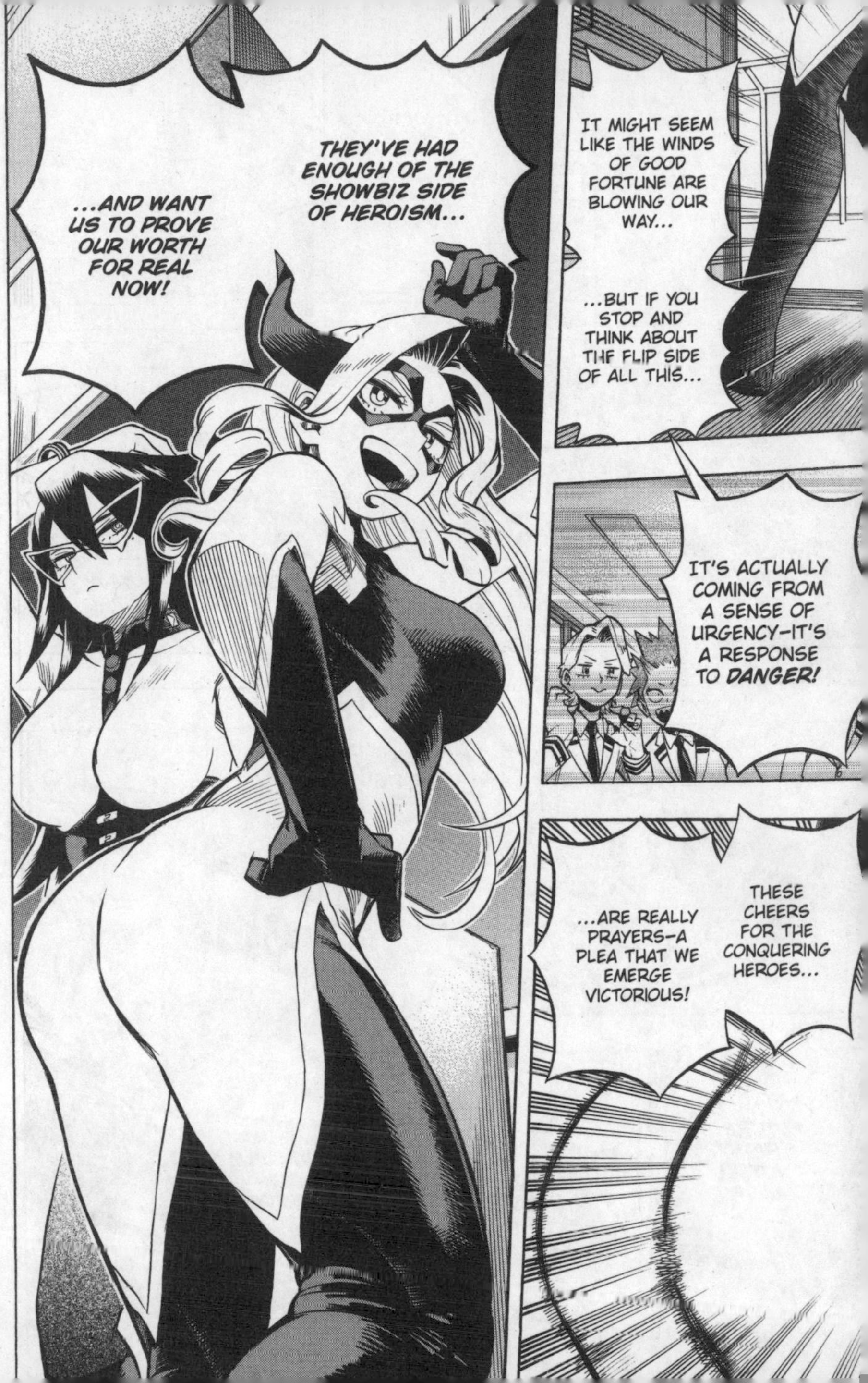
IT MIGHT SEEM LIKE THE WINDS OF GOOD FORTUNE ARE BLOWING OUR WAY...
...BUT IF YOU STOP AND THINK ABOUT THE FLIP SIDE OF ALL THIS...
IT'S ACTUALLY COMING FROM A SENSE OF URGENCY—IT'S A RESPONSE TO DANGER!
THESE CHEERS FOR THE CONQUERING HEROES...
...ARE REALLY PRAYERS—A PLEA THAT WE EMERGE VICTORIOUS!
THEY'VE HAD ENOUGH OF THE SHOWBIZ SIDE OF HEROISM...
...AND WANT US TO PROVE OUR WORTH FOR REAL NOW!

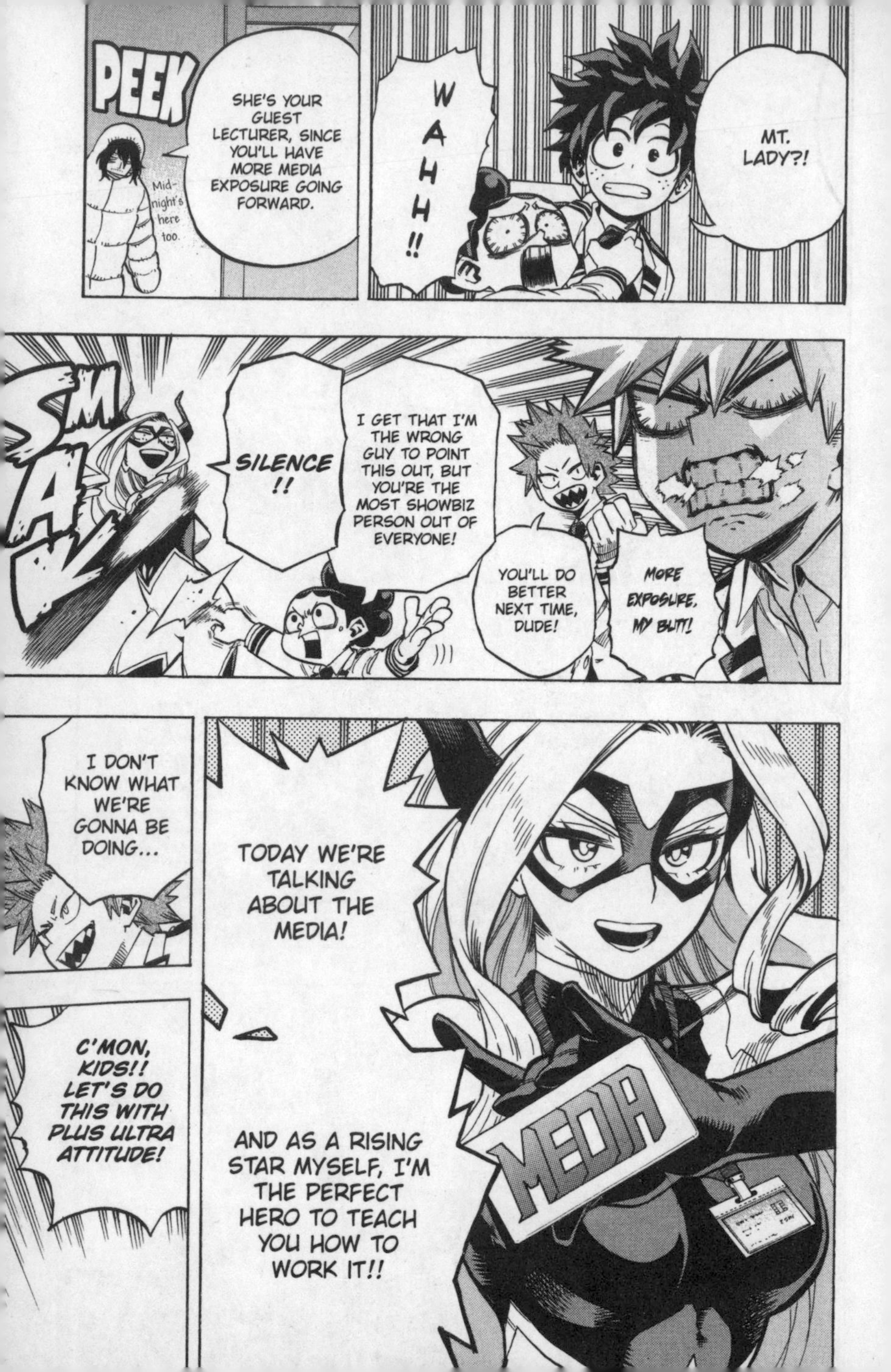
MT. LADY?!
WAHH!!
PEEK
SHE'S YOUR GUEST LECTURER, SINCE YOU'LL HAVE MORE MEDIA EXPOSURE GOING FORWARD.
Mid-night's here too.
MORE EXPOSURE, MY BUTT!
YOU'LL DO BETTER NEXT TIME, DUDE!
I GET THAT I'M THE WRONG GUY TO POINT THIS OUT, BUT YOU'RE THE MOST SHOWBIZ PERSON OUT OF EVERYONE!
SILENCE!!
TODAY WE'RE TALKING ABOUT THE MEDIA!
AND AS A RISING STAR MYSELF, I'M THE PERFECT HERO TO TEACH YOU HOW TO WORK IT!!
MEDIA
I DON'T KNOW WHAT WE'RE GONNA BE DOING...
C'MON, KIDS!! LET'S DO THIS WITH PLUS ULTRA ATTITUDE!

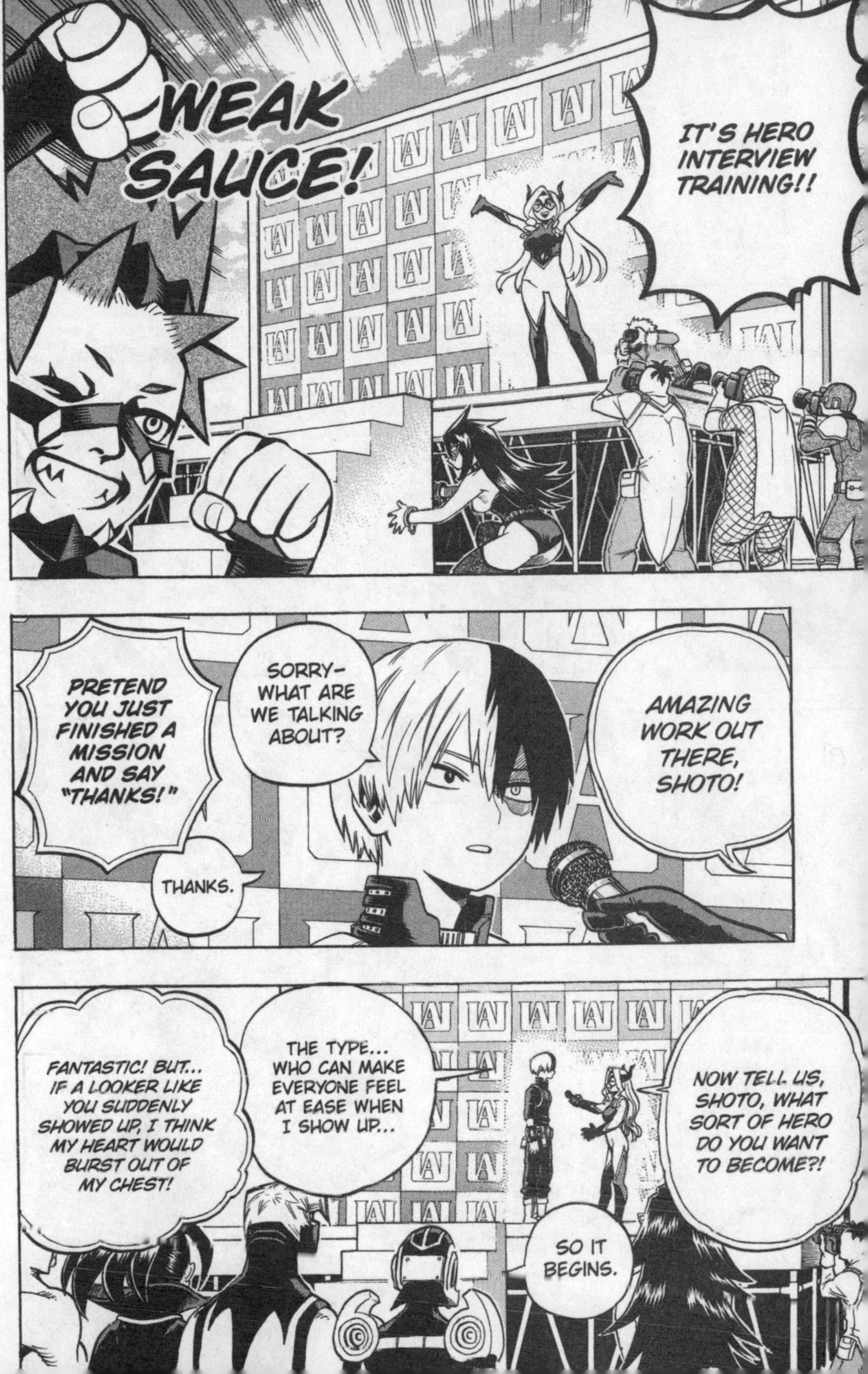
IT'S HERO INTERVIEW TRAINING!!
WEAK SAUCE!
AMAZING WORK OUT THERE, SHOTO!
SORRY- WHAT ARE WE TALKING ABOUT?
PRETEND YOU JUST FINISHED A MISSION AND SAY "THANKS!"
THANKS.
NOW TELL US, SHOTO, WHAT SORT OF HERO DO YOU WANT TO BECOME?!
THE TYPE... WHO CAN MAKE EVERYONE FEEL AT EASE WHEN I SHOW UP...
FANTASTIC! BUT... IF A LOOKER LIKE YOU SUDDENLY SHOWED UP, I THINK MY HEART WOULD BURST OUT OF MY CHEST!
SO IT BEGINS.

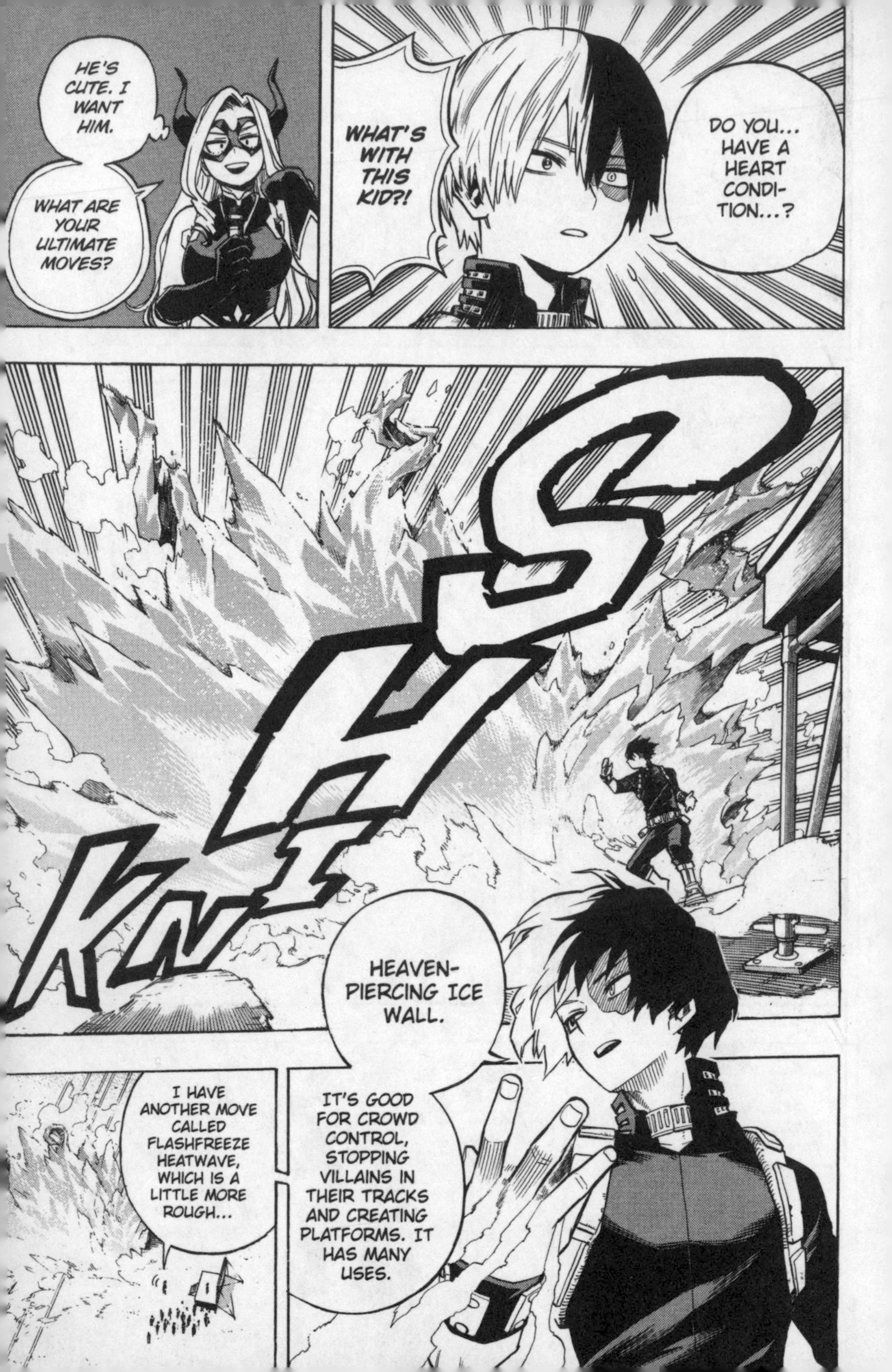

DO YOU... HAVE A HEART CONDITION...?
WHAT'S WITH THIS KID?!
HE'S CUTE. I WANT HIM.
WHAT ARE YOUR ULTIMATE MOVES?
HEAVEN-PIERCING ICE WALL.
IT'S GOOD FOR CROWD CONTROL, STOPPING VILLAINS IN THEIR TRACKS AND CREATING PLATFORMS. IT HAS MANY USES.
I HAVE ANOTHER MOVE CALLED FLASHFREEZE HEATWAVE, WHICH IS A LITTLE MORE ROUGH...

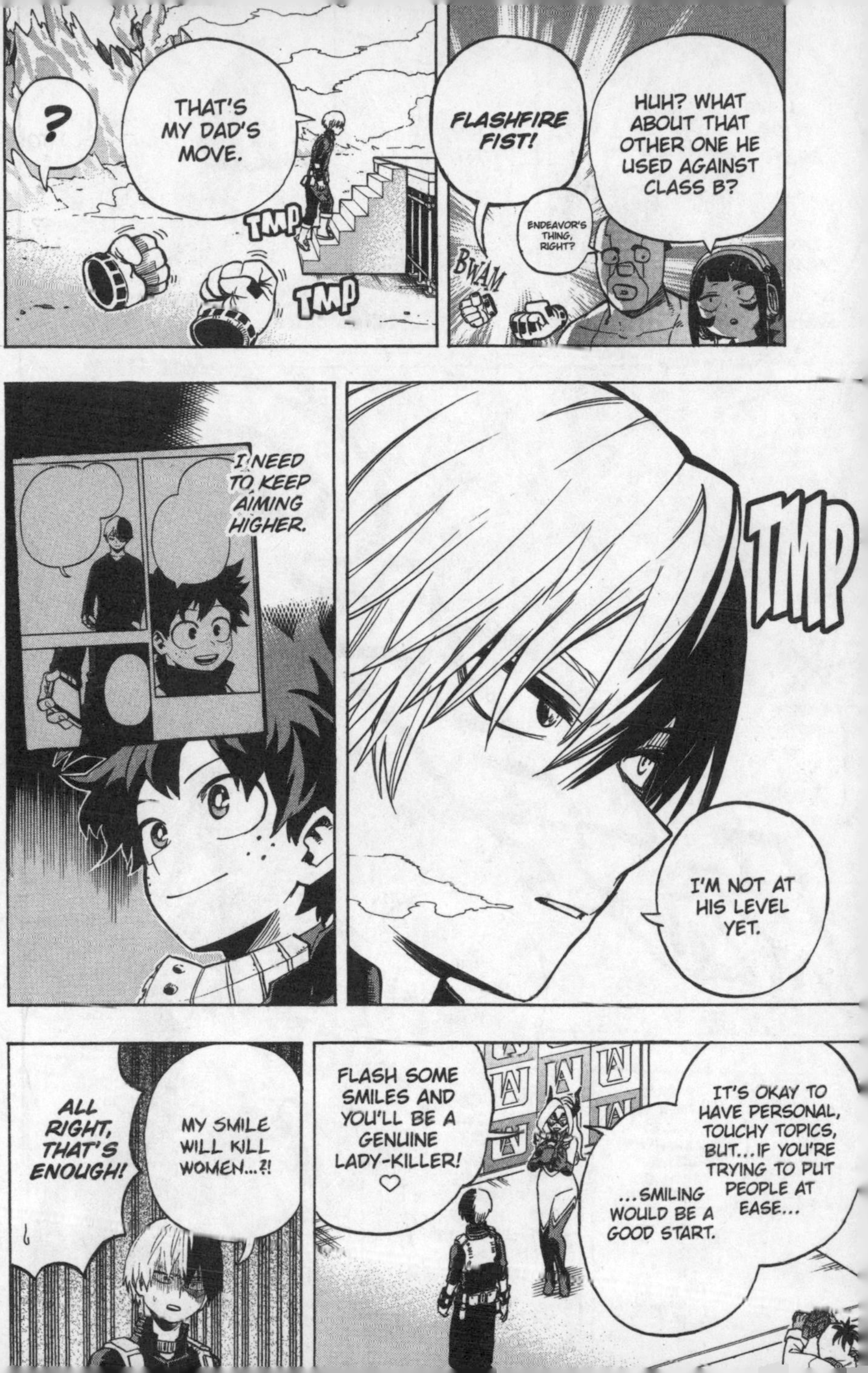
HUH? WHAT ABOUT THAT OTHER ONE HE USED AGAINST CLASS B?
ENDEAVOR'S THING, RIGHT?
FLASHFIRE FIST!
BWAM
THAT'S MY DAD'S MOVE.
?
TMP
TMP
TMP
I'M NOT AT HIS LEVEL YET.
I NEED TO KEEP AIMING HIGHER.
IT'S OKAY TO HAVE PERSONAL, TOUCHY TOPICS, BUT...IF YOU'RE TRYING TO PUT PEOPLE AT EASE...
...SMILING WOULD BE A GOOD START.
FLASH SOME SMILES AND YOU'LL BE A GENUINE LADY-KILLER! ♡
MY SMILE WILL KILL WOMEN...?!
ALL RIGHT, THAT'S ENOUGH!

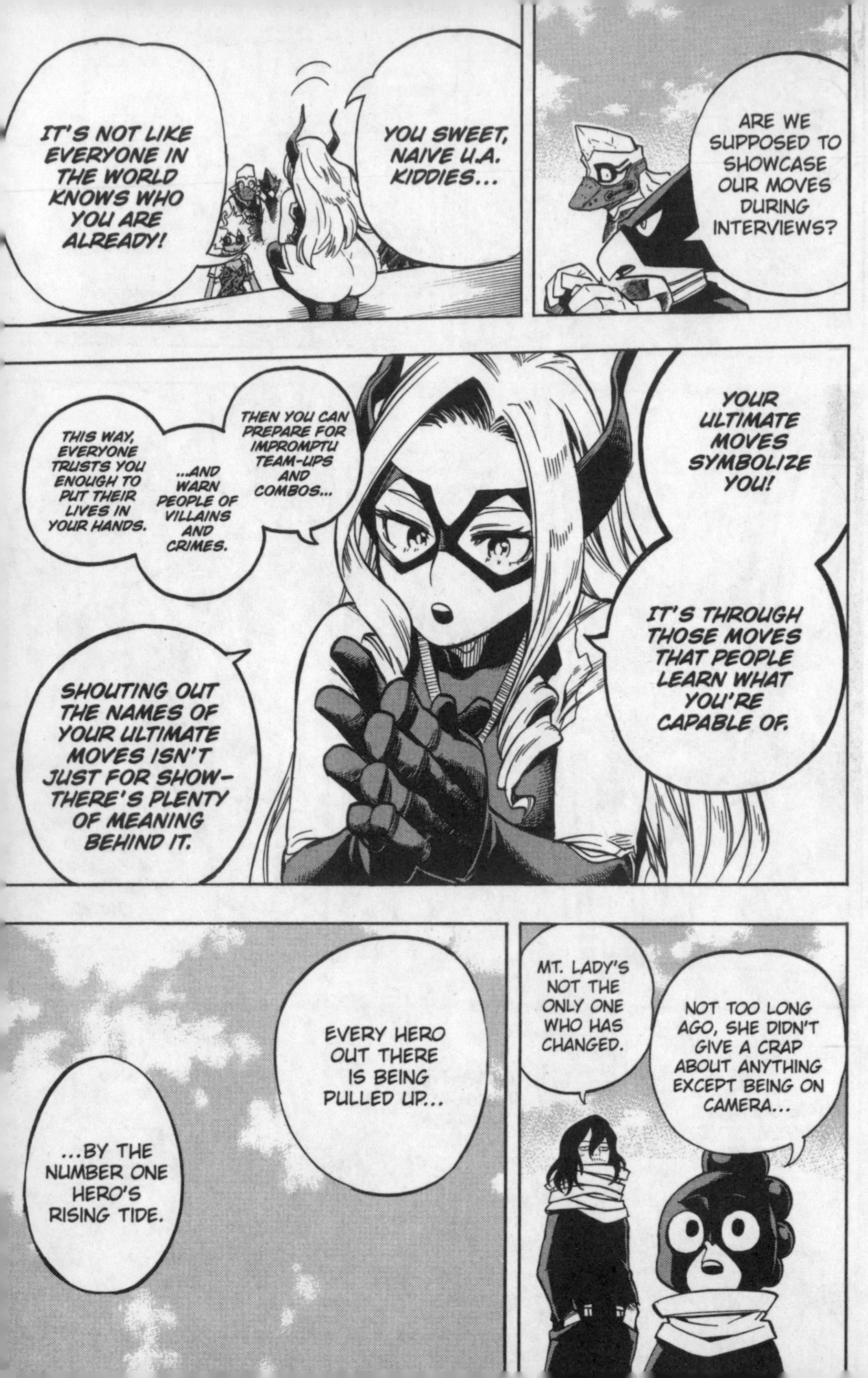
ARE WE SUPPOSED TO SHOWCASE OUR MOVES DURING INTERVIEWS?
YOU SWEET, NAIVE U.A. KIDDIES...
IT'S NOT LIKE EVERYONE IN THE WORLD KNOWS WHO YOU ARE ALREADY!
YOUR ULTIMATE MOVES SYMBOLIZE YOU!
IT'S THROUGH THOSE MOVES THAT PEOPLE LEARN WHAT YOU'RE CAPABLE OF.
THEN YOU CAN PREPARE FOR IMPROMPTU TEAM-UPS AND COMBOS...
...AND WARN PEOPLE OF VILLAINS AND CRIMES.
THIS WAY, EVERYONE TRUSTS YOU ENOUGH TO PUT THEIR LIVES IN YOUR HANDS.
SHOUTING OUT THE NAMES OF YOUR ULTIMATE MOVES ISN'T JUST FOR SHOW— THERE'S PLENTY OF MEANING BEHIND IT.
NOT TOO LONG AGO, SHE DIDN'T GIVE A CRAP ABOUT ANYTHING EXCEPT BEING ON CAMERA...
MT. LADY'S NOT THE ONLY ONE WHO HAS CHANGED.
EVERY HERO OUT THERE IS BEING PULLED UP...
...BY THE NUMBER ONE HERO'S RISING TIDE.

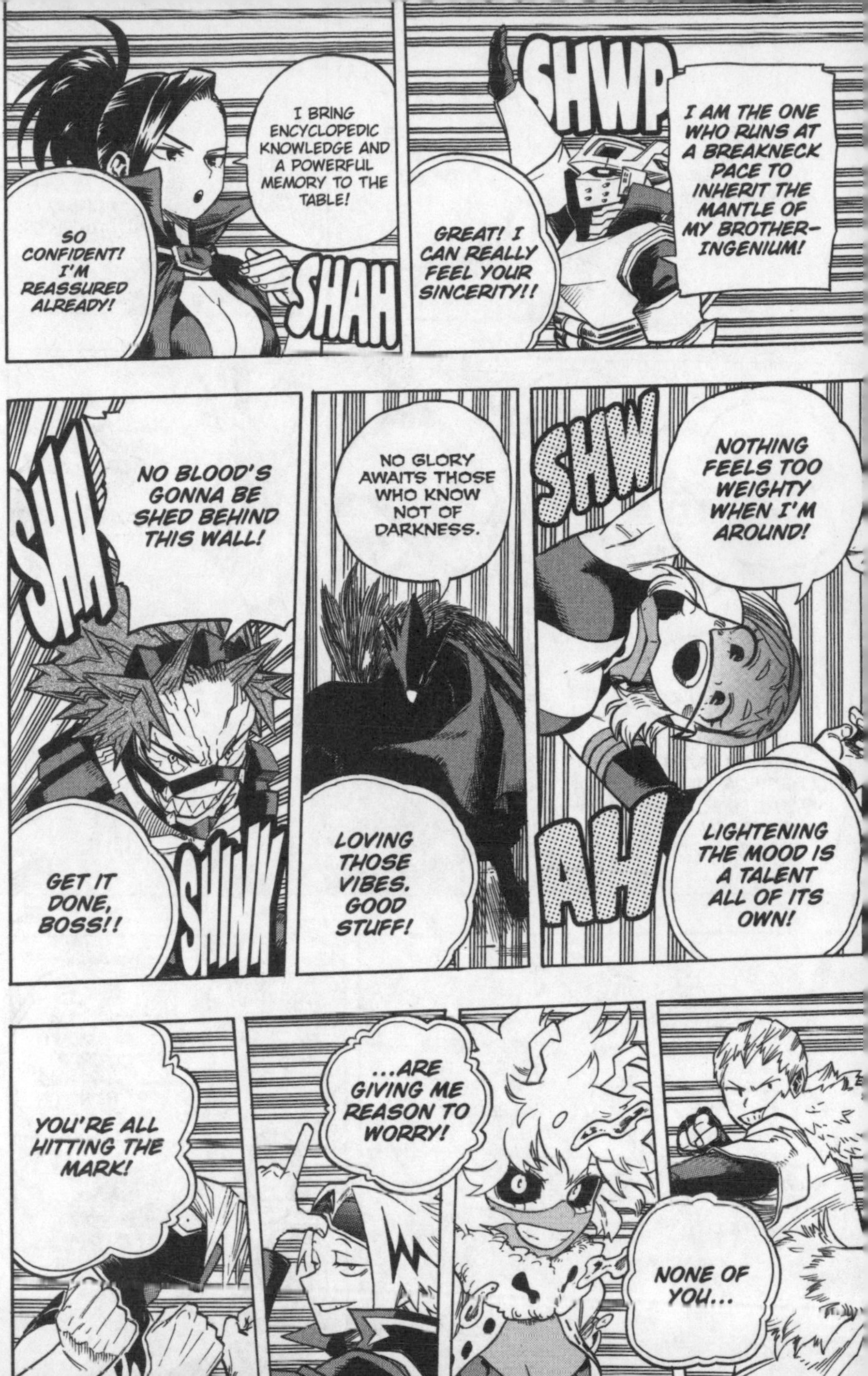
SHWP
I AM THE ONE WHO RUNS AT A BREAKNECK PACE TO INHERIT THE MANTLE OF MY BROTHER—INGENIUM!
GREAT! I CAN REALLY FEEL YOUR SINCERITY!!
I BRING ENCYCLOPEDIC KNOWLEDGE AND A POWERFUL MEMORY TO THE TABLE!
SHAH
SO CONFIDENT! I'M REASSURED ALREADY!
SHW
NOTHING FEELS TOO WEIGHTY WHEN I'M AROUND!
AH
LIGHTENING THE MOOD IS A TALENT ALL OF ITS OWN!
NO GLORY AWAITS THOSE WHO KNOW NOT OF DARKNESS.
LOVING THOSE VIBES. GOOD STUFF!
SHA
NO BLOOD'S GONNA BE SHED BEHIND THIS WALL!
SHINK
GET IT DONE, BOSS!!
NONE OF YOU...
...ARE GIVING ME REASON TO WORRY!
YOU'RE ALL HITTING THE MARK!

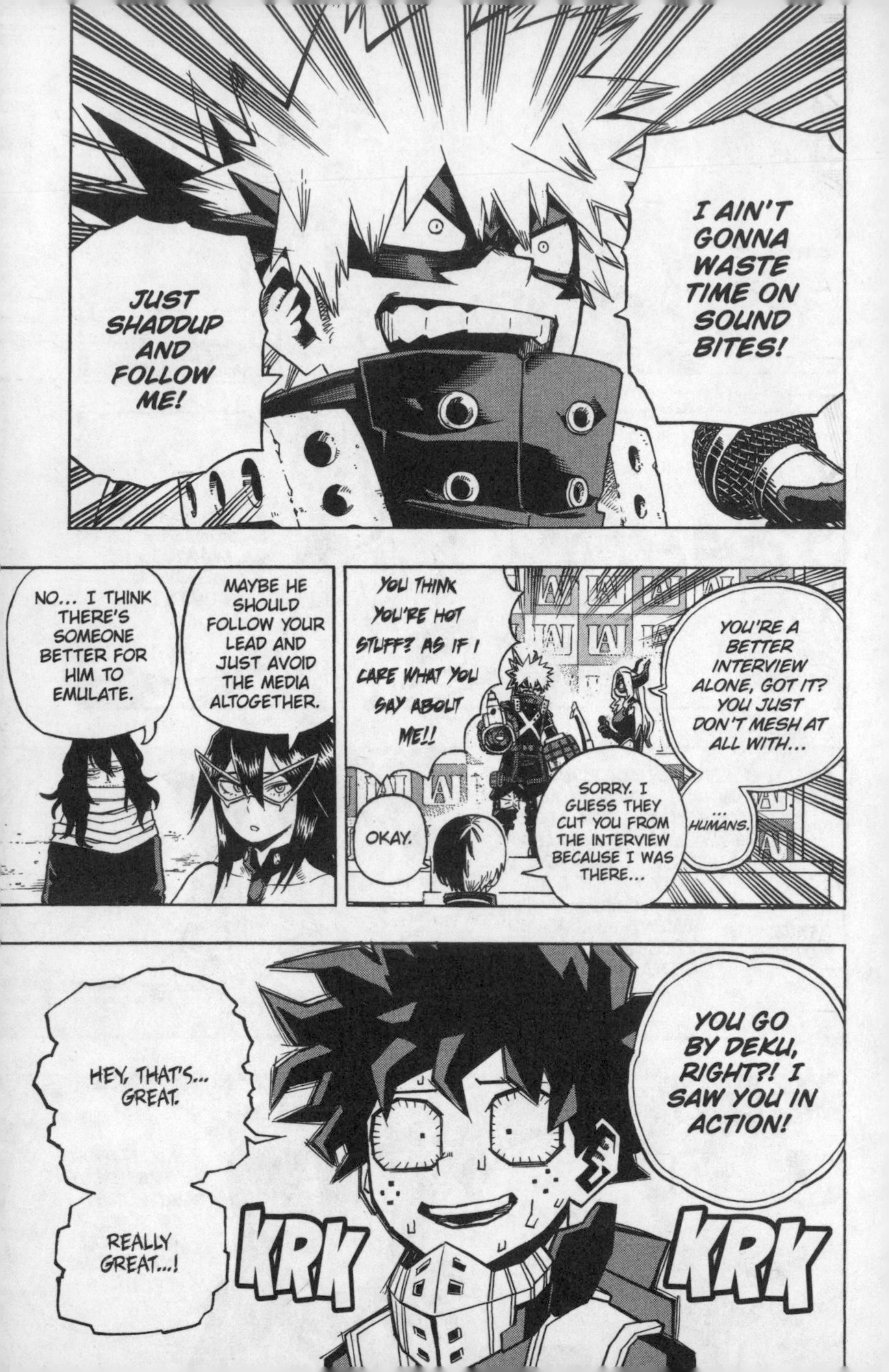

I AIN'T GONNA WASTE TIME ON SOUND BITES!
JUST SHADDUP AND FOLLOW ME!
YOU'RE A BETTER INTERVIEW ALONE, GOT IT? YOU JUST DON'T MESH AT ALL WITH...
...HUMANS.
YOU THINK YOU'RE HOT STUFF? AS IF I CARE WHAT YOU SAY ABOUT ME!!
SORRY. I GUESS THEY CUT YOU FROM THE INTERVIEW BECAUSE I WAS THERE...
OKAY.
MAYBE HE SHOULD FOLLOW YOUR LEAD AND JUST AVOID THE MEDIA ALTOGETHER.
NO... I THINK THERE'S SOMEONE BETTER FOR HIM TO EMULATE.
YOU GO BY DEKU, RIGHT?! I SAW YOU IN ACTION!
KRK
KRK
HEY, THAT'S... GREAT.
REALLY GREAT...!

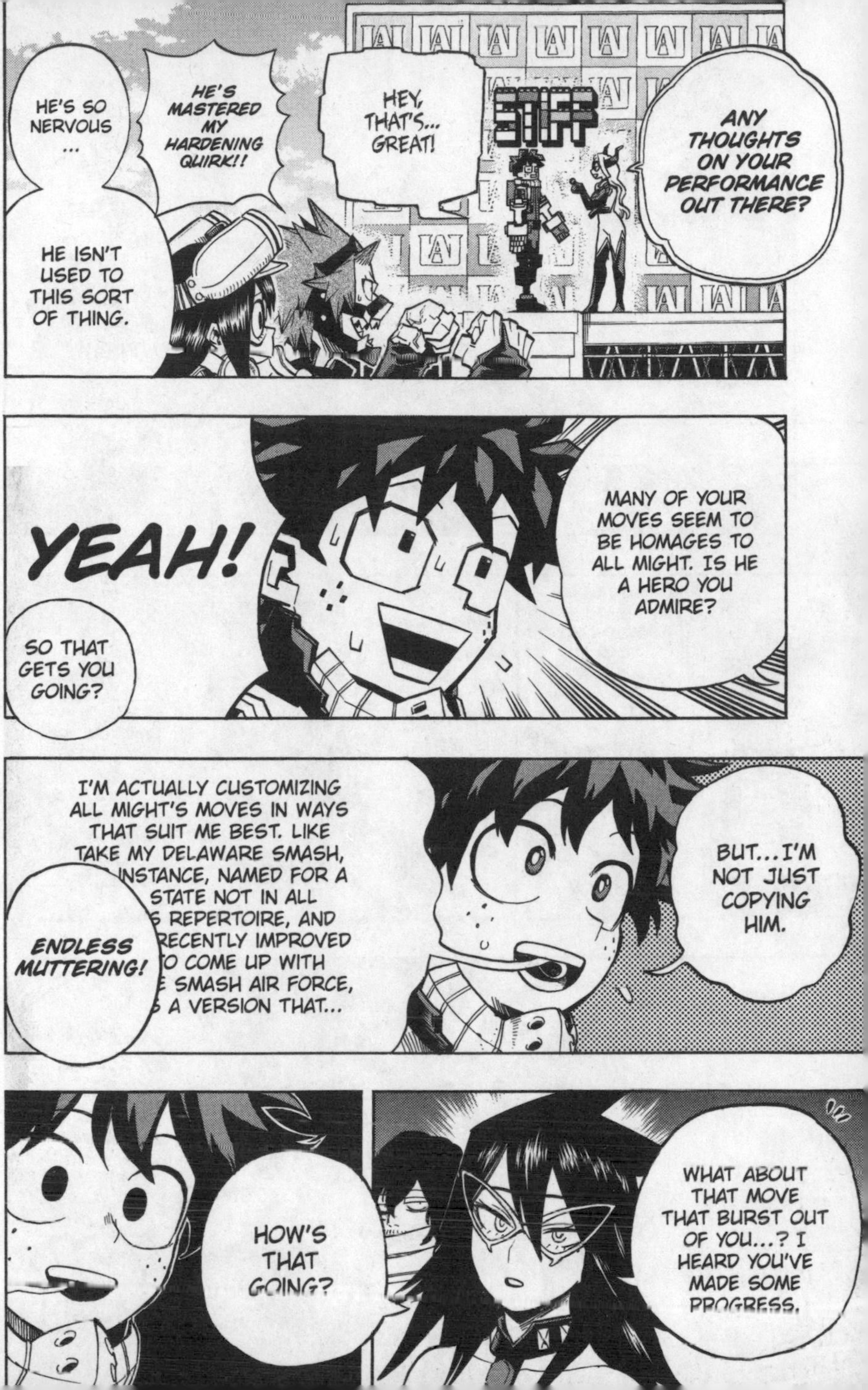
ANY THOUGHTS ON YOUR PERFORMANCE OUT THERE?
STIFF
HEY, THAT'S... GREAT!
HE'S MASTERED MY HARDENING QUIRK!!
HE'S SO NERVOUS ...
HE ISN'T USED TO THIS SORT OF THING.
MANY OF YOUR MOVES SEEM TO BE HOMAGES TO ALL MIGHT. IS HE A HERO YOU ADMIRE?
YEAH!
SO THAT GETS YOU GOING?
BUT...I'M NOT JUST COPYING HIM.
I'M ACTUALLY CUSTOMIZING ALL MIGHT'S MOVES IN WAYS THAT SUIT ME BEST. LIKE TAKE MY DELAWARE SMASH, INSTANCE, NAMED FOR A STATE NOT IN ALL S REPERTOIRE, AND RECENTLY IMPROVED TO COME UP WITH E SMASH AIR FORCE, S A VERSION THAT...
ENDLESS MUTTERING!
WHAT ABOUT THAT MOVE THAT BURST OUT OF YOU...? I HEARD YOU'VE MADE SOME PROGRESS.
HOW'S THAT GOING?

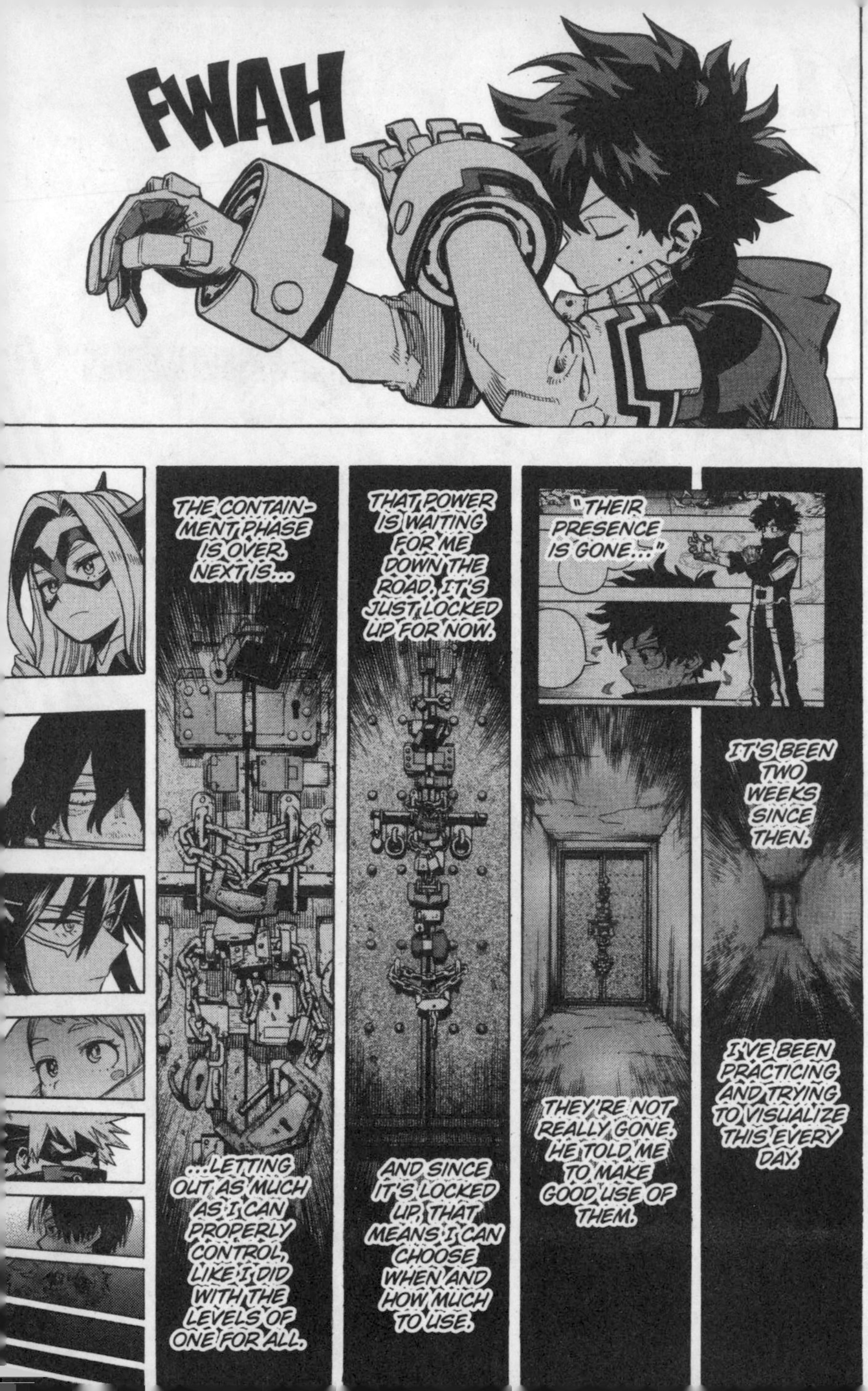
FWAH
IT'S BEEN TWO WEEKS SINCE THEN.
I'VE BEEN PRACTICING AND TRYING TO VISUALIZE THIS EVERY DAY.
"THEIR PRESENCE IS GONE..."
THEY'RE NOT REALLY GONE. HE TOLD ME TO MAKE GOOD USE OF THEM.
THAT POWER IS WAITING FOR ME DOWN THE ROAD. IT'S JUST LOCKED UP FOR NOW.
AND SINCE IT'S LOCKED UP, THAT MEANS I CAN CHOOSE WHEN AND HOW MUCH TO USE.
THE CONTAIN-MENT PHASE IS OVER. NEXT IS...
...LETTING OUT AS MUCH AS I CAN PROPERLY CONTROL, LIKE I DID WITH THE LEVELS OF ONE FOR ALL.

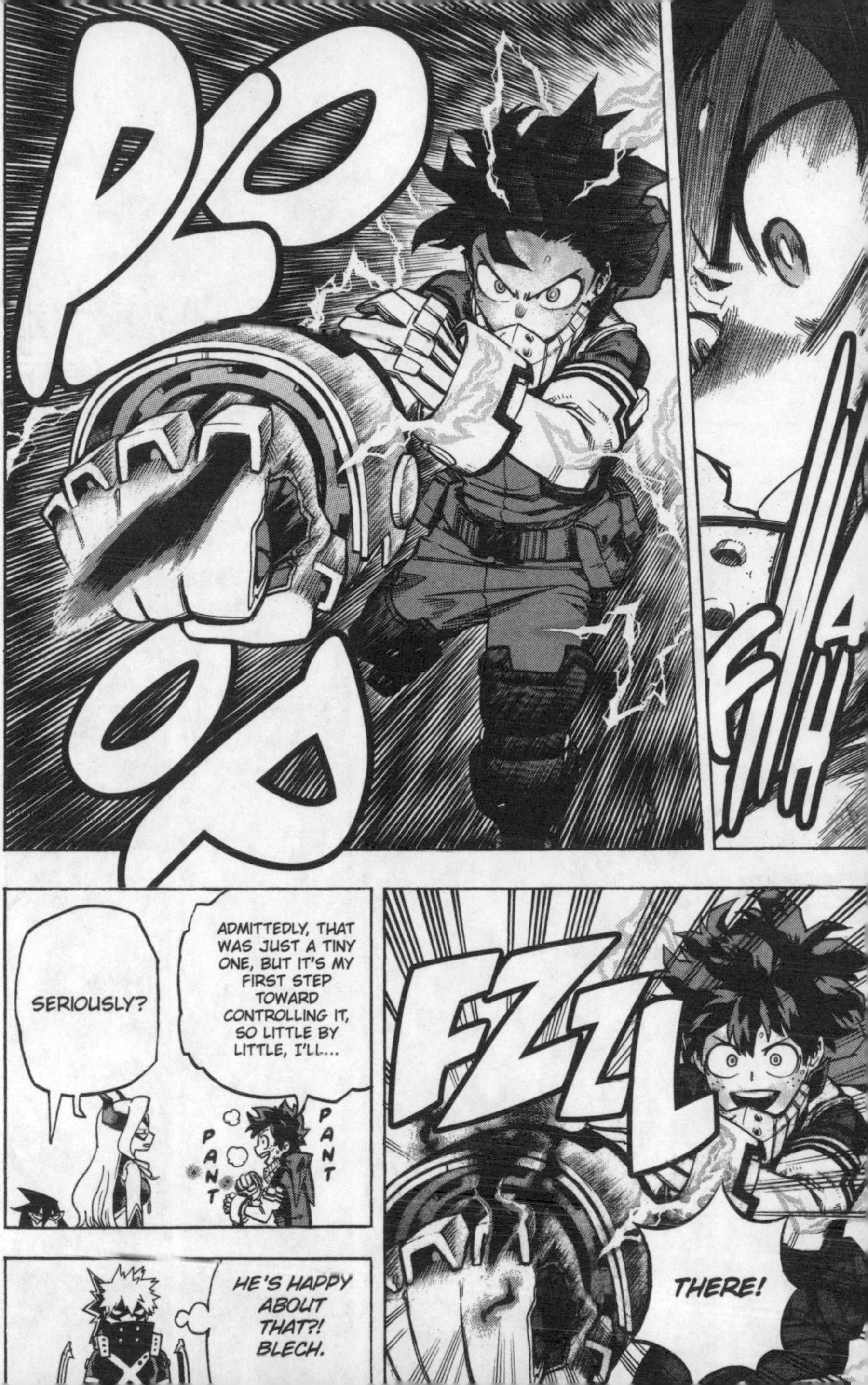
FZZL
THERE!
ADMITTEDLY, THAT WAS JUST A TINY ONE, BUT IT'S MY FIRST STEP TOWARD CONTROLLING IT, SO LITTLE BY LITTLE, I'LL...
SERIOUSLY?
PANT
PANT
HE'S HAPPY ABOUT THAT?! BLECH.

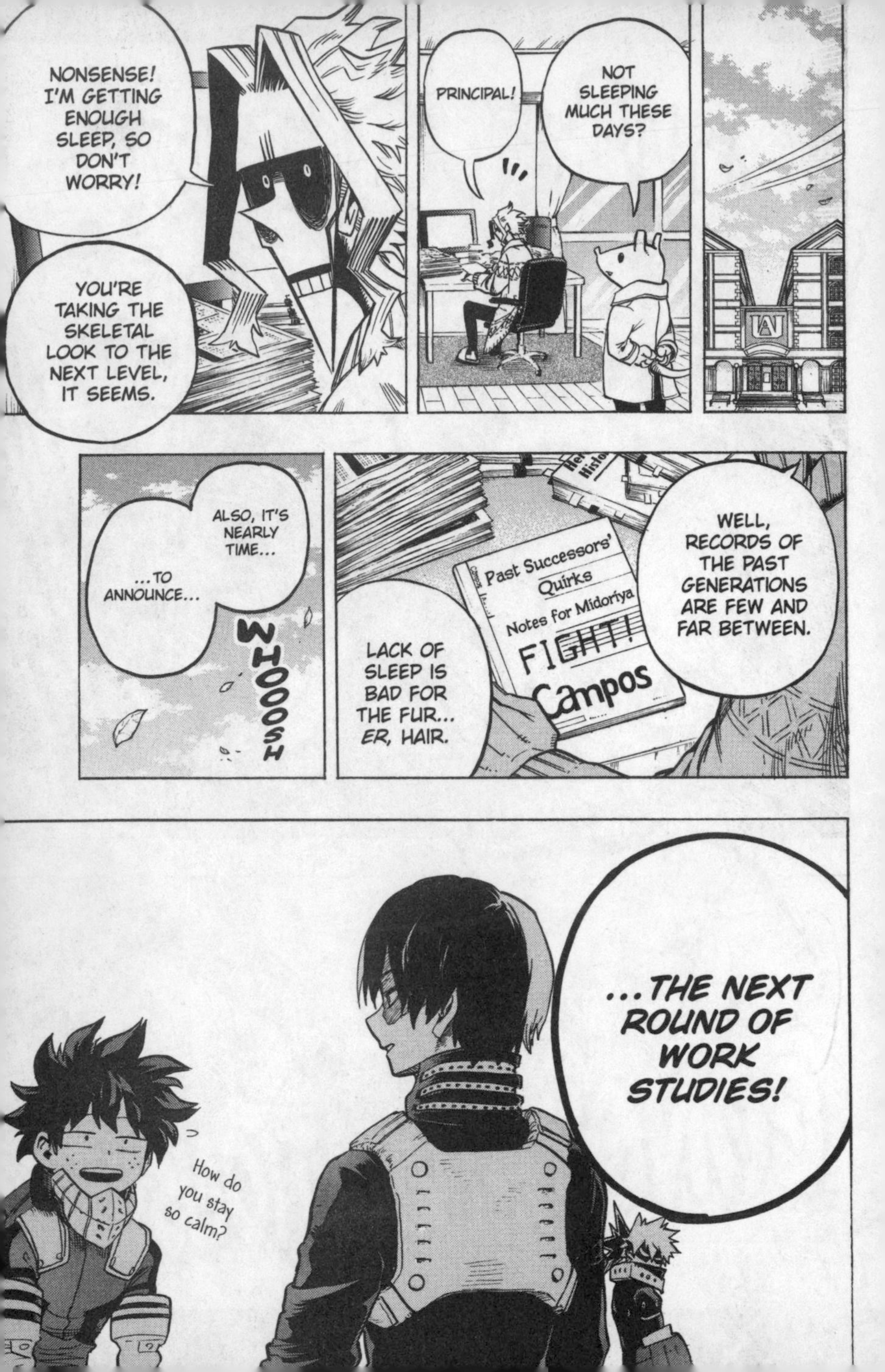
NOT SLEEPING MUCH THESE DAYS?
PRINCIPAL!
NONSENSE! I'M GETTING ENOUGH SLEEP, SO DON'T WORRY!
YOU'RE TAKING THE SKELETAL LOOK TO THE NEXT LEVEL, IT SEEMS.
WELL, RECORDS OF THE PAST GENERATIONS ARE FEW AND FAR BETWEEN.
Past Successors' Quirks
Notes for Midoriya
FIGHT!
Campos
LACK OF SLEEP IS BAD FOR THE FUR... ER, HAIR.
ALSO, IT'S NEARLY TIME...
...TO ANNOUNCE...
WHOOOOSH
...THE NEXT ROUND OF WORK STUDIES!
How do you stay so calm?

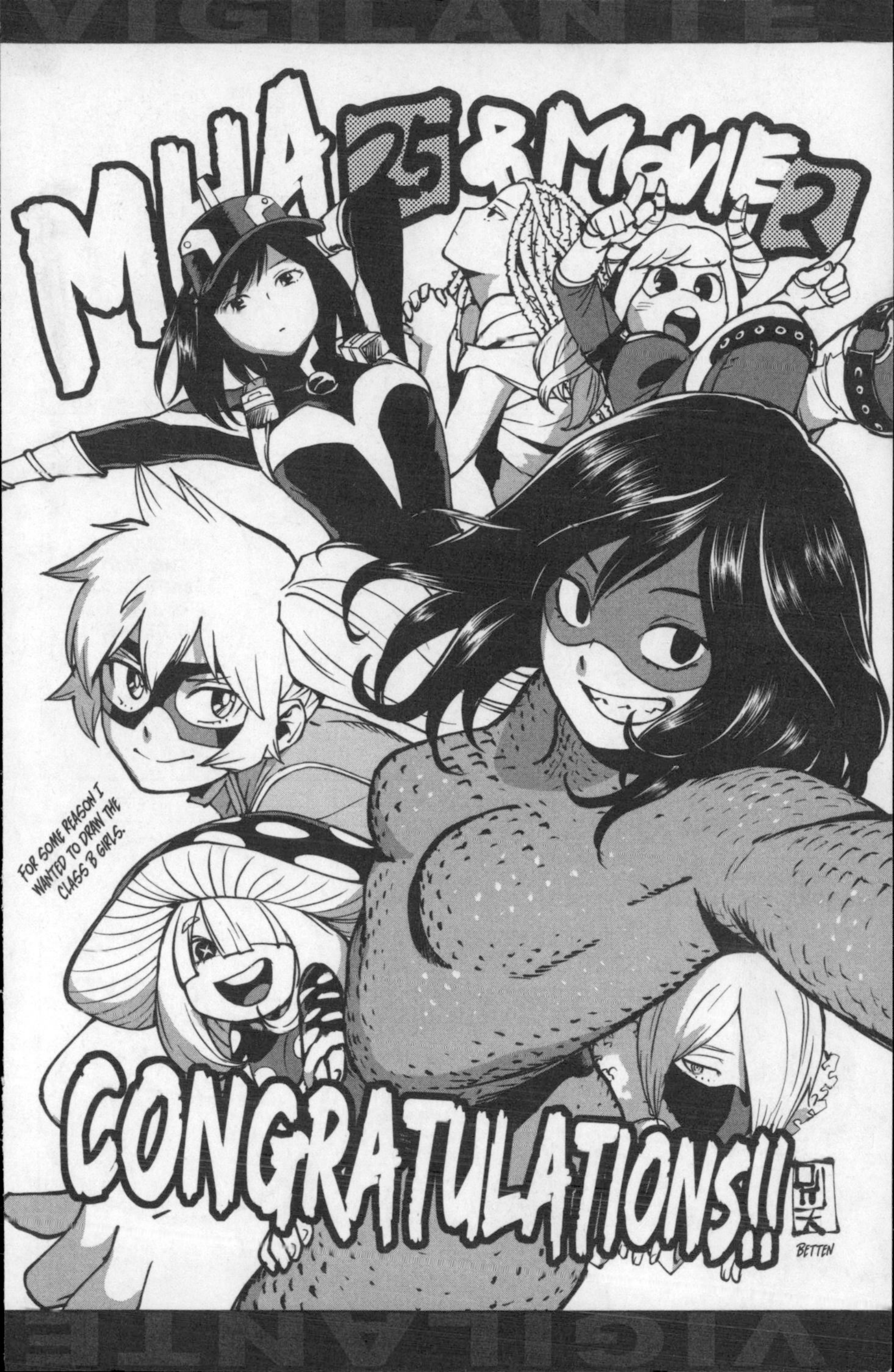
VIGILANTES
MHA 25 & MOVIE 2
FOR SOME REASON I WANTED TO DRAW THE CLASS B GIRLS.
CONGRATULATIONS!!
BETTEN

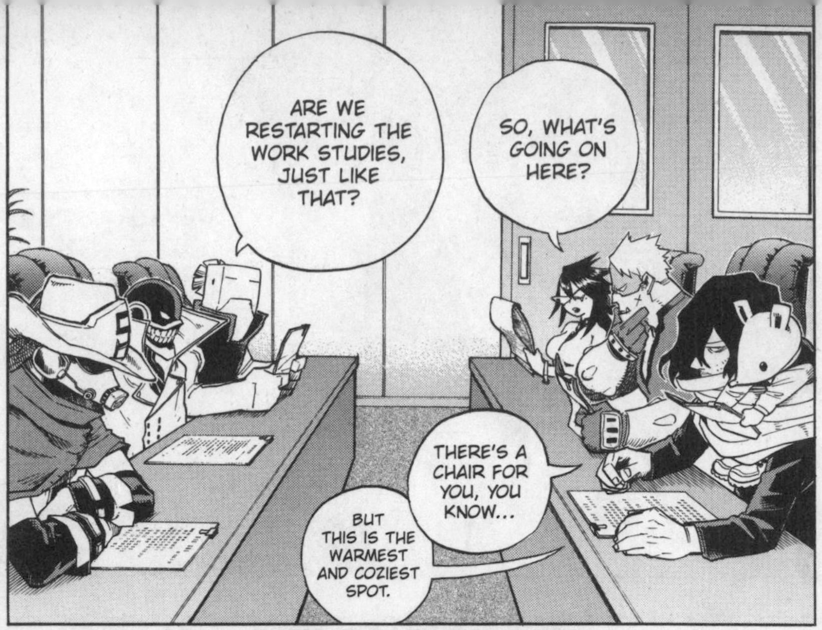
SO, WHAT'S GOING ON HERE?
ARE WE RESTARTING THE WORK STUDIES, JUST LIKE THAT?
THERE'S A CHAIR FOR YOU, YOU KNOW...
BUT THIS IS THE WARMEST AND COZIEST SPOT.

NO. 242 - HAVE A MERRY CHRISTMAS!

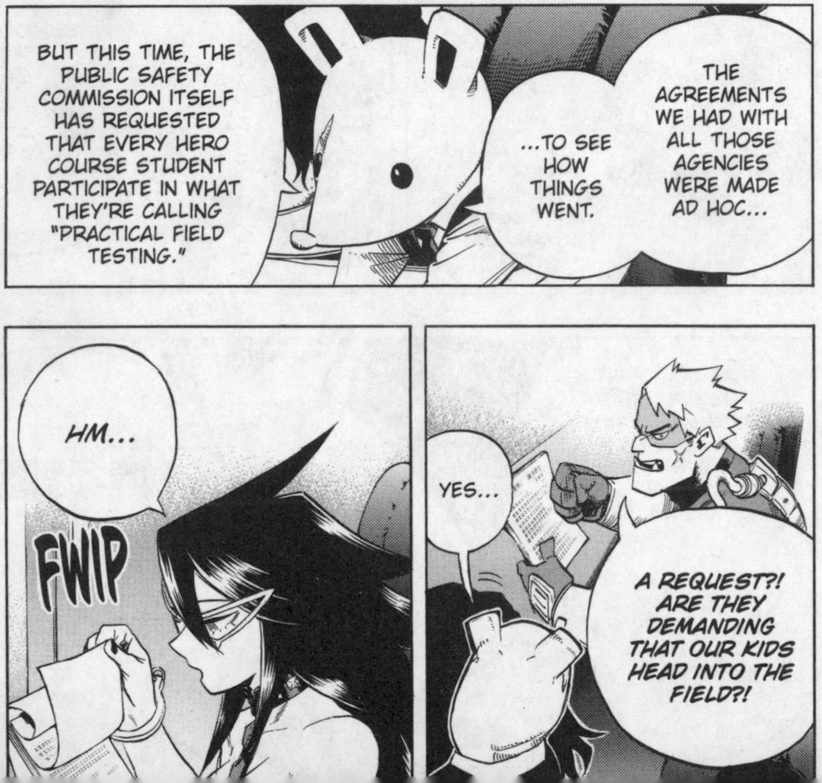
THE AGREEMENTS WE HAD WITH ALL THOSE AGENCIES WERE MADE AD HOC...
...TO SEE HOW THINGS WENT.
BUT THIS TIME, THE PUBLIC SAFETY COMMISSION ITSELF HAS REQUESTED THAT EVERY HERO COURSE STUDENT PARTICIPATE IN WHAT THEY'RE CALLING "PRACTICAL FIELD TESTING."
A REQUEST?! ARE THEY DEMANDING THAT OUR KIDS HEAD INTO THE FIELD?!
YES...
HM...
FWIP

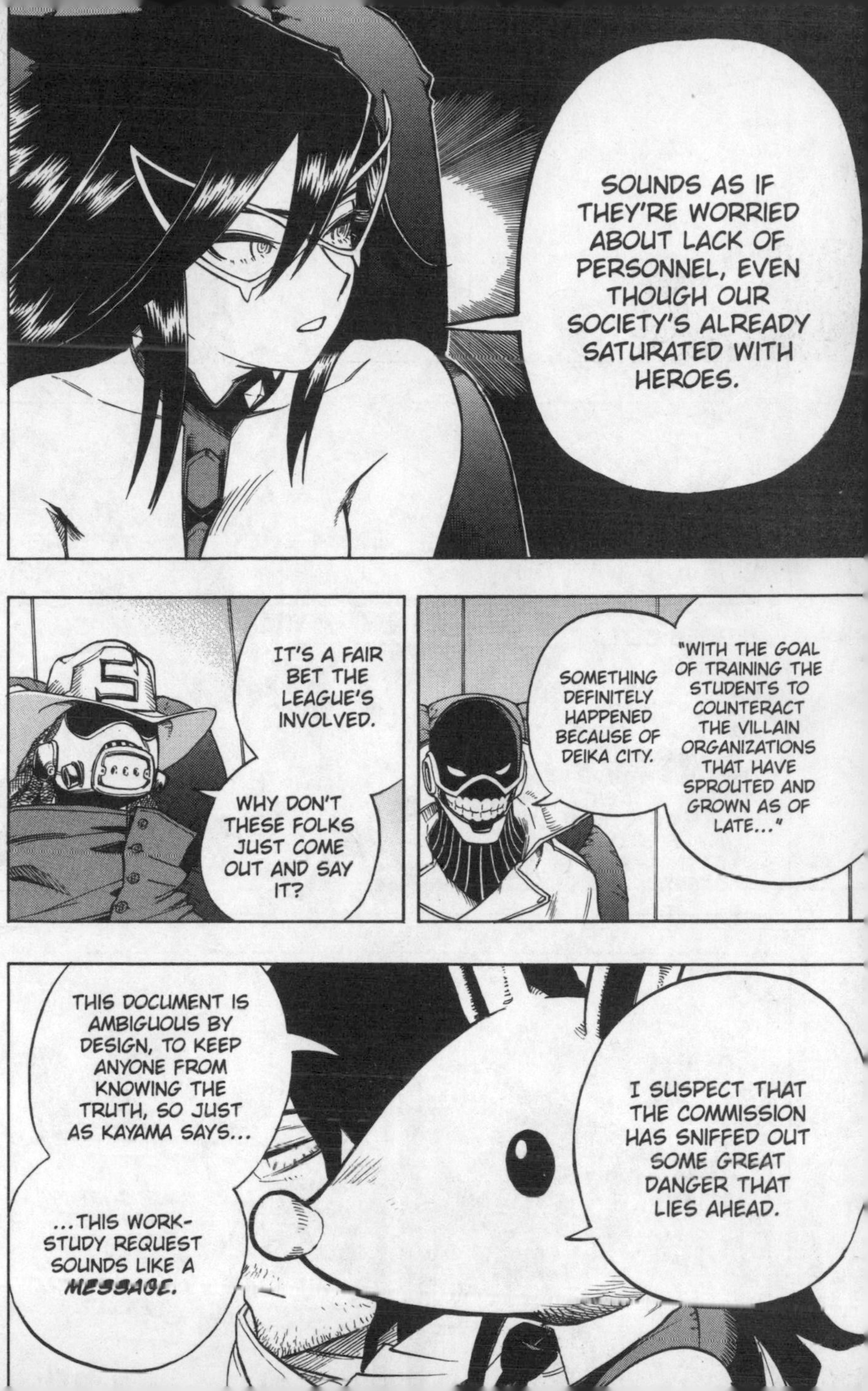

SOUNDS AS IF THEY'RE WORRIED ABOUT LACK OF PERSONNEL, EVEN THOUGH OUR SOCIETY'S ALREADY SATURATED WITH HEROES.
"WITH THE GOAL OF TRAINING THE STUDENTS TO COUNTERACT THE VILLAIN ORGANIZATIONS THAT HAVE SPROUTED AND GROWN AS OF LATE..."
SOMETHING DEFINITELY HAPPENED BECAUSE OF DEIKA CITY.
IT'S A FAIR BET THE LEAGUE'S INVOLVED.
WHY DON'T THESE FOLKS JUST COME OUT AND SAY IT?
THIS DOCUMENT IS AMBIGUOUS BY DESIGN, TO KEEP ANYONE FROM KNOWING THE TRUTH, SO JUST AS KAYAMA SAYS...
...THIS WORK-STUDY REQUEST SOUNDS LIKE A MESSAGE.
I SUSPECT THAT THE COMMISSION HAS SNIFFED OUT SOME GREAT DANGER THAT LIES AHEAD.

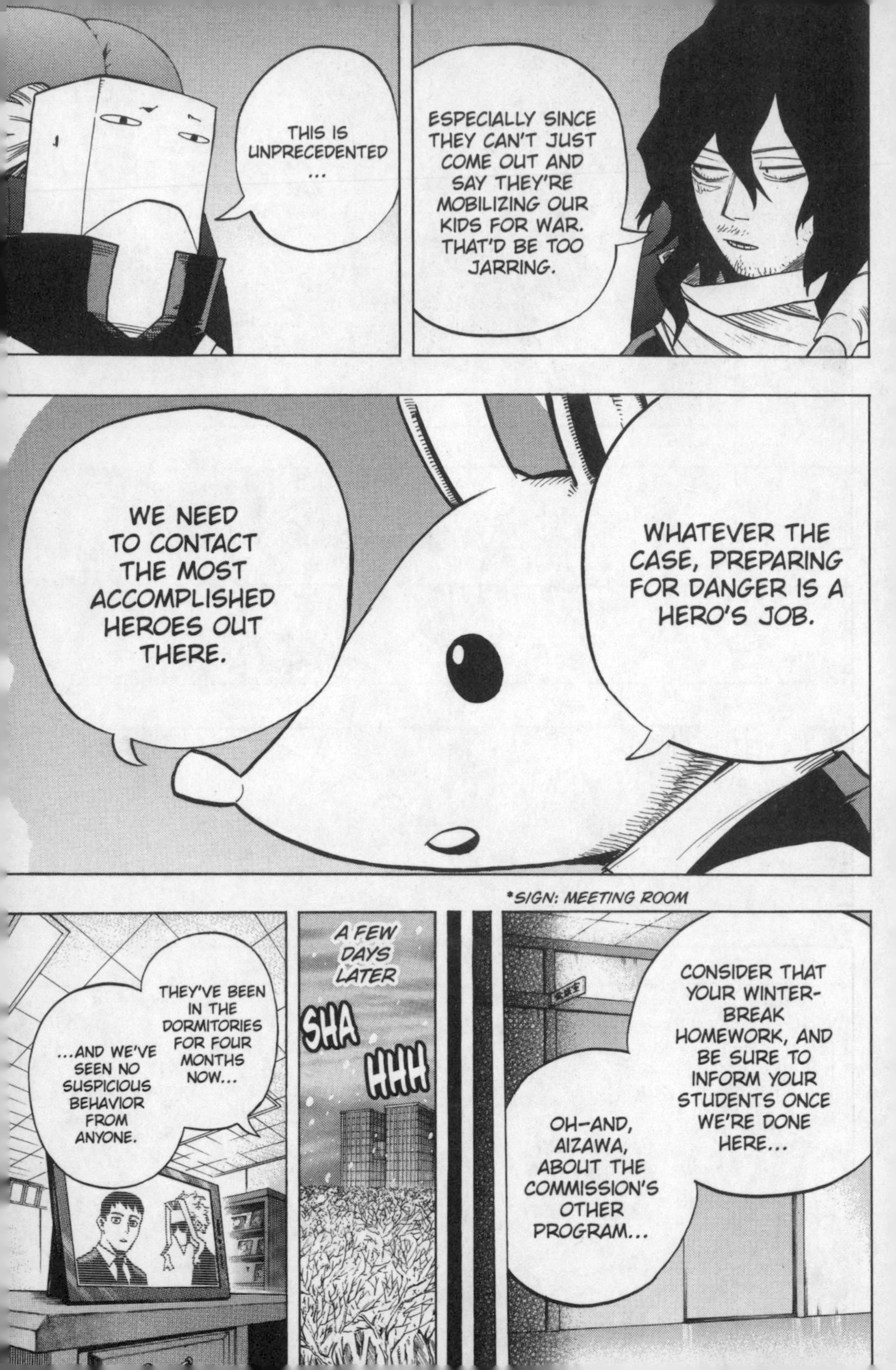
ESPECIALLY SINCE THEY CAN'T JUST COME OUT AND SAY THEY'RE MOBILIZING OUR KIDS FOR WAR. THAT'D BE TOO JARRING.
THIS IS UNPRECEDENTED ...
WHATEVER THE CASE, PREPARING FOR DANGER IS A HERO'S JOB.
WE NEED TO CONTACT THE MOST ACCOMPLISHED HEROES OUT THERE.
*SIGN: MEETING ROOM
CONSIDER THAT YOUR WINTER-BREAK HOMEWORK, AND BE SURE TO INFORM YOUR STUDENTS ONCE WE'RE DONE HERE...
OH—AND, AIZAWA, ABOUT THE COMMISSION'S OTHER PROGRAM...
A FEW DAYS LATER
SHA HHH
THEY'VE BEEN IN THE DORMITORIES FOR FOUR MONTHS NOW...
...AND WE'VE SEEN NO SUSPICIOUS BEHAVIOR FROM ANYONE.

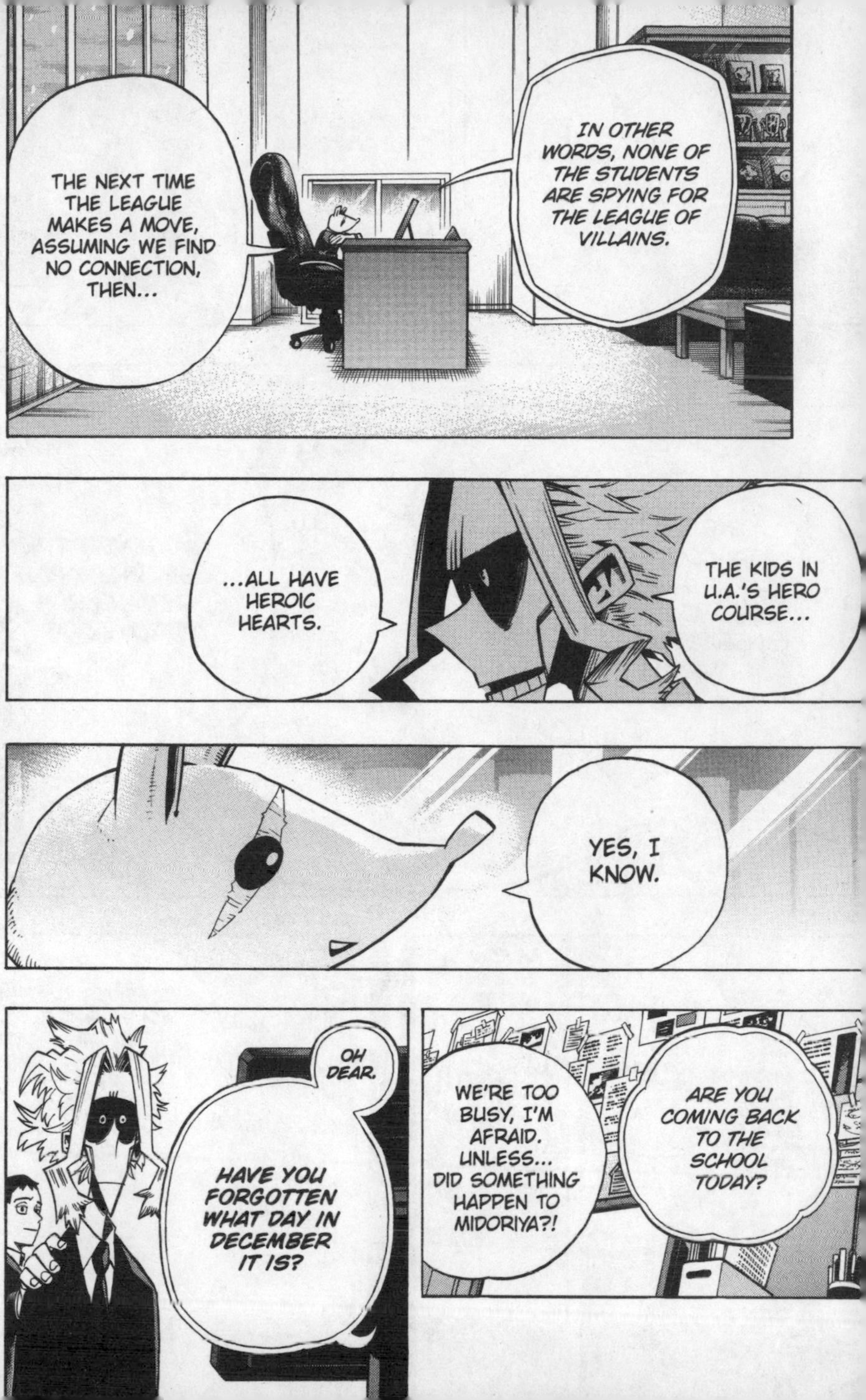
IN OTHER WORDS, NONE OF THE STUDENTS ARE SPYING FOR THE LEAGUE OF VILLAINS.
THE NEXT TIME THE LEAGUE MAKES A MOVE, ASSUMING WE FIND NO CONNECTION, THEN...
THE KIDS IN U.A.'S HERO COURSE...
...ALL HAVE HEROIC HEARTS.
YES, I KNOW.
ARE YOU COMING BACK TO THE SCHOOL TODAY?
WE'RE TOO BUSY, I'M AFRAID. UNLESS... DID SOMETHING HAPPEN TO MIDORIYA?!
OH DEAR.
HAVE YOU FORGOTTEN WHAT DAY IN DECEMBER IT IS?

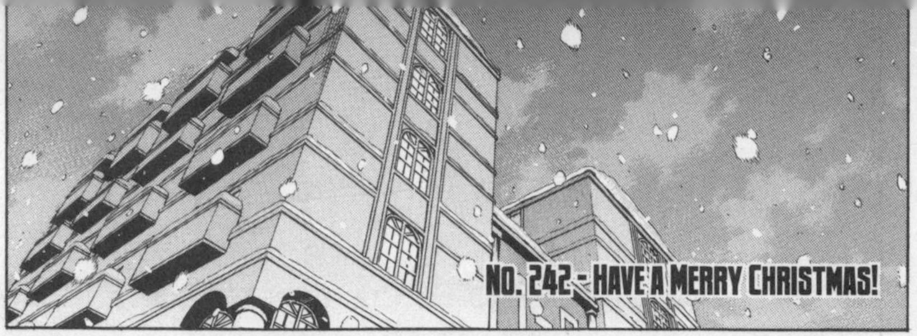
No. 242 - Have a Merry Christmas!

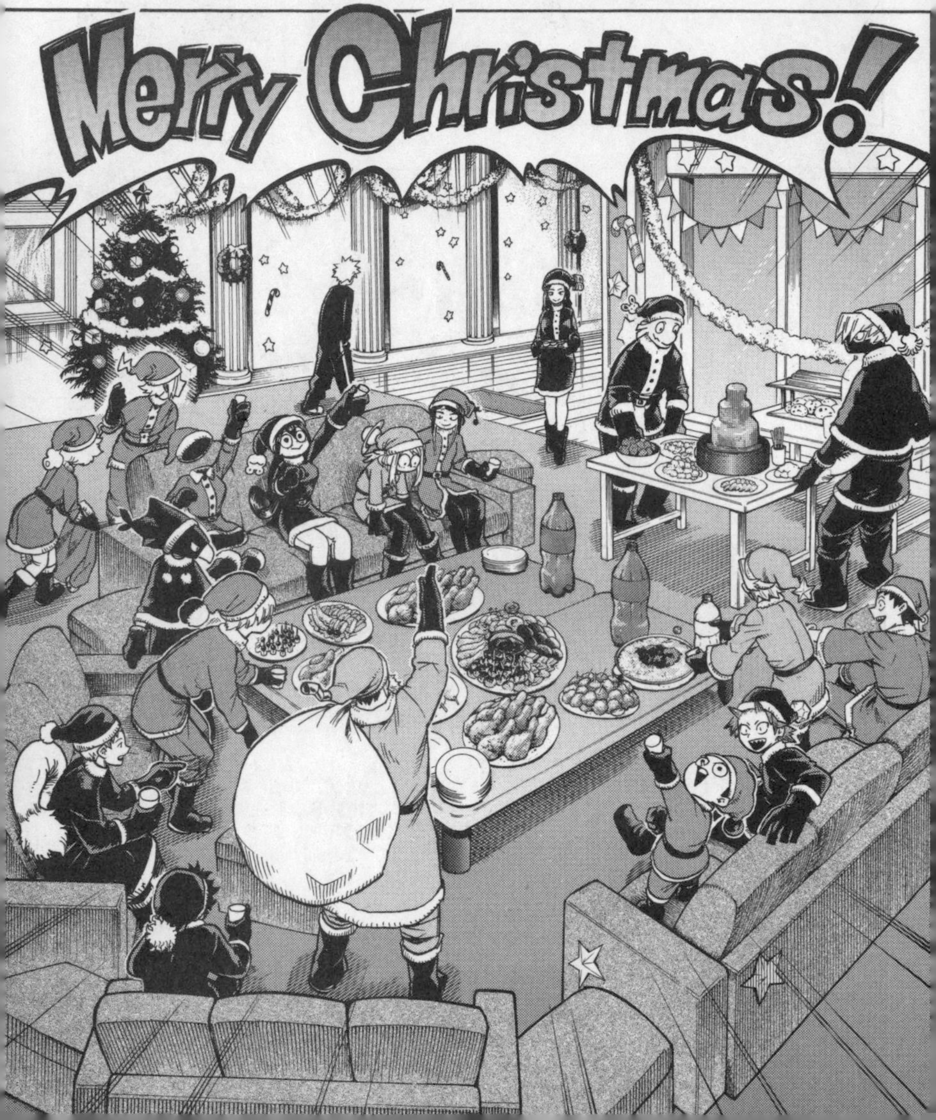
Merry Christmas!

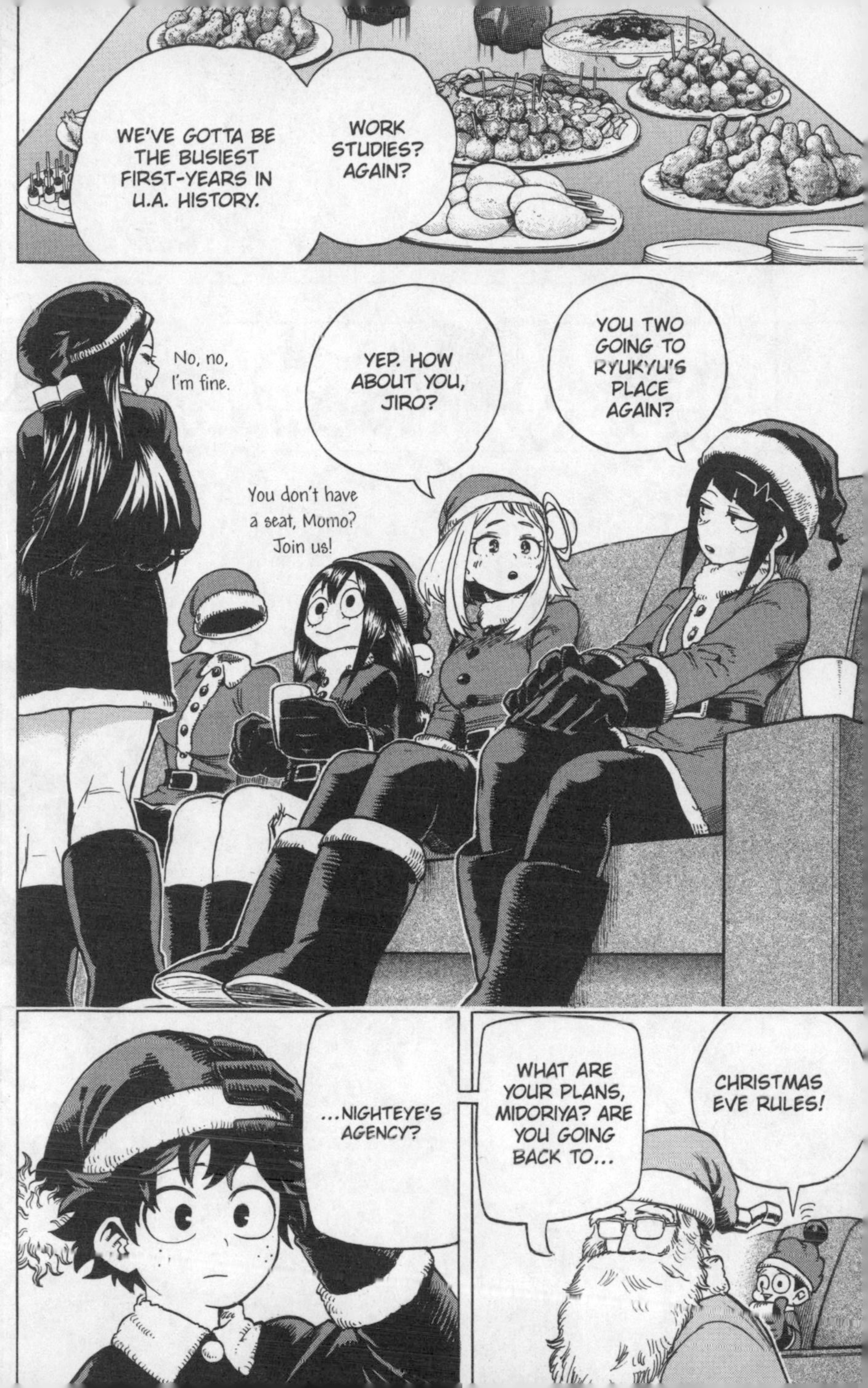
WORK STUDIES? AGAIN?
WE'VE GOTTA BE THE BUSIEST FIRST-YEARS IN U.A. HISTORY.
YOU TWO GOING TO RYUKYU'S PLACE AGAIN?
YEP. HOW ABOUT YOU, JIRO?
You don't have a seat, Momo? Join us!
No, no, I'm fine.
CHRISTMAS EVE RULES!
WHAT ARE YOUR PLANS, MIDORIYA? ARE YOU GOING BACK TO...
...NIGHTEYE'S AGENCY?

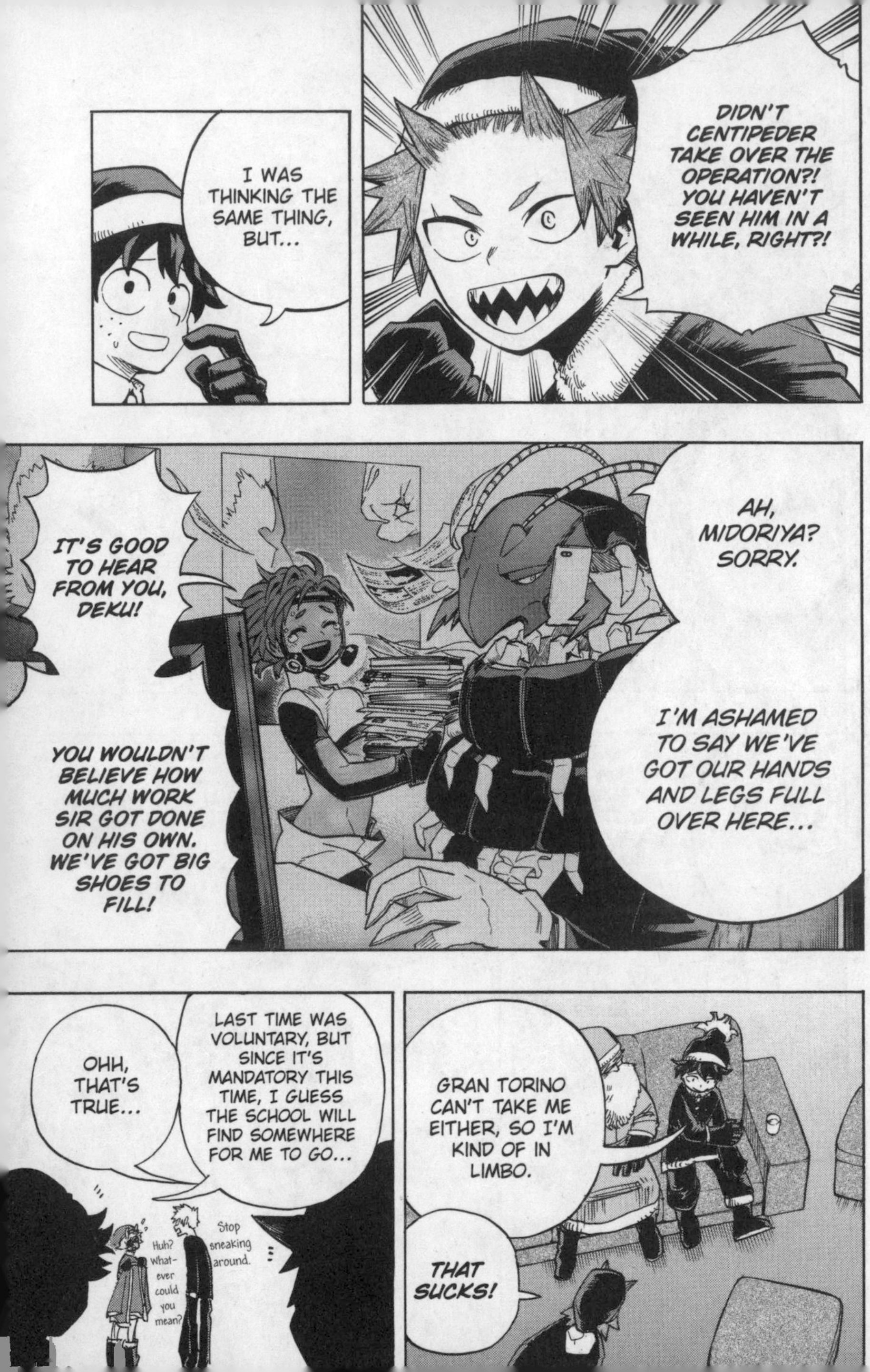
DIDN'T CENTIPEDER TAKE OVER THE OPERATION?! YOU HAVEN'T SEEN HIM IN A WHILE, RIGHT?!
I WAS THINKING THE SAME THING, BUT...
AH, MIDORIYA? SORRY.
I'M ASHAMED TO SAY WE'VE GOT OUR HANDS AND LEGS FULL OVER HERE...
IT'S GOOD TO HEAR FROM YOU, DEKU!
YOU WOULDN'T BELIEVE HOW MUCH WORK SIR GOT DONE ON HIS OWN. WE'VE GOT BIG SHOES TO FILL!
GRAN TORINO CAN'T TAKE ME EITHER, SO I'M KIND OF IN LIMBO.
THAT SUCKS!
LAST TIME WAS VOLUNTARY, BUT SINCE IT'S MANDATORY THIS TIME, I GUESS THE SCHOOL WILL FIND SOMEWHERE FOR ME TO GO...
OHH, THAT'S TRUE...
Stop sneaking around.
Huh? Whatever could you mean?

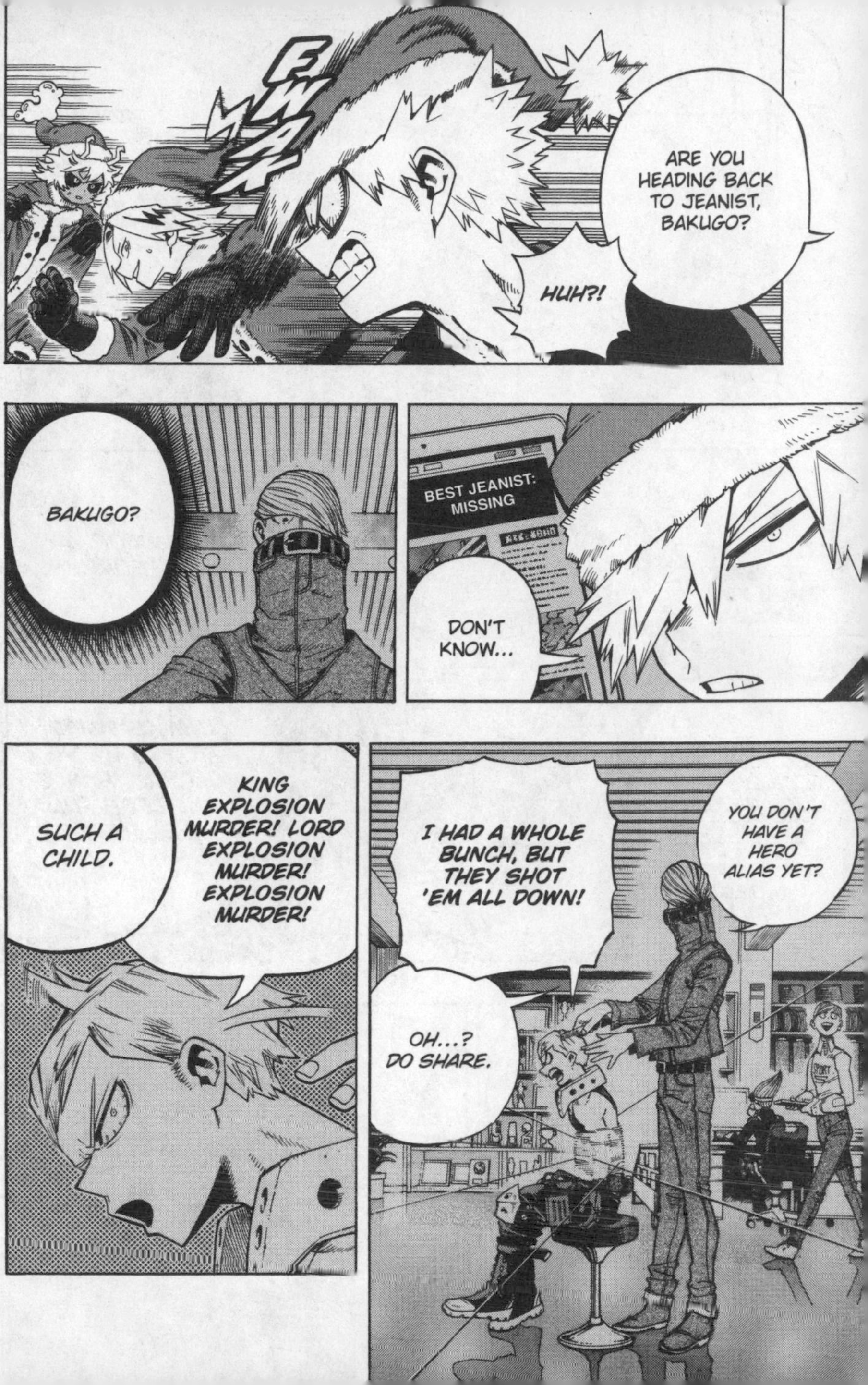
ARE YOU HEADING BACK TO JEANIST, BAKUGO?
HUH?!
BEST JEANIST: MISSING
DON'T KNOW...
BAKUGO?
YOU DON'T HAVE A HERO ALIAS YET?
I HAD A WHOLE BUNCH, BUT THEY SHOT 'EM ALL DOWN!
OH...? DO SHARE.
KING EXPLOSION MURDER! LORD EXPLOSION MURDER! EXPLOSION MURDER!
SUCH A CHILD.

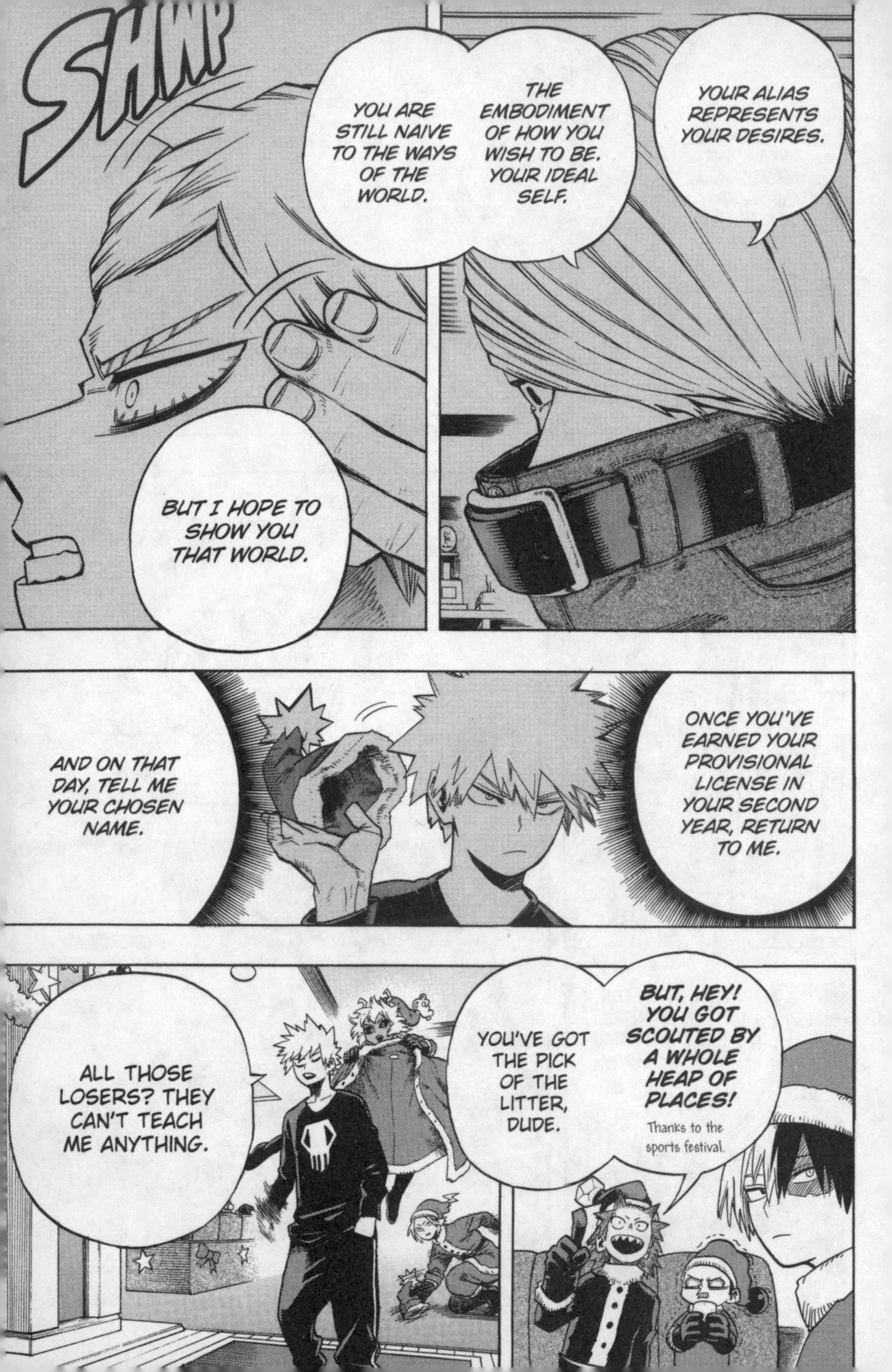

YOUR ALIAS REPRESENTS YOUR DESIRES.
THE EMBODIMENT OF HOW YOU WISH TO BE. YOUR IDEAL SELF.
YOU ARE STILL NAIVE TO THE WAYS OF THE WORLD.
SHMP
BUT I HOPE TO SHOW YOU THAT WORLD.
ONCE YOU'VE EARNED YOUR PROVISIONAL LICENSE IN YOUR SECOND YEAR, RETURN TO ME.
AND ON THAT DAY, TELL ME YOUR CHOSEN NAME.
BUT, HEY! YOU GOT SCOUTED BY A WHOLE HEAP OF PLACES!
Thanks to the sports festival.
YOU'VE GOT THE PICK OF THE LITTER, DUDE.
ALL THOSE LOSERS? THEY CAN'T TEACH ME ANYTHING.

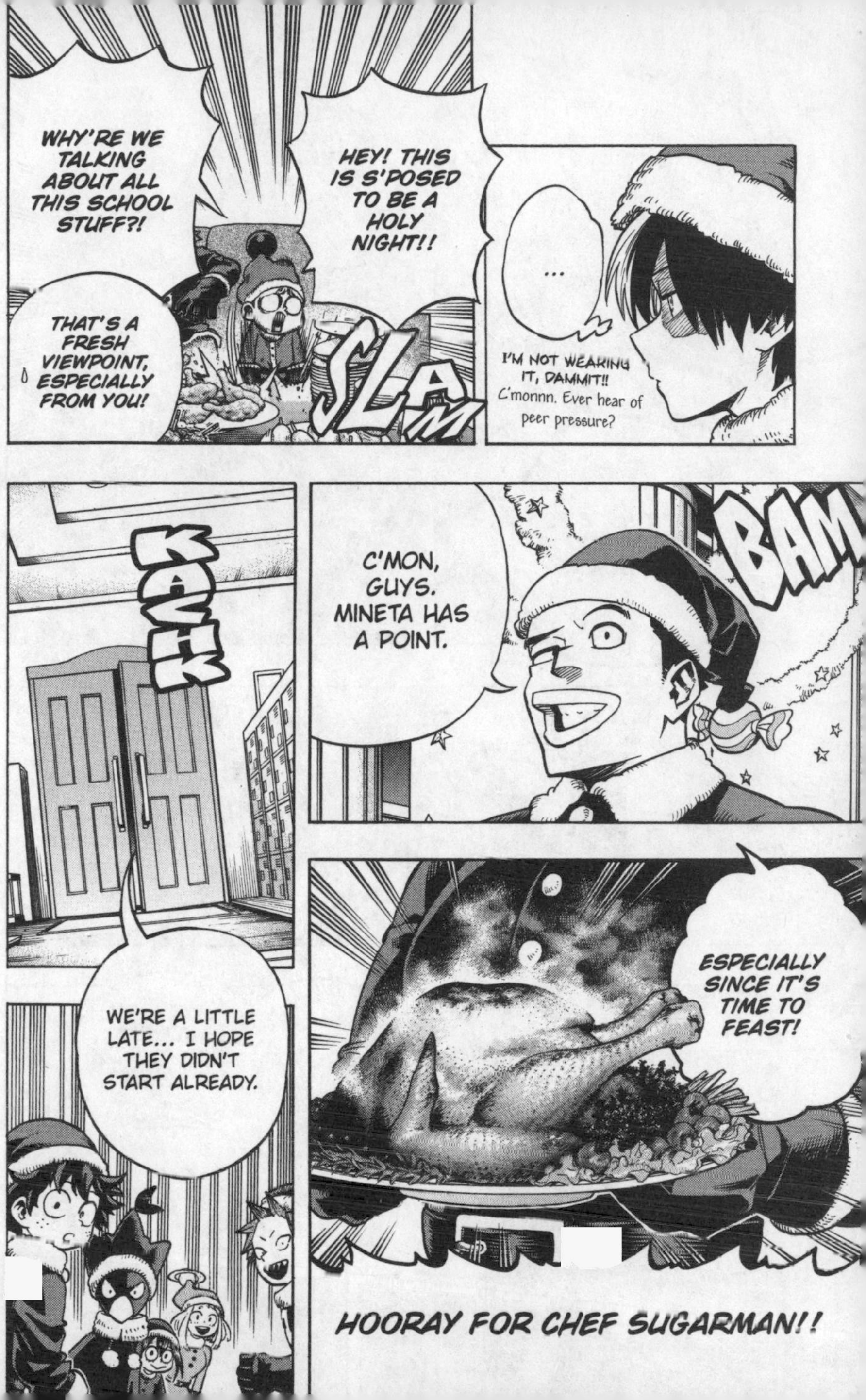
...
I'M NOT WEARING IT, DAMMIT!!
C'monnn. Ever hear of peer pressure?
HEY! THIS IS S'POSED TO BE A HOLY NIGHT!!
WHY'RE WE TALKING ABOUT ALL THIS SCHOOL STUFF?!
SLAM
THAT'S A FRESH VIEWPOINT, ESPECIALLY FROM YOU!
BAM
C'MON, GUYS. MINETA HAS A POINT.
ESPECIALLY SINCE IT'S TIME TO FEAST!
HOORAY FOR CHEF SUGARMAN!!
KACHK
WE'RE A LITTLE LATE... I HOPE THEY DIDN'T START ALREADY.

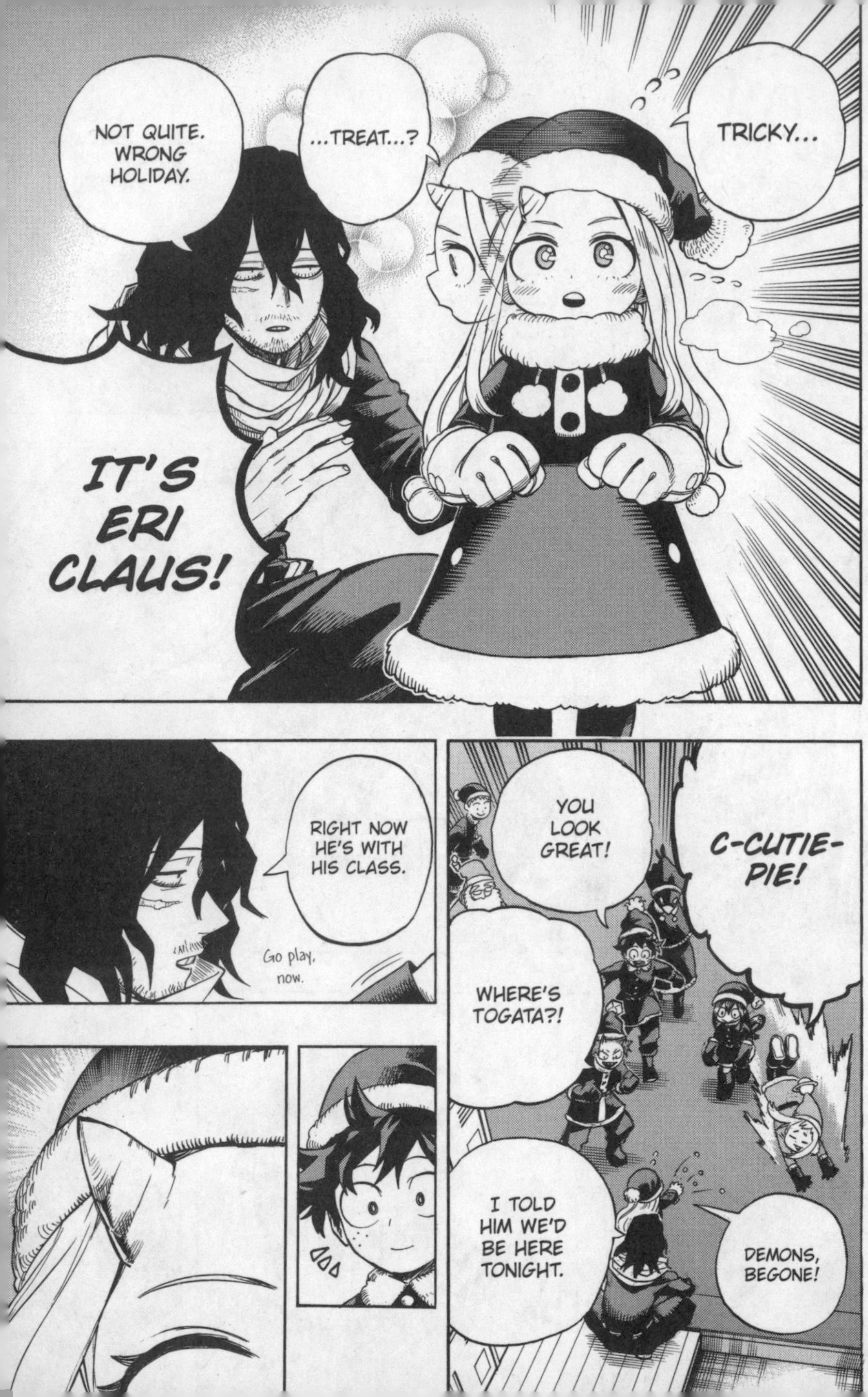
TRICKY...
...TREAT...?
NOT QUITE. WRONG HOLIDAY.
IT'S ERI CLAUS!
C-CUTIE-PIE!
YOU LOOK GREAT!
WHERE'S TOGATA?!
DEMONS, BEGONE!
I TOLD HIM WE'D BE HERE TONIGHT.
RIGHT NOW HE'S WITH HIS CLASS.
Go play, now.

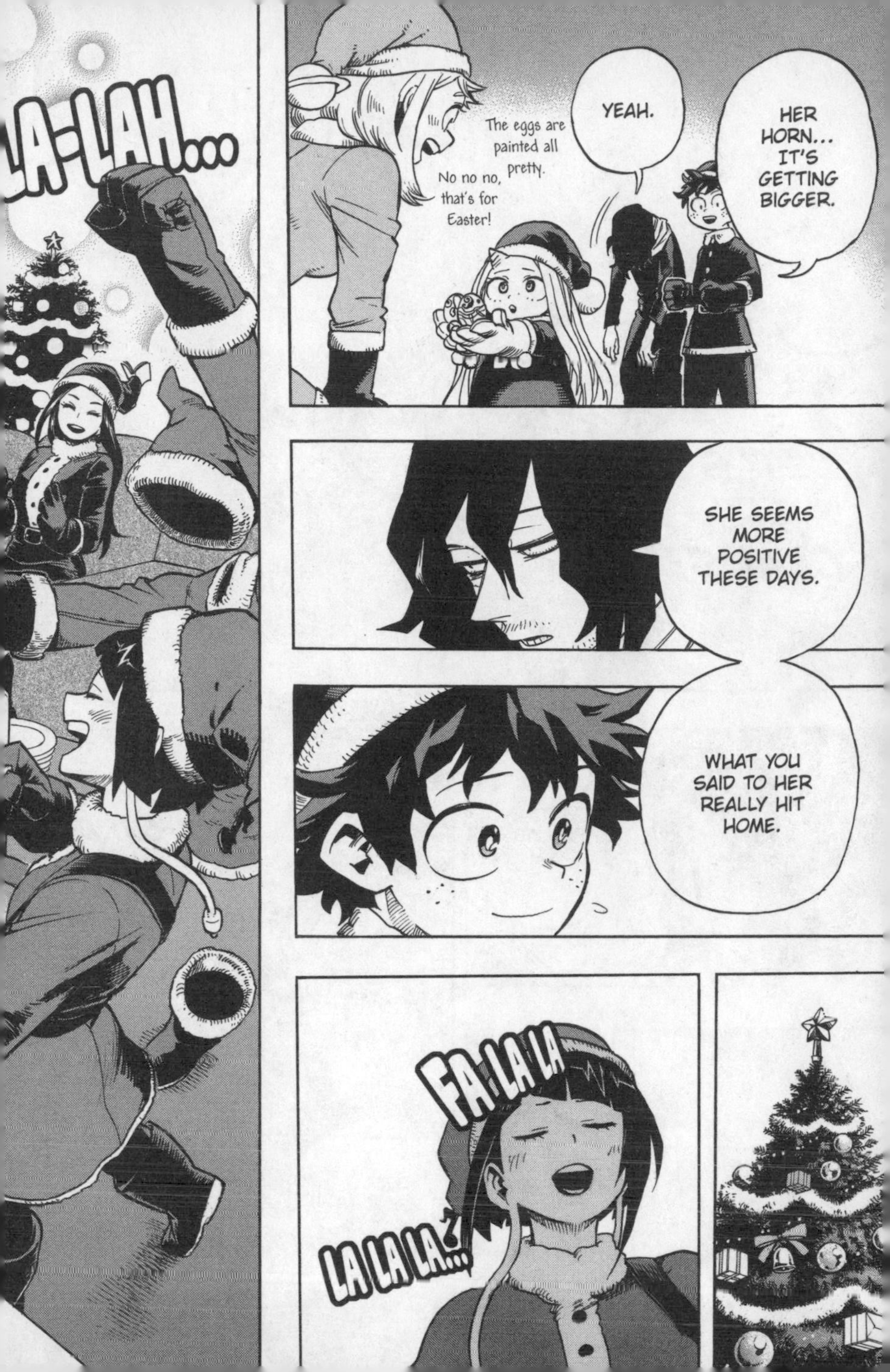
HER HORN... IT'S GETTING BIGGER.
YEAH.
The eggs are painted all pretty.
No no no, that's for Easter!
SHE SEEMS MORE POSITIVE THESE DAYS.
WHAT YOU SAID TO HER REALLY HIT HOME.
FA-LA LA LA
LA LA LA...
LA-LAH...

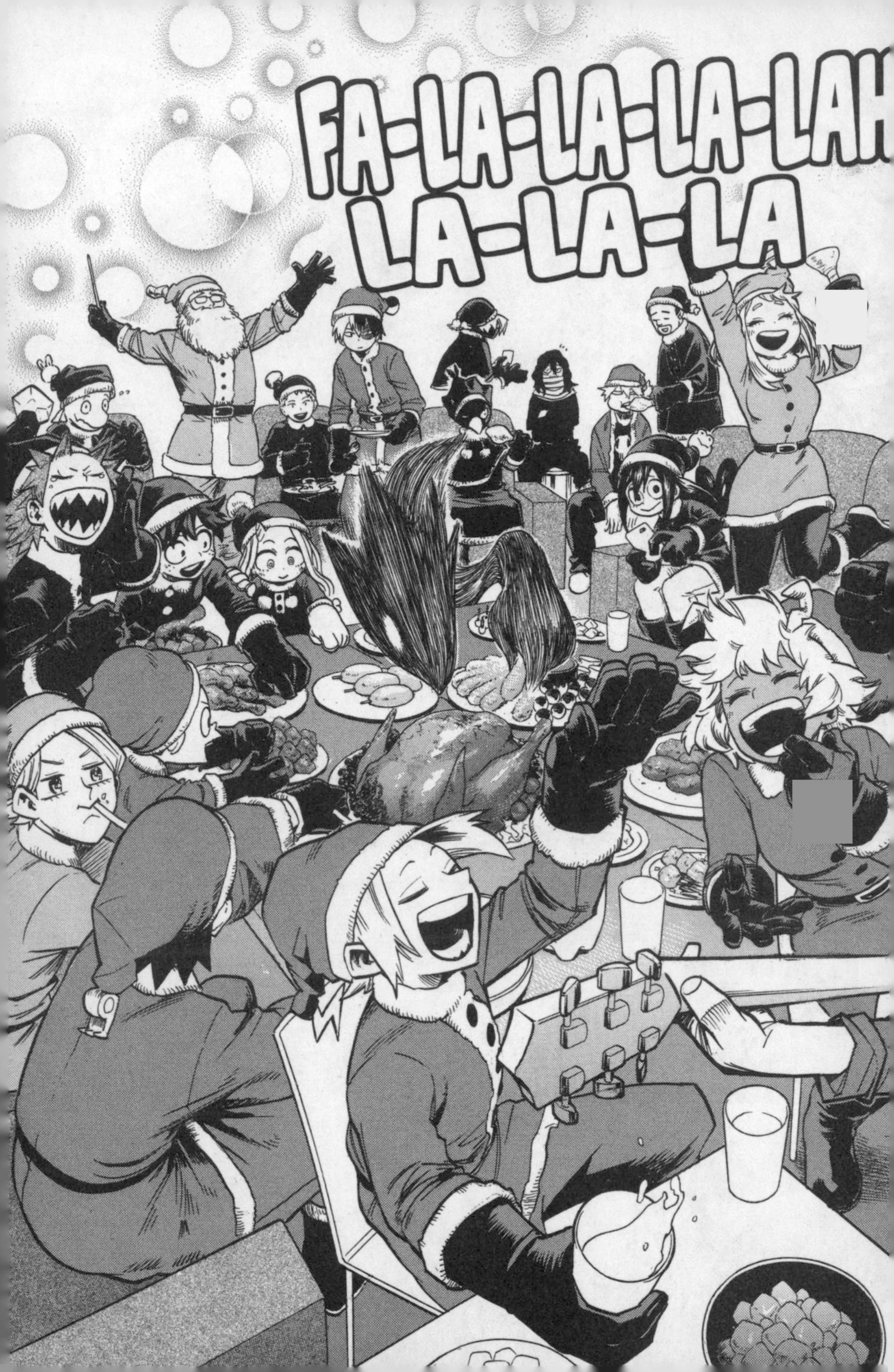
FA-LA-LA-LA-LAH
LA-LA-LA

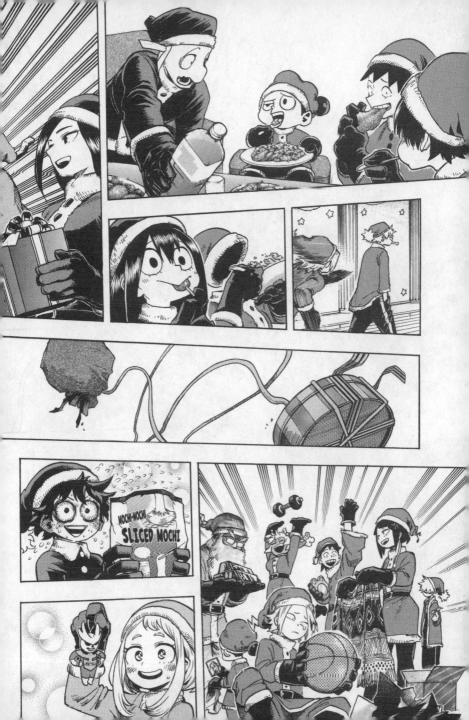

NOCHI-NOCHI
SLICED MOCHI

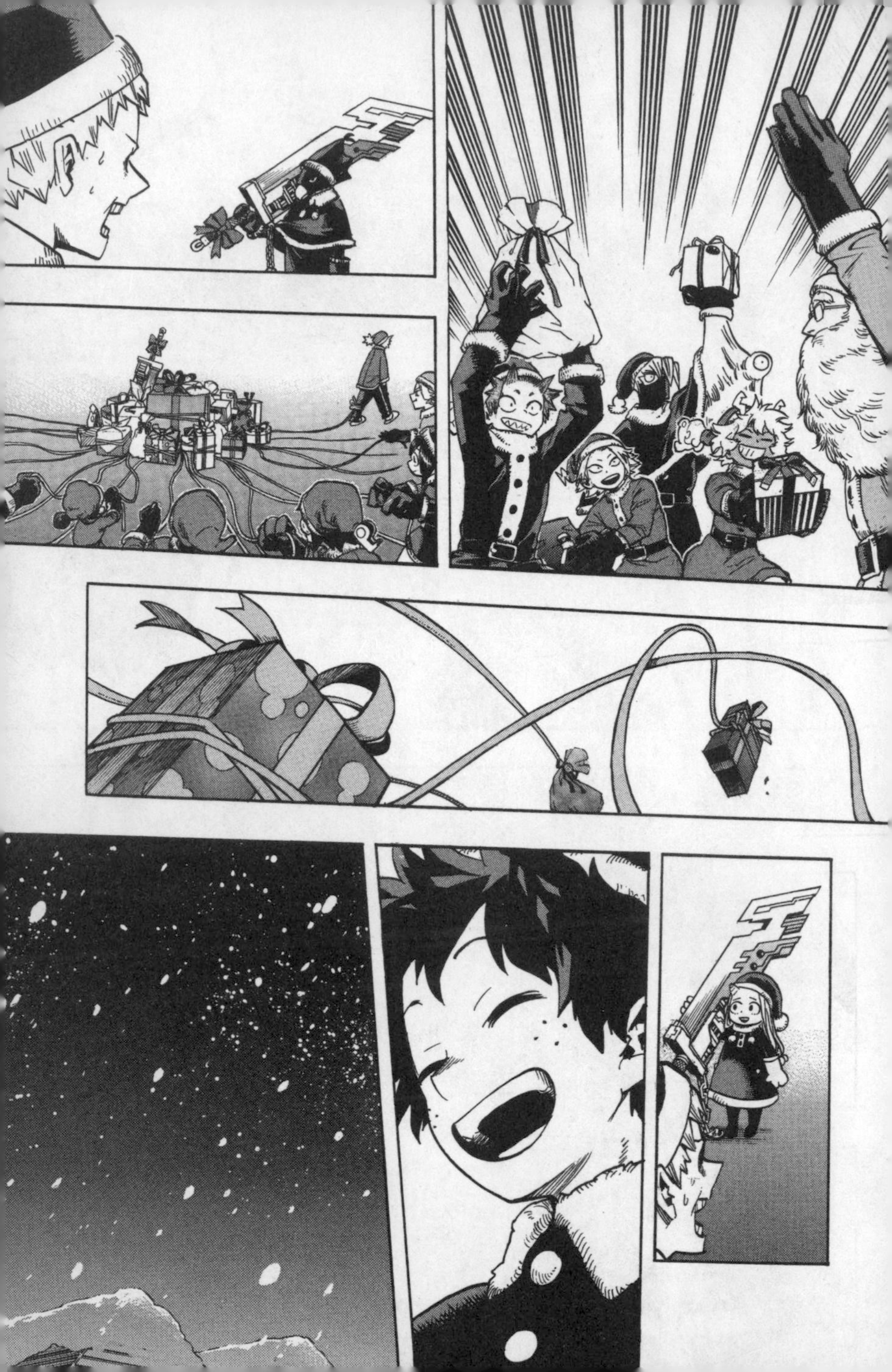

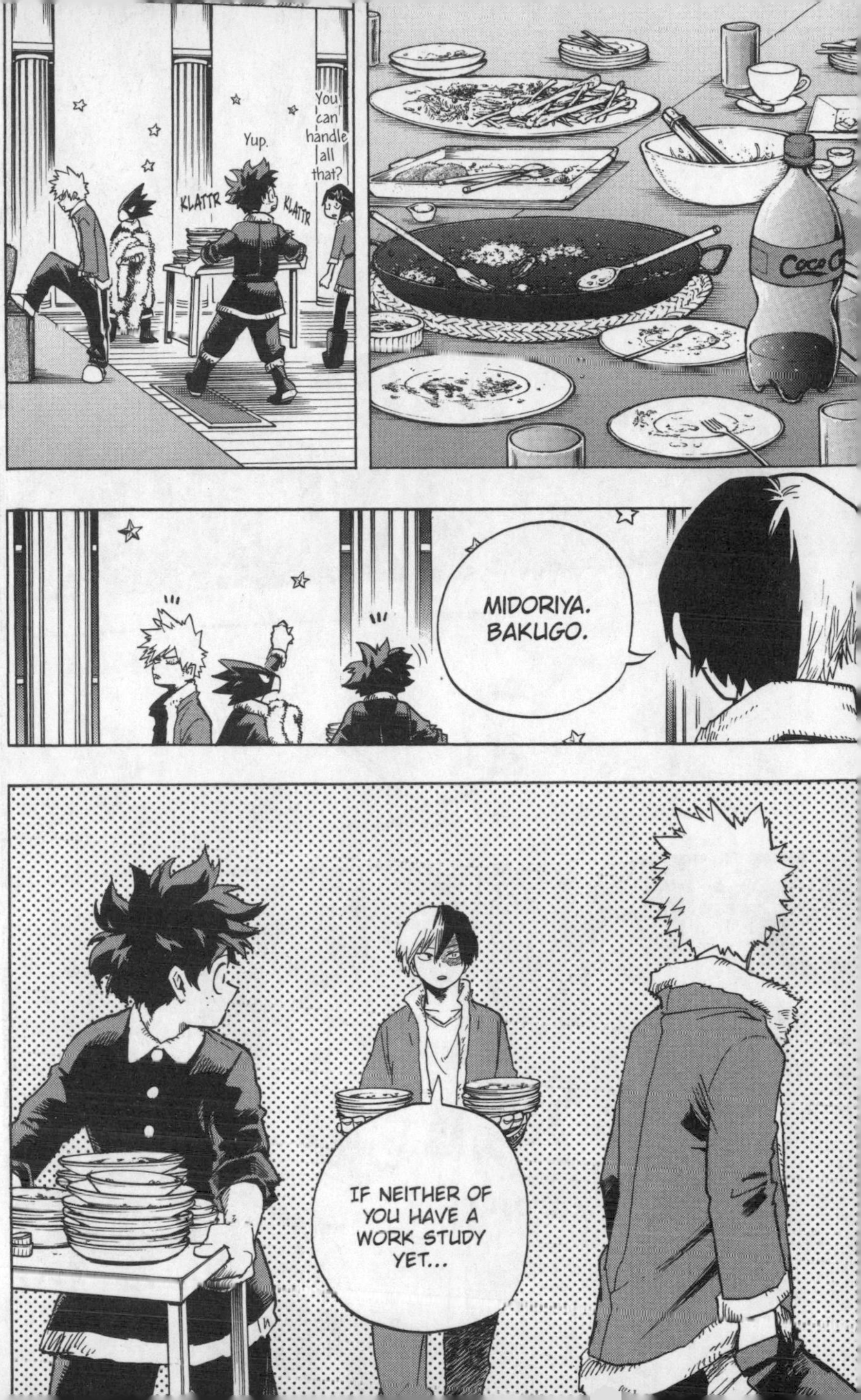
You can handle all that?
Yup.
KLATTR
KLATTR
MIDORIYA. BAKUGO.
IF NEITHER OF YOU HAVE A WORK STUDY YET...

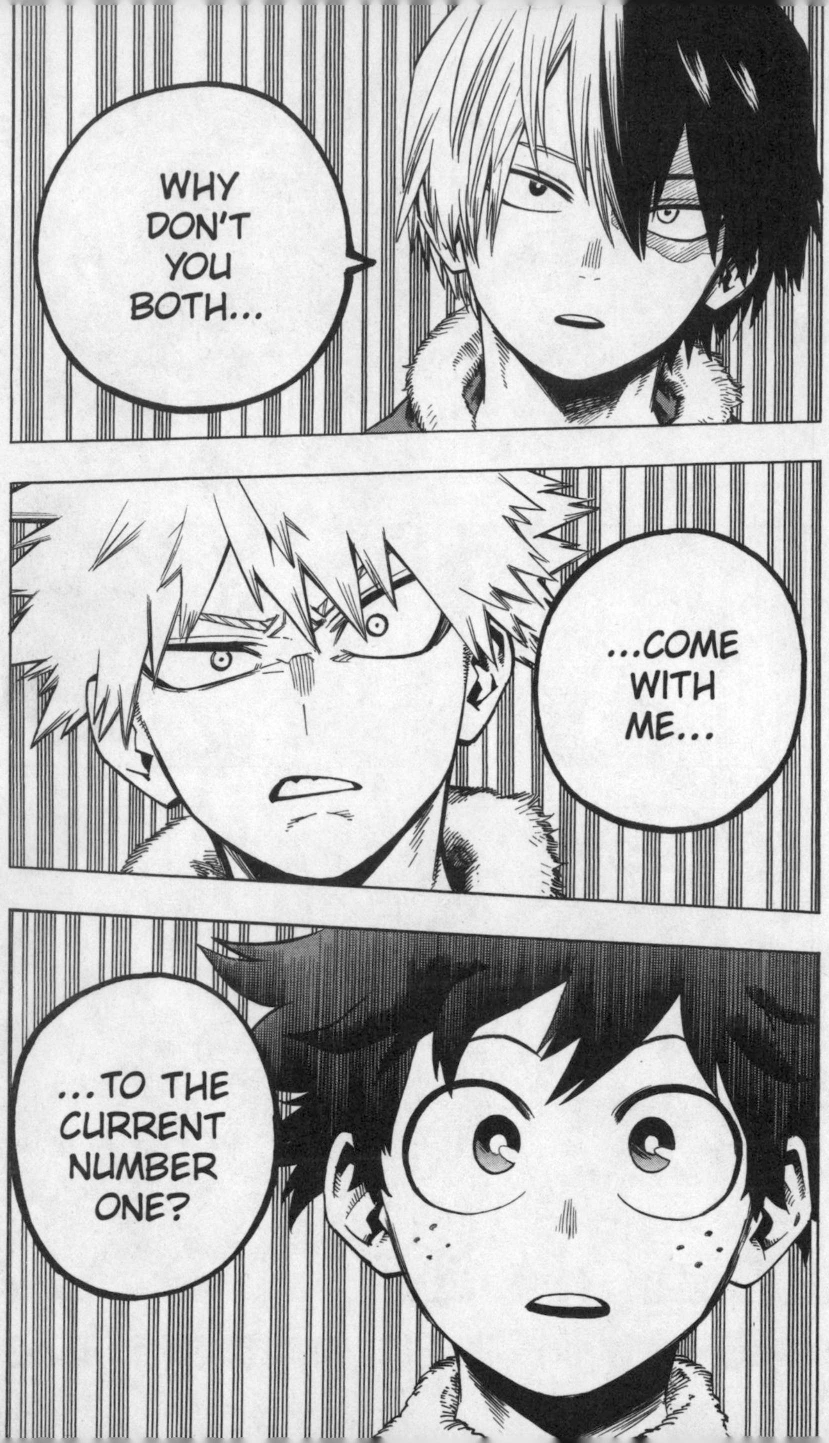
WHY DON'T YOU BOTH...
...COME WITH ME...
...TO THE CURRENT NUMBER ONE?

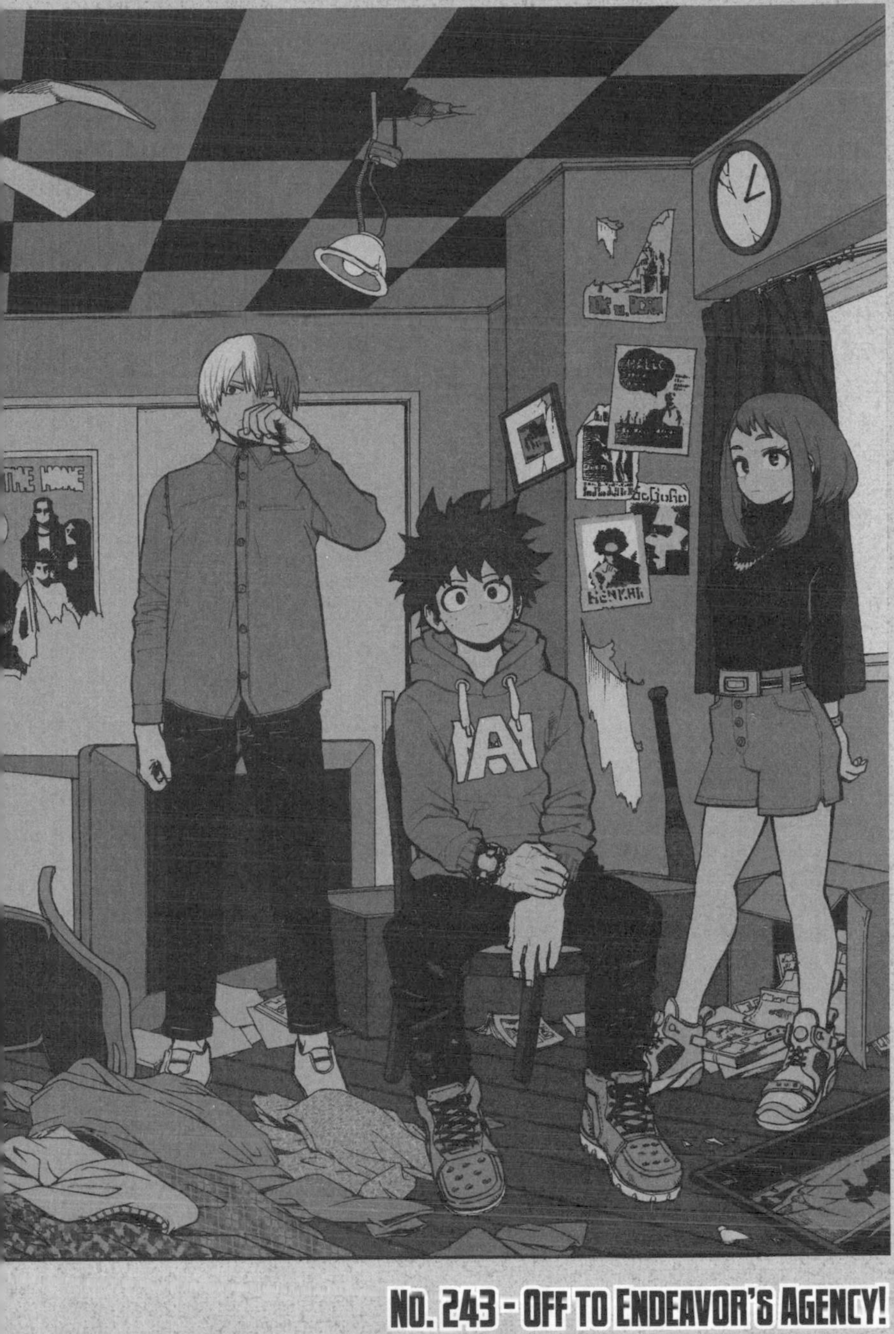

No. 243 - Off to Endeavor's Agency!

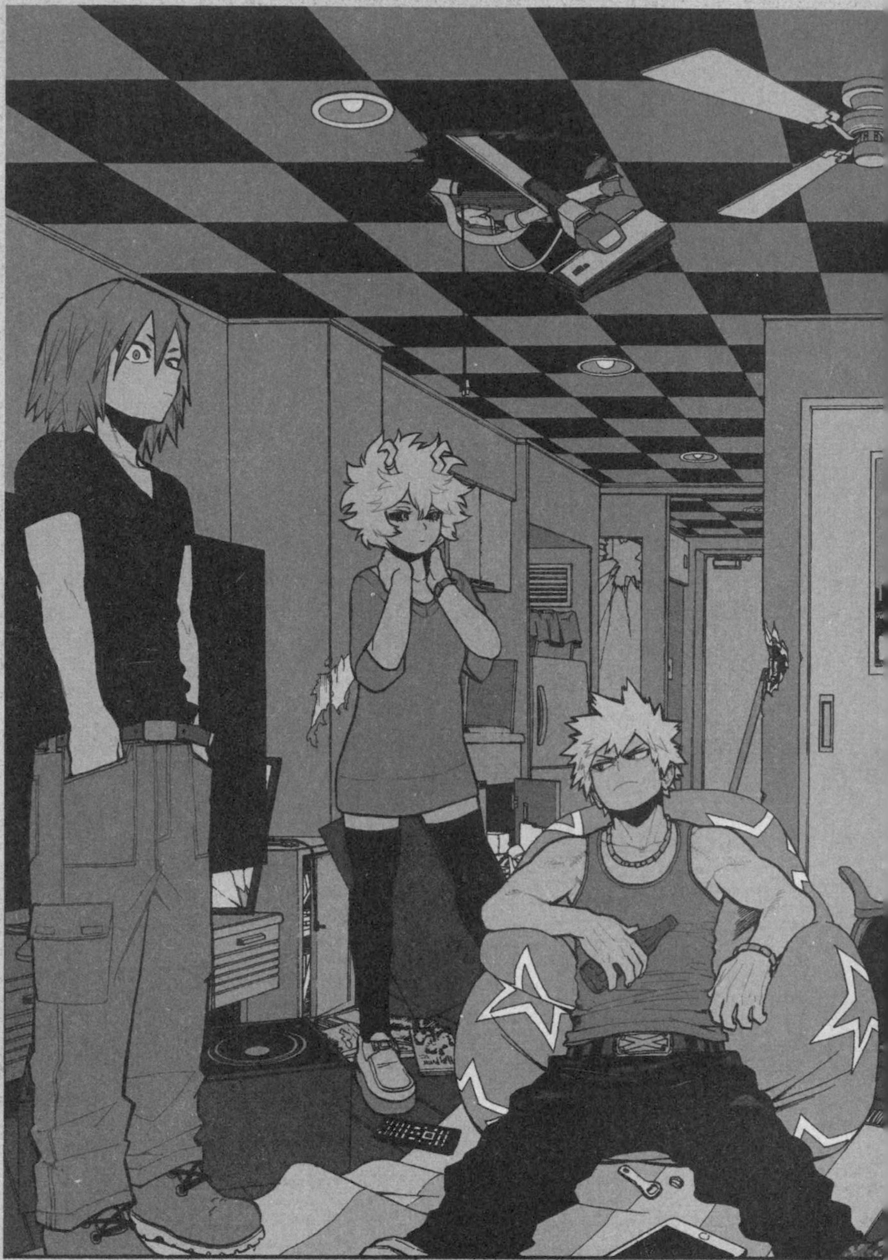

MY HERO ACADEMIA

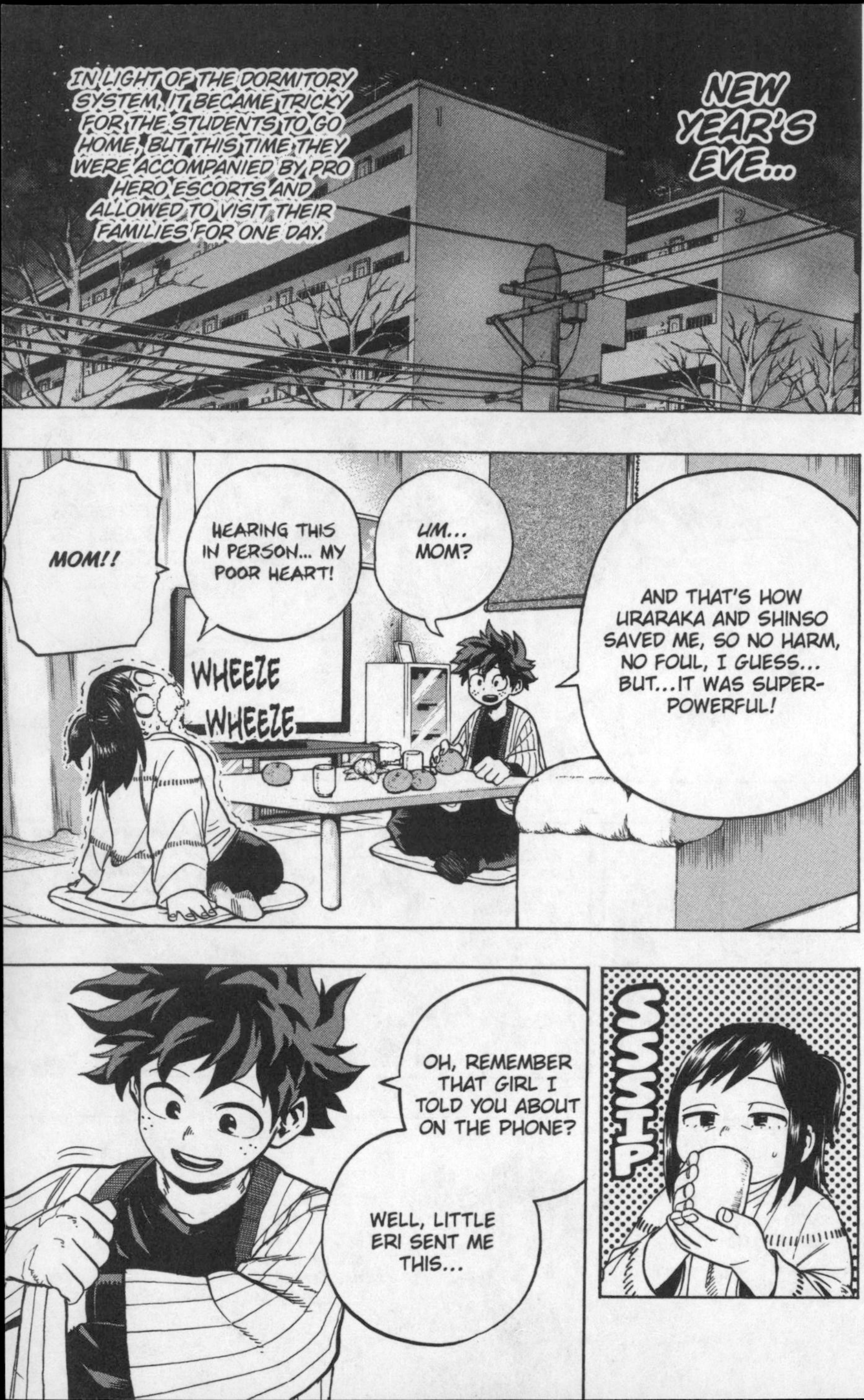
NEW YEAR'S EVE...
IN LIGHT OF THE DORMITORY SYSTEM, IT BECAME TRICKY FOR THE STUDENTS TO GO HOME, BUT THIS TIME THEY WERE ACCOMPANIED BY PRO HERO ESCORTS AND ALLOWED TO VISIT THEIR FAMILIES FOR ONE DAY.
AND THAT'S HOW URARAKA AND SHINSO SAVED ME, SO NO HARM, NO FOUL, I GUESS... BUT...IT WAS SUPER-POWERFUL!
UM... MOM?
HEARING THIS IN PERSON... MY POOR HEART!
WHEEZE WHEEZE
MOM!!
SSSIP
OH, REMEMBER THAT GIRL I TOLD YOU ABOUT ON THE PHONE?
WELL, LITTLE ERI SENT ME THIS...

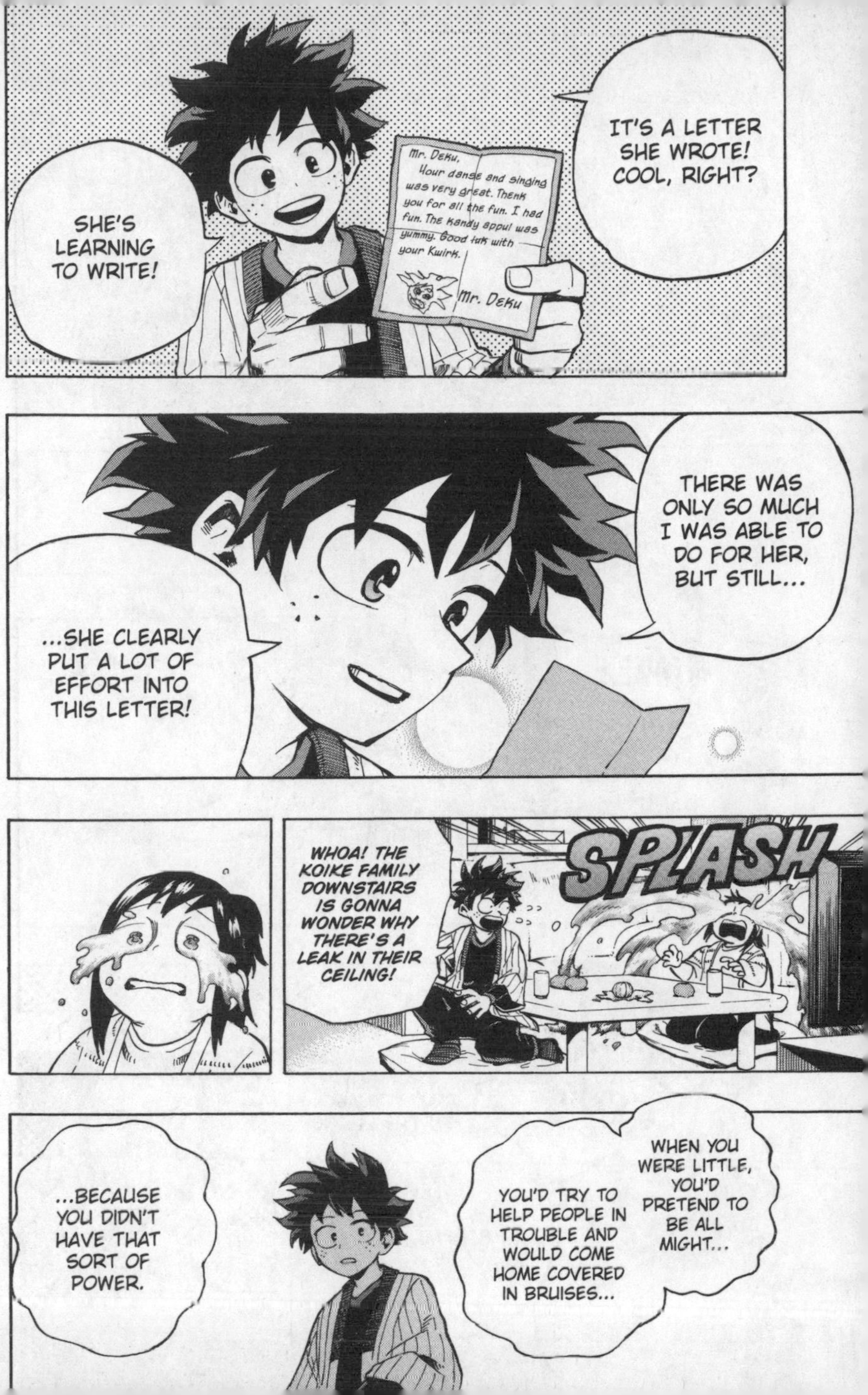
IT'S A LETTER SHE WROTE! COOL, RIGHT?
Mr. Deku,
Your danse and singing was very great. Thenk you for all the fun. I had fun. The kandy sppul was yummy. Good luk with your Kwirk.
Mr. Deku
SHE'S LEARNING TO WRITE!
THERE WAS ONLY SO MUCH I WAS ABLE TO DO FOR HER, BUT STILL...
...SHE CLEARLY PUT A LOT OF EFFORT INTO THIS LETTER!
SPLASH
WHOA! THE KOIKE FAMILY DOWNSTAIRS IS GONNA WONDER WHY THERE'S A LEAK IN THEIR CEILING!
WHEN YOU WERE LITTLE, YOU'D PRETEND TO BE ALL MIGHT...
YOU'D TRY TO HELP PEOPLE IN TROUBLE AND WOULD COME HOME COVERED IN BRUISES...
...BECAUSE YOU DIDN'T HAVE THAT SORT OF POWER.

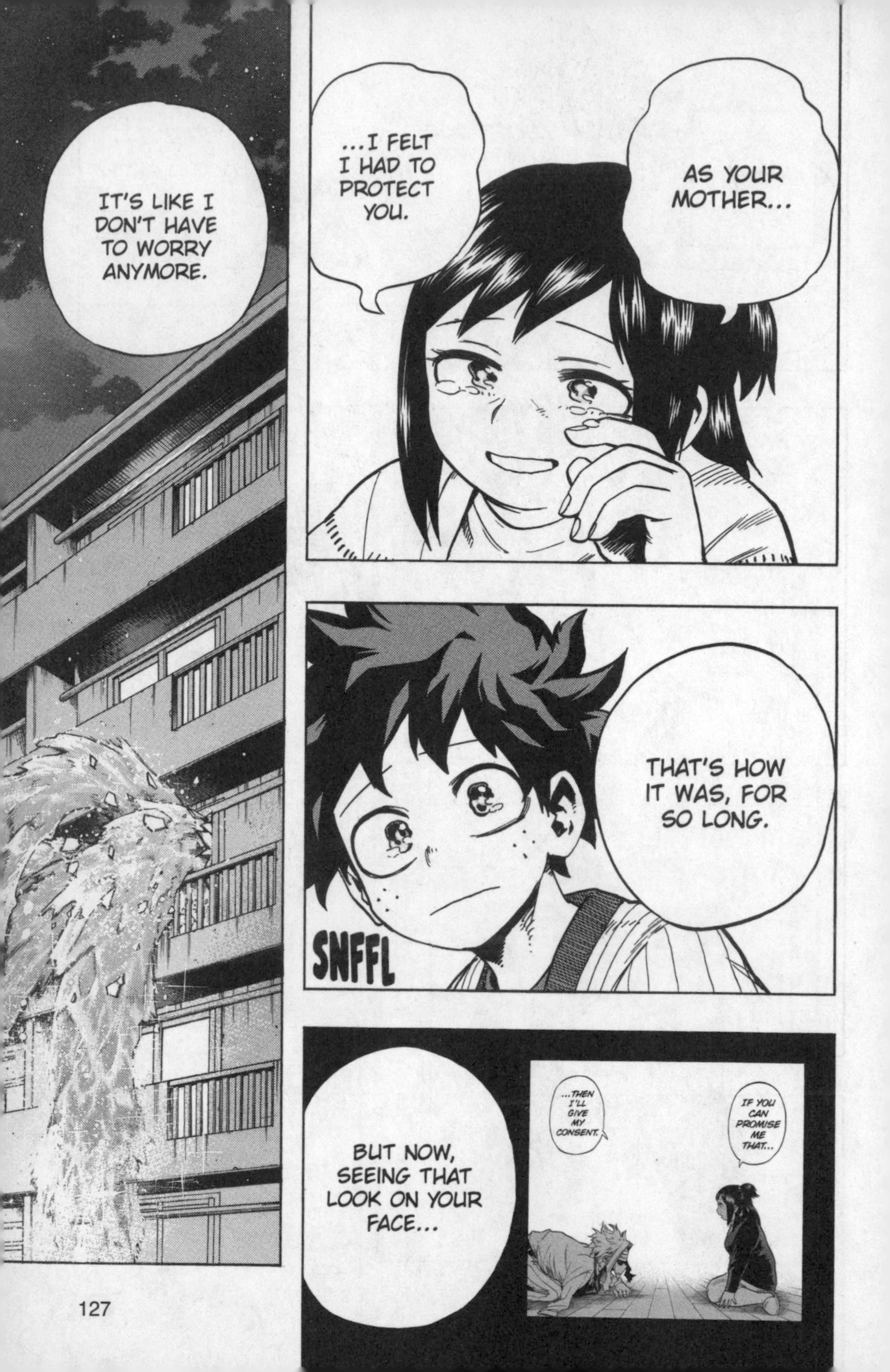
AS YOUR MOTHER...
...I FELT I HAD TO PROTECT YOU.
THAT'S HOW IT WAS, FOR SO LONG.
SNFFL
IF YOU CAN PROMISE ME THAT...
...THEN I'LL GIVE MY CONSENT.
BUT NOW, SEEING THAT LOOK ON YOUR FACE...
IT'S LIKE I DON'T HAVE TO WORRY ANYMORE.

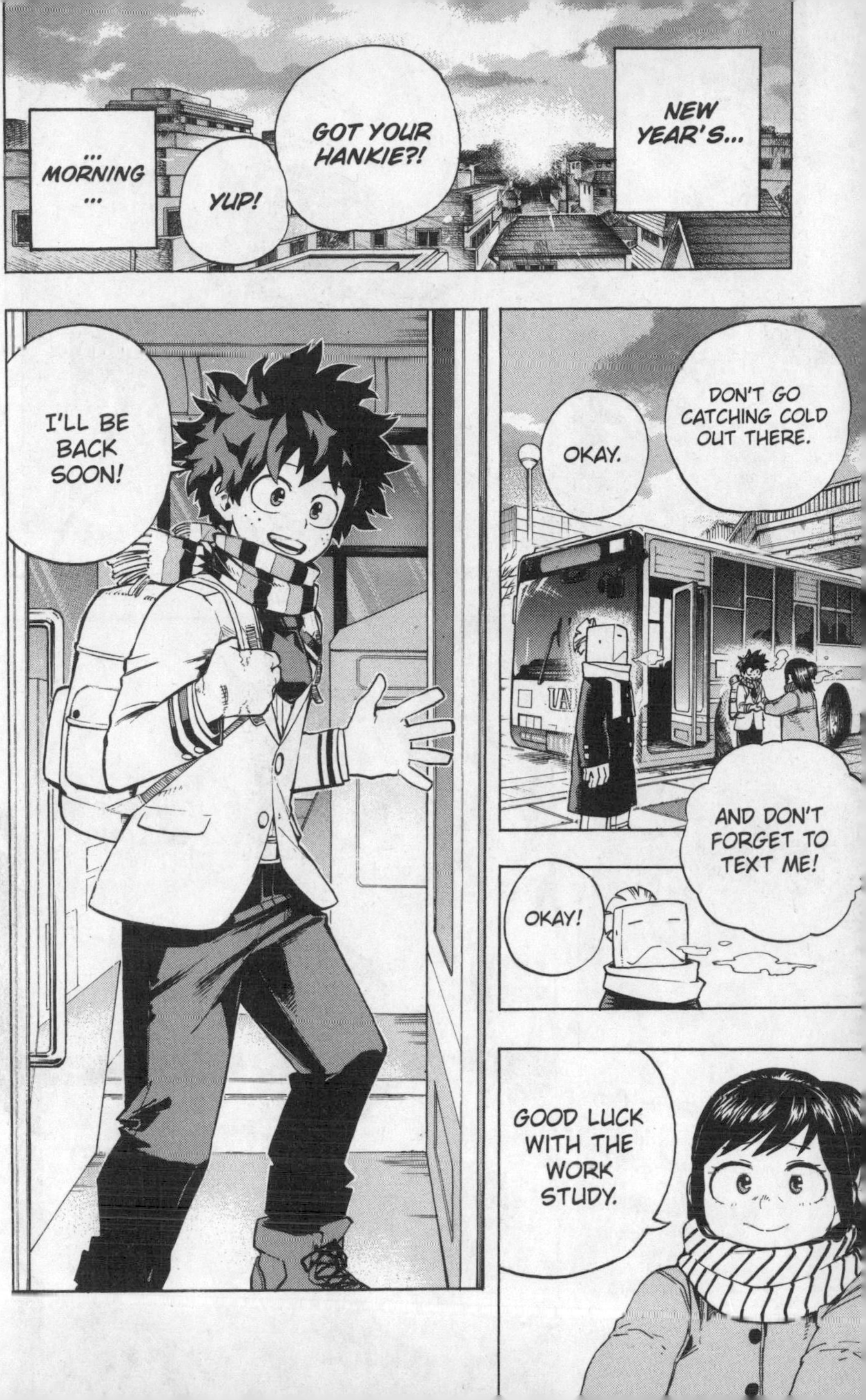
NEW YEAR'S...
GOT YOUR HANKIE?!
YUP!
... MORNING ...
DON'T GO CATCHING COLD OUT THERE.
OKAY.
AND DON'T FORGET TO TEXT ME!
OKAY!
GOOD LUCK WITH THE WORK STUDY.
I'LL BE BACK SOON!

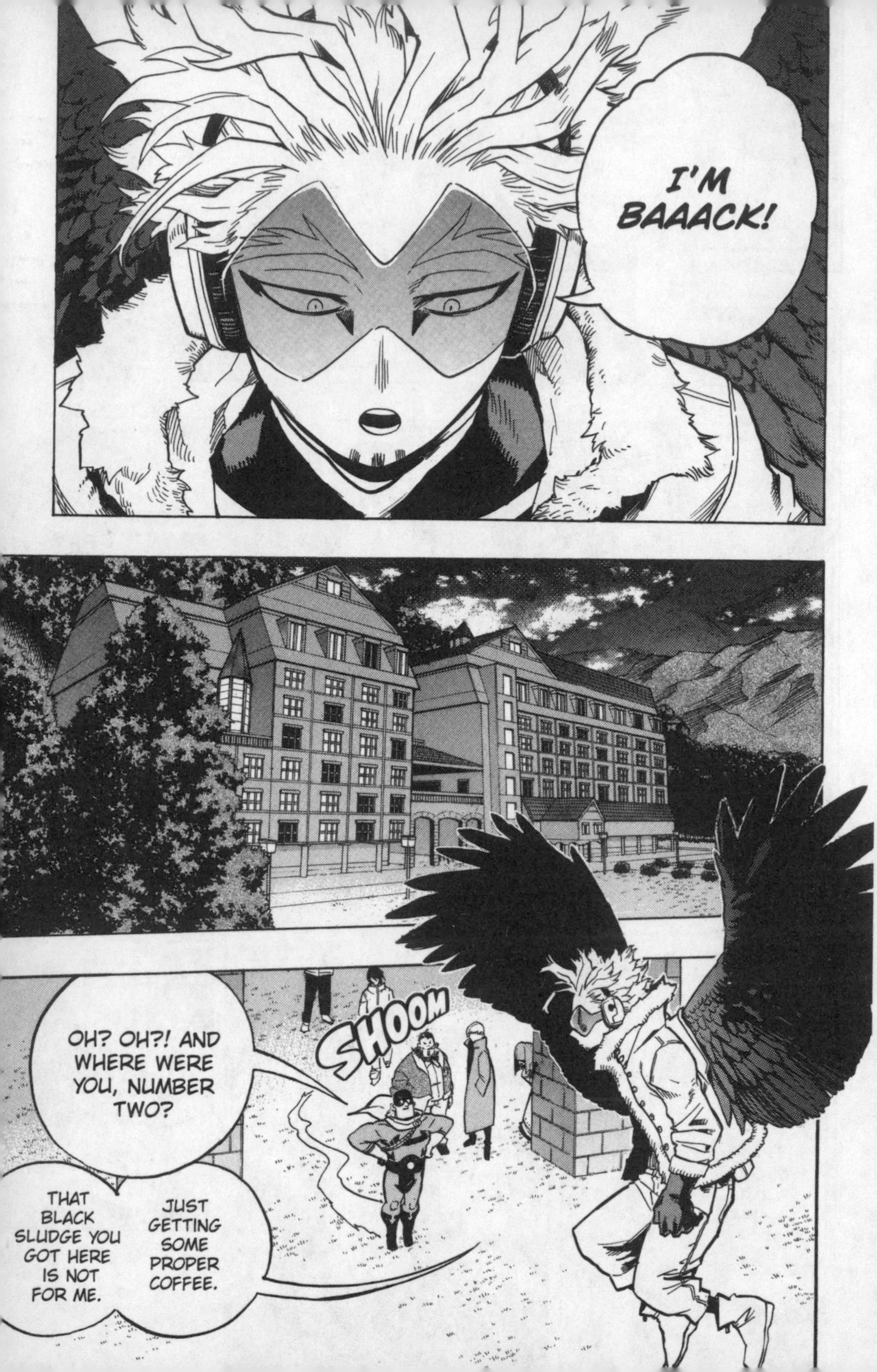
I'M BAAACK!
SHOOM
OH? OH?! AND WHERE WERE YOU, NUMBER TWO?
JUST GETTING SOME PROPER COFFEE.
THAT BLACK SLUDGE YOU GOT HERE IS NOT FOR ME.

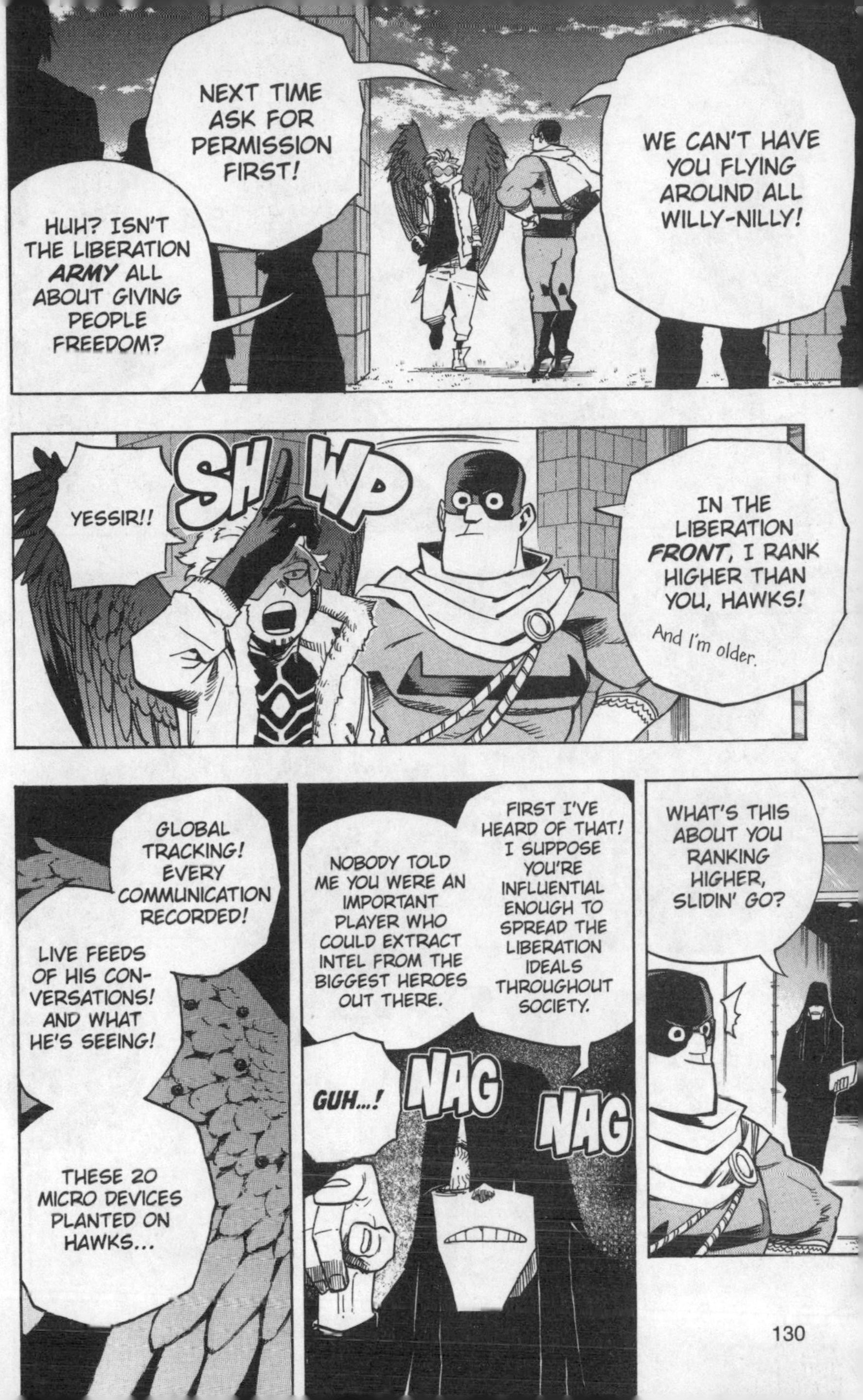
WE CAN'T HAVE YOU FLYING AROUND ALL WILLY-NILLY!
NEXT TIME ASK FOR PERMISSION FIRST!
HUH? ISN'T THE LIBERATION ARMY ALL ABOUT GIVING PEOPLE FREEDOM?
IN THE LIBERATION FRONT, I RANK HIGHER THAN YOU, HAWKS!
And I'm older.
SHWP
YESSIR!!
WHAT'S THIS ABOUT YOU RANKING HIGHER, SLIDIN' GO?
FIRST I'VE HEARD OF THAT! I SUPPOSE YOU'RE INFLUENTIAL ENOUGH TO SPREAD THE LIBERATION IDEALS THROUGHOUT SOCIETY.
NOBODY TOLD ME YOU WERE AN IMPORTANT PLAYER WHO COULD EXTRACT INTEL FROM THE BIGGEST HEROES OUT THERE.
NAG
NAG
GUH...!
GLOBAL TRACKING! EVERY COMMUNICATION RECORDED!
LIVE FEEDS OF HIS CON- VERSATIONS! AND WHAT HE'S SEEING!
THESE 20 MICRO DEVICES PLANTED ON HAWKS...

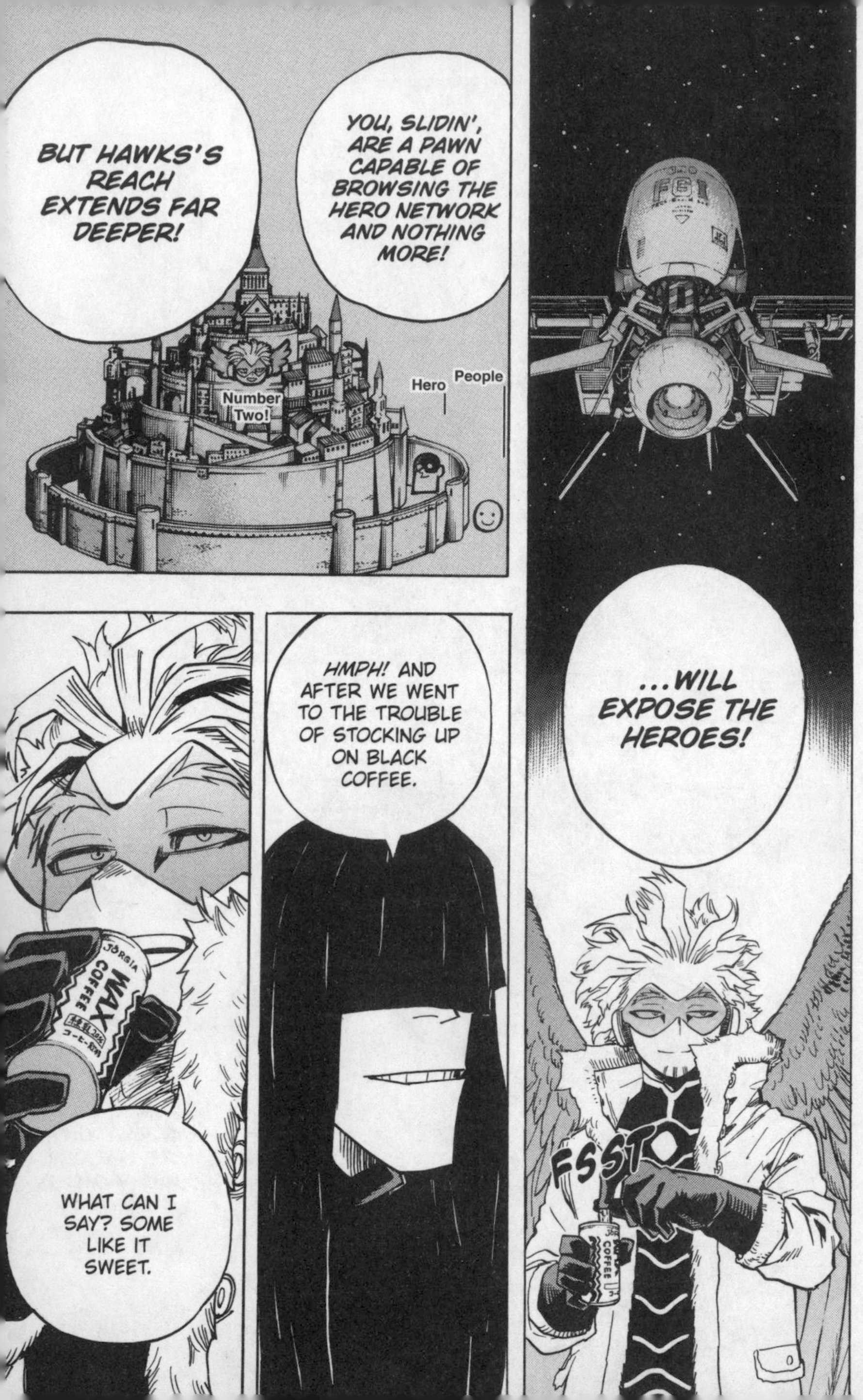

YOU, SLIDIN', ARE A PAWN CAPABLE OF BROWSING THE HERO NETWORK AND NOTHING MORE!
BUT HAWKS'S REACH EXTENDS FAR DEEPER!
People
Hero
Number Two!
...WILL EXPOSE THE HEROES!
FSST
HMPH! AND AFTER WE WENT TO THE TROUBLE OF STOCKING UP ON BLACK COFFEE.
WHAT CAN I SAY? SOME LIKE IT SWEET.

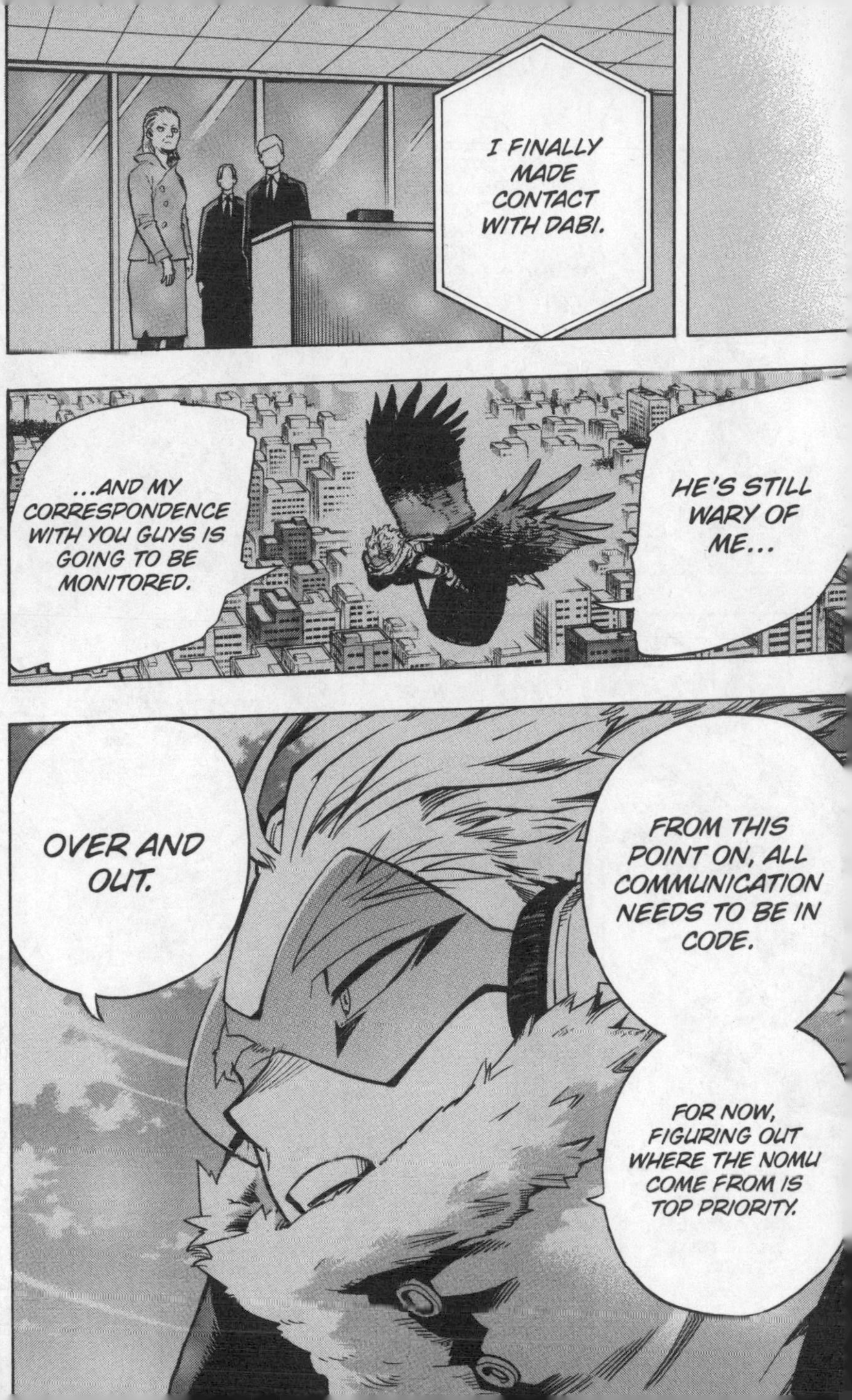
I FINALLY MADE CONTACT WITH DABI.
HE'S STILL WARY OF ME...
...AND MY CORRESPONDENCE WITH YOU GUYS IS GOING TO BE MONITORED.
FROM THIS POINT ON, ALL COMMUNICATION NEEDS TO BE IN CODE.
FOR NOW, FIGURING OUT WHERE THE NOMU COME FROM IS TOP PRIORITY.
OVER AND OUT.

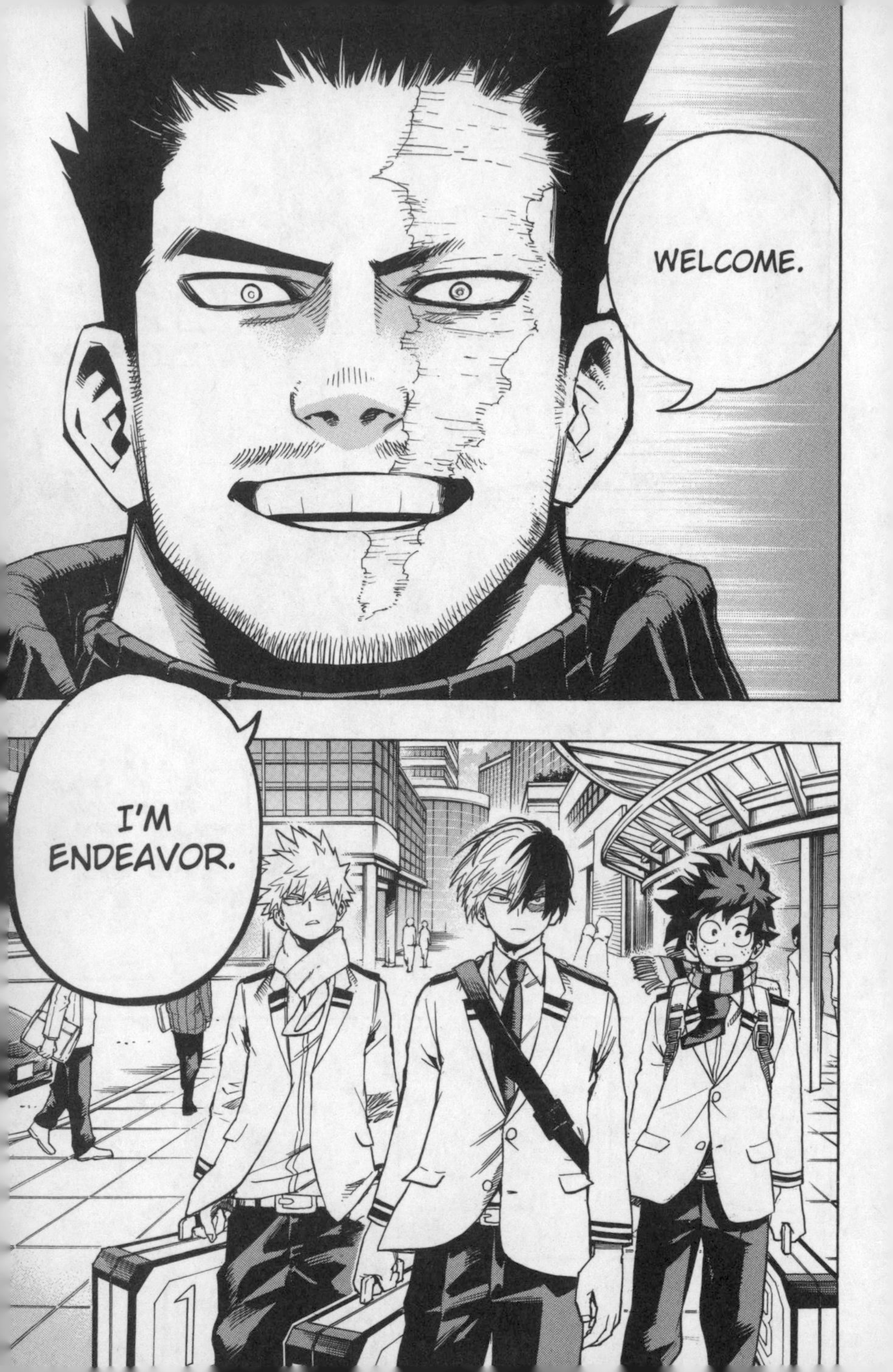
WELCOME.
I'M ENDEAVOR.

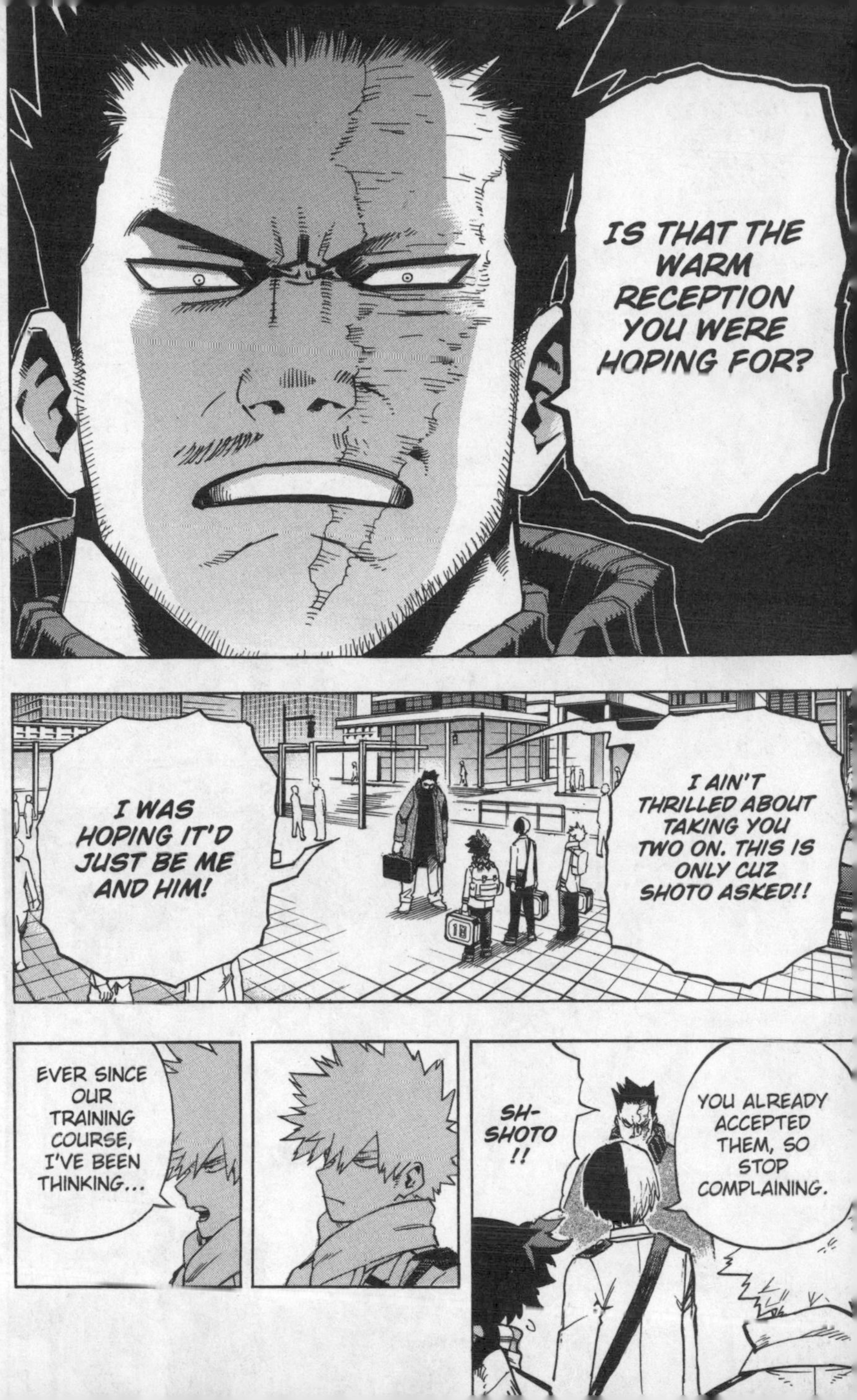
IS THAT THE WARM RECEPTION YOU WERE HOPING FOR?
I AIN'T THRILLED ABOUT TAKING YOU TWO ON. THIS IS ONLY CUZ SHOTO ASKED!!
I WAS HOPING IT'D JUST BE ME AND HIM!
YOU ALREADY ACCEPTED THEM, SO STOP COMPLAINING.
SH-SHOTO!!
EVER SINCE OUR TRAINING COURSE, I'VE BEEN THINKING...

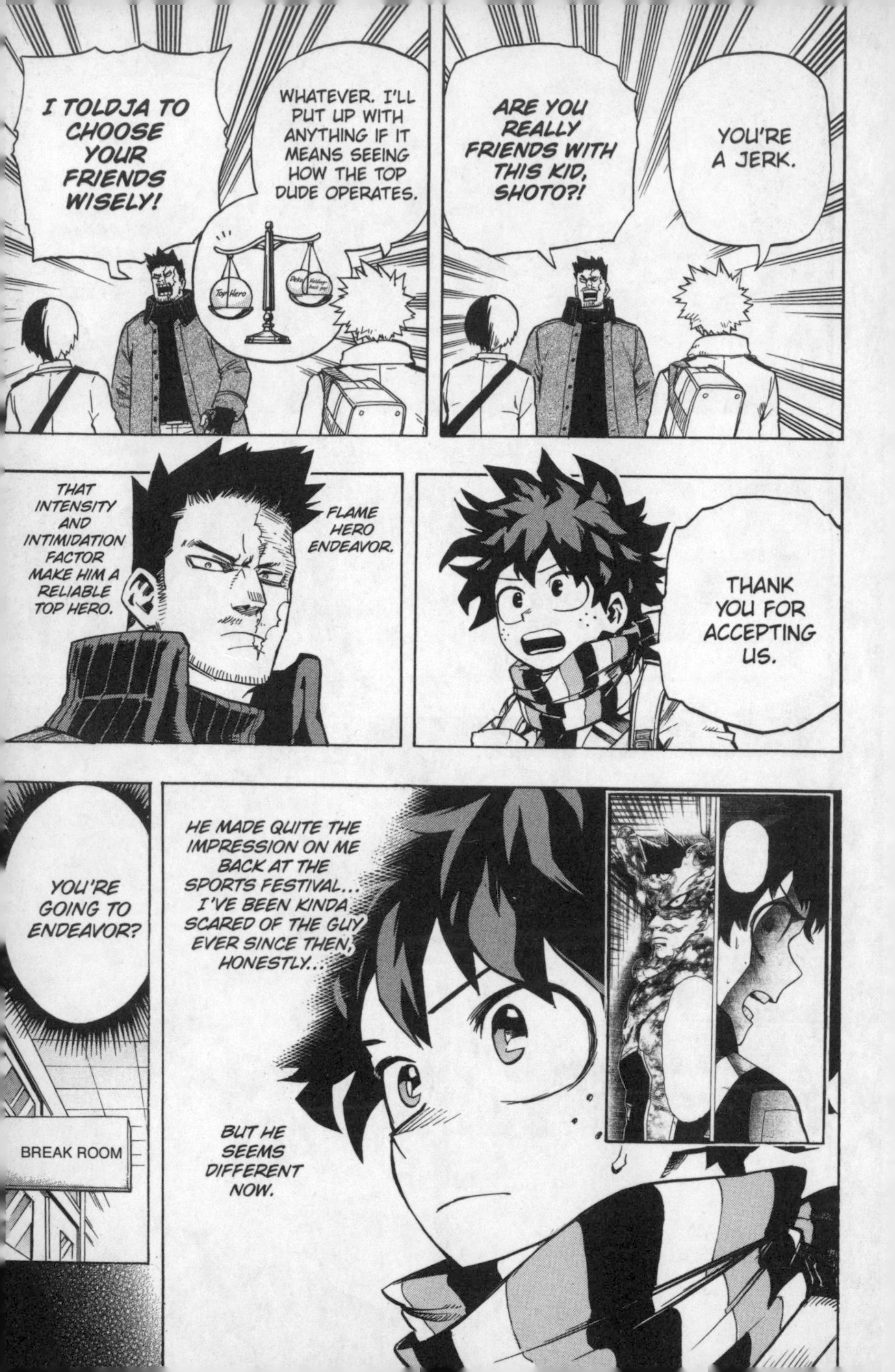
YOU'RE A JERK.
ARE YOU REALLY FRIENDS WITH THIS KID, SHOTO?!
WHATEVER. I'LL PUT UP WITH ANYTHING IF IT MEANS SEEING HOW THE TOP DUDE OPERATES.
I TOLDJA TO CHOOSE YOUR FRIENDS WISELY!
Top Hero
THANK YOU FOR ACCEPTING US.
FLAME HERO ENDEAVOR.
THAT INTENSITY AND INTIMIDATION FACTOR MAKE HIM A RELIABLE TOP HERO.
HE MADE QUITE THE IMPRESSION ON ME BACK AT THE SPORTS FESTIVAL... I'VE BEEN KINDA SCARED OF THE GUY EVER SINCE THEN, HONESTLY...
BUT HE SEEMS DIFFERENT NOW.
YOU'RE GOING TO ENDEAVOR?
BREAK ROOM

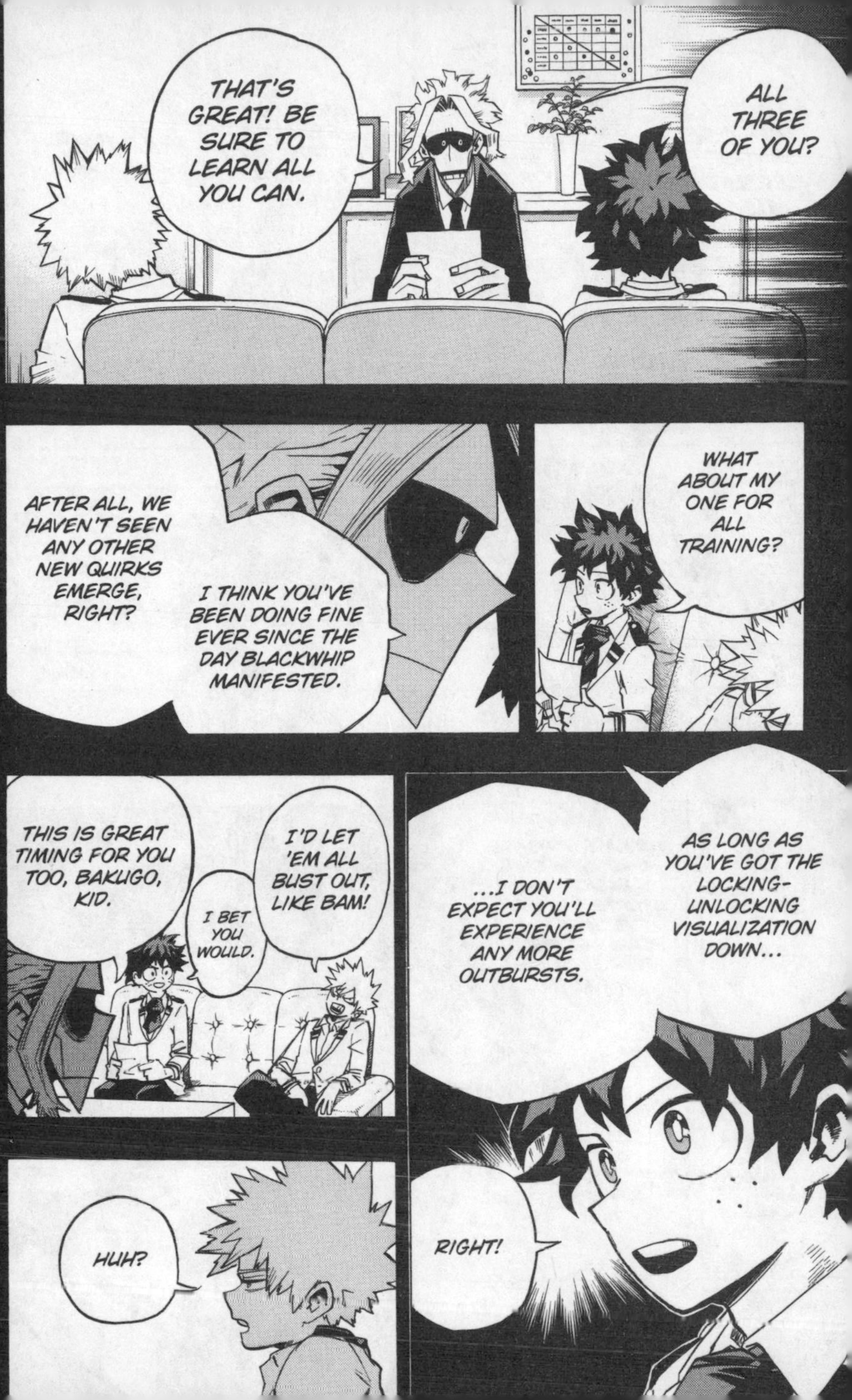
ALL THREE OF YOU?
THAT'S GREAT! BE SURE TO LEARN ALL YOU CAN.
WHAT ABOUT MY ONE FOR ALL TRAINING?
I THINK YOU'VE BEEN DOING FINE EVER SINCE THE DAY BLACKWHIP MANIFESTED.
AFTER ALL, WE HAVEN'T SEEN ANY OTHER NEW QUIRKS EMERGE, RIGHT?
AS LONG AS YOU'VE GOT THE LOCKING-UNLOCKING VISUALIZATION DOWN...
...I DON'T EXPECT YOU'LL EXPERIENCE ANY MORE OUTBURSTS.
RIGHT!
I'D LET 'EM ALL BUST OUT, LIKE BAM!
I BET YOU WOULD.
THIS IS GREAT TIMING FOR YOU TOO, BAKUGO, KID.
HUH?

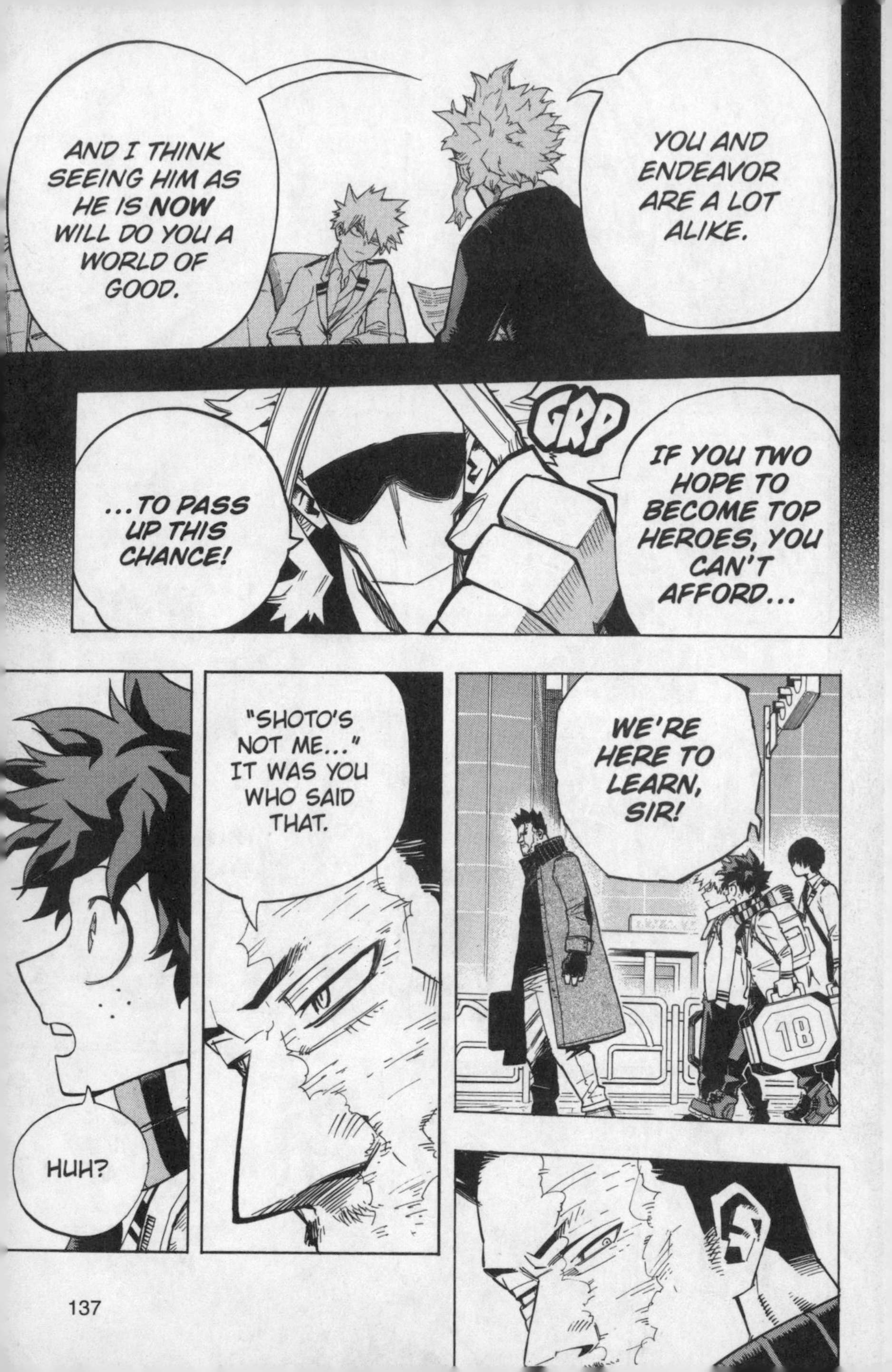
YOU AND ENDEAVOR ARE A LOT ALIKE.
AND I THINK SEEING HIM AS HE IS **NOW** WILL DO YOU A WORLD OF GOOD.
GRP
IF YOU TWO HOPE TO BECOME TOP HEROES, YOU CAN'T AFFORD...
...TO PASS UP THIS CHANCE!
WE'RE HERE TO LEARN, SIR!
18
"SHOTO'S NOT ME..." IT WAS YOU WHO SAID THAT.
HUH?

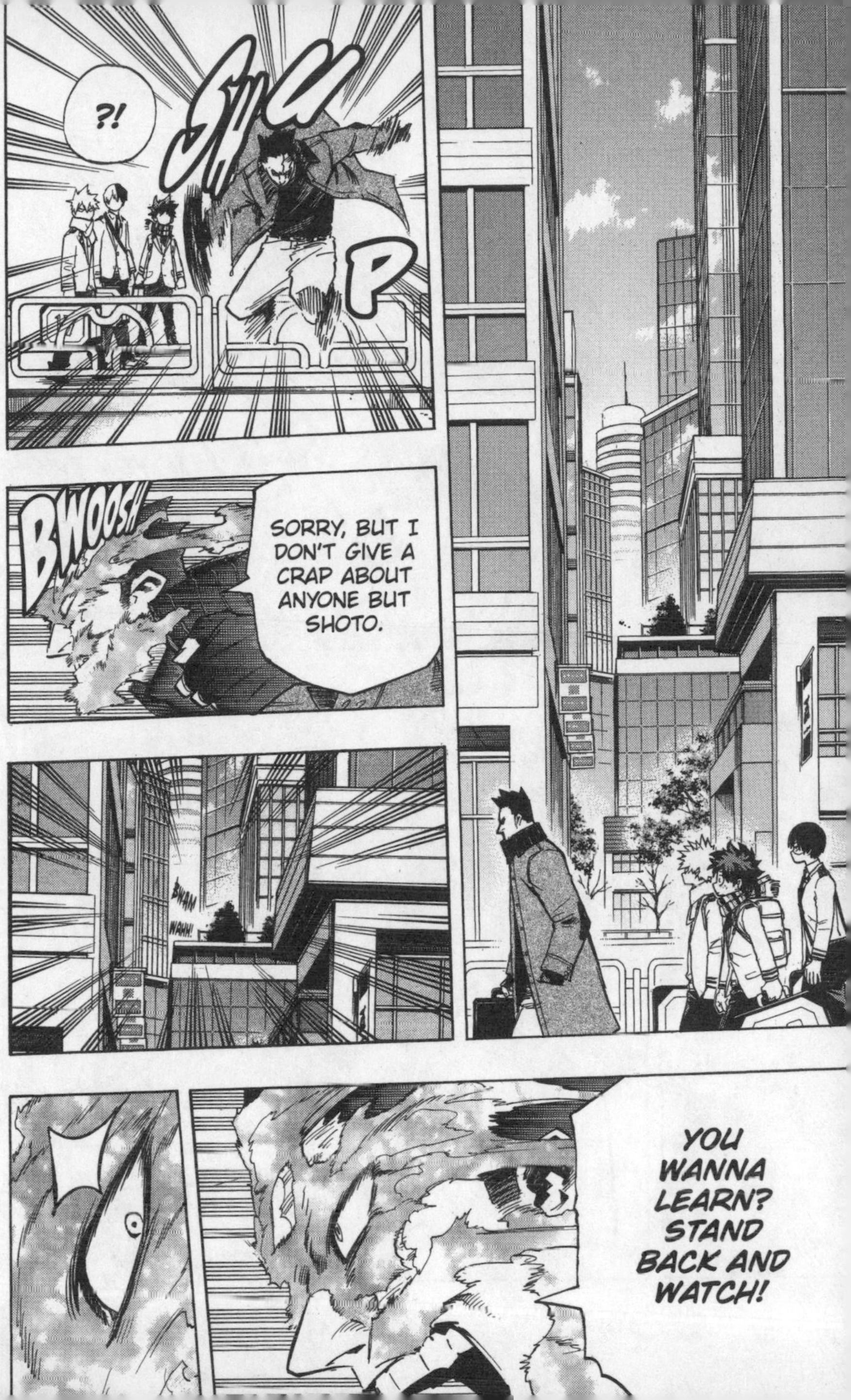
?!
BWOOSH
SORRY, BUT I DON'T GIVE A CRAP ABOUT ANYONE BUT SHOTO.
BWAM
WAHH!
YOU WANNA LEARN? STAND BACK AND WATCH!

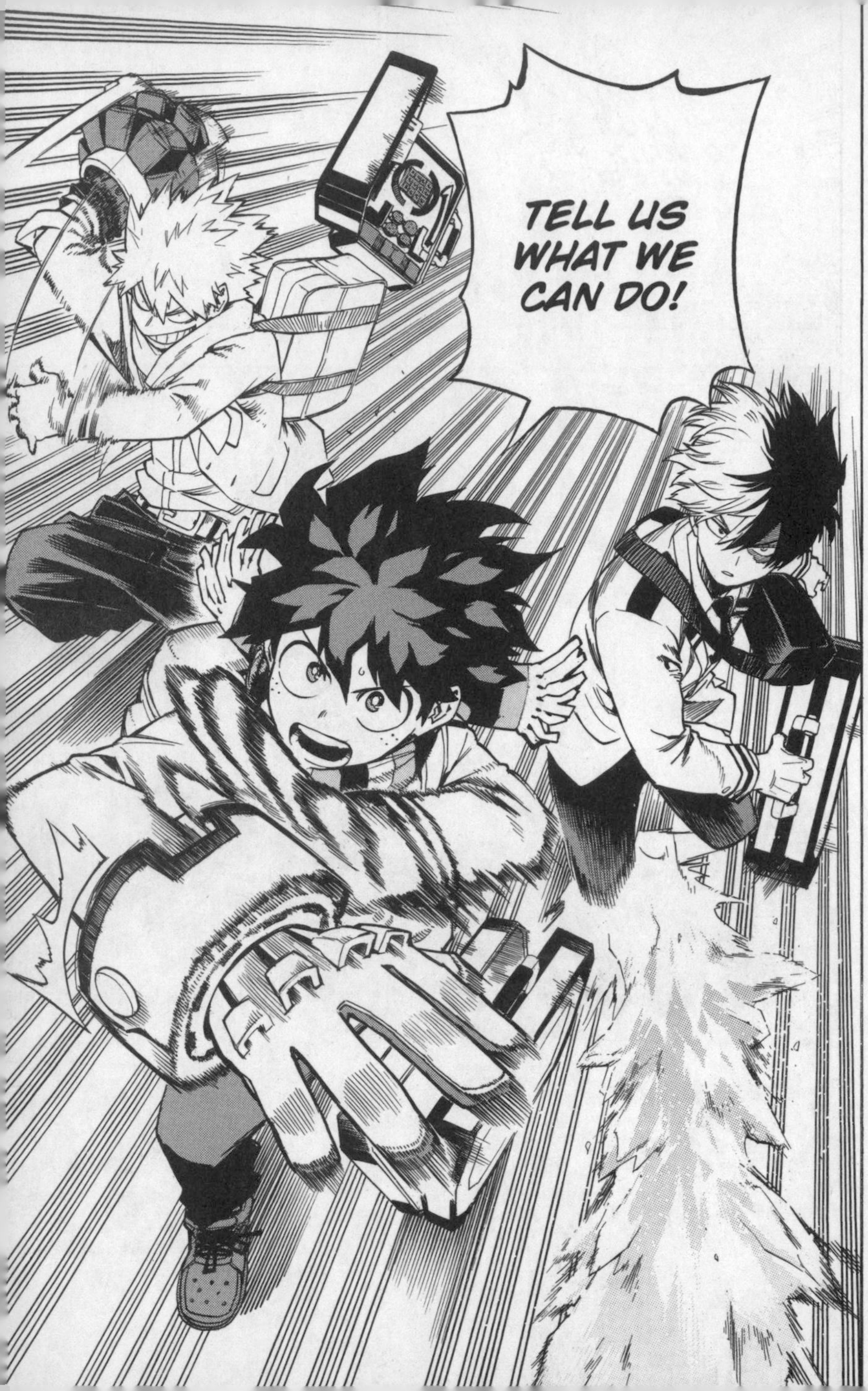
TELL US WHAT WE CAN DO!

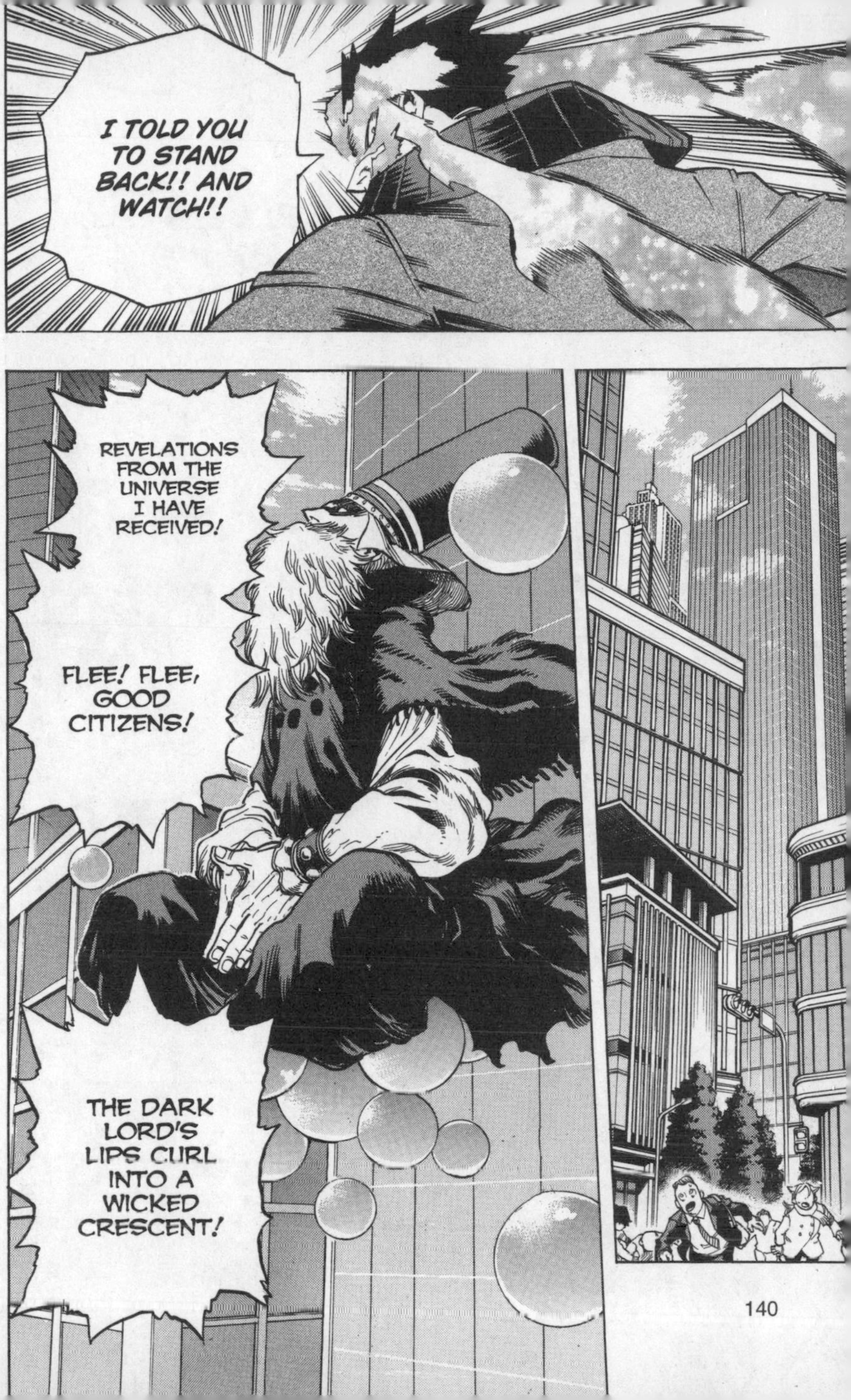
I TOLD YOU TO STAND BACK!! AND WATCH!!
REVELATIONS FROM THE UNIVERSE I HAVE RECEIVED!
FLEE! FLEE, GOOD CITIZENS!
THE DARK LORD'S LIPS CURL INTO A WICKED CRESCENT!

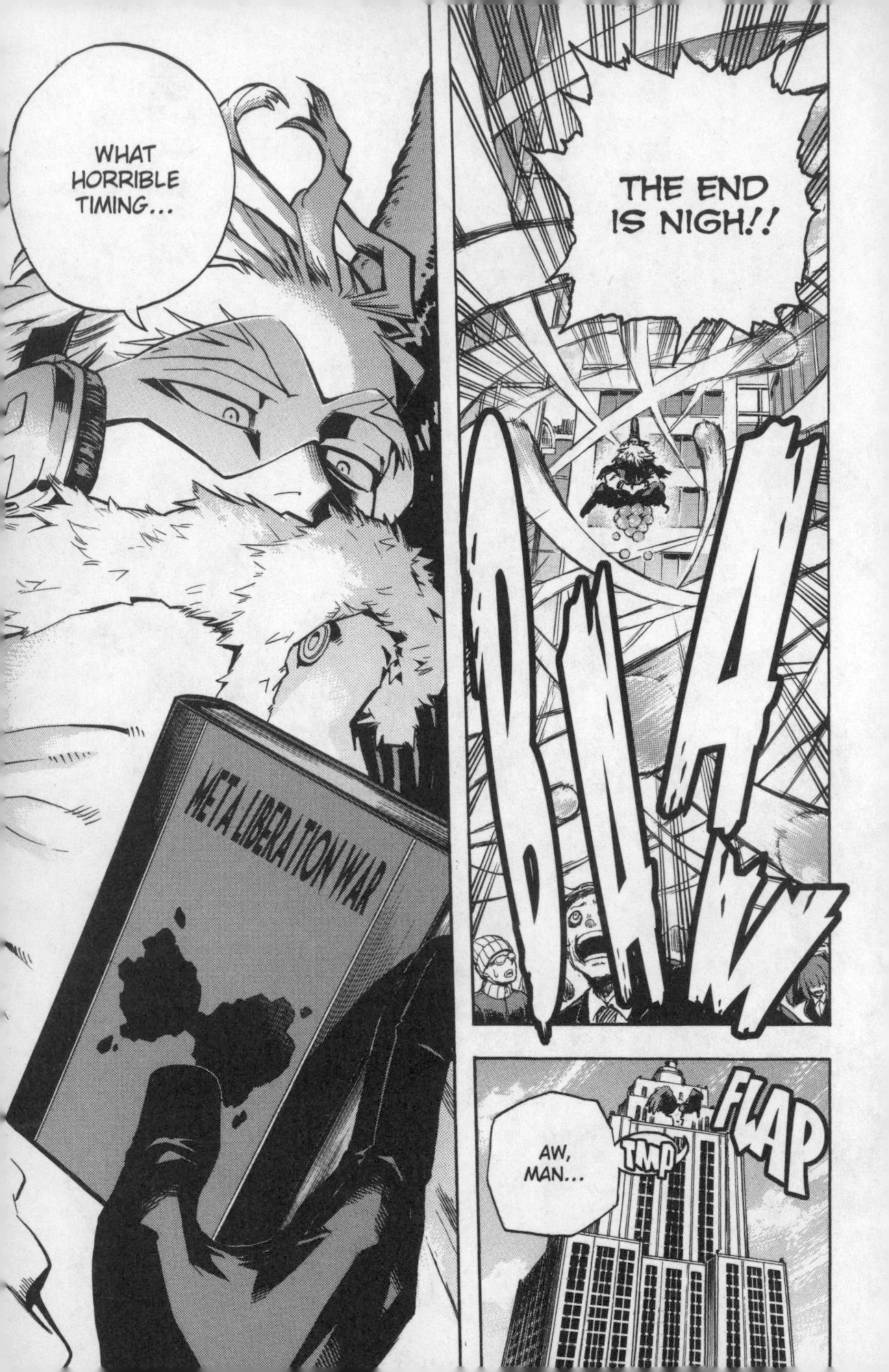
THE END IS NIGH!!
FLAP
TMP
AW, MAN...
WHAT HORRIBLE TIMING...
META LIBERATION WAR

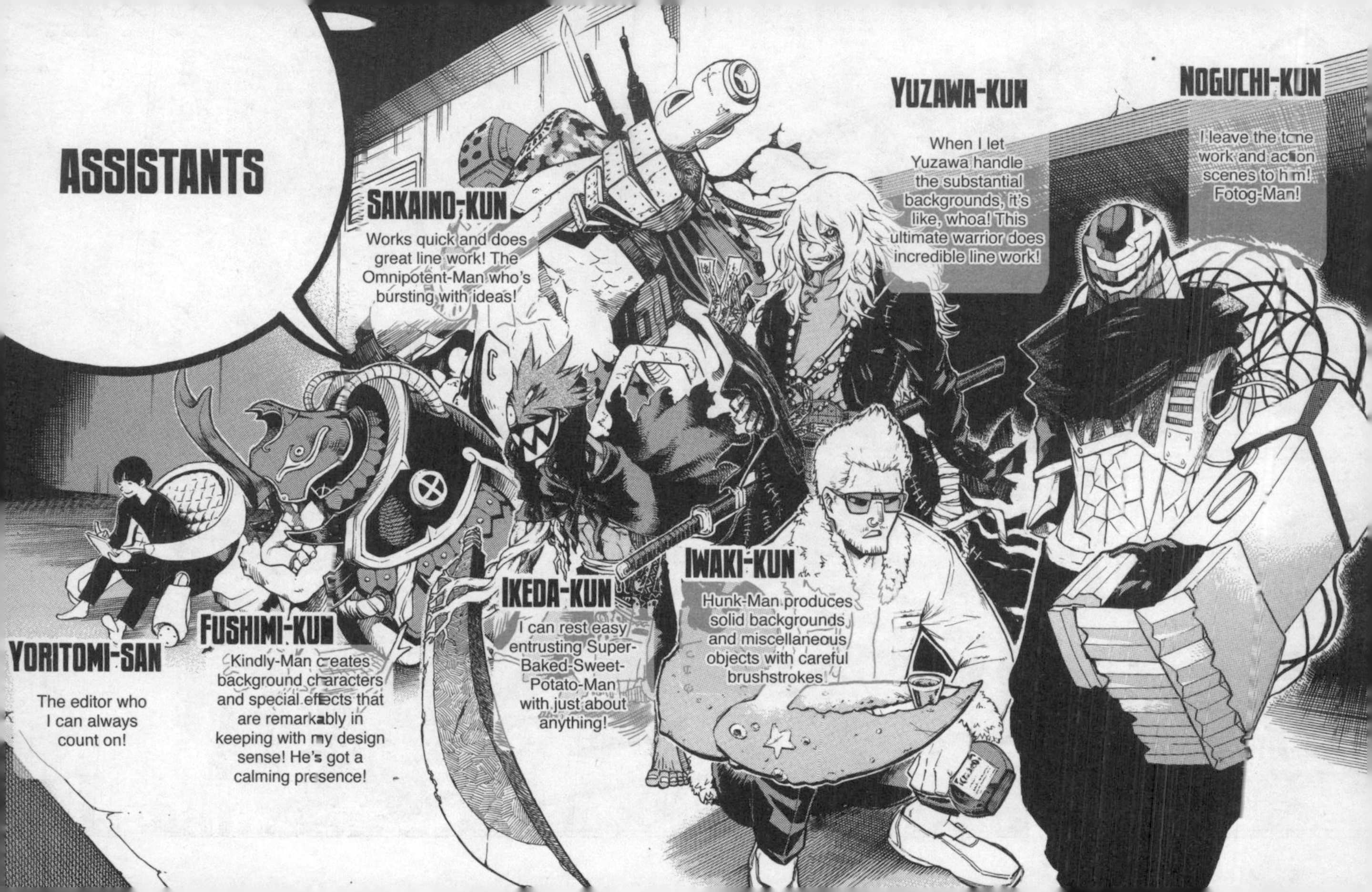
ASSISTANTS
NOGUCHI-KUN
I leave the tone work and action scenes to him! Fotog-Man!
YUZAWA-KUN
When I let Yuzawa handle the substantial backgrounds, it's like, whoa! This ultimate warrior does incredible line work!
SAKAINO-KUN
Works quick and does great line work! The Omnipotent-Man who's bursting with ideas!
IWAKI-KUN
Hunk-Man produces solid backgrounds and miscellaneous objects with careful brushstrokes!
IKEDA-KUN
I can rest easy entrusting Super-Baked-Sweet-Potato-Man with just about anything!
FUSHIMI-KUN
Kindly-Man creates background characters and special effects that are remarkably in keeping with my design sense! He's got a calming presence!
YORITOMI-SAN
The editor who I can always count on!

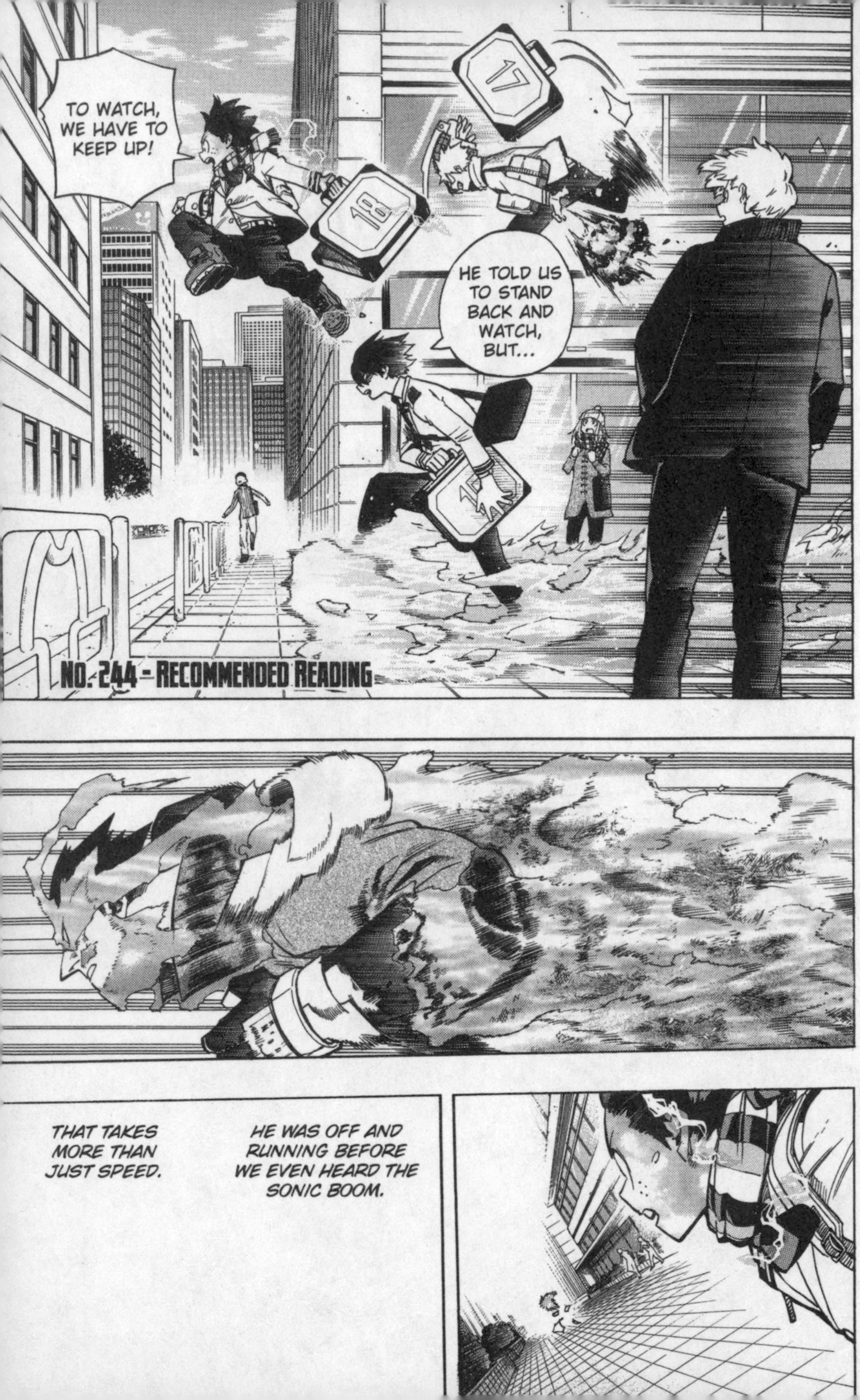
HE TOLD US TO STAND BACK AND WATCH, BUT...
TO WATCH, WE HAVE TO KEEP UP!
No. 244 - Recommended Reading
HE WAS OFF AND RUNNING BEFORE WE EVEN HEARD THE SONIC BOOM.
THAT TAKES MORE THAN JUST SPEED.

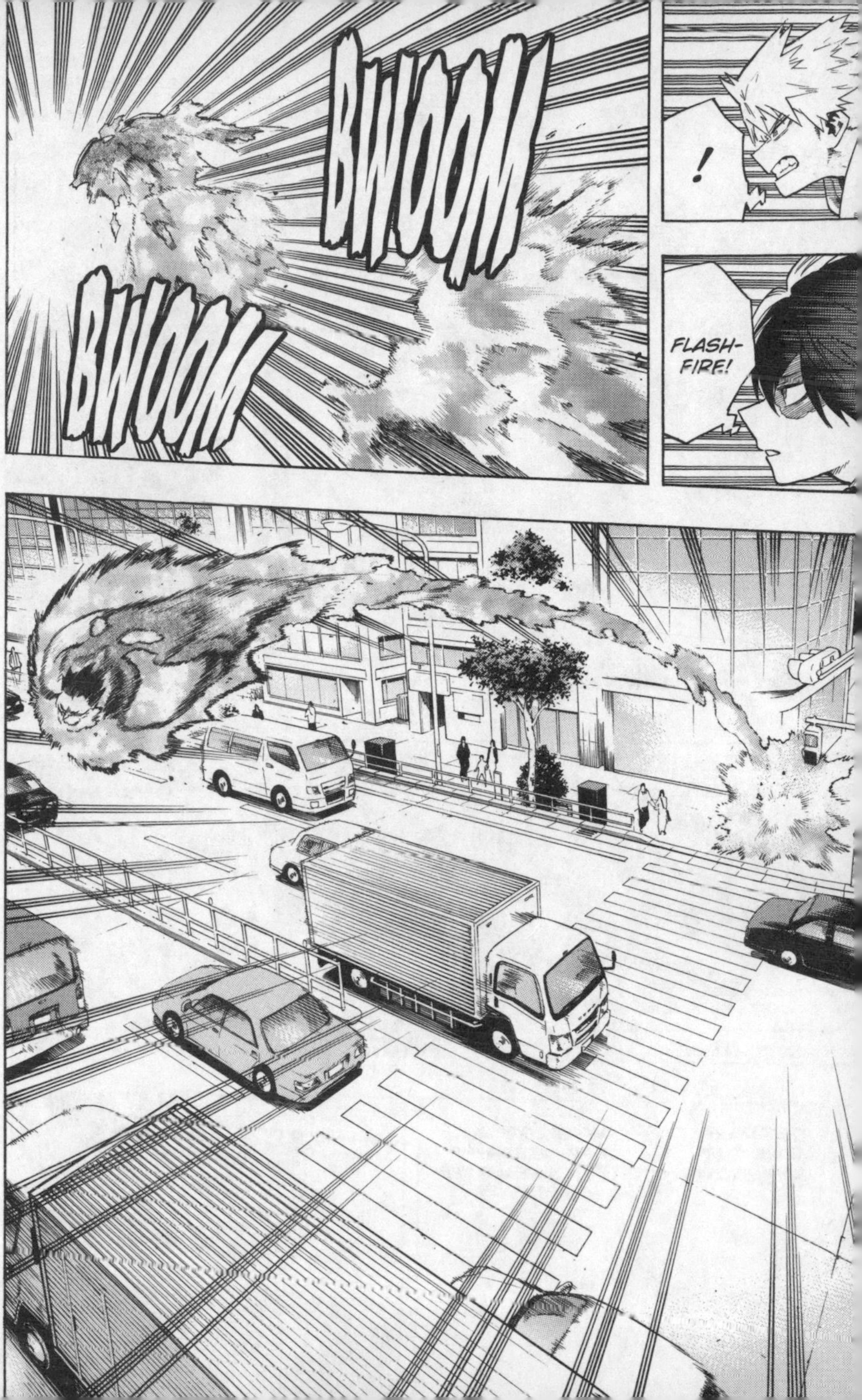
!
FLASH-FIRE!
BWOOM
BWOOM

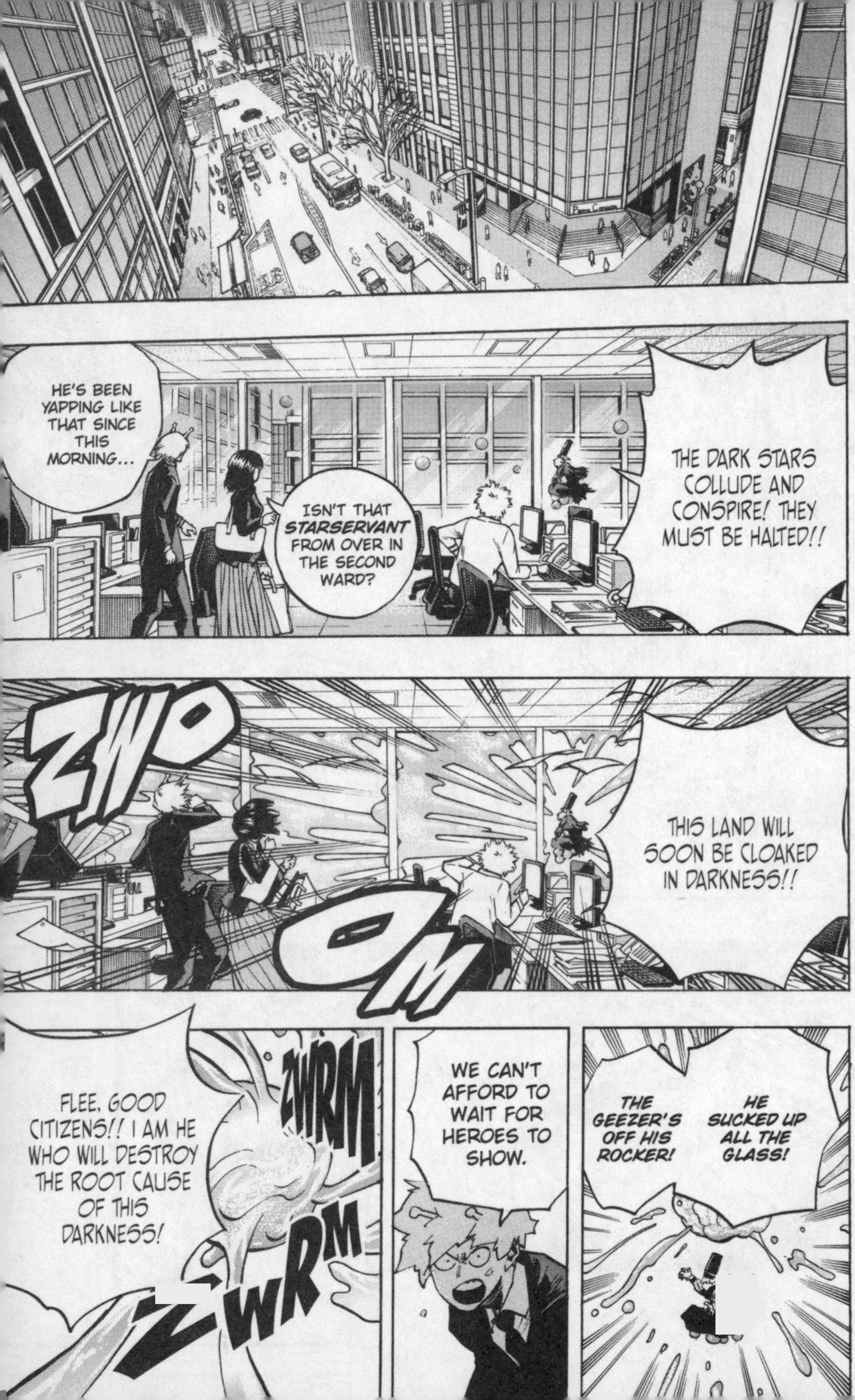
THE DARK STARS COLLUDE AND CONSPIRE! THEY MUST BE HALTED!!
ISN'T THAT STARSERVANT FROM OVER IN THE SECOND WARD?
HE'S BEEN YAPPING LIKE THAT SINCE THIS MORNING...
THIS LAND WILL SOON BE CLOAKED IN DARKNESS!!
ZWOOM
HE SUCKED UP ALL THE GLASS!
THE GEEZER'S OFF HIS ROCKER!
WE CAN'T AFFORD TO WAIT FOR HEROES TO SHOW.
ZWRM
FLEE, GOOD CITIZENS!! I AM HE WHO WILL DESTROY THE ROOT CAUSE OF THIS DARKNESS!
ZWRM

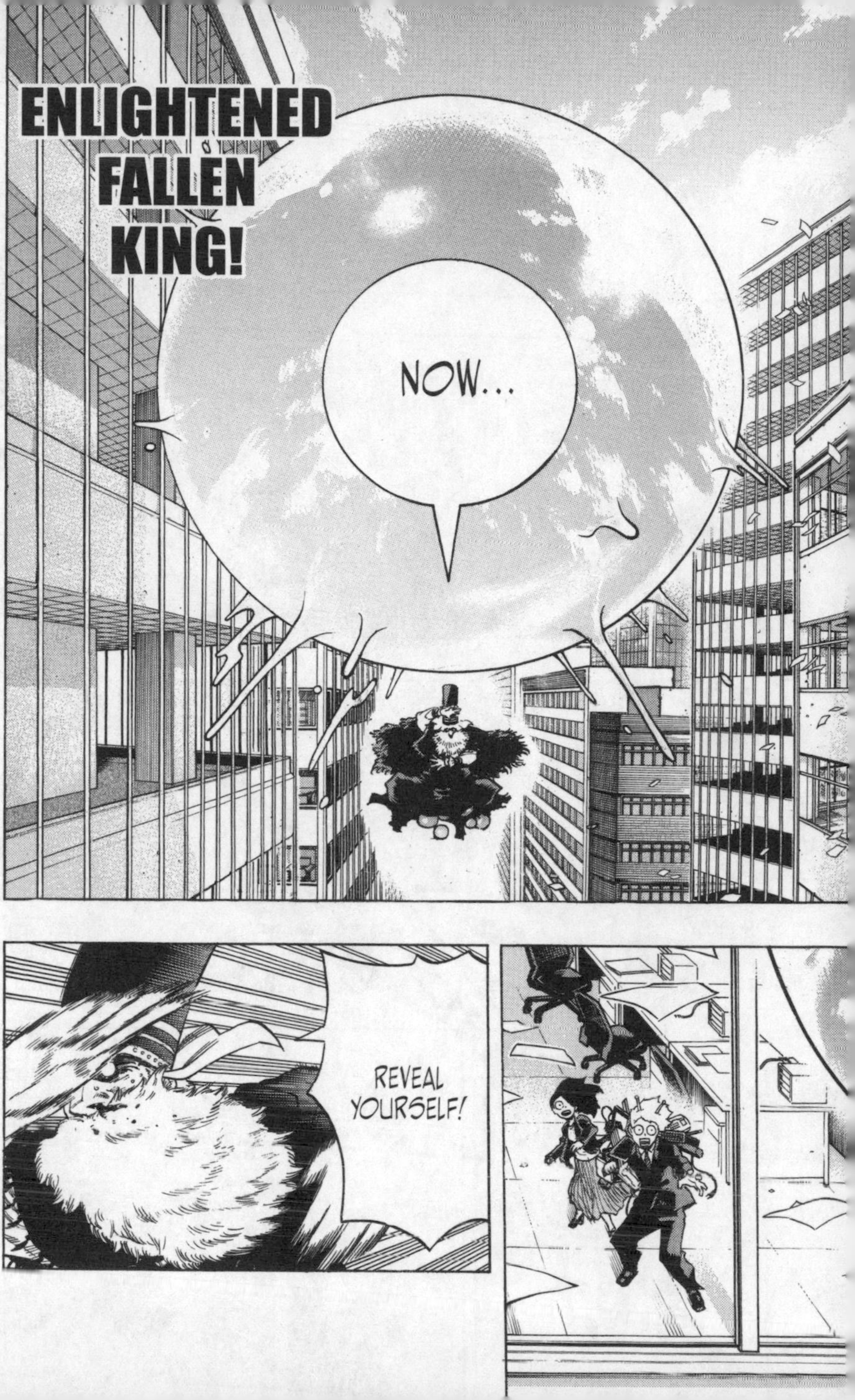
ENLIGHTENED FALLEN KING!
NOW...
REVEAL YOURSELF!

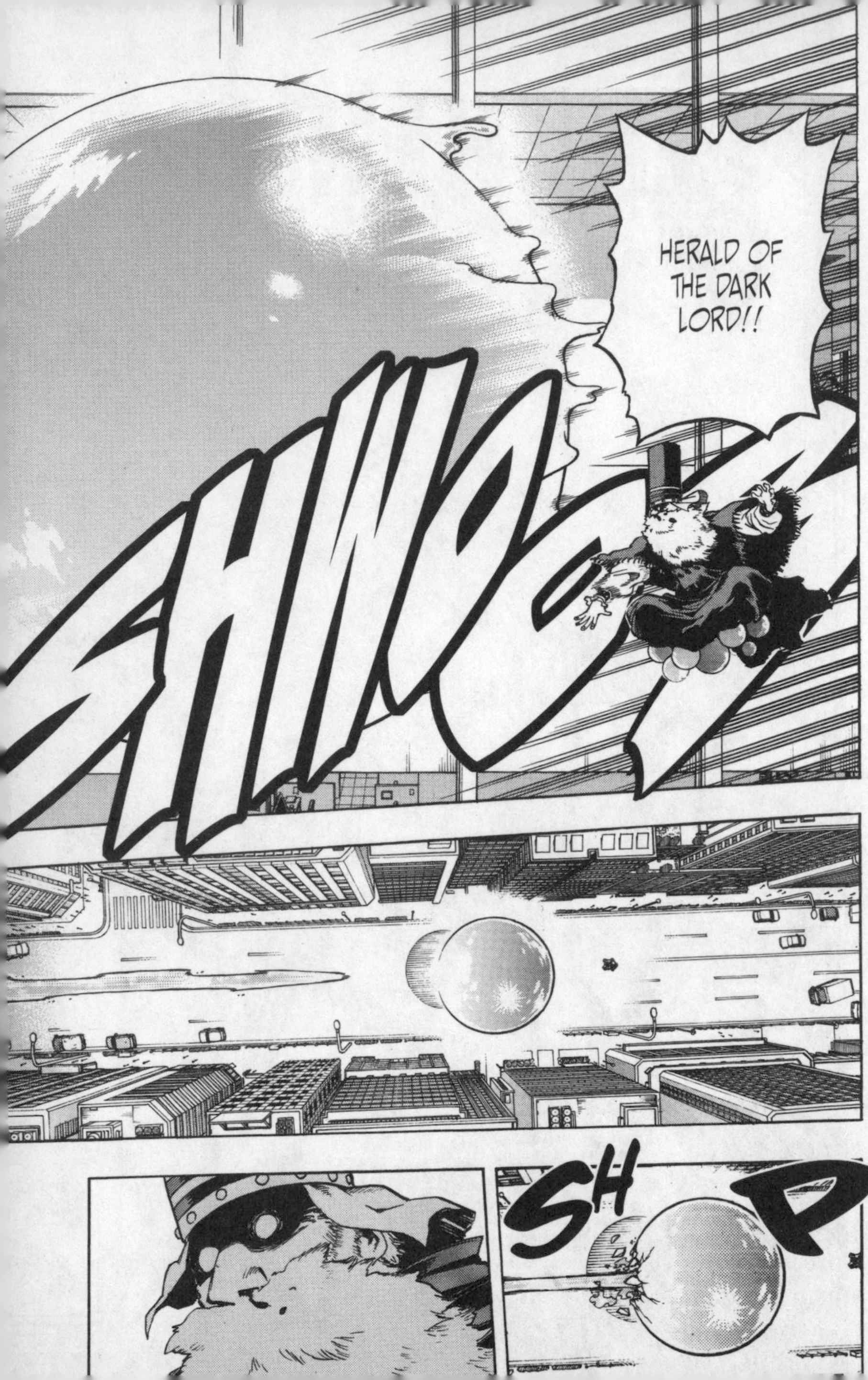
HERALD OF THE DARK LORD!!

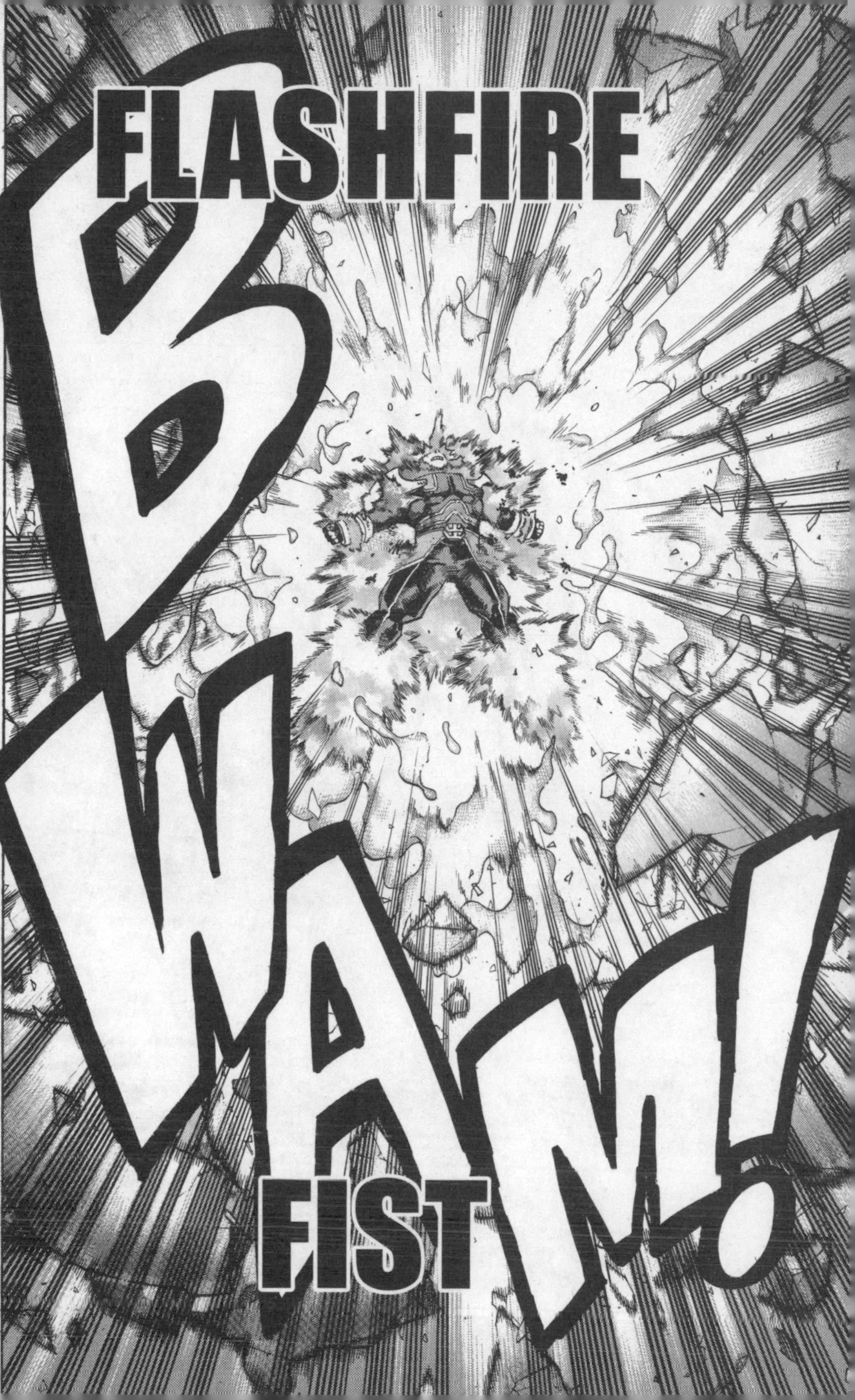
FLASHFIRE
BAM!
FIST

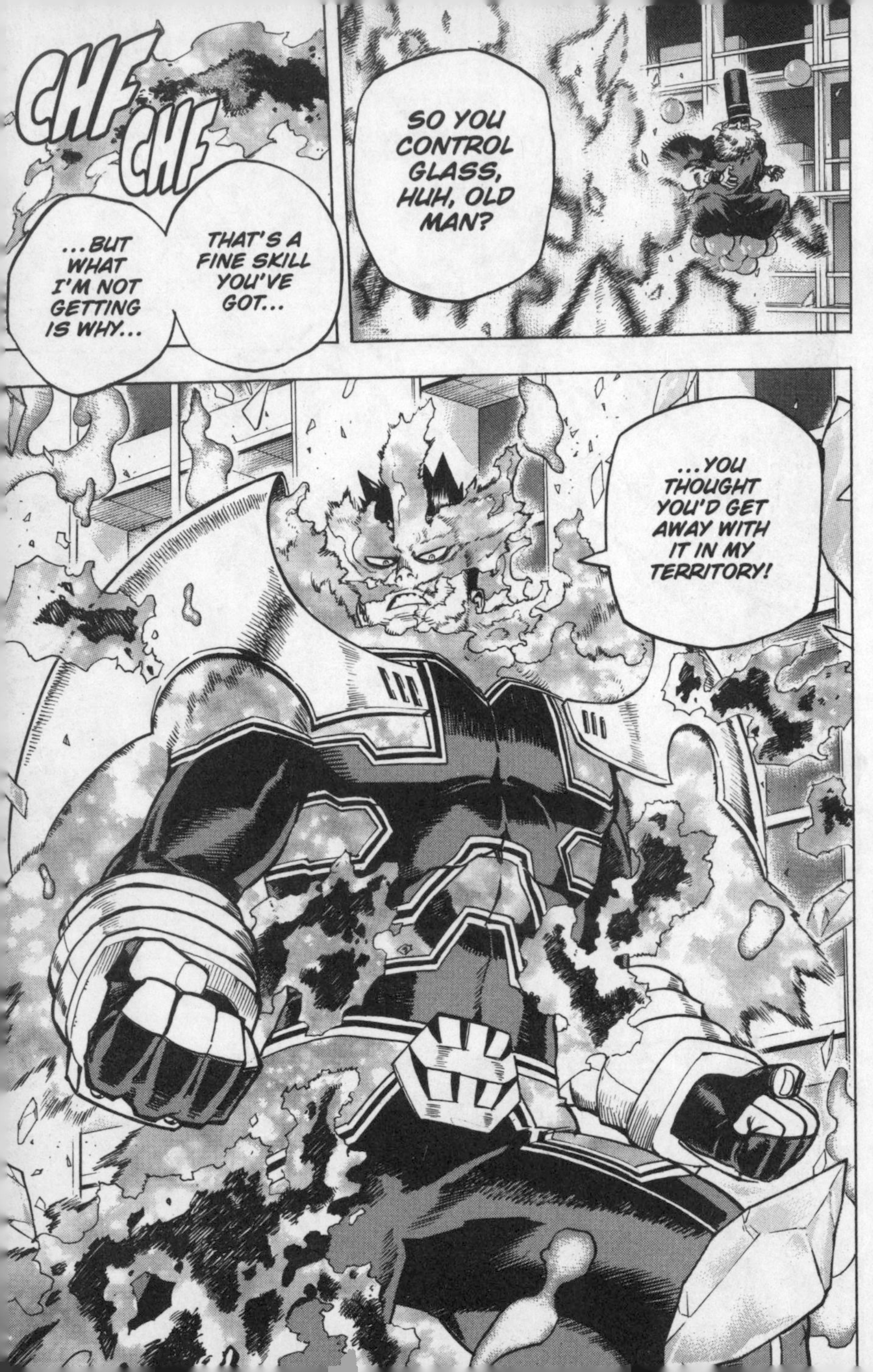
SO YOU CONTROL GLASS, HUH, OLD MAN?
CHF CHF
THAT'S A FINE SKILL YOU'VE GOT...
...BUT WHAT I'M NOT GETTING IS WHY...
...YOU THOUGHT YOU'D GET AWAY WITH IT IN MY TERRITORY!

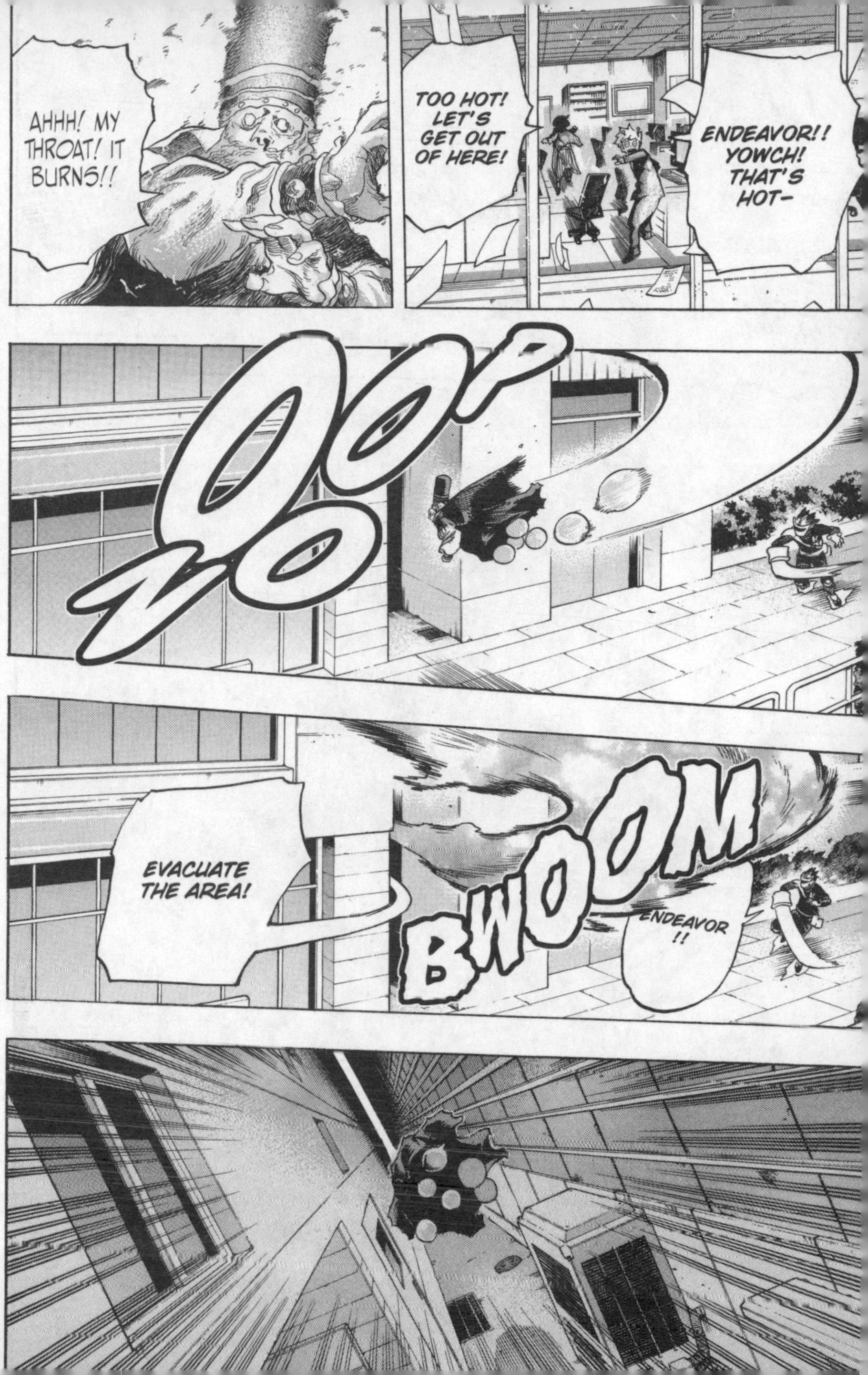
ENDEAVOR!! YOWCH! THAT'S HOT-
TOO HOT! LET'S GET OUT OF HERE!
AHHH! MY THROAT! IT BURNS!!
ZOOP
ENDEAVOR !!
BWOOM
EVACUATE THE AREA!

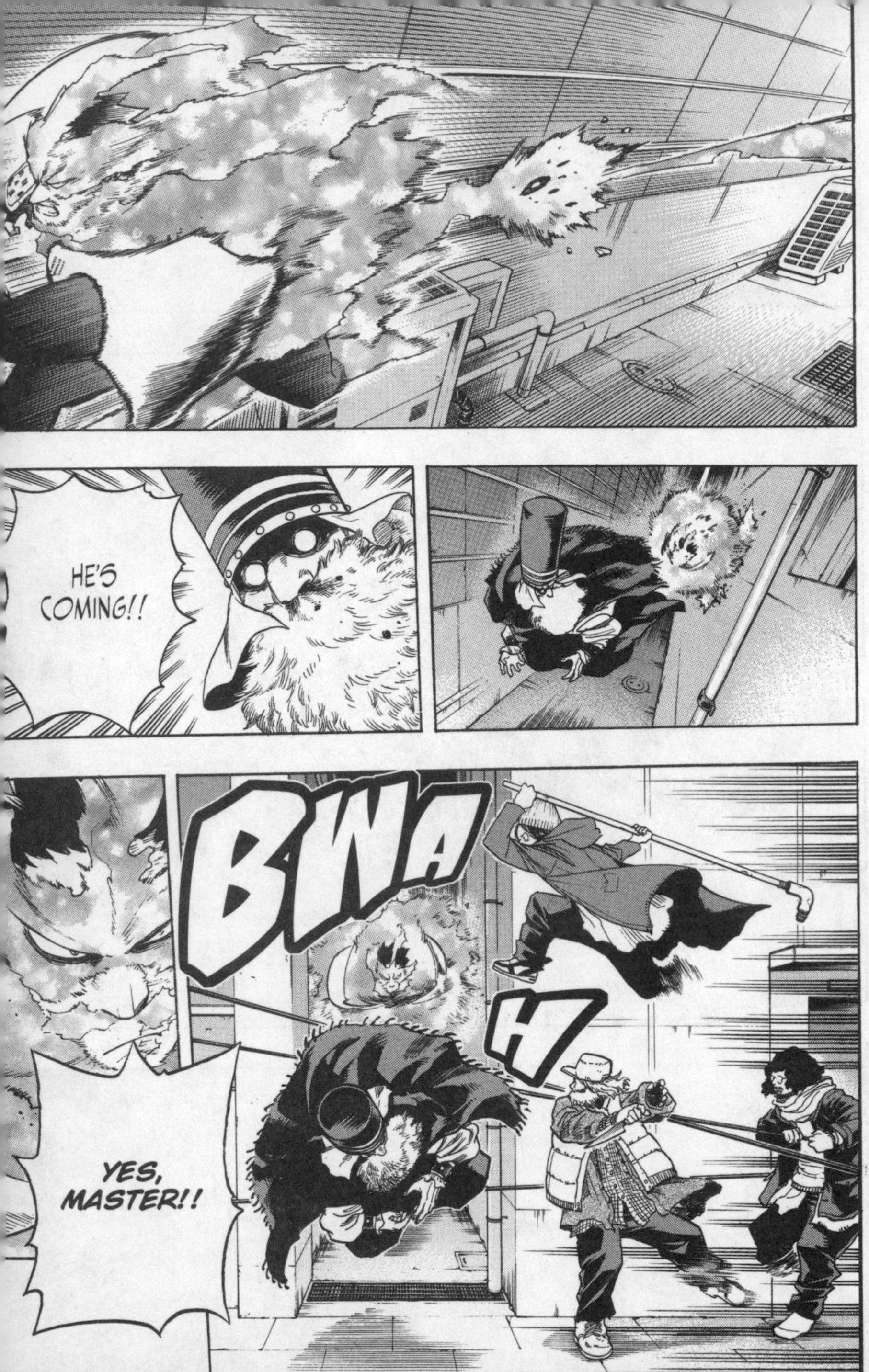
HE'S COMING!!
BWAH
YES, MASTER!!

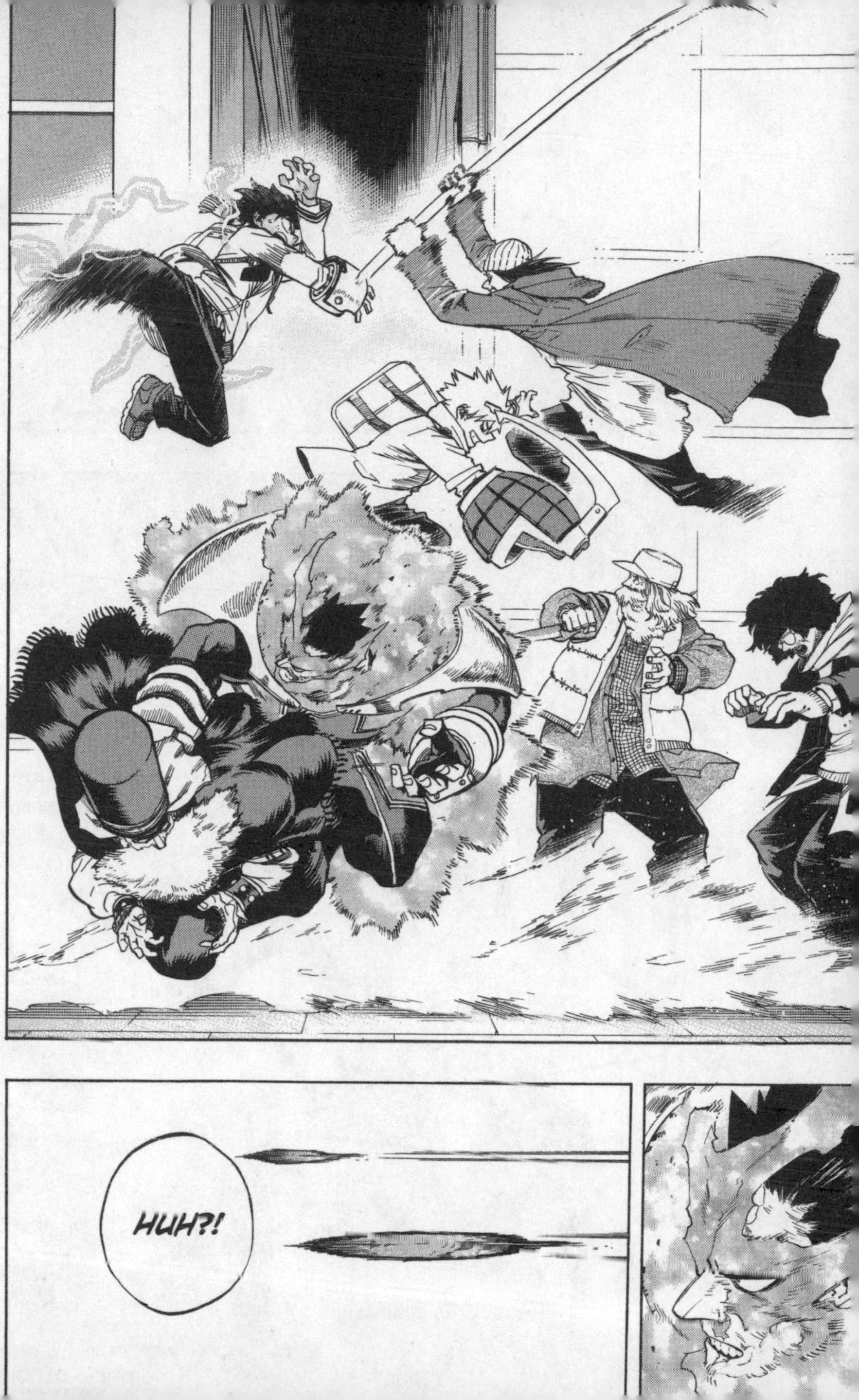
HUH?!

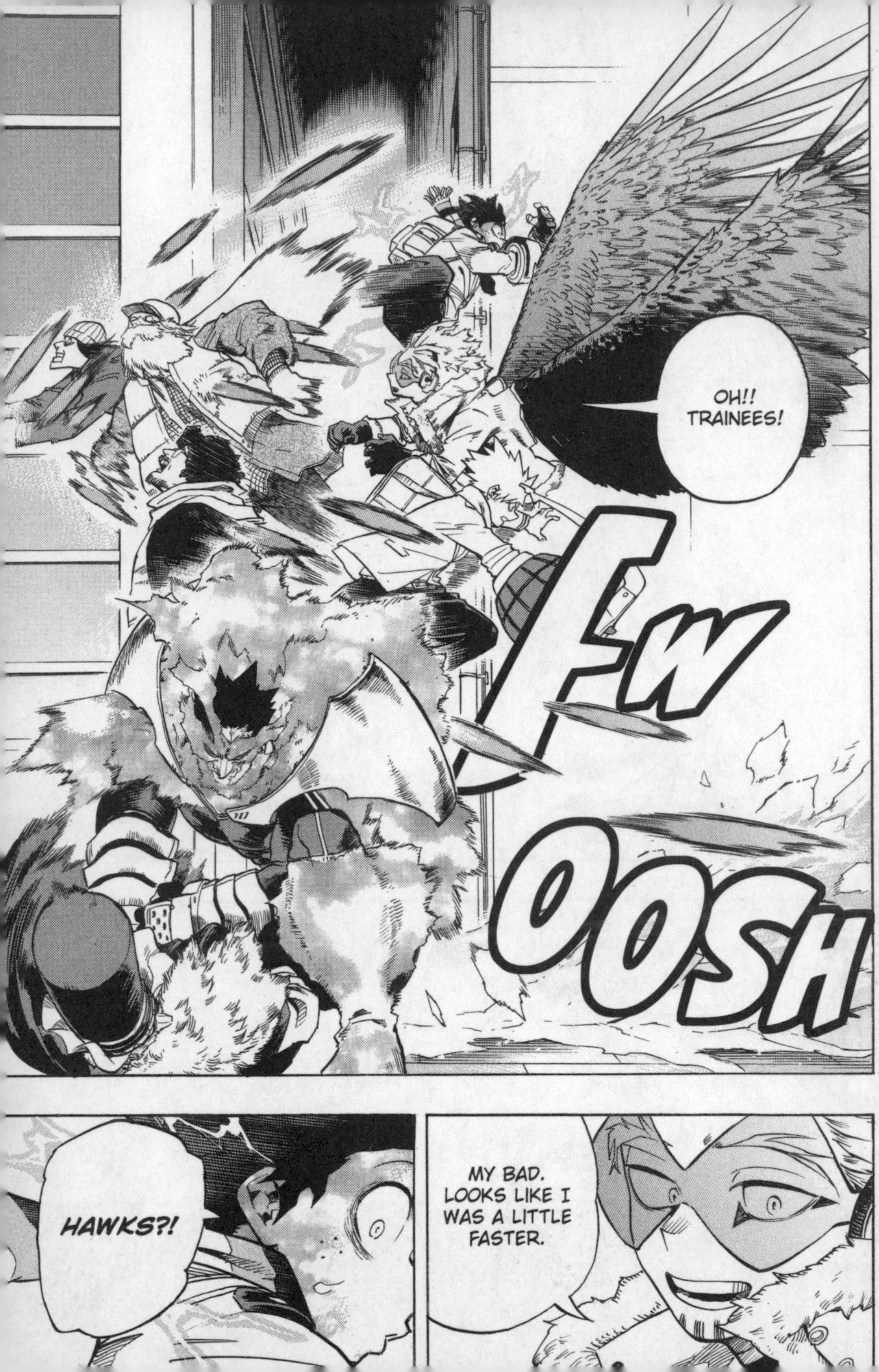
OH!! TRAINEES!
FWOOSH
MY BAD. LOOKS LIKE I WAS A LITTLE FASTER.
HAWKS?!

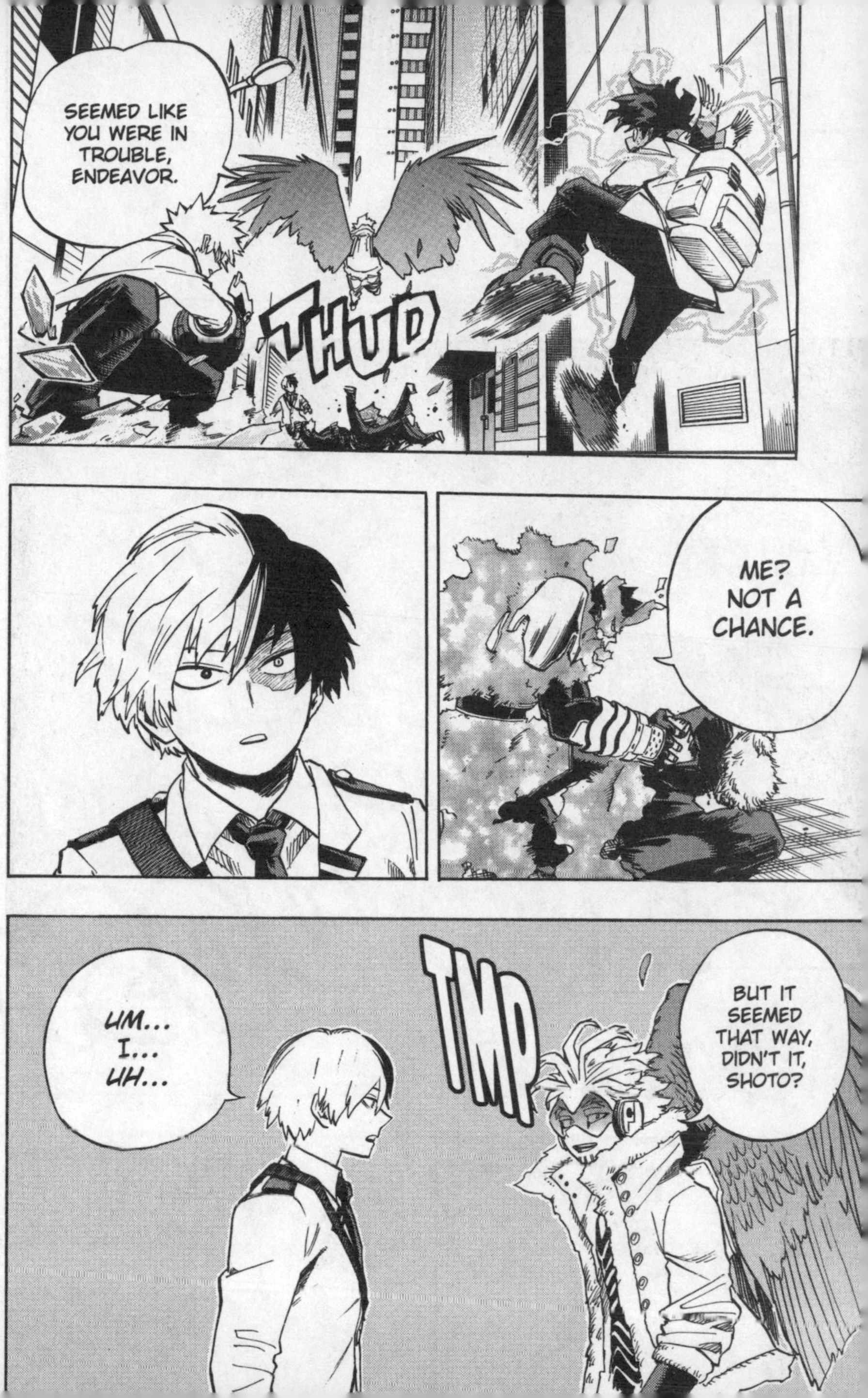
SEEMED LIKE YOU WERE IN TROUBLE, ENDEAVOR.
THUD
ME? NOT A CHANCE.
BUT IT SEEMED THAT WAY, DIDN'T IT, SHOTO?
TMP
UM... I... UH...

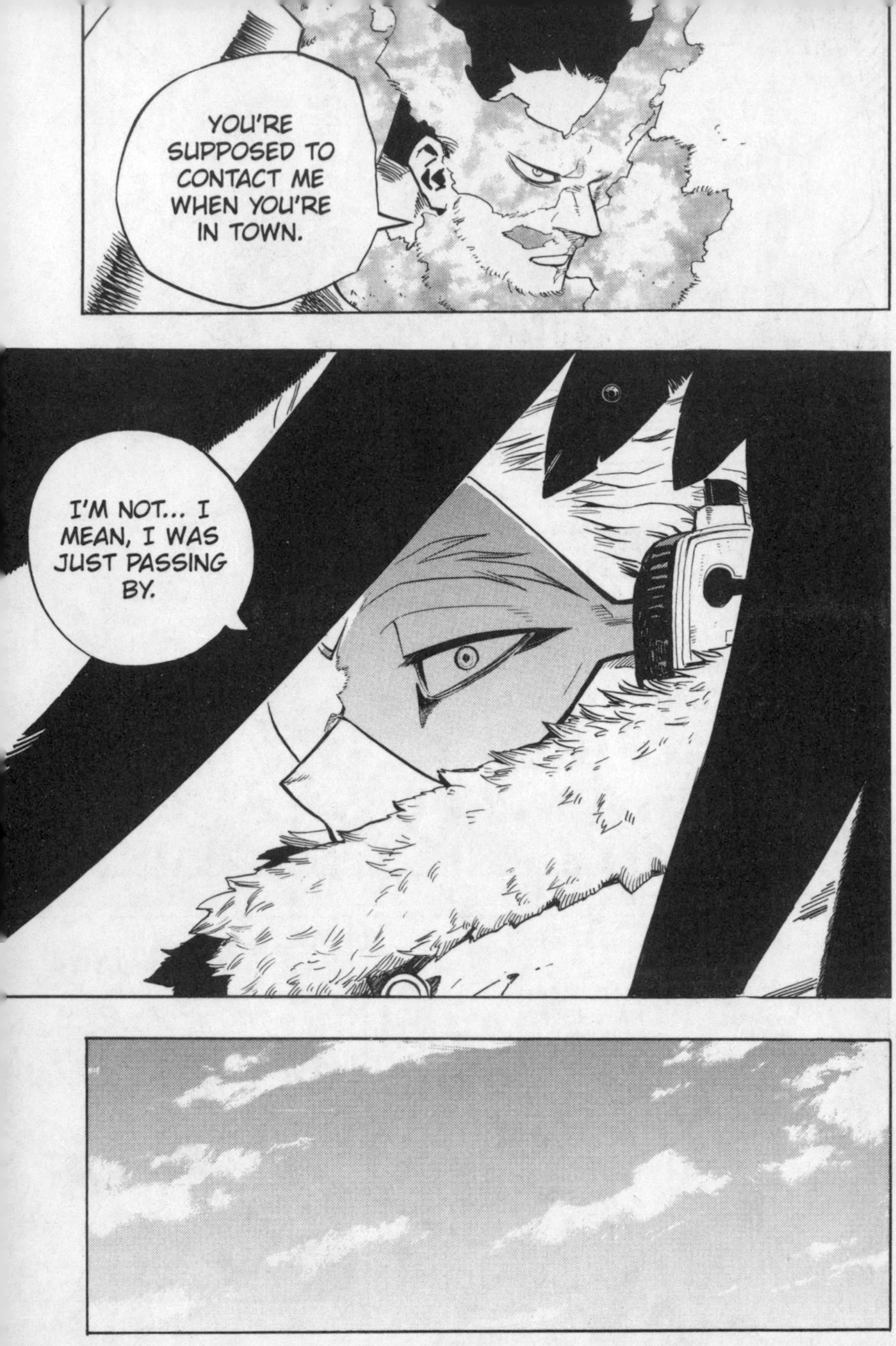
YOU'RE SUPPOSED TO CONTACT ME WHEN YOU'RE IN TOWN.
I'M NOT... I MEAN, I WAS JUST PASSING BY.

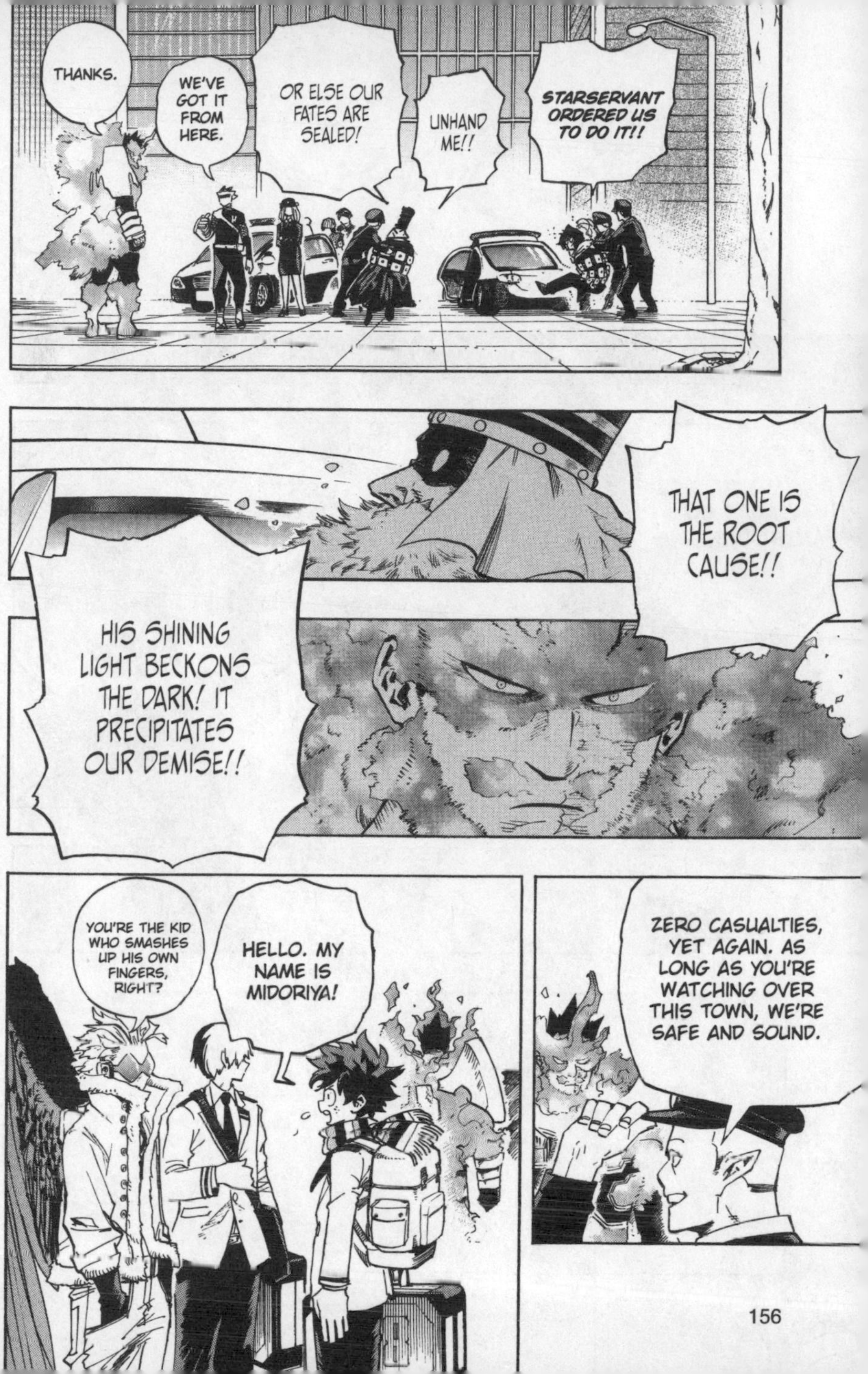
STARSERVANT ORDERED US TO DO IT!!
UNHAND ME!!
OR ELSE OUR FATES ARE SEALED!
WE'VE GOT IT FROM HERE.
THANKS.
THAT ONE IS THE ROOT CAUSE!!
HIS SHINING LIGHT BECKONS THE DARK! IT PRECIPITATES OUR DEMISE!!
ZERO CASUALTIES, YET AGAIN. AS LONG AS YOU'RE WATCHING OVER THIS TOWN, WE'RE SAFE AND SOUND.
HELLO. MY NAME IS MIDORIYA!
YOU'RE THE KID WHO SMASHES UP HIS OWN FINGERS, RIGHT?

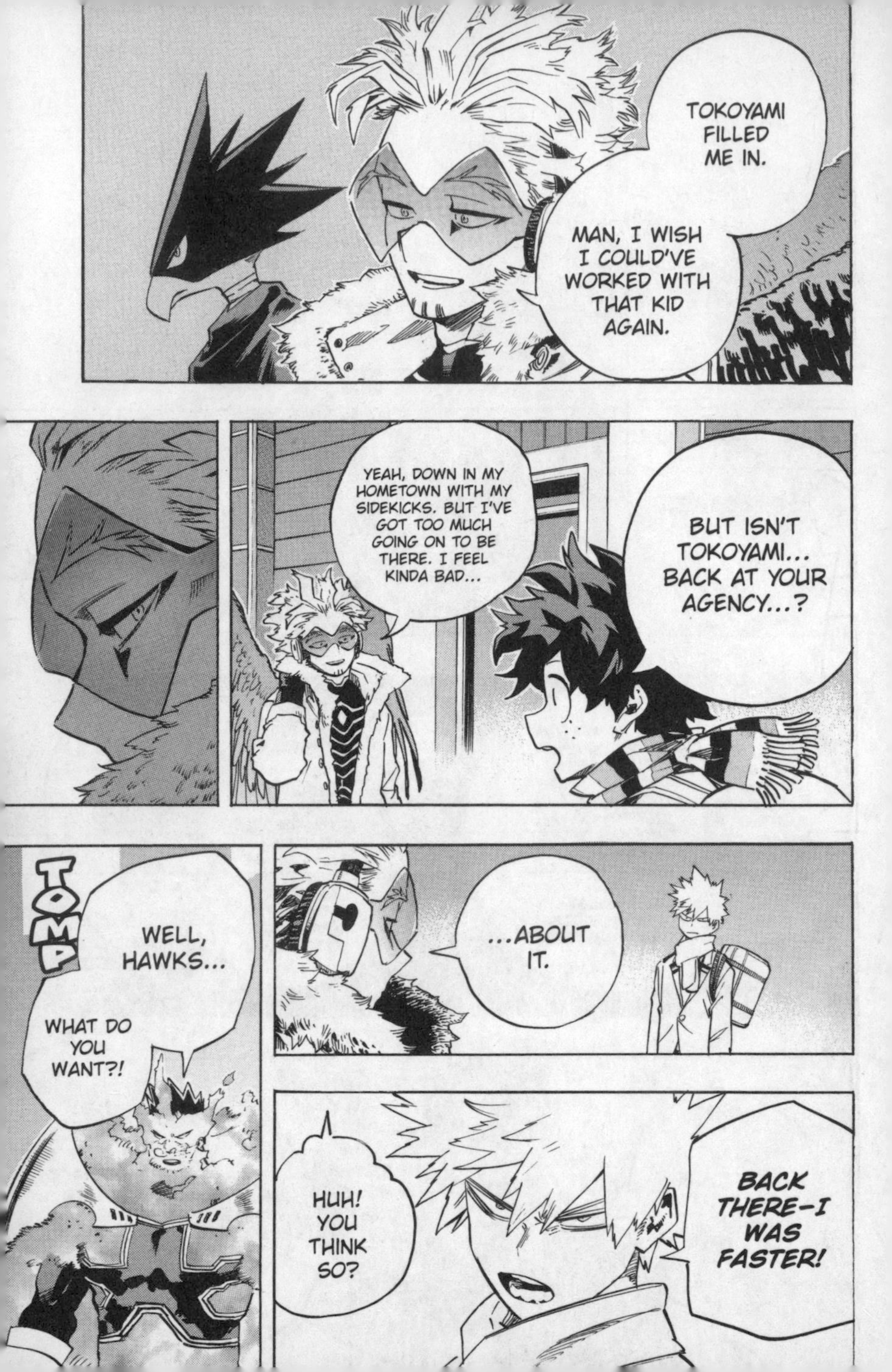
TOKOYAMI FILLED ME IN.
MAN, I WISH I COULD'VE WORKED WITH THAT KID AGAIN.
BUT ISN'T TOKOYAMI... BACK AT YOUR AGENCY...?
YEAH, DOWN IN MY HOMETOWN WITH MY SIDEKICKS. BUT I'VE GOT TOO MUCH GOING ON TO BE THERE. I FEEL KINDA BAD...
...ABOUT IT.
BACK THERE—I WAS FASTER!
HUH! YOU THINK SO?
TOMP
WELL, HAWKS...
WHAT DO YOU WANT?!

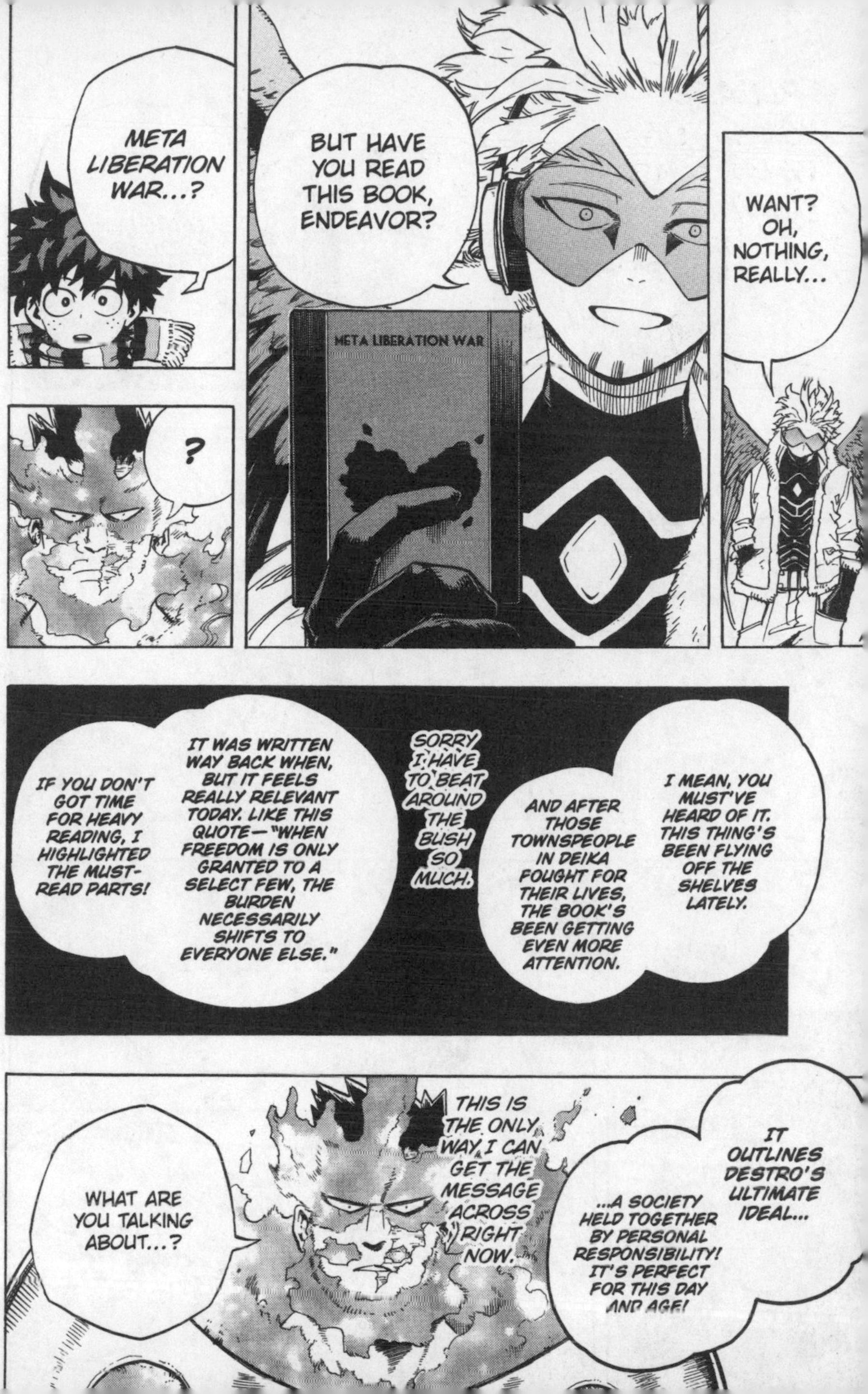
WANT? OH, NOTHING, REALLY...
BUT HAVE YOU READ THIS BOOK, ENDEAVOR?
META LIBERATION WAR
META LIBERATION WAR...?
?
I MEAN, YOU MUST'VE HEARD OF IT. THIS THING'S BEEN FLYING OFF THE SHELVES LATELY.
AND AFTER THOSE TOWNSPEOPLE IN DEIKA FOUGHT FOR THEIR LIVES, THE BOOK'S BEEN GETTING EVEN MORE ATTENTION.
SORRY I HAVE TO BEAT AROUND THE BUSH SO MUCH.
IT WAS WRITTEN WAY BACK WHEN, BUT IT FEELS REALLY RELEVANT TODAY. LIKE THIS QUOTE—"WHEN FREEDOM IS ONLY GRANTED TO A SELECT FEW, THE BURDEN NECESSARILY SHIFTS TO EVERYONE ELSE."
IF YOU DON'T GOT TIME FOR HEAVY READING, I HIGHLIGHTED THE MUST-READ PARTS!
IT OUTLINES DESTRO'S ULTIMATE IDEAL...
...A SOCIETY HELD TOGETHER BY PERSONAL RESPONSIBILITY! IT'S PERFECT FOR THIS DAY AND AGE!
THIS IS THE ONLY WAY I CAN GET THE MESSAGE ACROSS RIGHT NOW.
WHAT ARE YOU TALKING ABOUT...?

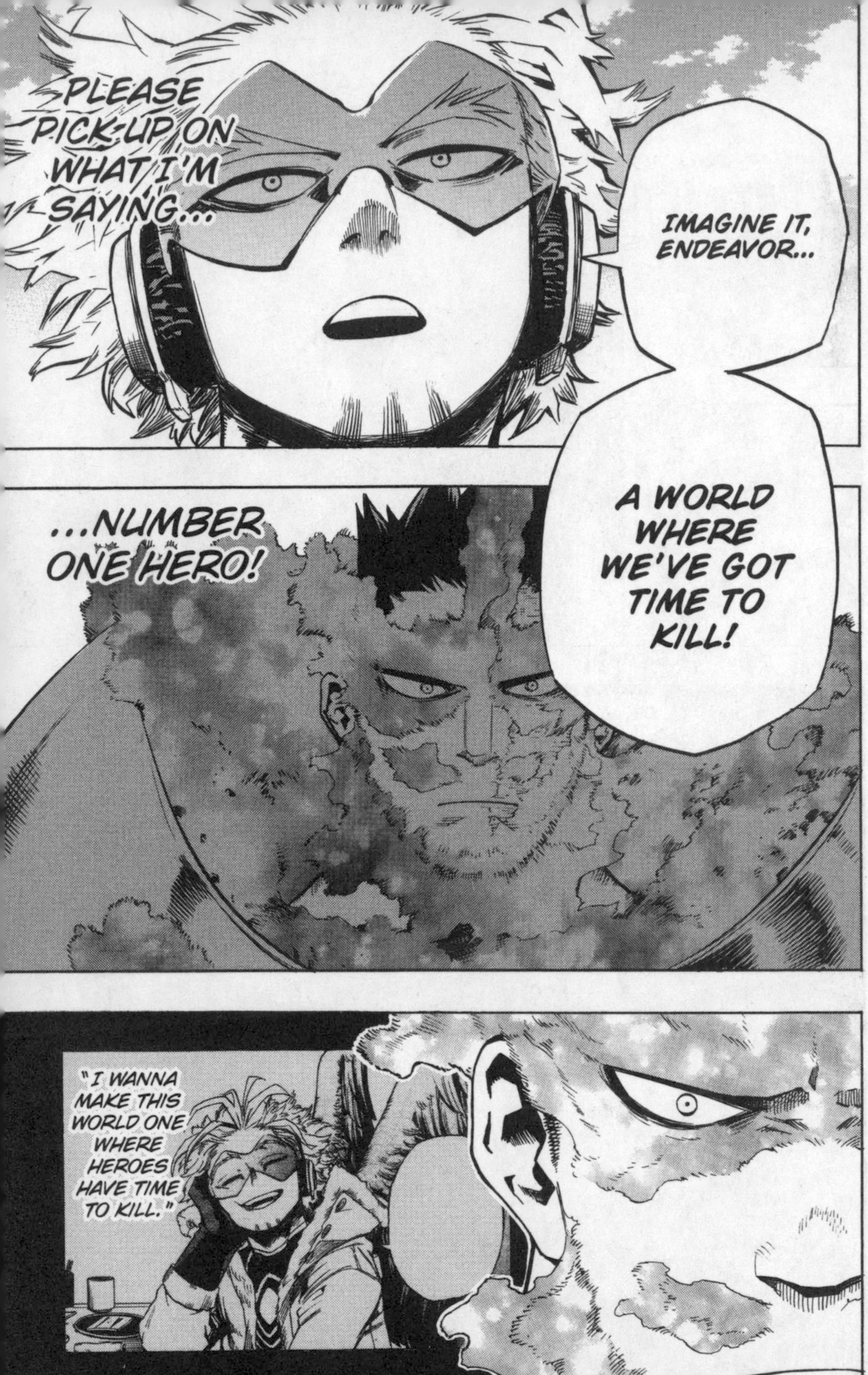
IMAGINE IT, ENDEAVOR...
A WORLD WHERE WE'VE GOT TIME TO KILL!
PLEASE PICK UP ON WHAT I'M SAYING...
...NUMBER ONE HERO!
"I WANNA MAKE THIS WORLD ONE WHERE HEROES HAVE TIME TO KILL."

HERO

BURNIN (25) (MOE KAMIJI)

STREET CLOTHES

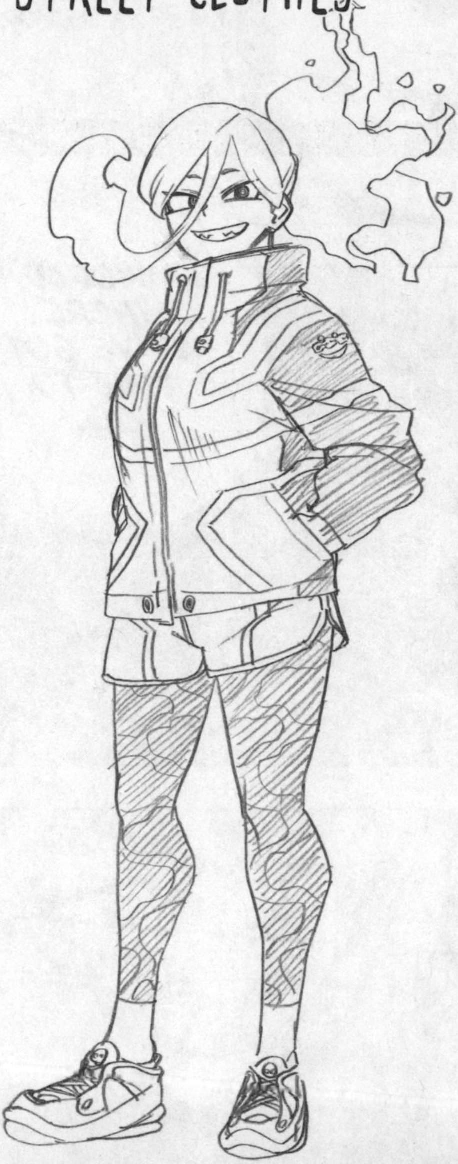

Birthday: 1/18
Height: 169 cm
Favorite Thing: Festivals

THE SIDEKICK

People with strong ambitions find their way to Endeavor's agency, and it didn't take long after joining for Moe to make it clear she was going places. She wasn't necessarily an Endeavor fan to start with, but she gained respect for the man while watching him perform hero work in the flesh.

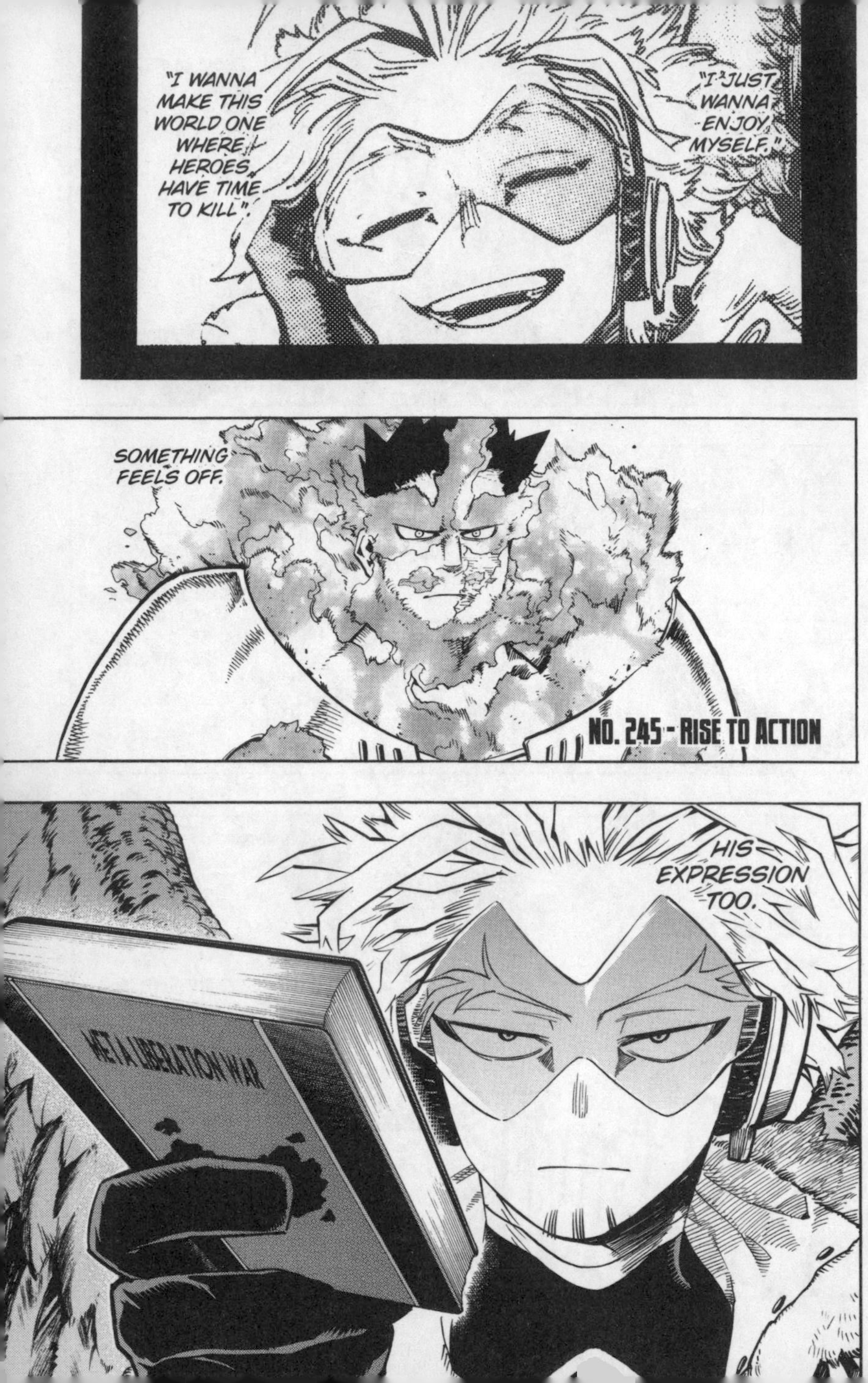
"I JUST WANNA ENJOY MYSELF."
"I WANNA MAKE THIS WORLD ONE WHERE HEROES HAVE TIME TO KILL".
SOMETHING FEELS OFF.
NO. 245 - RISE TO ACTION
HIS EXPRESSION TOO.
LIBERATION WAR

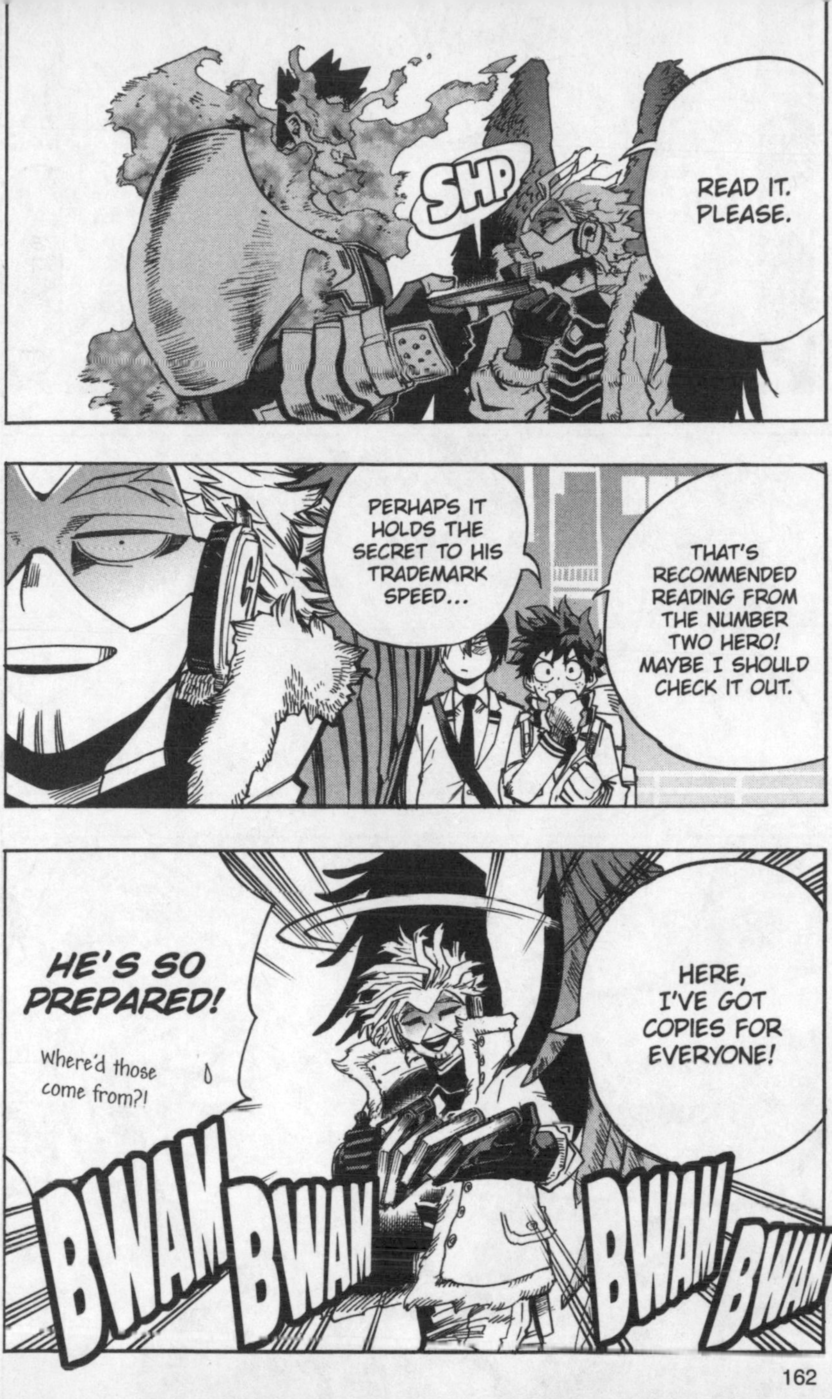
READ IT. PLEASE.
SHP
THAT'S RECOMMENDED READING FROM THE NUMBER TWO HERO! MAYBE I SHOULD CHECK IT OUT.
PERHAPS IT HOLDS THE SECRET TO HIS TRADEMARK SPEED...
HERE, I'VE GOT COPIES FOR EVERYONE!
HE'S SO PREPARED!
Where'd those come from?!
BWAM
BWAM
BWAM
BWAM

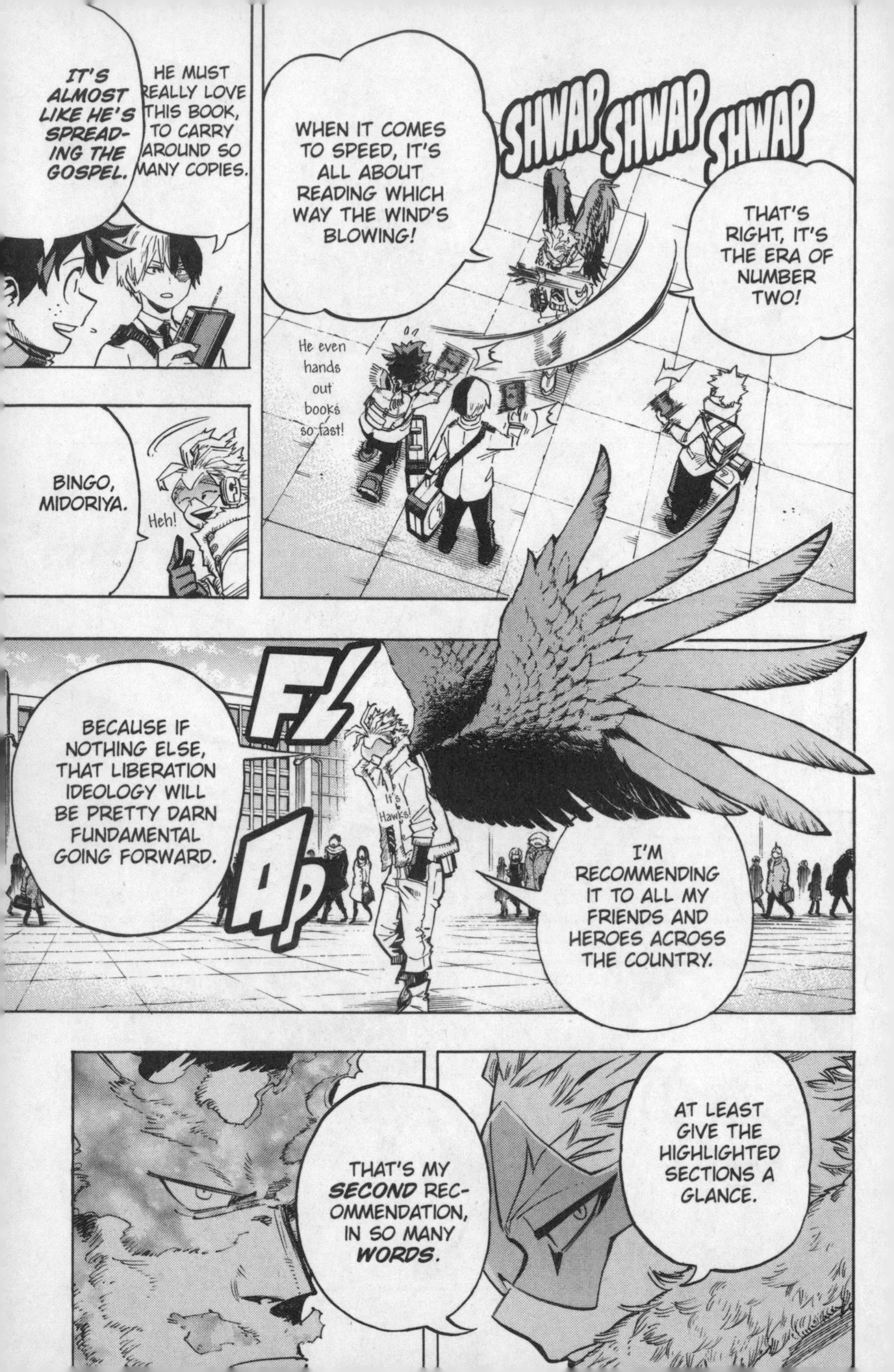
SHWAP SHWAP SHWAP
WHEN IT COMES TO SPEED, IT'S ALL ABOUT READING WHICH WAY THE WIND'S BLOWING!
THAT'S RIGHT, IT'S THE ERA OF NUMBER TWO!
He even hands out books so fast!
HE MUST REALLY LOVE THIS BOOK, TO CARRY AROUND SO MANY COPIES.
IT'S ALMOST LIKE HE'S SPREADING THE GOSPEL.
BINGO, MIDORIYA.
Heh!
FL
AP
I'M RECOMMENDING IT TO ALL MY FRIENDS AND HEROES ACROSS THE COUNTRY.
BECAUSE IF NOTHING ELSE, THAT LIBERATION IDEOLOGY WILL BE PRETTY DARN FUNDAMENTAL GOING FORWARD.
It's Hawks!
AT LEAST GIVE THE HIGHLIGHTED SECTIONS A GLANCE.
THAT'S MY SECOND RECOMMENDATION, IN SO MANY WORDS.

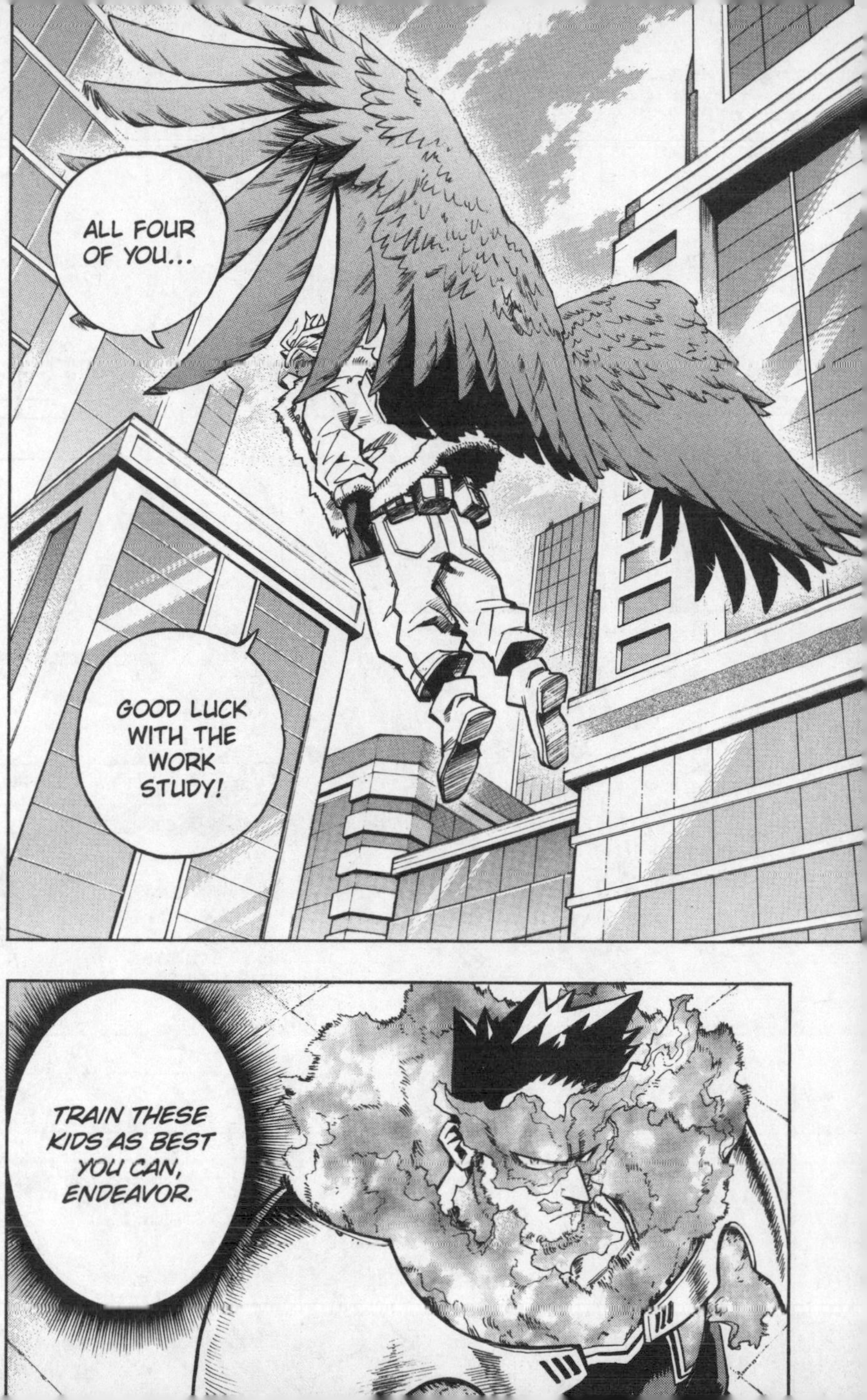
ALL FOUR OF YOU...
GOOD LUCK WITH THE WORK STUDY!
TRAIN THESE KIDS AS BEST YOU CAN, ENDEAVOR.

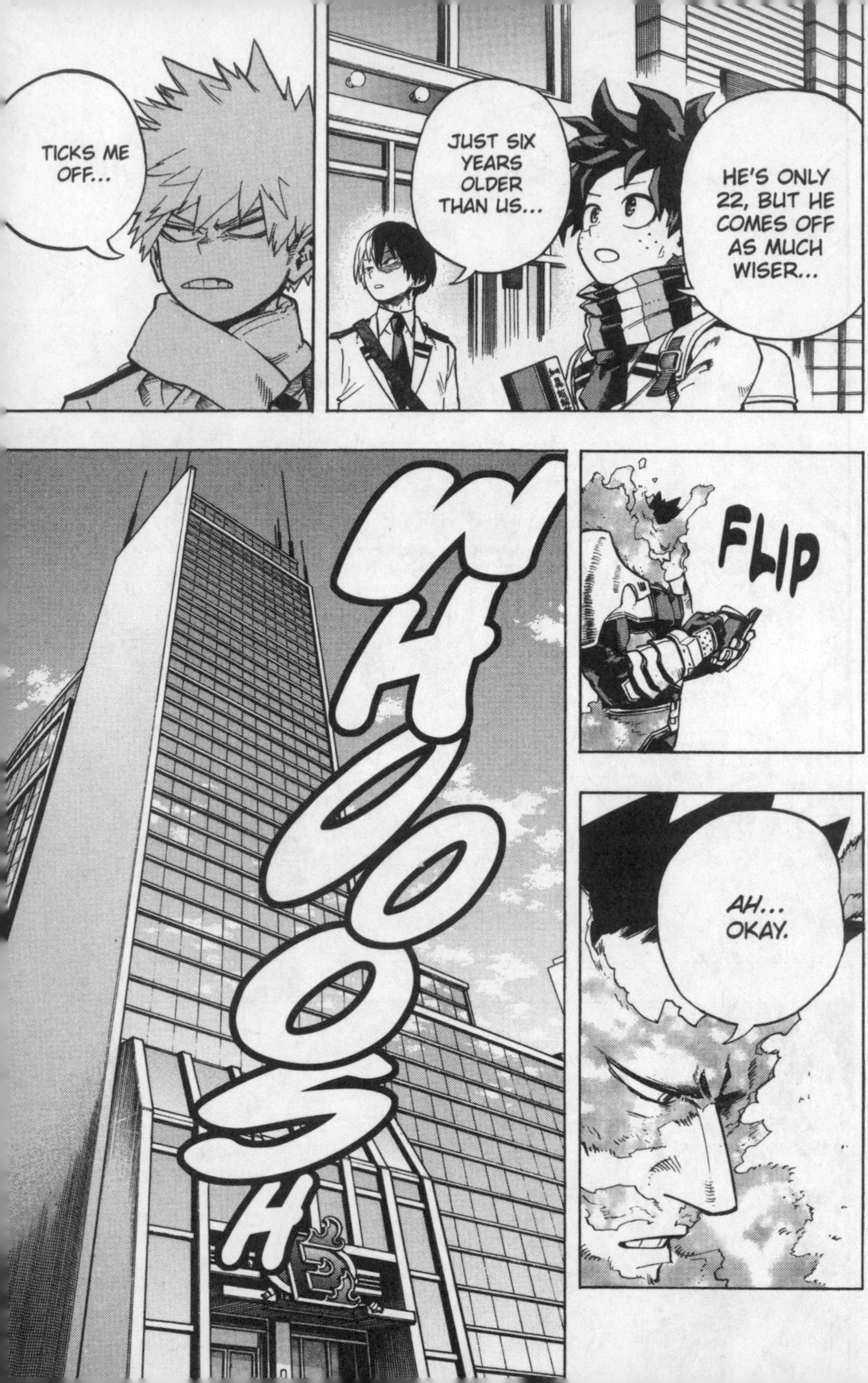
HE'S ONLY 22, BUT HE COMES OFF AS MUCH WISER...
JUST SIX YEARS OLDER THAN US...
TICKS ME OFF...
FLIP
AH... OKAY.
WHOOSH

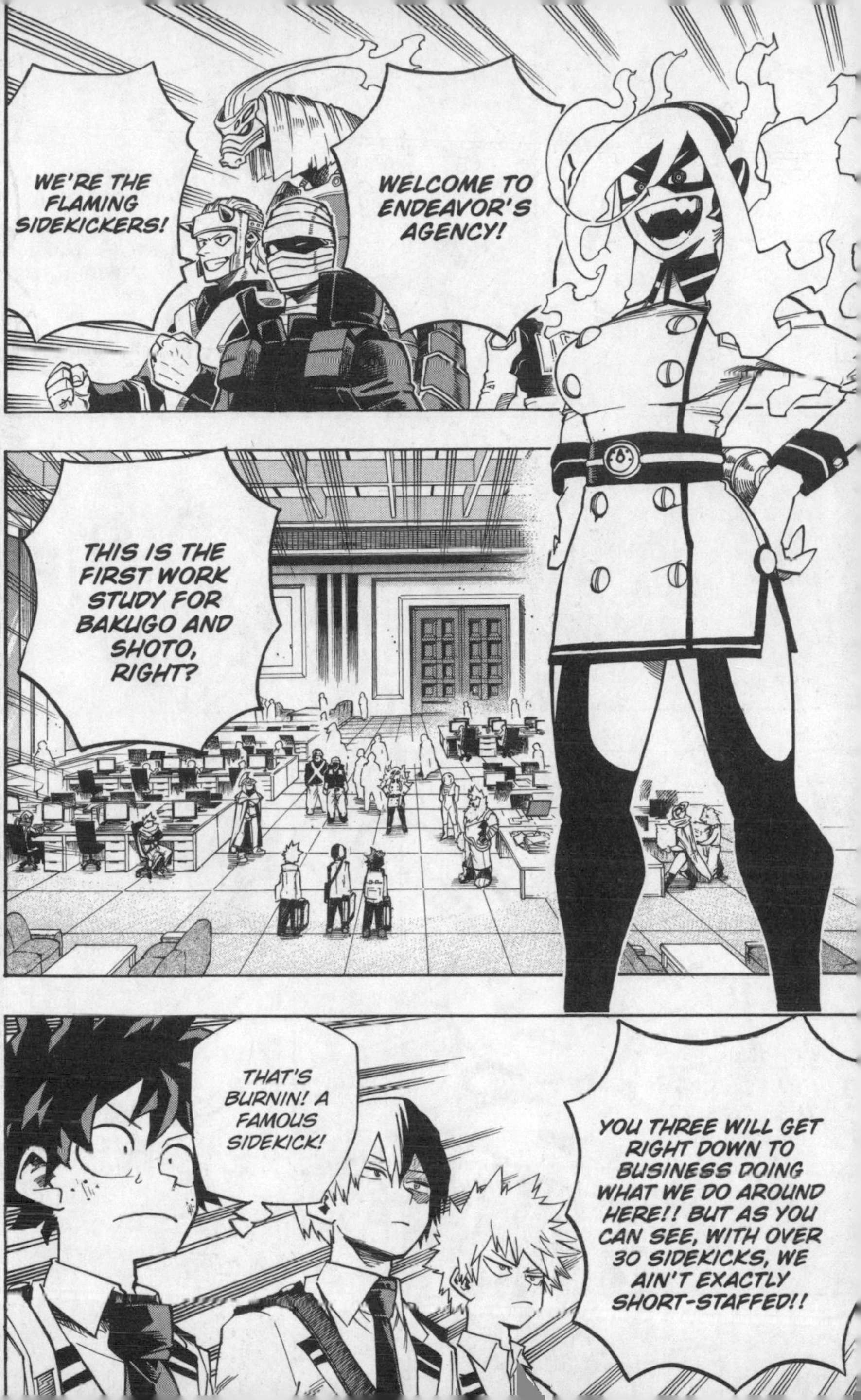
WELCOME TO ENDEAVOR'S AGENCY!
WE'RE THE FLAMING SIDEKICKERS!
THIS IS THE FIRST WORK STUDY FOR BAKUGO AND SHOTO, RIGHT?
YOU THREE WILL GET RIGHT DOWN TO BUSINESS DOING WHAT WE DO AROUND HERE!! BUT AS YOU CAN SEE, WITH OVER 30 SIDEKICKS, WE AIN'T EXACTLY SHORT-STAFFED!!
THAT'S BURNIN! A FAMOUS SIDEKICK!

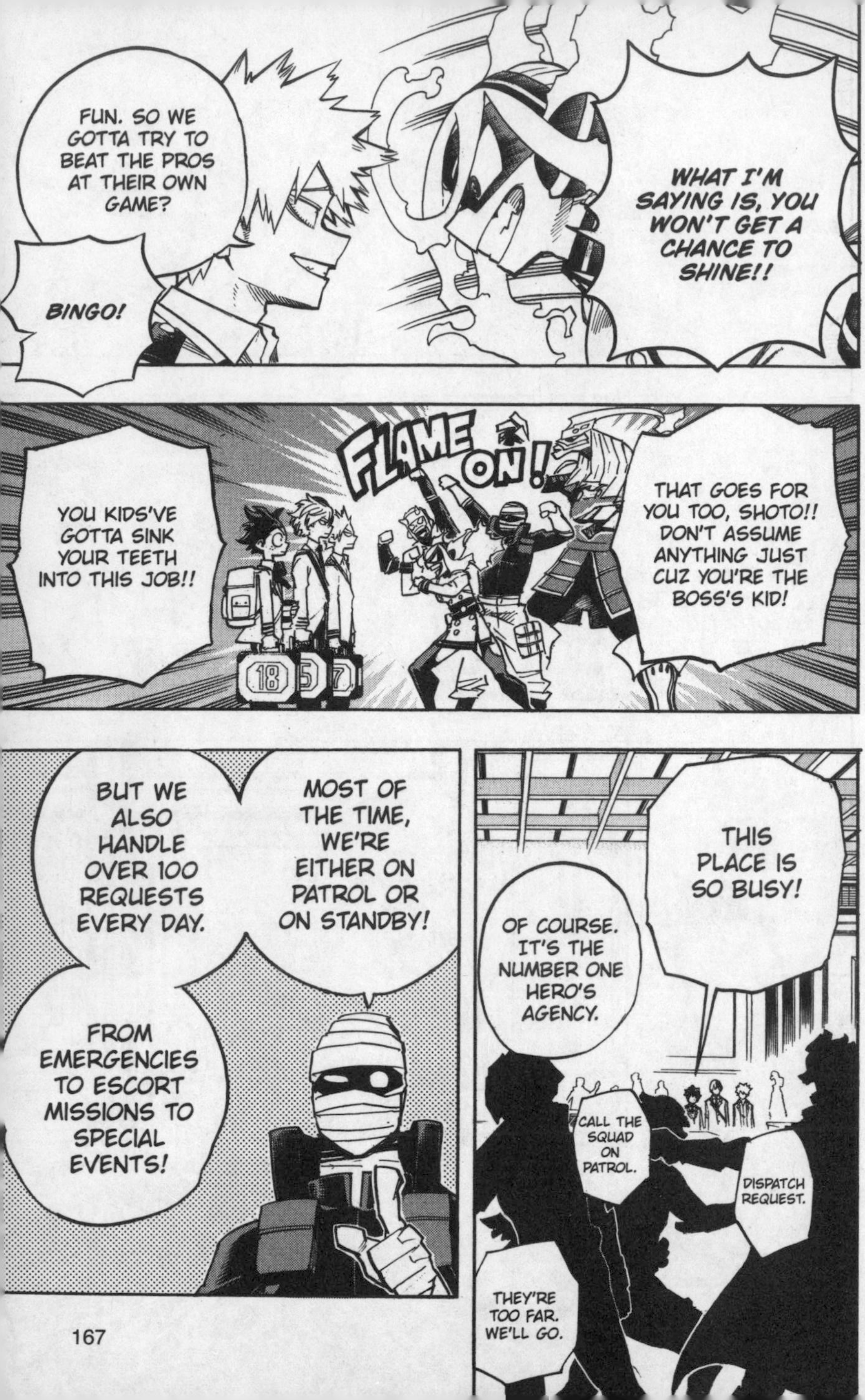
WHAT I'M SAYING IS, YOU WON'T GET A CHANCE TO SHINE!!
FUN. SO WE GOTTA TRY TO BEAT THE PROS AT THEIR OWN GAME?
BINGO!
THAT GOES FOR YOU TOO, SHOTO!! DON'T ASSUME ANYTHING JUST CUZ YOU'RE THE BOSS'S KID!
FLAME ON!
YOU KIDS'VE GOTTA SINK YOUR TEETH INTO THIS JOB!!
THIS PLACE IS SO BUSY!
OF COURSE. IT'S THE NUMBER ONE HERO'S AGENCY.
DISPATCH REQUEST.
CALL THE SQUAD ON PATROL.
THEY'RE TOO FAR. WE'LL GO.
MOST OF THE TIME, WE'RE EITHER ON PATROL OR ON STANDBY!
BUT WE ALSO HANDLE OVER 100 REQUESTS EVERY DAY.
FROM EMERGENCIES TO ESCORT MISSIONS TO SPECIAL EVENTS!

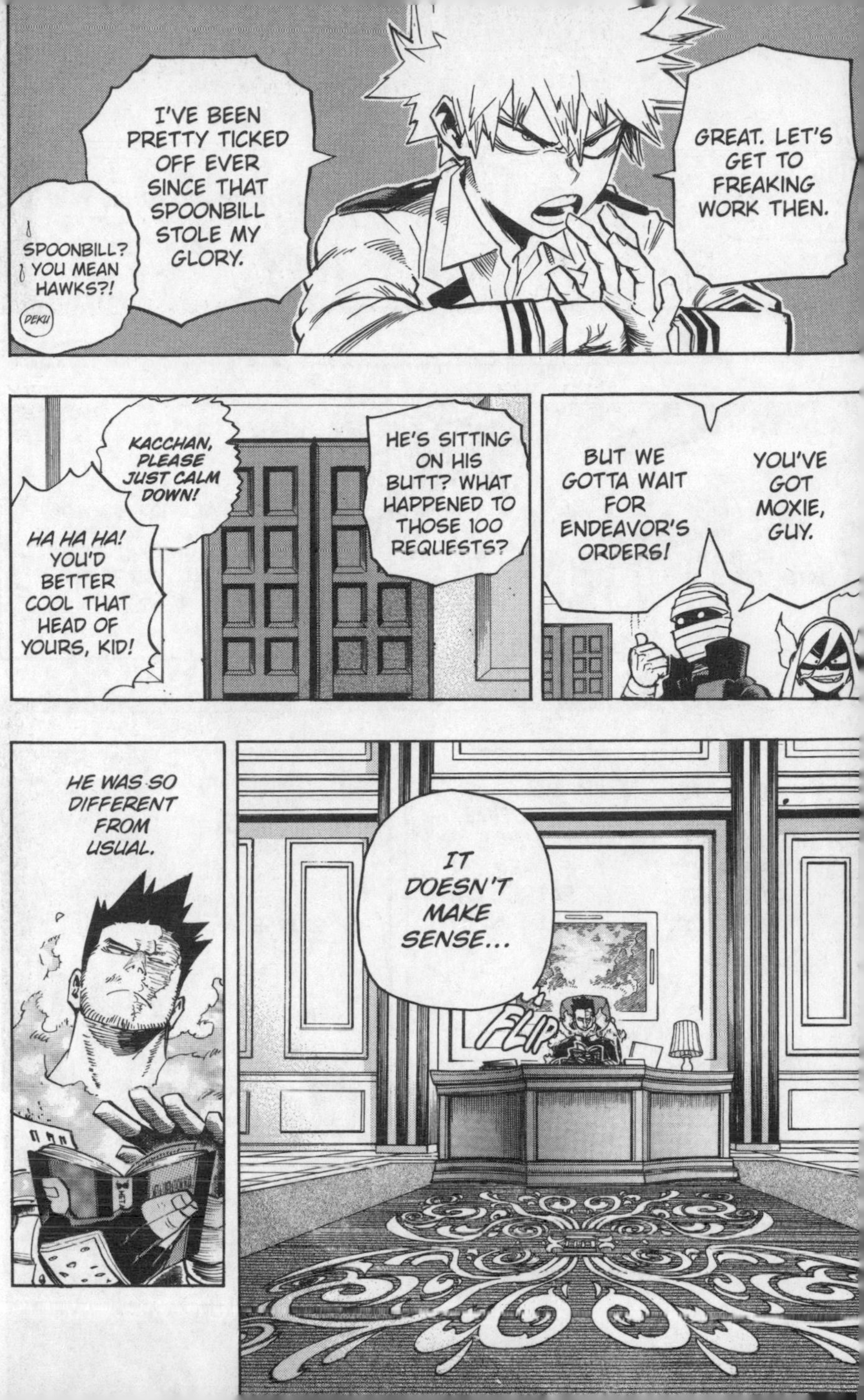
GREAT. LET'S GET TO FREAKING WORK THEN.
I'VE BEEN PRETTY TICKED OFF EVER SINCE THAT SPOONBILL STOLE MY GLORY.
SPOONBILL? YOU MEAN HAWKS?!
DEKU
YOU'VE GOT MOXIE, GUY.
BUT WE GOTTA WAIT FOR ENDEAVOR'S ORDERS!
HE'S SITTING ON HIS BUTT? WHAT HAPPENED TO THOSE 100 REQUESTS?
KACCHAN, PLEASE JUST CALM DOWN!
HA HA HA! YOU'D BETTER COOL THAT HEAD OF YOURS, KID!
IT DOESN'T MAKE SENSE...
FLIP
HE WAS SO DIFFERENT FROM USUAL.

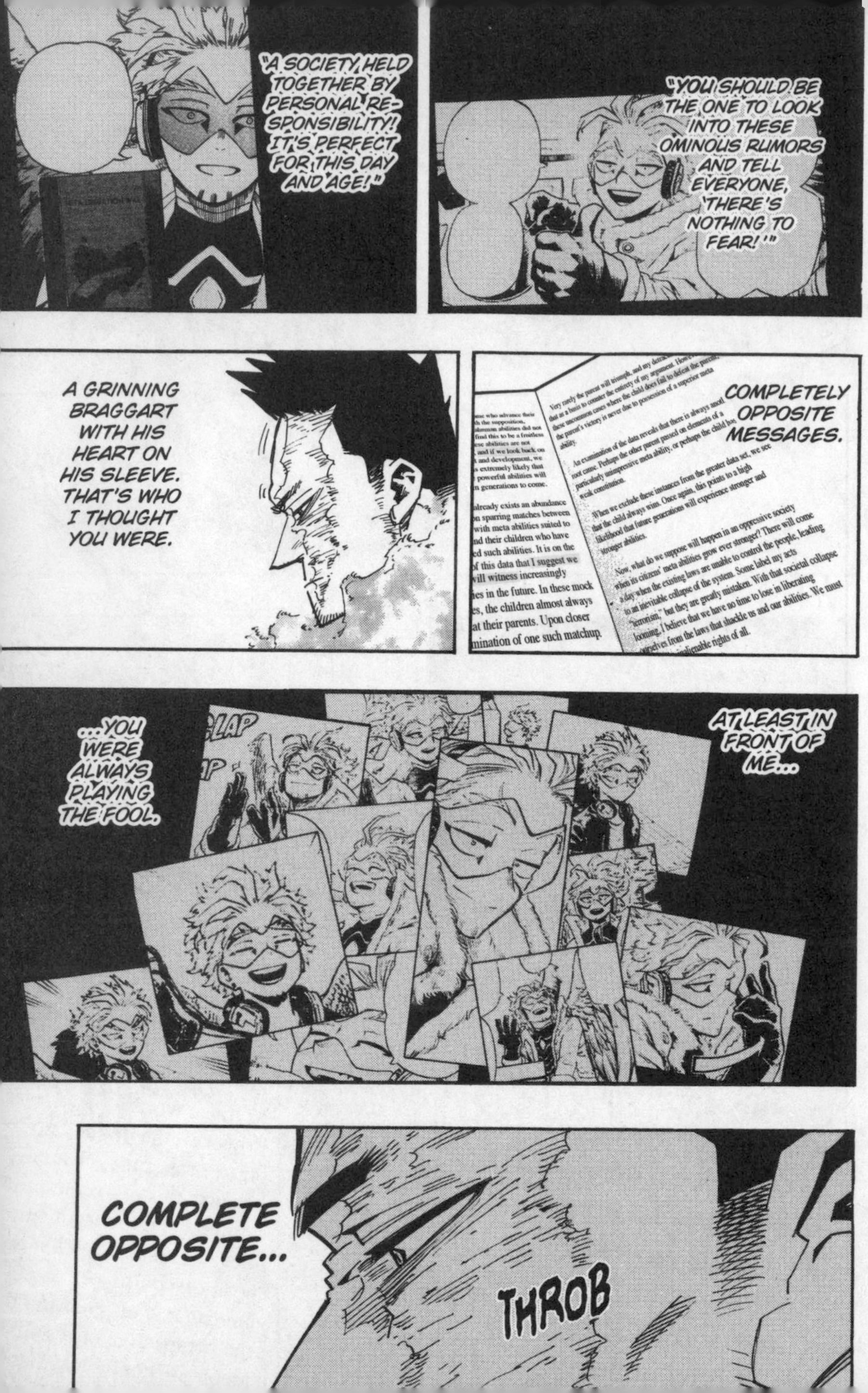
"YOU SHOULD BE THE ONE TO LOOK INTO THESE OMINOUS RUMORS AND TELL EVERYONE, 'THERE'S NOTHING TO FEAR!'"
"A SOCIETY HELD TOGETHER BY PERSONAL RE-SPONSIBILITY! IT'S PERFECT FOR THIS DAY AND AGE!"
COMPLETELY OPPOSITE MESSAGES.
Very rarely the parent will triumph, and my detra
that as a basis to counter the entirety of my argument. Howe
these uncommon cases where the child does fail to defeat the parent
the parent's victory is never due to possession of a superior meta
ability.
An examination of the data reveals that there is always anot
root cause. Perhaps the other parent passed on elements of a
particularly unimpressive meta ability, or perhaps the child has
weak constitution.
When we exclude these instances from the greater data set, we see
that the child always wins. Once again, this points to a high
likelihood that future generations will experience stronger and
stronger abilities.
Now, what do we suppose will happen in an oppressive society
when its citizens' meta abilities grow ever stronger? There will come
a day when the existing laws are unable to control the people, leading
to an inevitable collapse of the system. Some label my acts
"terrorism," but they are greatly mistaken. With that societal collapse
looming, I believe that we have no time to lose in liberating
ourselves from the laws that shackle us and our abilities. We must
inalienable rights of all.
already exists an abundance
on sparring matches between
with meta abilities suited to
nd their children who have
ed such abilities. It is on the
of this data that I suggest we
will witness increasingly
ies in the future. In these mock
es, the children almost always
at their parents. Upon closer
mination of one such matchup.
A GRINNING BRAGGART WITH HIS HEART ON HIS SLEEVE. THAT'S WHO I THOUGHT YOU WERE.
AT LEAST IN FRONT OF ME...
...YOU WERE ALWAYS PLAYING THE FOOL.
COMPLETE OPPOSITE...
THROB

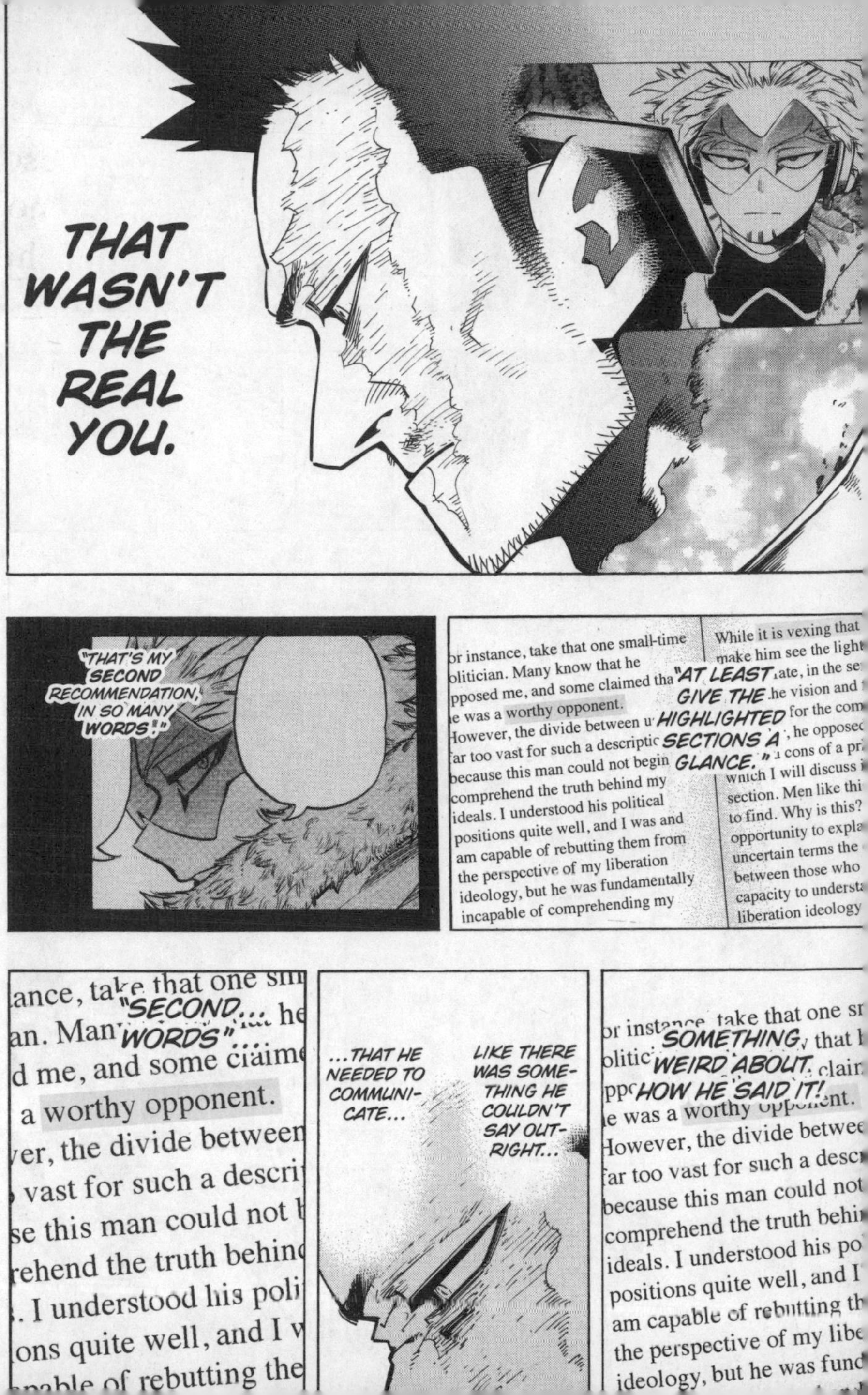
THAT WASN'T THE REAL YOU.
or instance, take that one small-time politician. Many know that he pposed me, and some claimed tha e was a worthy opponent. However, the divide between u far too vast for such a descriptic because this man could not begin comprehend the truth behind my ideals. I understood his political positions quite well, and I was and am capable of rebutting them from the perspective of my liberation ideology, but he was fundamentally incapable of comprehending my
While it is vexing that make him see the light
"AT LEAST GIVE THE HIGHLIGHTED SECTIONS A GLANCE."
"THAT'S MY SECOND RECOMMENDATION, IN SO MANY WORDS!"
SOMETHING WEIRD ABOUT HOW HE SAID IT!
LIKE THERE WAS SOMETHING HE COULDN'T SAY OUTRIGHT...
...THAT HE NEEDED TO COMMUNICATE...
"SECOND... WORDS"...

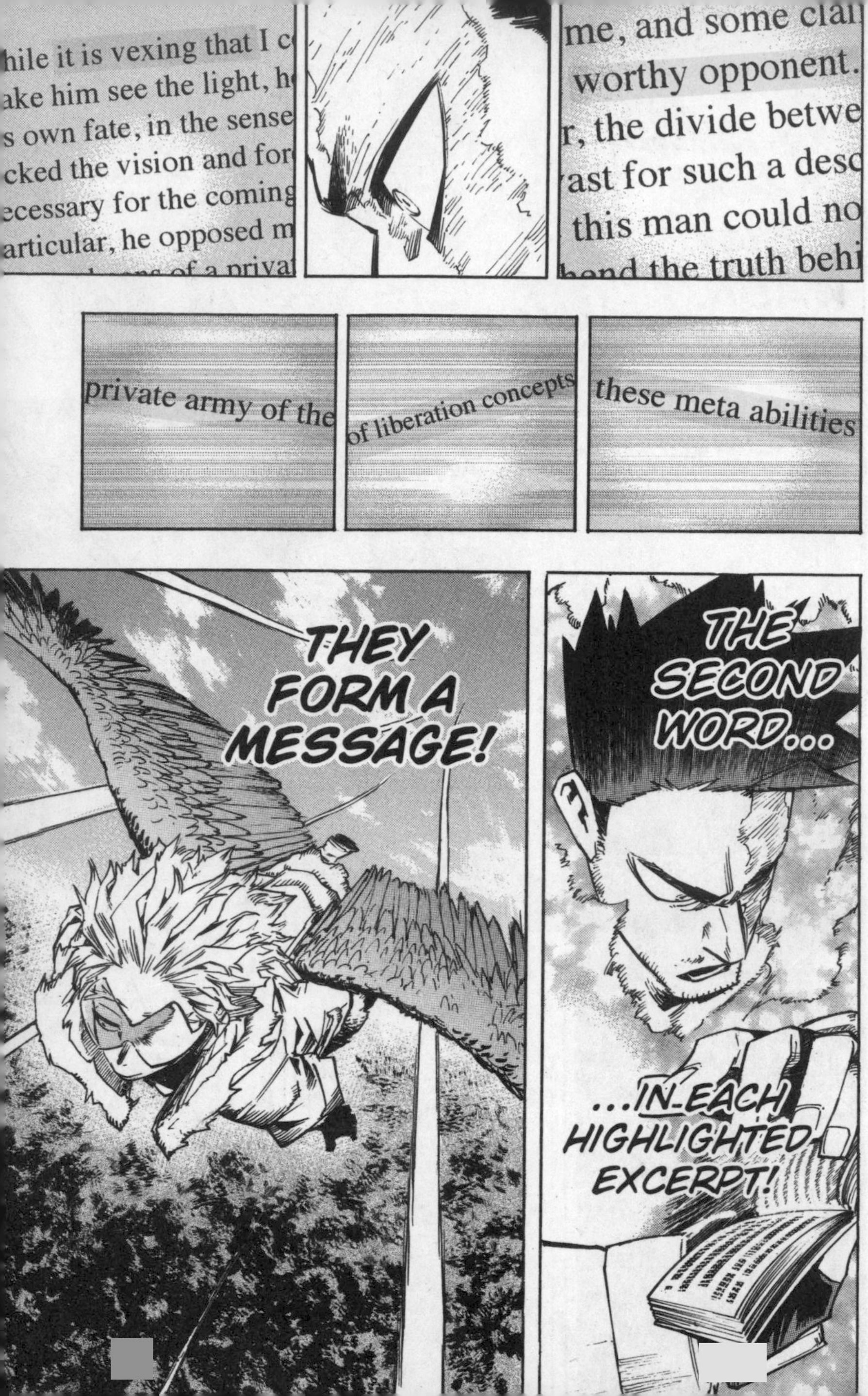

me, and some clai
worthy opponent.
r, the divide betwe
ast for such a desc
this man could no
hend the truth behi
hile it is vexing that I c
ake him see the light, h
s own fate, in the sense
cked the vision and for
ecessary for the coming
articular, he opposed m
these meta abilities
of liberation concepts
private army of the
THE SECOND WORD...
...IN EACH HIGHLIGHTED EXCERPT!
THEY FORM A MESSAGE!

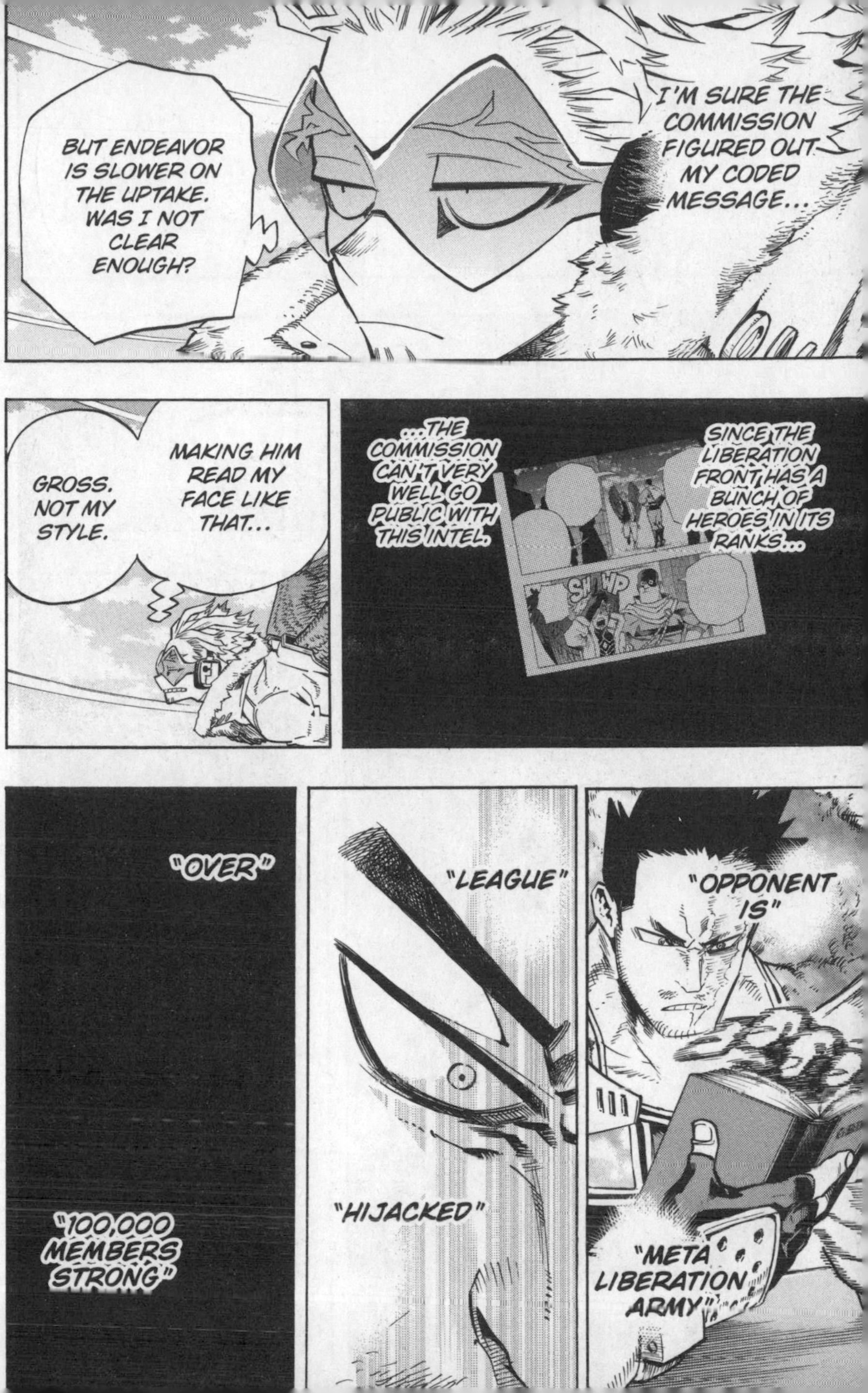
I'M SURE THE COMMISSION FIGURED OUT MY CODED MESSAGE...
BUT ENDEAVOR IS SLOWER ON THE UPTAKE. WAS I NOT CLEAR ENOUGH?
SINCE THE LIBERATION FRONT HAS A BUNCH OF HEROES IN ITS RANKS...
...THE COMMISSION CAN'T VERY WELL GO PUBLIC WITH THIS INTEL.
MAKING HIM READ MY FACE LIKE THAT...
GROSS. NOT MY STYLE.
"OPPONENT IS"
"META LIBERATION ARMY"
"LEAGUE"
"HIJACKED"
"OVER"
"100,000 MEMBERS STRONG"

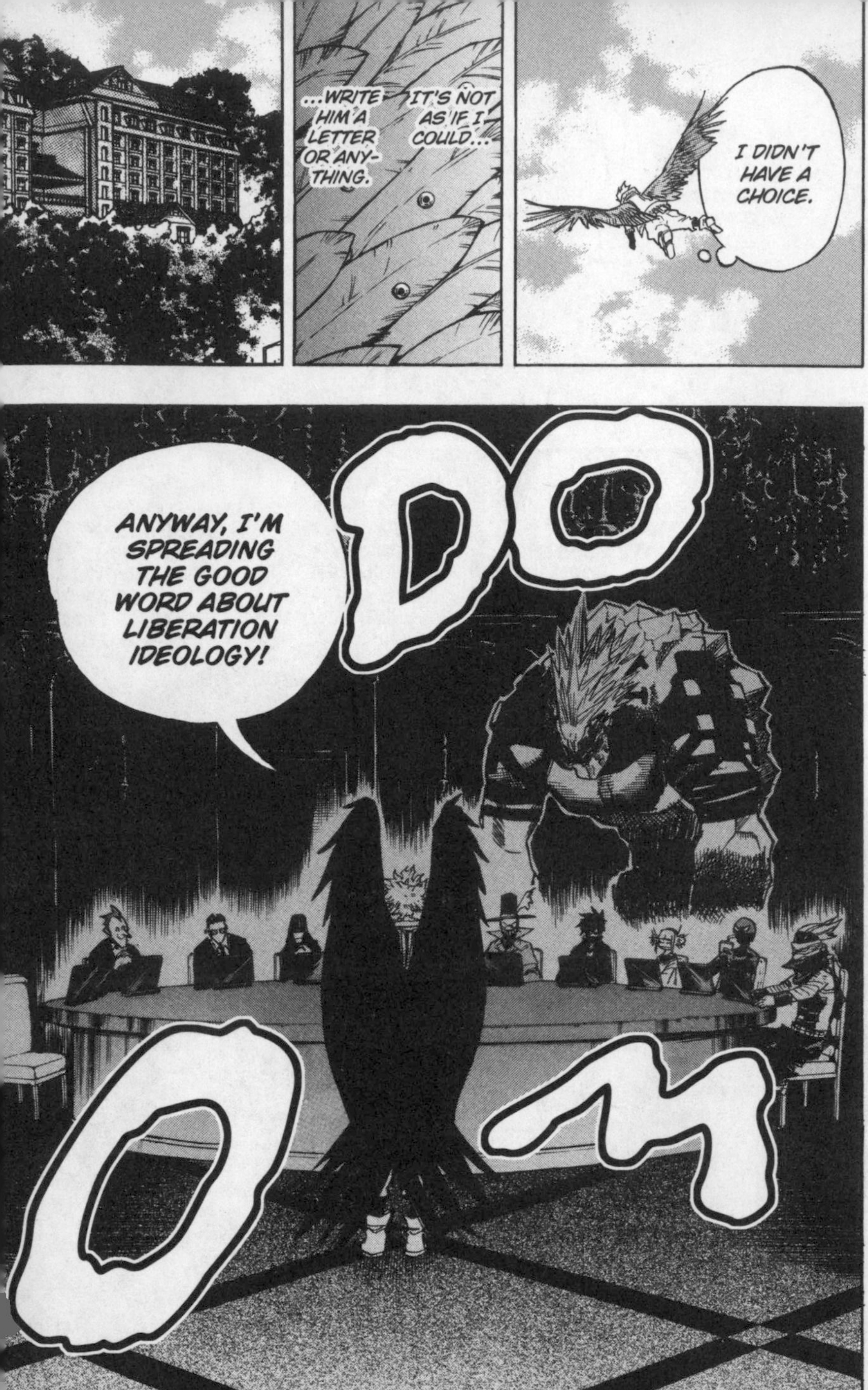
I DIDN'T HAVE A CHOICE.
IT'S NOT AS IF I COULD...
...WRITE HIM A LETTER OR ANYTHING.
ANYWAY, I'M SPREADING THE GOOD WORD ABOUT LIBERATION IDEOLOGY!
DOOM

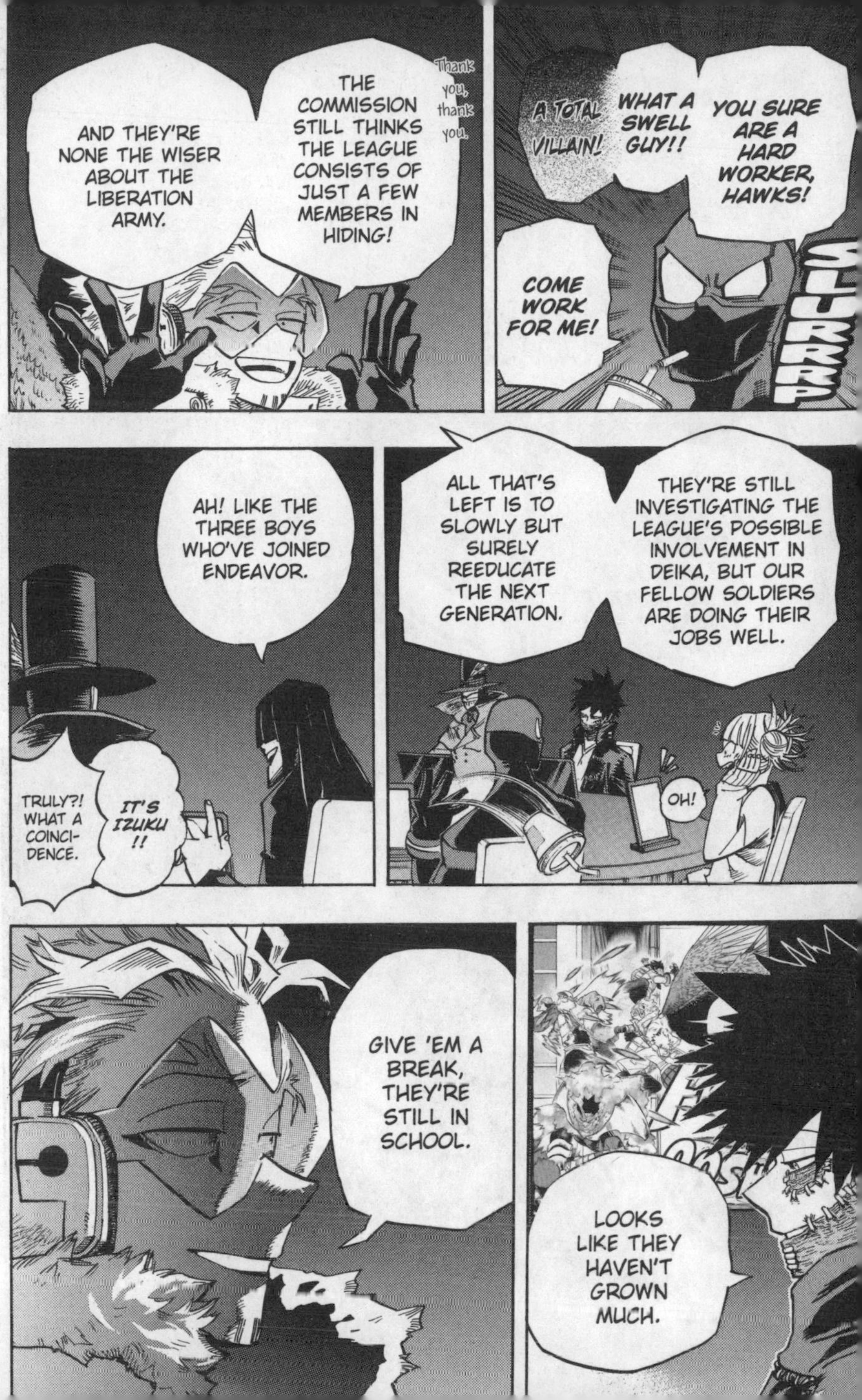
YOU SURE ARE A HARD WORKER, HAWKS!
WHAT A SWELL GUY!!
A TOTAL VILLAIN!
COME WORK FOR ME!
SLURRP
THE COMMISSION STILL THINKS THE LEAGUE CONSISTS OF JUST A FEW MEMBERS IN HIDING!
Thank you, thank you.
AND THEY'RE NONE THE WISER ABOUT THE LIBERATION ARMY.
THEY'RE STILL INVESTIGATING THE LEAGUE'S POSSIBLE INVOLVEMENT IN DEIKA, BUT OUR FELLOW SOLDIERS ARE DOING THEIR JOBS WELL.
ALL THAT'S LEFT IS TO SLOWLY BUT SURELY REEDUCATE THE NEXT GENERATION.
OH!
AH! LIKE THE THREE BOYS WHO'VE JOINED ENDEAVOR.
IT'S IZUKU!!
TRULY?! WHAT A COINCIDENCE.
LOOKS LIKE THEY HAVEN'T GROWN MUCH.
GIVE 'EM A BREAK, THEY'RE STILL IN SCHOOL.

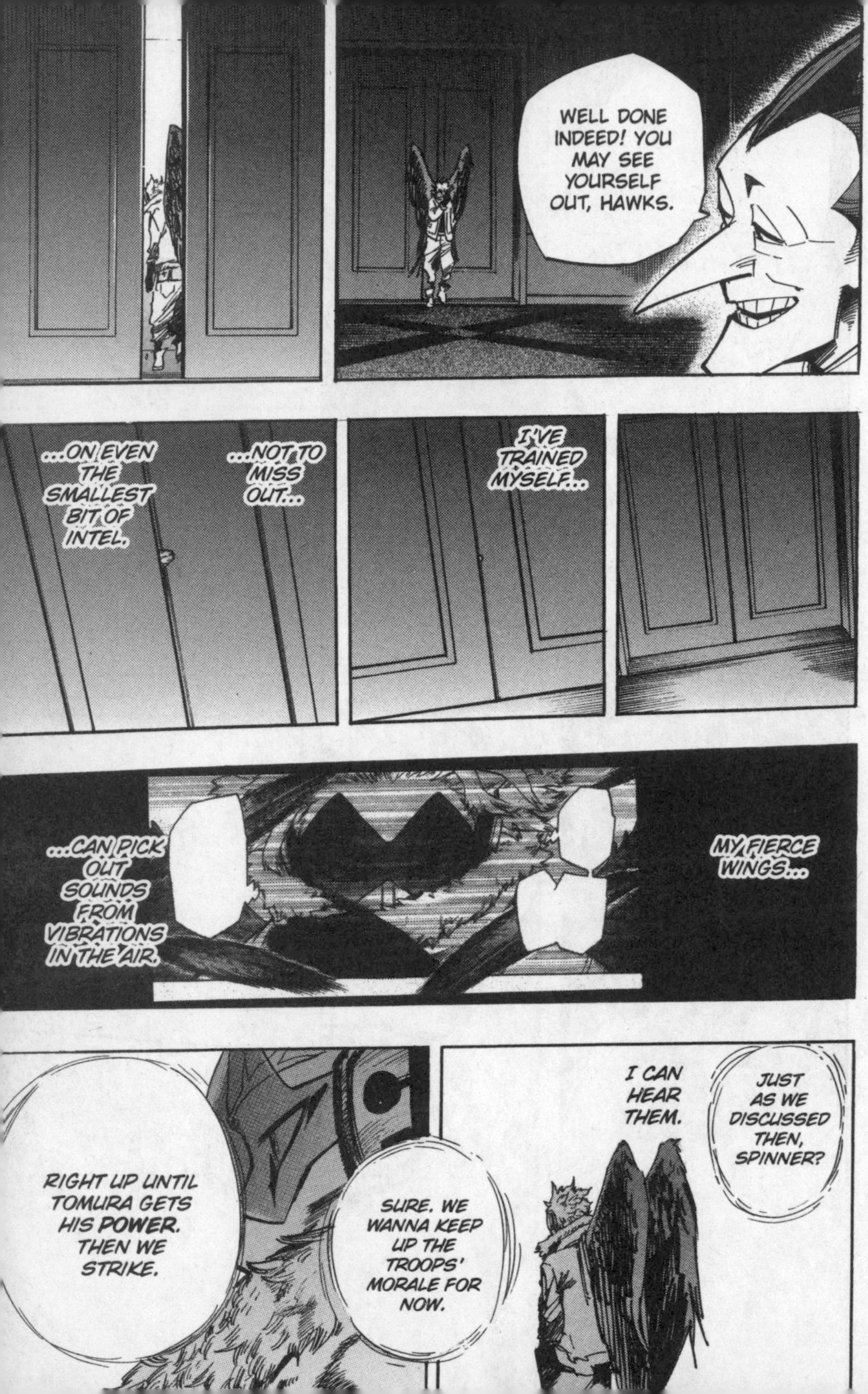
WELL DONE INDEED! YOU MAY SEE YOURSELF OUT, HAWKS.
I'VE TRAINED MYSELF...
...NOT TO MISS OUT...
...ON EVEN THE SMALLEST BIT OF INTEL.
MY FIERCE WINGS...
...CAN PICK OUT SOUNDS FROM VIBRATIONS IN THE AIR.
JUST AS WE DISCUSSED THEN, SPINNER?
I CAN HEAR THEM.
SURE. WE WANNA KEEP UP THE TROOPS' MORALE FOR NOW.
RIGHT UP UNTIL TOMURA GETS HIS POWER. THEN WE STRIKE.

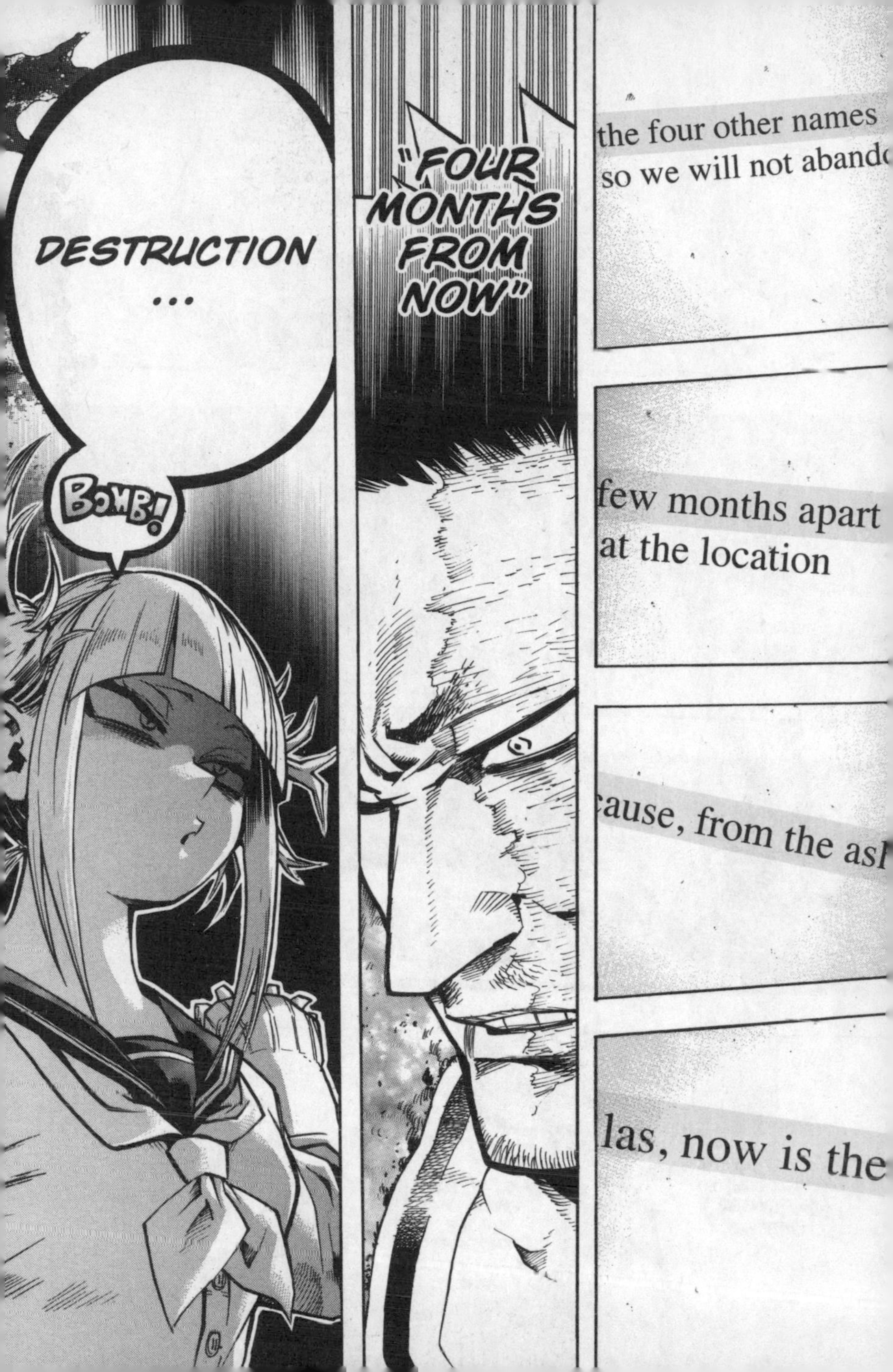

the four other names
so we will not aband
few months apart
at the location
ause, from the as
las, now is the
"FOUR MONTHS FROM NOW"
DESTRUCTION ...
BOMB!

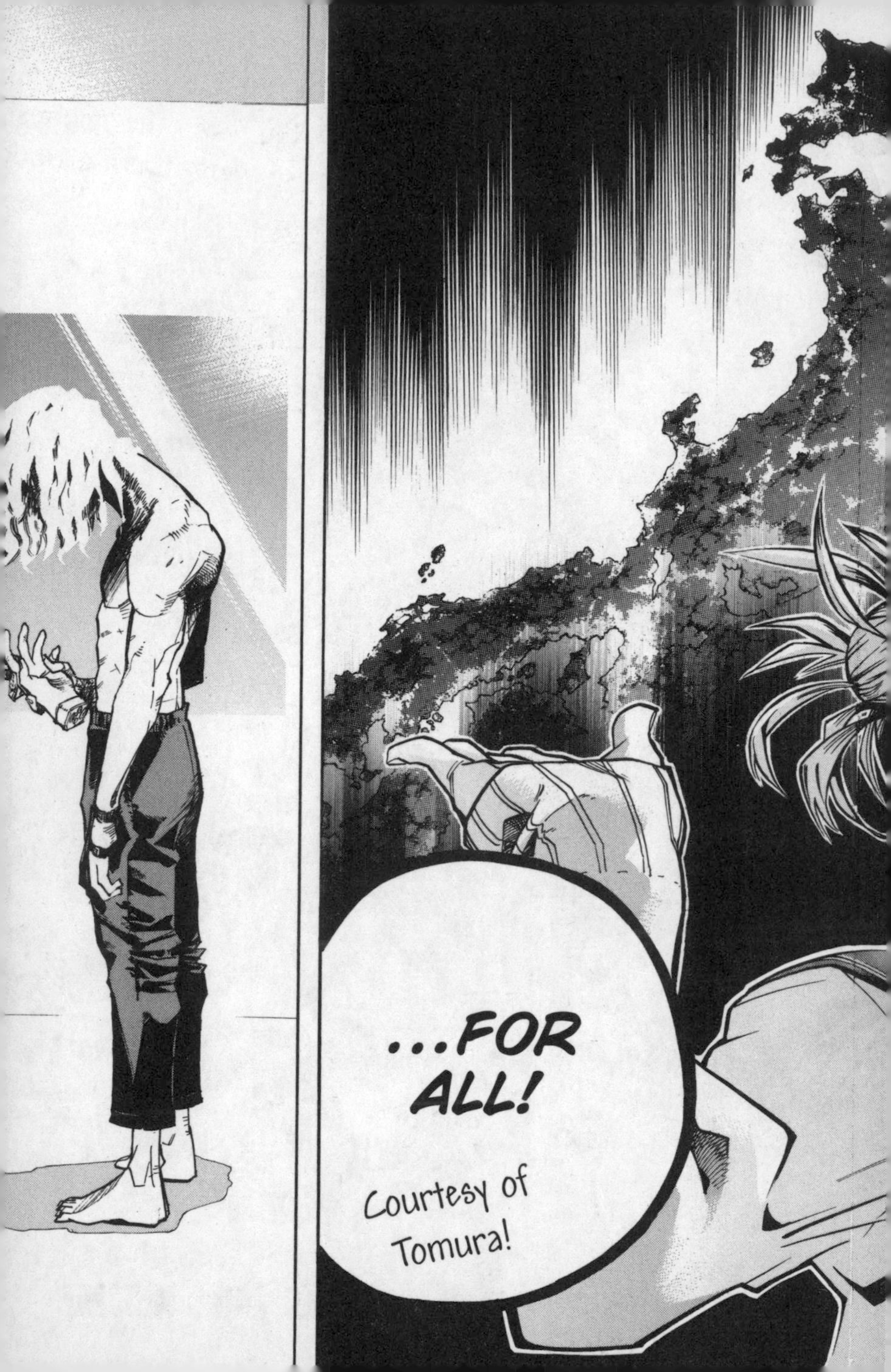
...FOR ALL!
Courtesy of Tomura!

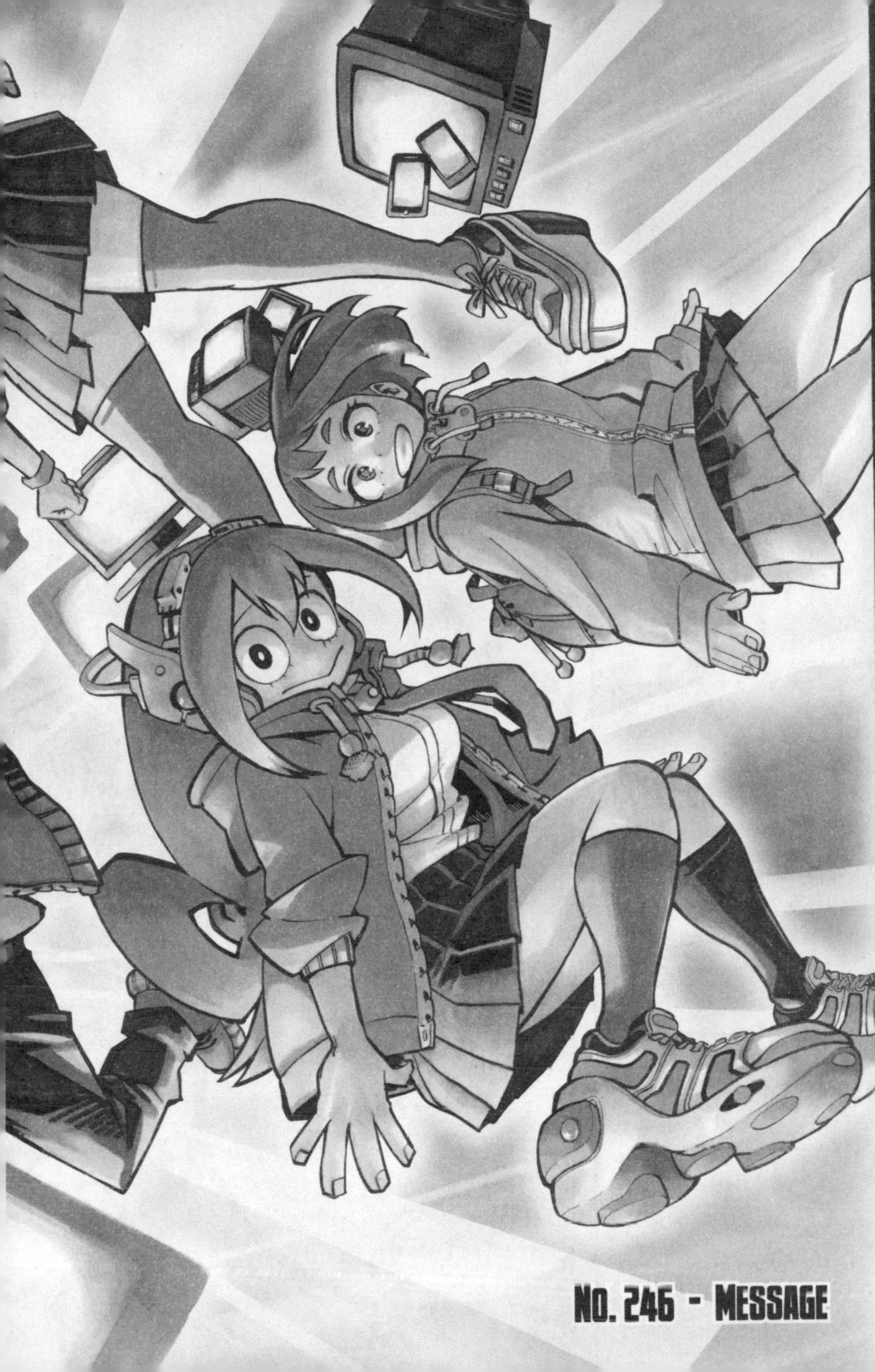

NO. 246 - MESSAGE

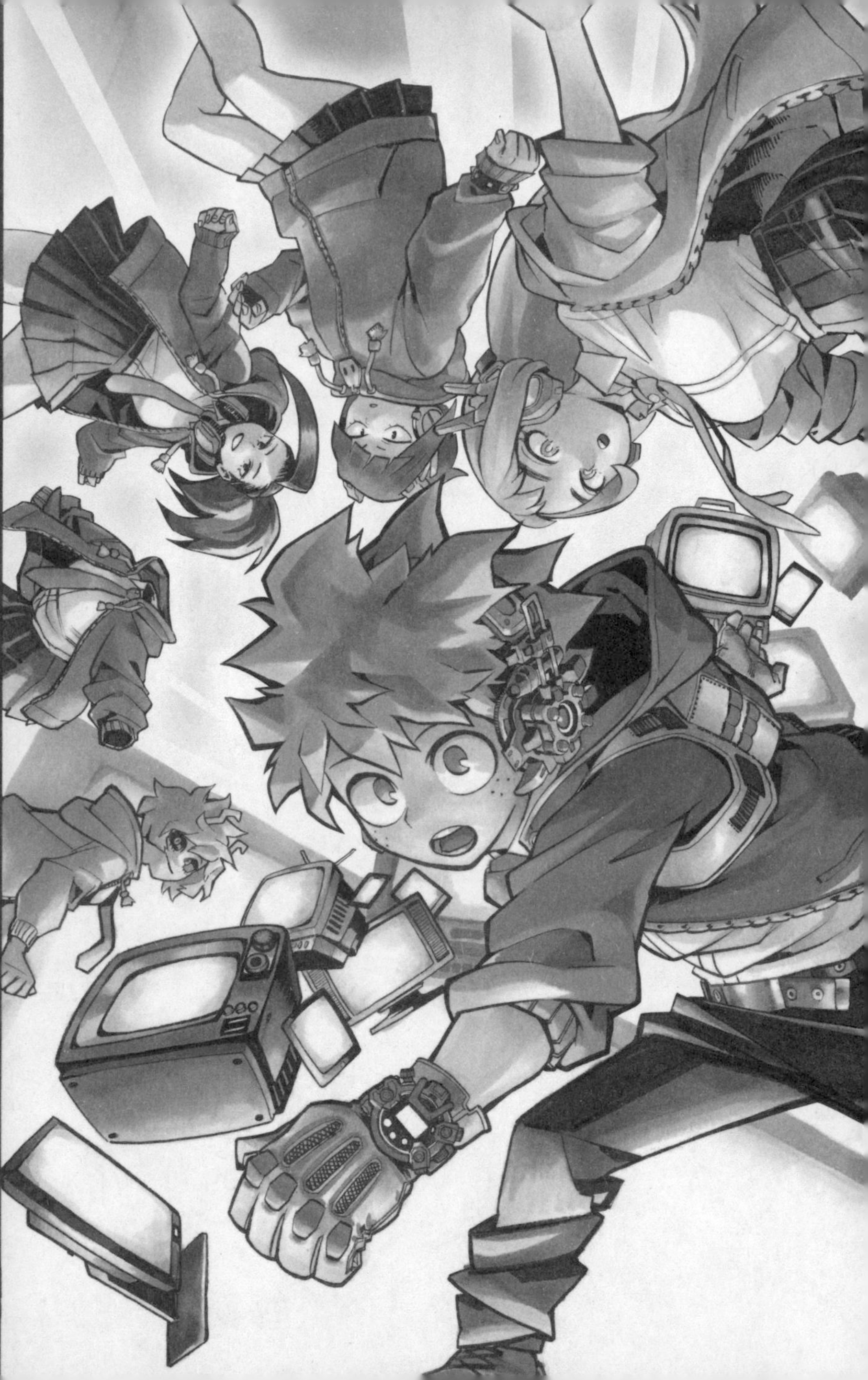

MY HERO ACADEMIA

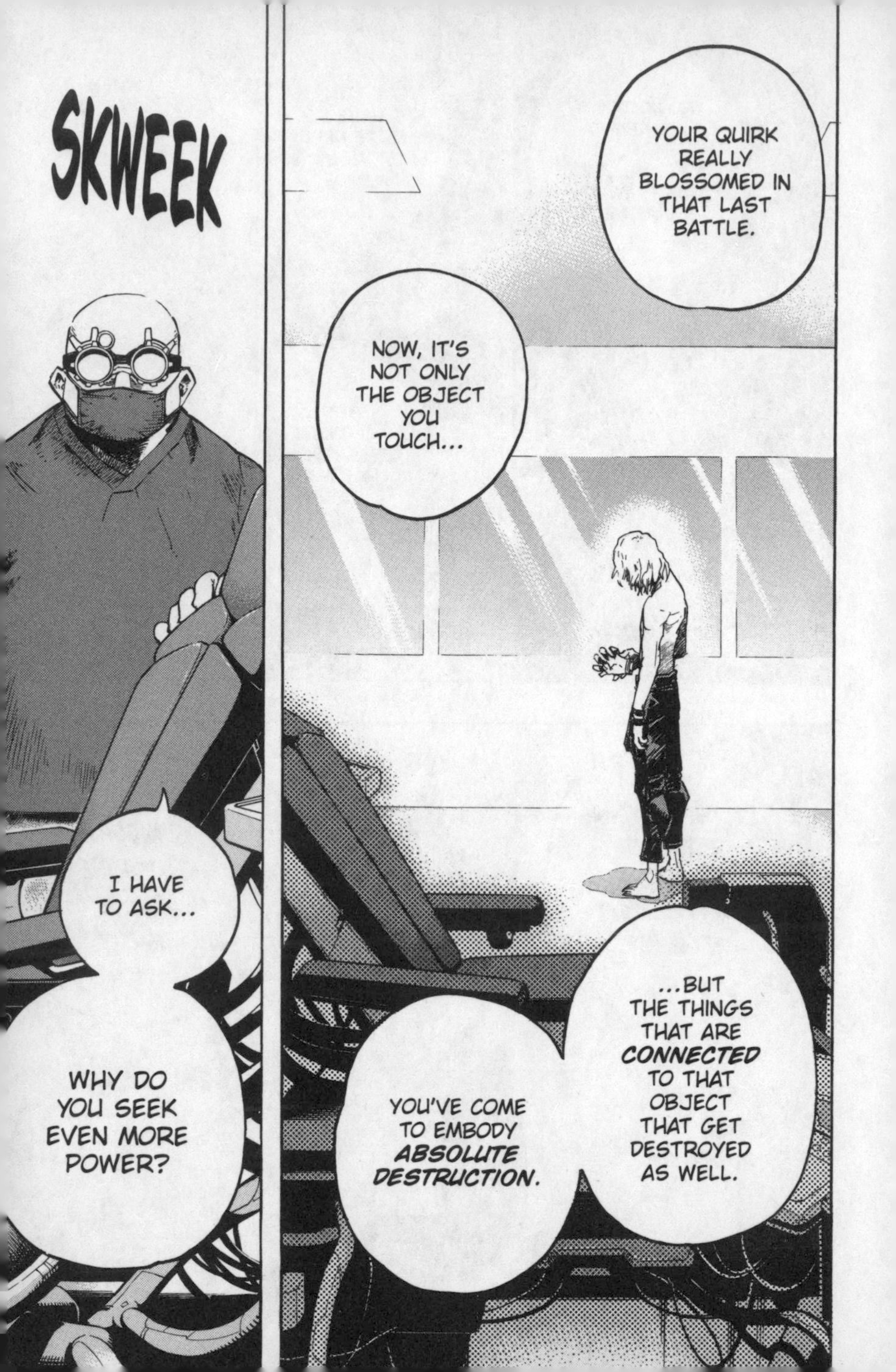
YOUR QUIRK REALLY BLOSSOMED IN THAT LAST BATTLE.
NOW, IT'S NOT ONLY THE OBJECT YOU TOUCH...
...BUT THE THINGS THAT ARE *CONNECTED* TO THAT OBJECT THAT GET DESTROYED AS WELL.
YOU'VE COME TO EMBODY *ABSOLUTE DESTRUCTION*.
SKWEEK
I HAVE TO ASK...
WHY DO YOU SEEK EVEN MORE POWER?

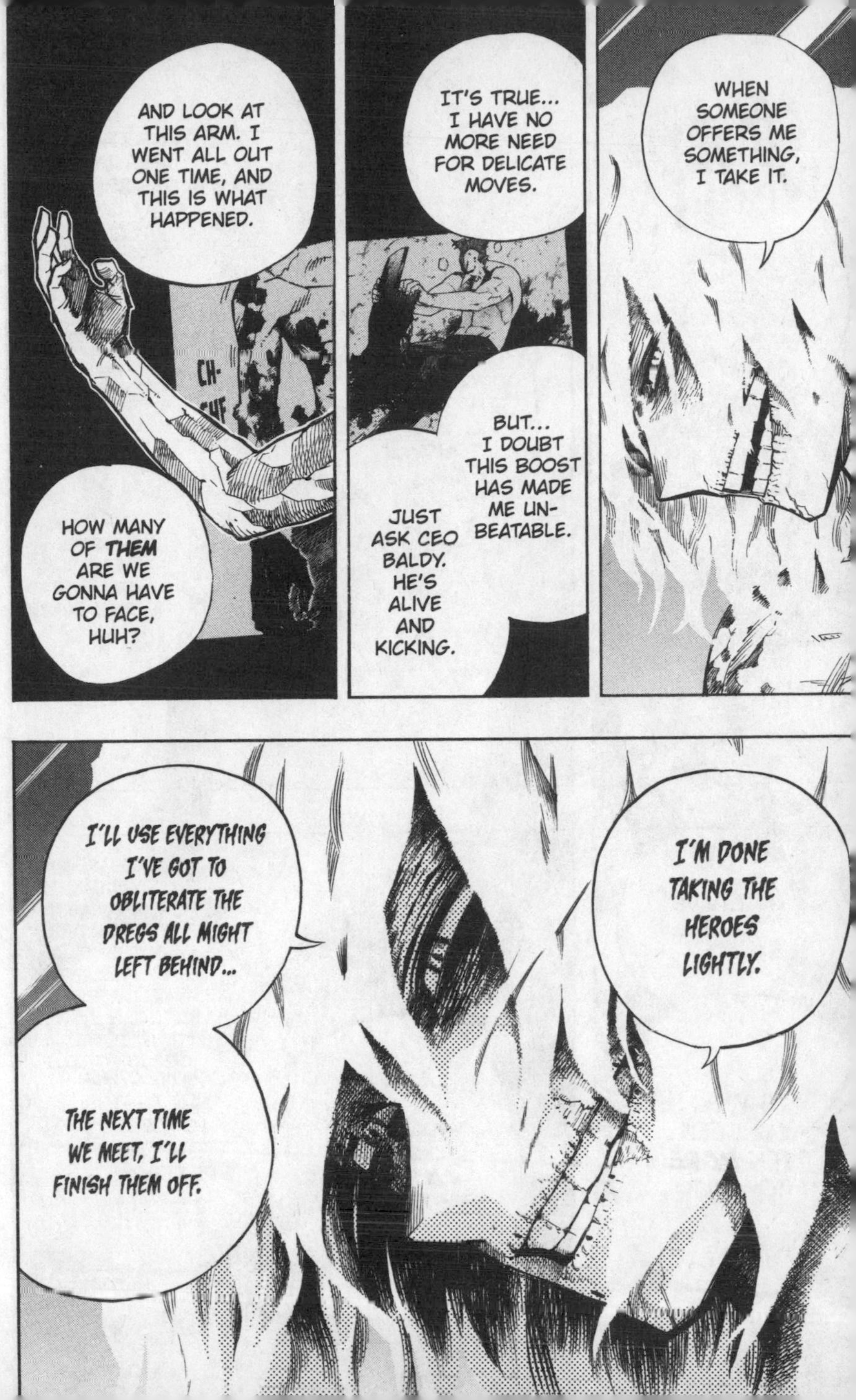
WHEN SOMEONE OFFERS ME SOMETHING, I TAKE IT.
IT'S TRUE... I HAVE NO MORE NEED FOR DELICATE MOVES.
BUT... I DOUBT THIS BOOST HAS MADE ME UN-BEATABLE.
JUST ASK CEO BALDY. HE'S ALIVE AND KICKING.
AND LOOK AT THIS ARM. I WENT ALL OUT ONE TIME, AND THIS IS WHAT HAPPENED.
HOW MANY OF THEM ARE WE GONNA HAVE TO FACE, HUH?
I'M DONE TAKING THE HEROES LIGHTLY.
I'LL USE EVERYTHING I'VE GOT TO OBLITERATE THE DREGS ALL MIGHT LEFT BEHIND...
THE NEXT TIME WE MEET, I'LL FINISH THEM OFF.

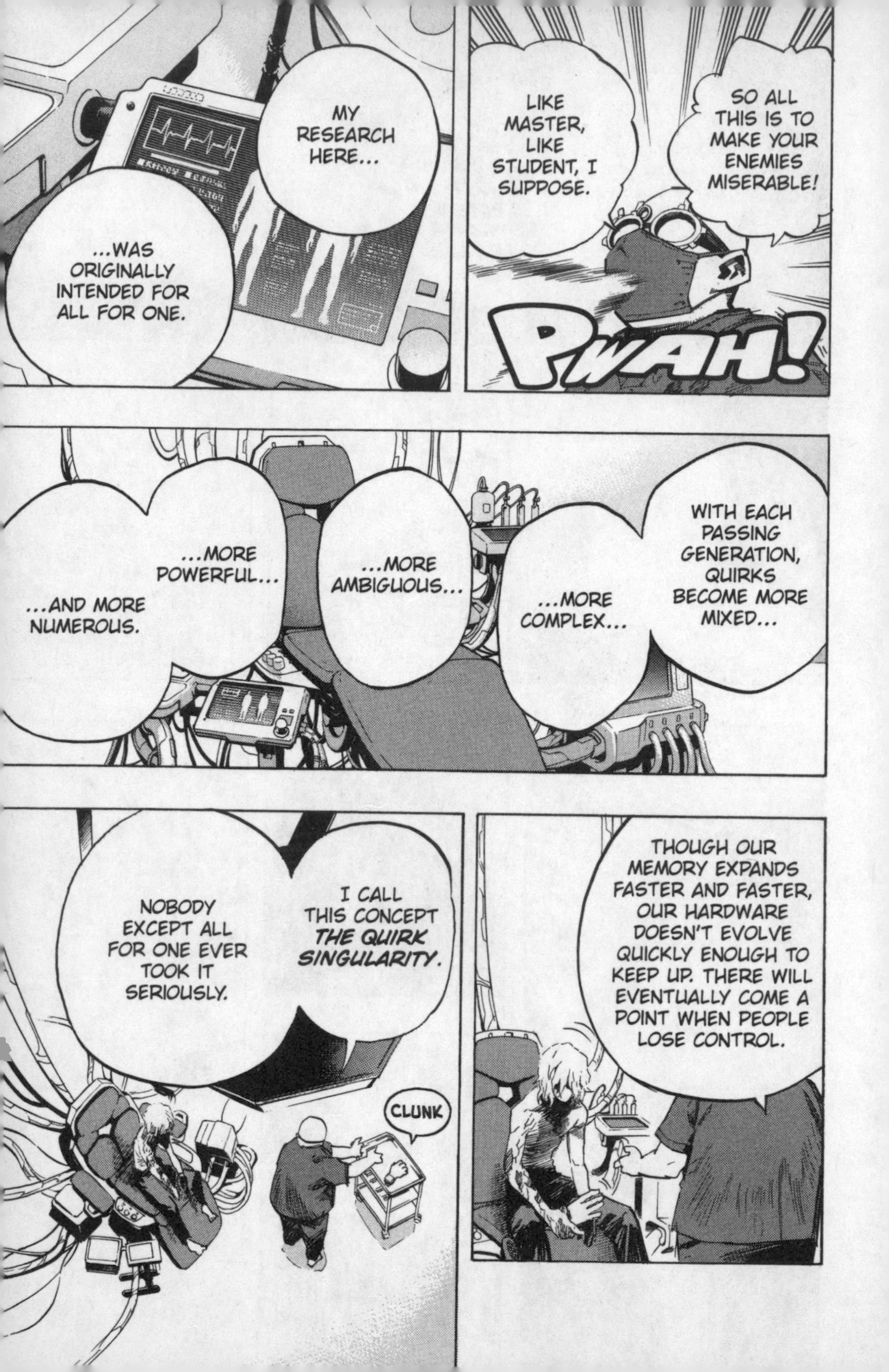
SO ALL THIS IS TO MAKE YOUR ENEMIES MISERABLE!
LIKE MASTER, LIKE STUDENT, I SUPPOSE.
PWAH!
MY RESEARCH HERE...
...WAS ORIGINALLY INTENDED FOR ALL FOR ONE.
WITH EACH PASSING GENERATION, QUIRKS BECOME MORE MIXED...
...MORE COMPLEX...
...MORE AMBIGUOUS...
...MORE POWERFUL...
...AND MORE NUMEROUS.
THOUGH OUR MEMORY EXPANDS FASTER AND FASTER, OUR HARDWARE DOESN'T EVOLVE QUICKLY ENOUGH TO KEEP UP. THERE WILL EVENTUALLY COME A POINT WHEN PEOPLE LOSE CONTROL.
I CALL THIS CONCEPT *THE QUIRK SINGULARITY*.
NOBODY EXCEPT ALL FOR ONE EVER TOOK IT SERIOUSLY.
CLUNK

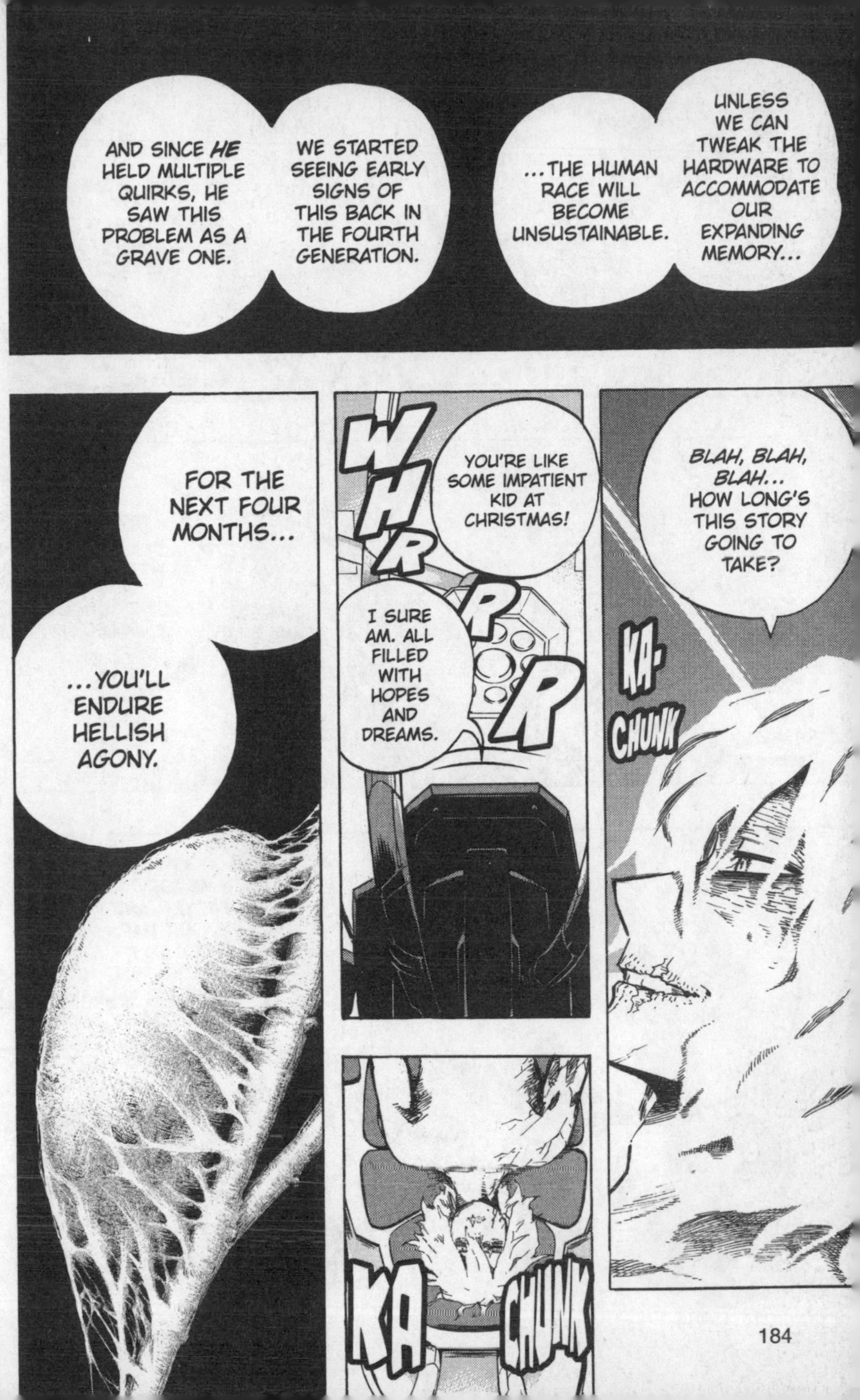
UNLESS WE CAN TWEAK THE HARDWARE TO ACCOMMODATE OUR EXPANDING MEMORY...
...THE HUMAN RACE WILL BECOME UNSUSTAINABLE.
WE STARTED SEEING EARLY SIGNS OF THIS BACK IN THE FOURTH GENERATION.
AND SINCE *HE* HELD MULTIPLE QUIRKS, HE SAW THIS PROBLEM AS A GRAVE ONE.
BLAH, BLAH, BLAH... HOW LONG'S THIS STORY GOING TO TAKE?
KA-CHUNK
WHRRR
YOU'RE LIKE SOME IMPATIENT KID AT CHRISTMAS!
I SURE AM. ALL FILLED WITH HOPES AND DREAMS.
KA CHUNK
FOR THE NEXT FOUR MONTHS...
...YOU'LL ENDURE HELLISH AGONY.

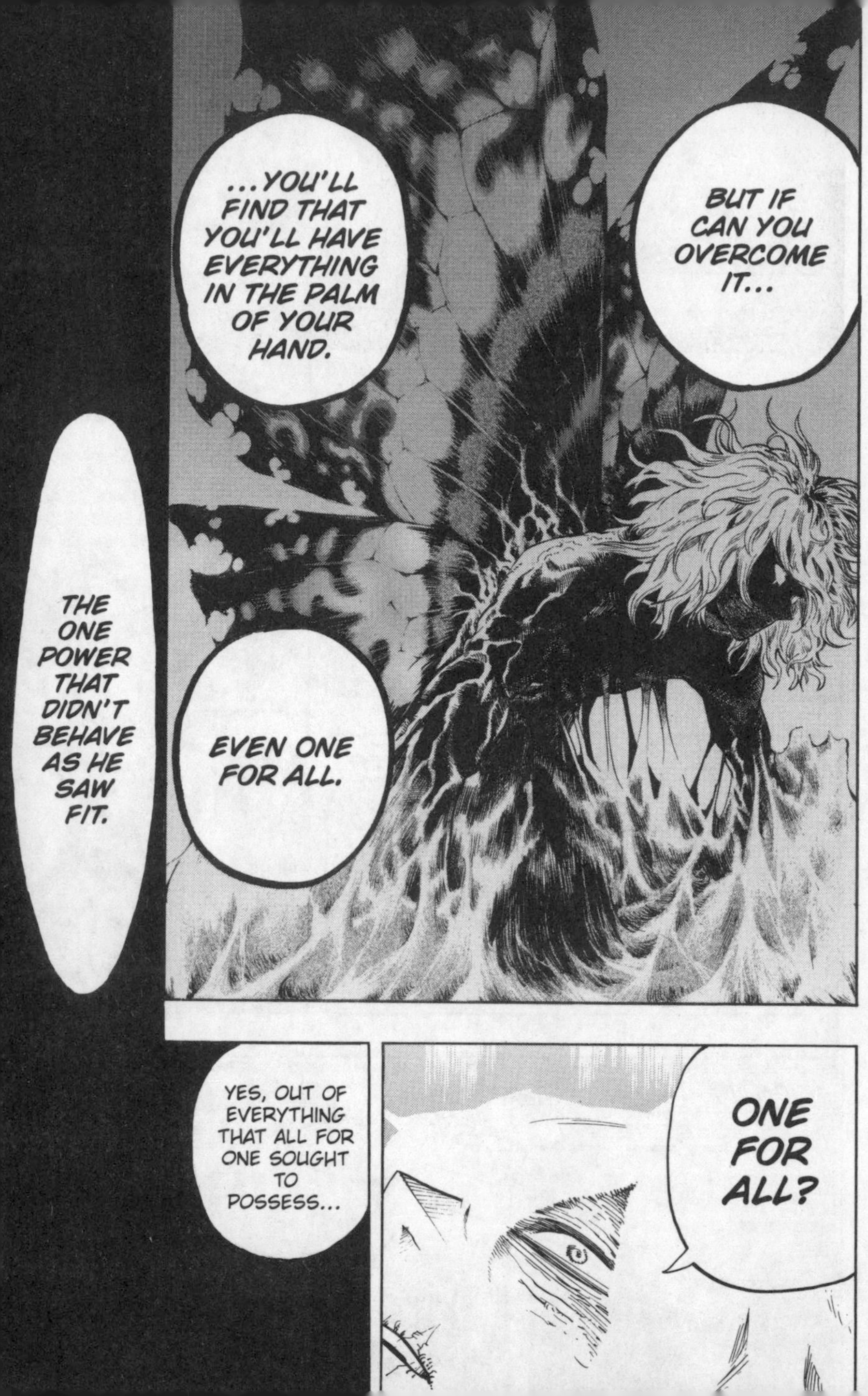
BUT IF CAN YOU OVERCOME IT...
...YOU'LL FIND THAT YOU'LL HAVE EVERYTHING IN THE PALM OF YOUR HAND.
EVEN ONE FOR ALL.
ONE FOR ALL?
YES, OUT OF EVERYTHING THAT ALL FOR ONE SOUGHT TO POSSESS...
THE ONE POWER THAT DIDN'T BEHAVE AS HE SAW FIT.

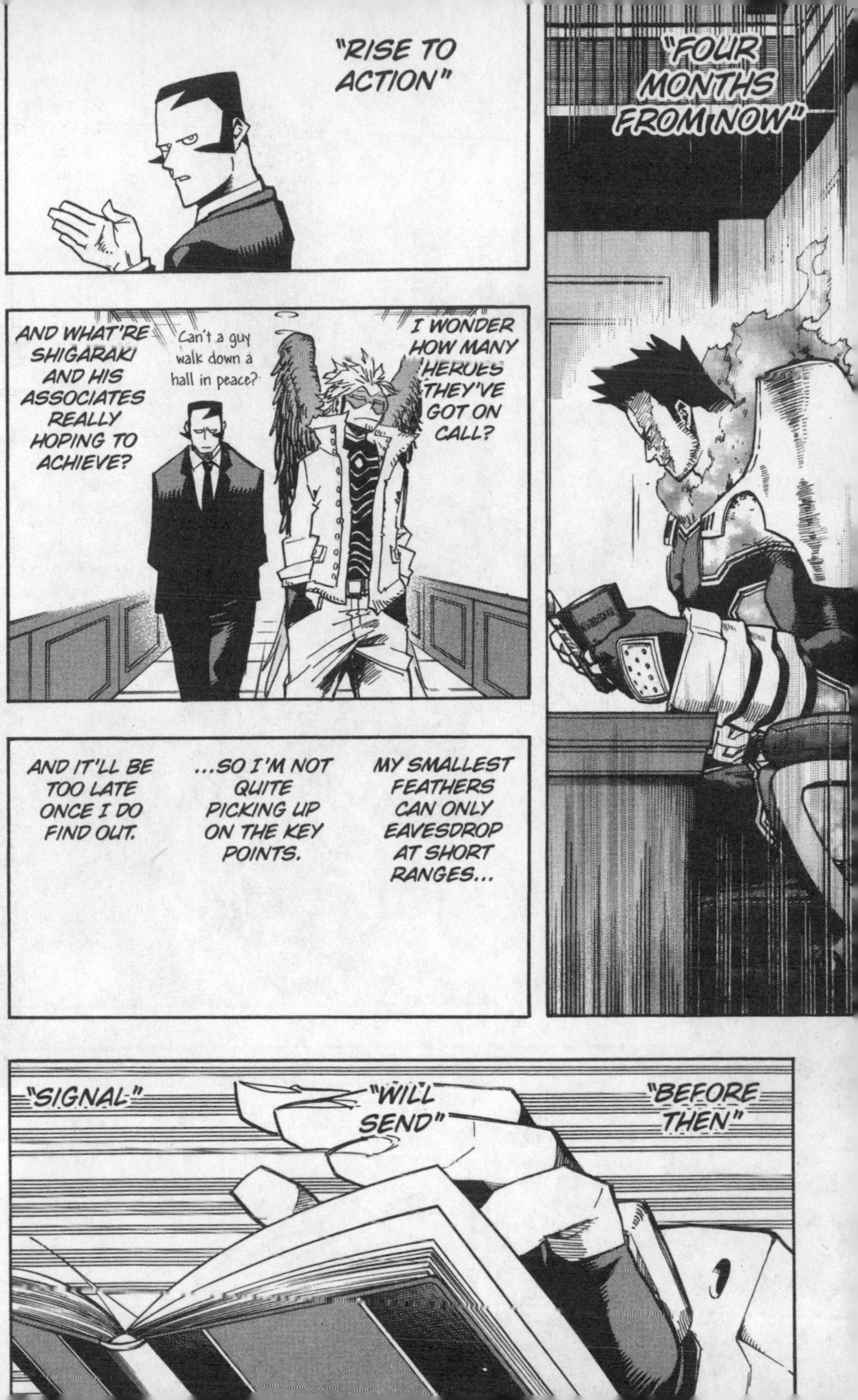
"FOUR MONTHS FROM NOW"
"RISE TO ACTION"
I WONDER HOW MANY HEROES THEY'VE GOT ON CALL?
Can't a guy walk down a hall in peace?
AND WHAT'RE SHIGARAKI AND HIS ASSOCIATES REALLY HOPING TO ACHIEVE?
MY SMALLEST FEATHERS CAN ONLY EAVESDROP AT SHORT RANGES...
...SO I'M NOT QUITE PICKING UP ON THE KEY POINTS.
AND IT'LL BE TOO LATE ONCE I DO FIND OUT.
"BEFORE THEN"
"WILL SEND"
"SIGNAL"

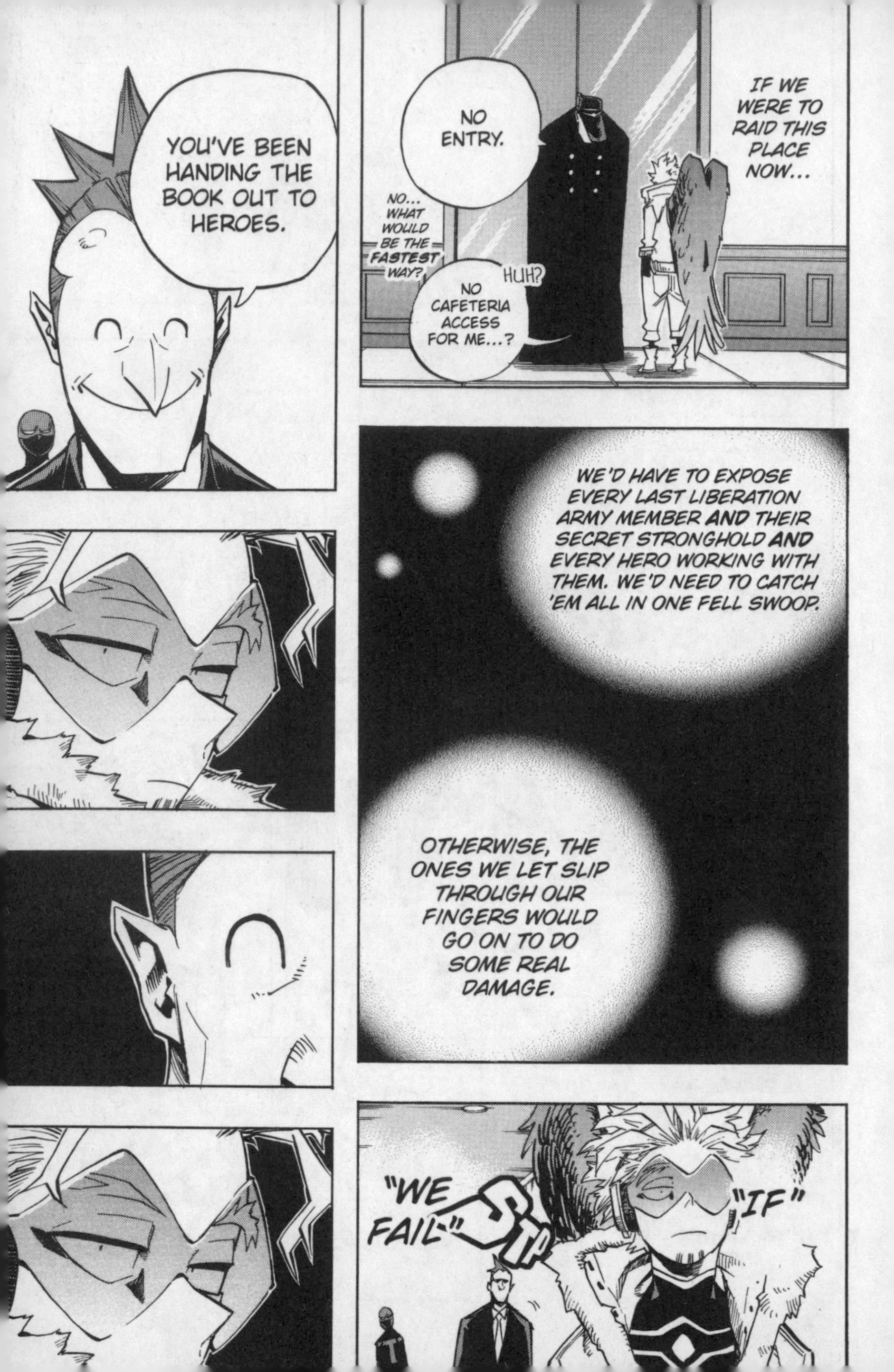
IF WE WERE TO RAID THIS PLACE NOW...
NO ENTRY.
HUH?
NO CAFETERIA ACCESS FOR ME...?
NO... WHAT WOULD BE THE FASTEST WAY?
YOU'VE BEEN HANDING THE BOOK OUT TO HEROES.
WE'D HAVE TO EXPOSE EVERY LAST LIBERATION ARMY MEMBER AND THEIR SECRET STRONGHOLD AND EVERY HERO WORKING WITH THEM. WE'D NEED TO CATCH 'EM ALL IN ONE FELL SWOOP.
OTHERWISE, THE ONES WE LET SLIP THROUGH OUR FINGERS WOULD GO ON TO DO SOME REAL DAMAGE.
"IF"
STP
"WE FAIL"

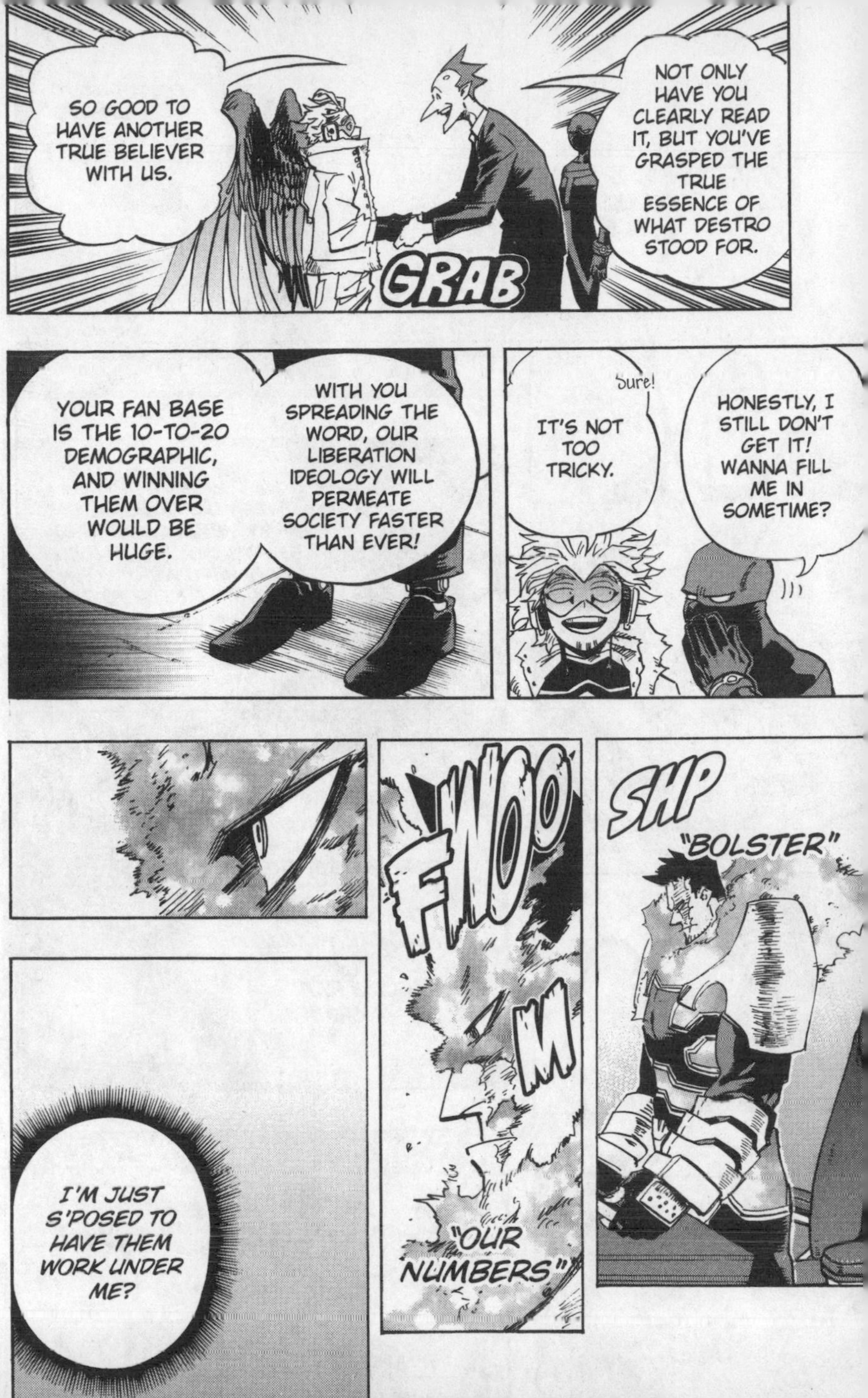
NOT ONLY HAVE YOU CLEARLY READ IT, BUT YOU'VE GRASPED THE TRUE ESSENCE OF WHAT DESTRO STOOD FOR.
SO GOOD TO HAVE ANOTHER TRUE BELIEVER WITH US.
GRAB
HONESTLY, I STILL DON'T GET IT! WANNA FILL ME IN SOMETIME?
Sure!
IT'S NOT TOO TRICKY.
YOUR FAN BASE IS THE 10-TO-20 DEMOGRAPHIC, AND WINNING THEM OVER WOULD BE HUGE.
WITH YOU SPREADING THE WORD, OUR LIBERATION IDEOLOGY WILL PERMEATE SOCIETY FASTER THAN EVER!
SHP
"BOLSTER"
FWOOM
"OUR NUMBERS"
I'M JUST S'POSED TO HAVE THEM WORK UNDER ME?

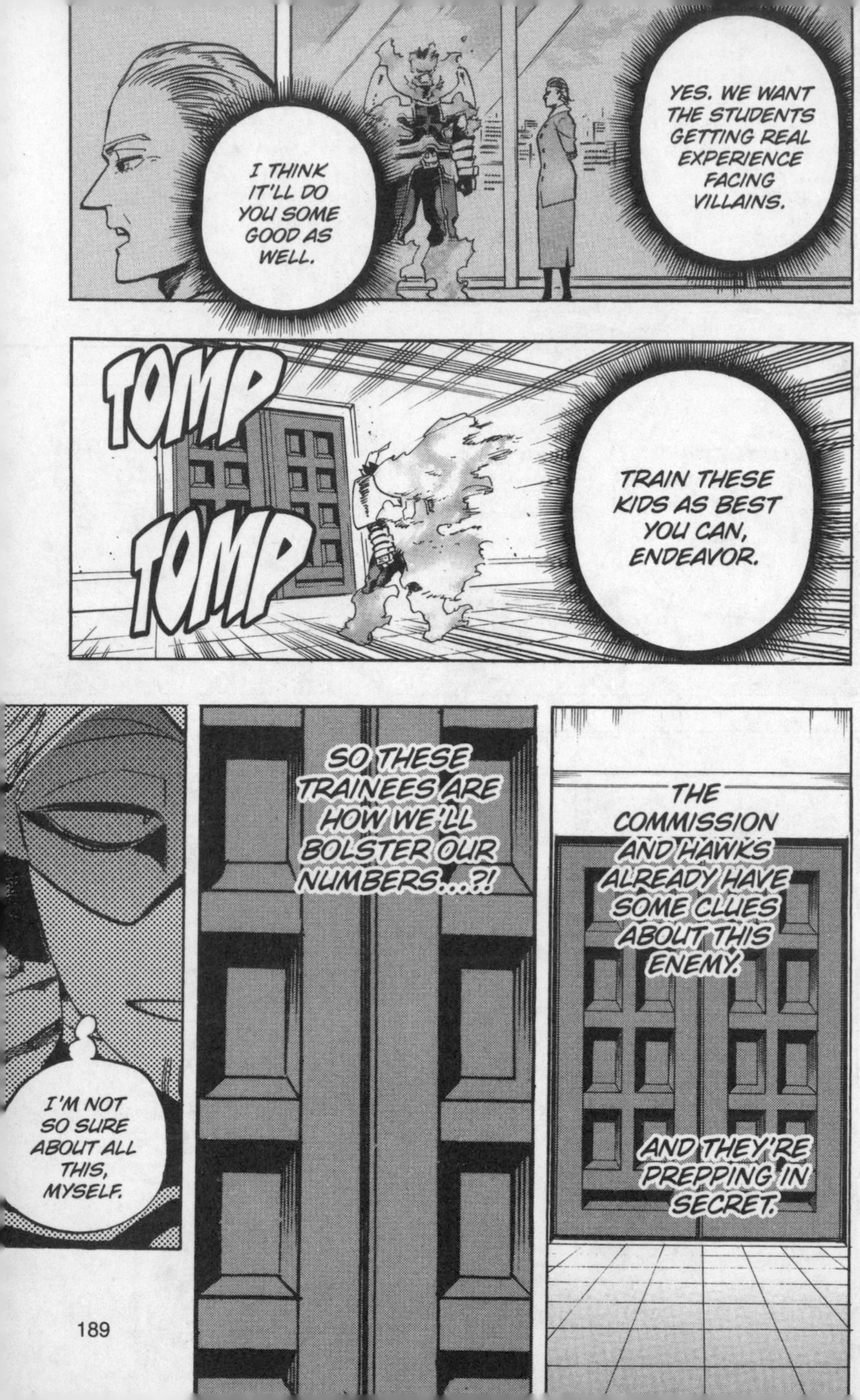
YES. WE WANT THE STUDENTS GETTING REAL EXPERIENCE FACING VILLAINS.
I THINK IT'LL DO YOU SOME GOOD AS WELL.
TRAIN THESE KIDS AS BEST YOU CAN, ENDEAVOR.
TOMP
TOMP
THE COMMISSION AND HAWKS ALREADY HAVE SOME CLUES ABOUT THIS ENEMY.
AND THEY'RE PREPPING IN SECRET.
SO THESE TRAINEES ARE HOW WE'LL BOLSTER OUR NUMBERS...?!
I'M NOT SO SURE ABOUT ALL THIS, MYSELF.

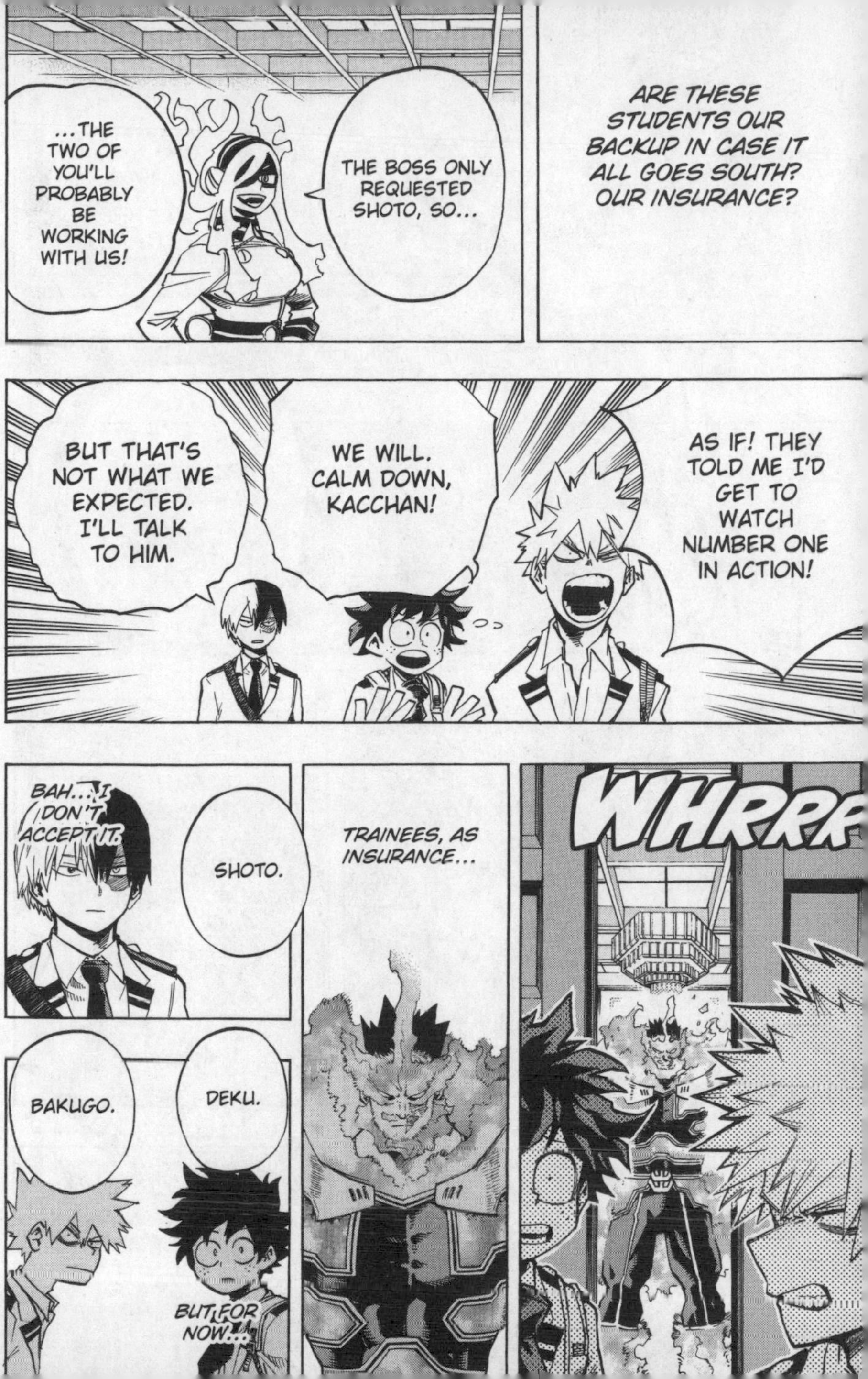
ARE THESE STUDENTS OUR BACKUP IN CASE IT ALL GOES SOUTH? OUR INSURANCE?
THE BOSS ONLY REQUESTED SHOTO, SO...
...THE TWO OF YOU'LL PROBABLY BE WORKING WITH US!
AS IF! THEY TOLD ME I'D GET TO WATCH NUMBER ONE IN ACTION!
WE WILL. CALM DOWN, KACCHAN!
BUT THAT'S NOT WHAT WE EXPECTED. I'LL TALK TO HIM.
WHRR
TRAINEES, AS INSURANCE...
SHOTO.
BAH... I DON'T ACCEPT IT.
DEKU.
BAKUGO.
BUT FOR NOW...

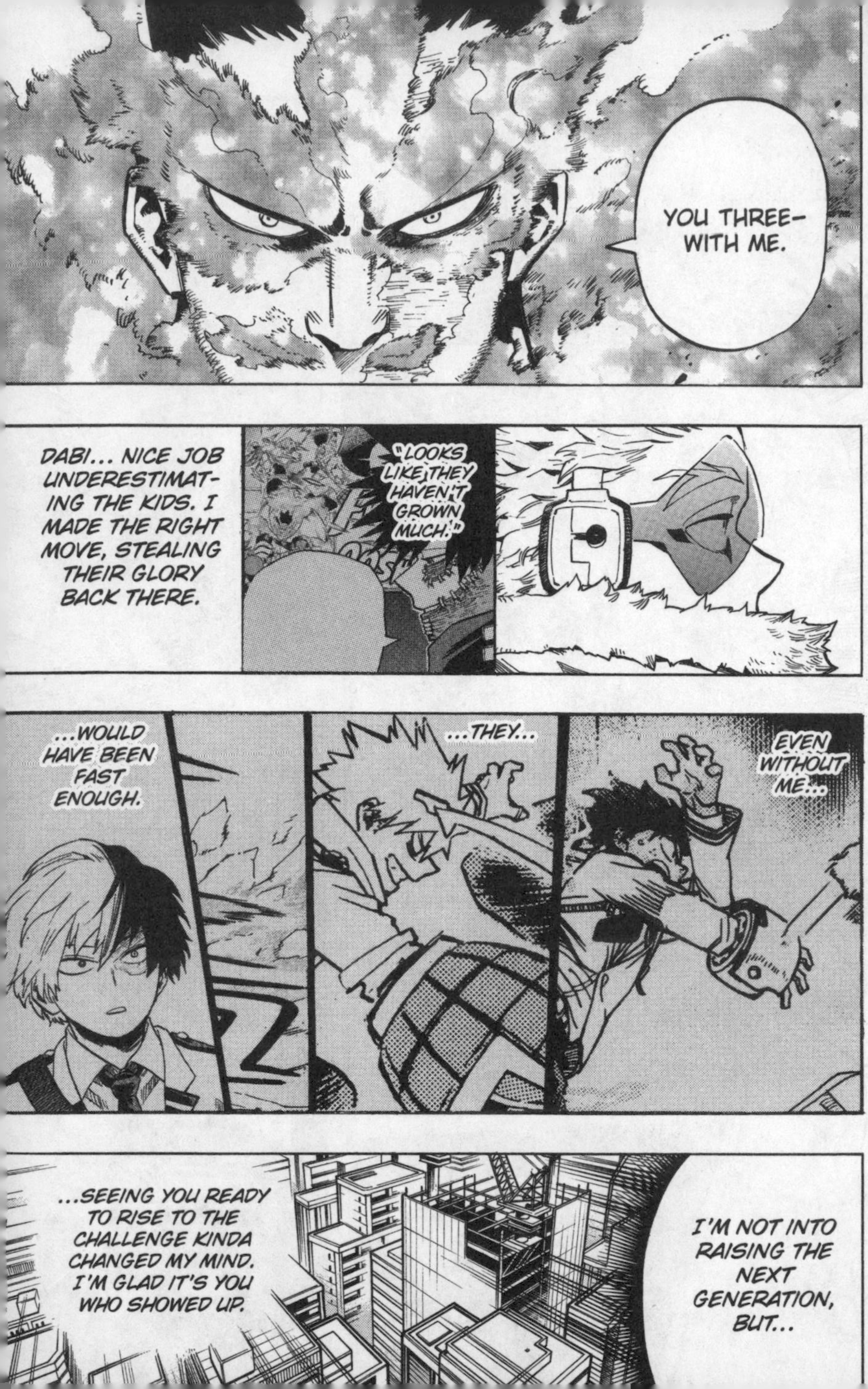
YOU THREE—WITH ME.
"LOOKS LIKE THEY HAVEN'T GROWN MUCH."
DABI... NICE JOB UNDERESTIMATING THE KIDS. I MADE THE RIGHT MOVE, STEALING THEIR GLORY BACK THERE.
EVEN WITHOUT ME...
...THEY...
...WOULD HAVE BEEN FAST ENOUGH.
I'M NOT INTO RAISING THE NEXT GENERATION, BUT...
...SEEING YOU READY TO RISE TO THE CHALLENGE KINDA CHANGED MY MIND. I'M GLAD IT'S YOU WHO SHOWED UP.

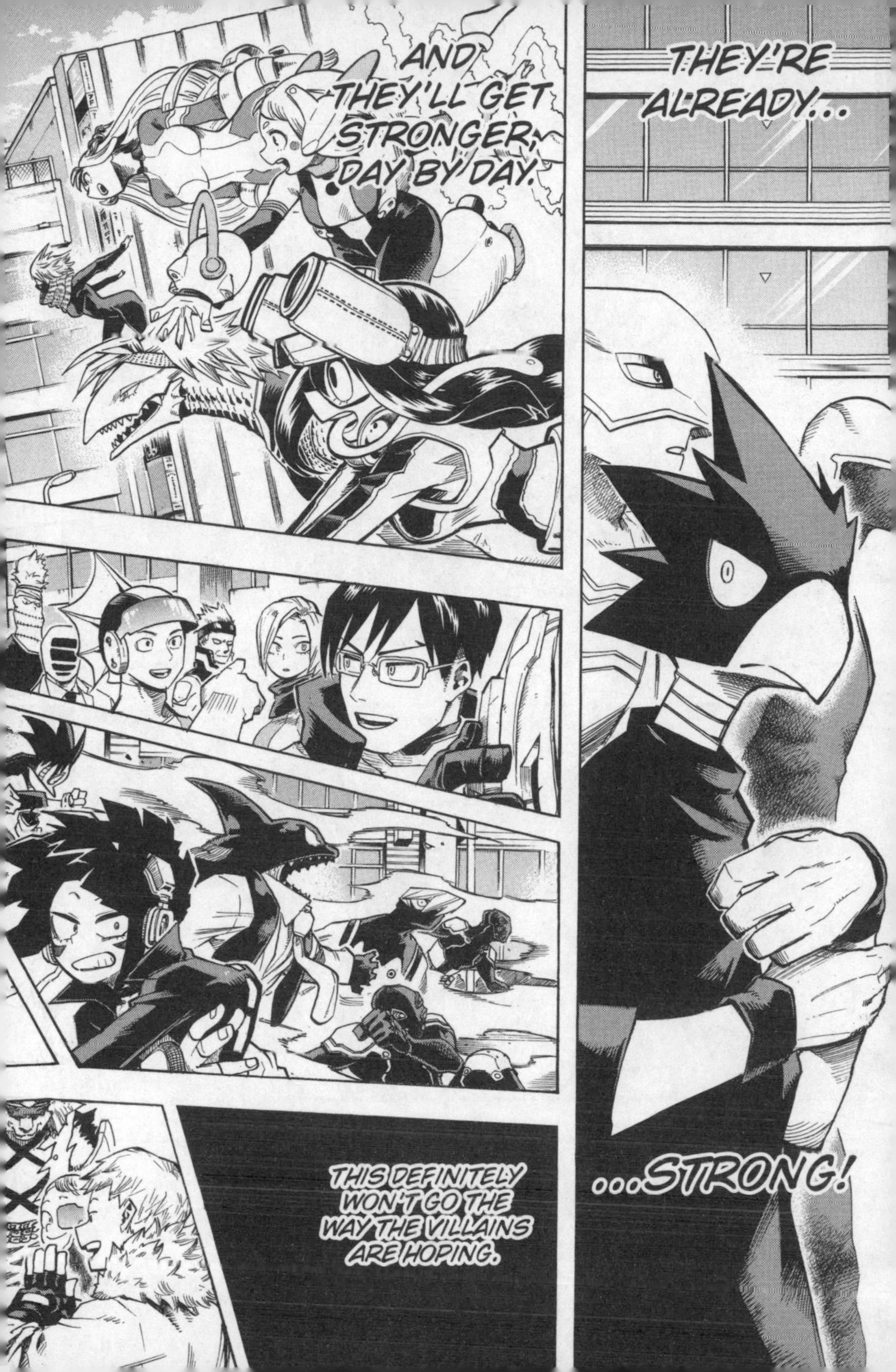
THEY'RE ALREADY...
...STRONG!
AND THEY'LL GET STRONGER, DAY BY DAY.
THIS DEFINITELY WON'T GO THE WAY THE VILLAINS ARE HOPING.

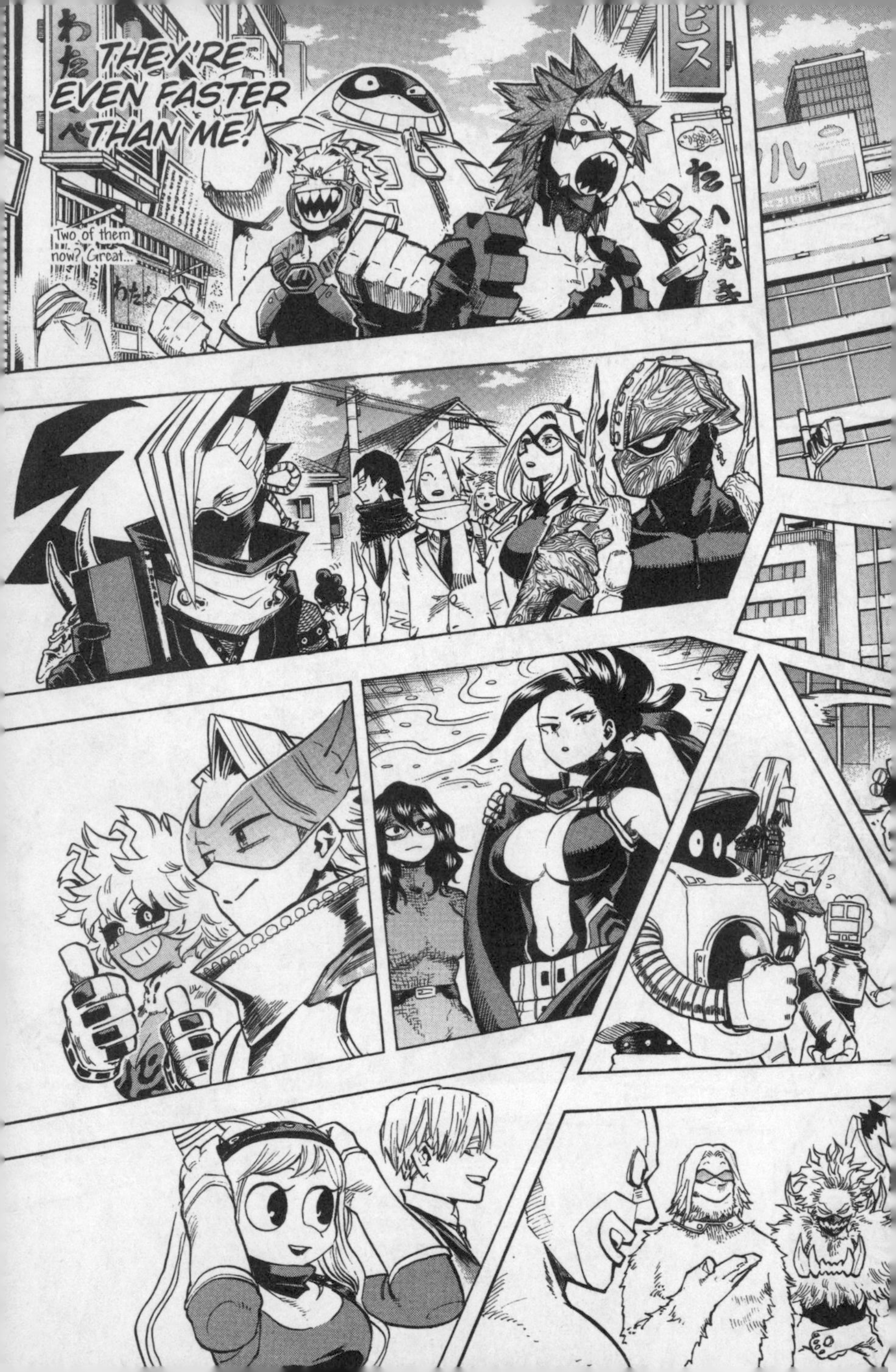
THEY'RE EVEN FASTER THAN ME!
Two of them now? Great...

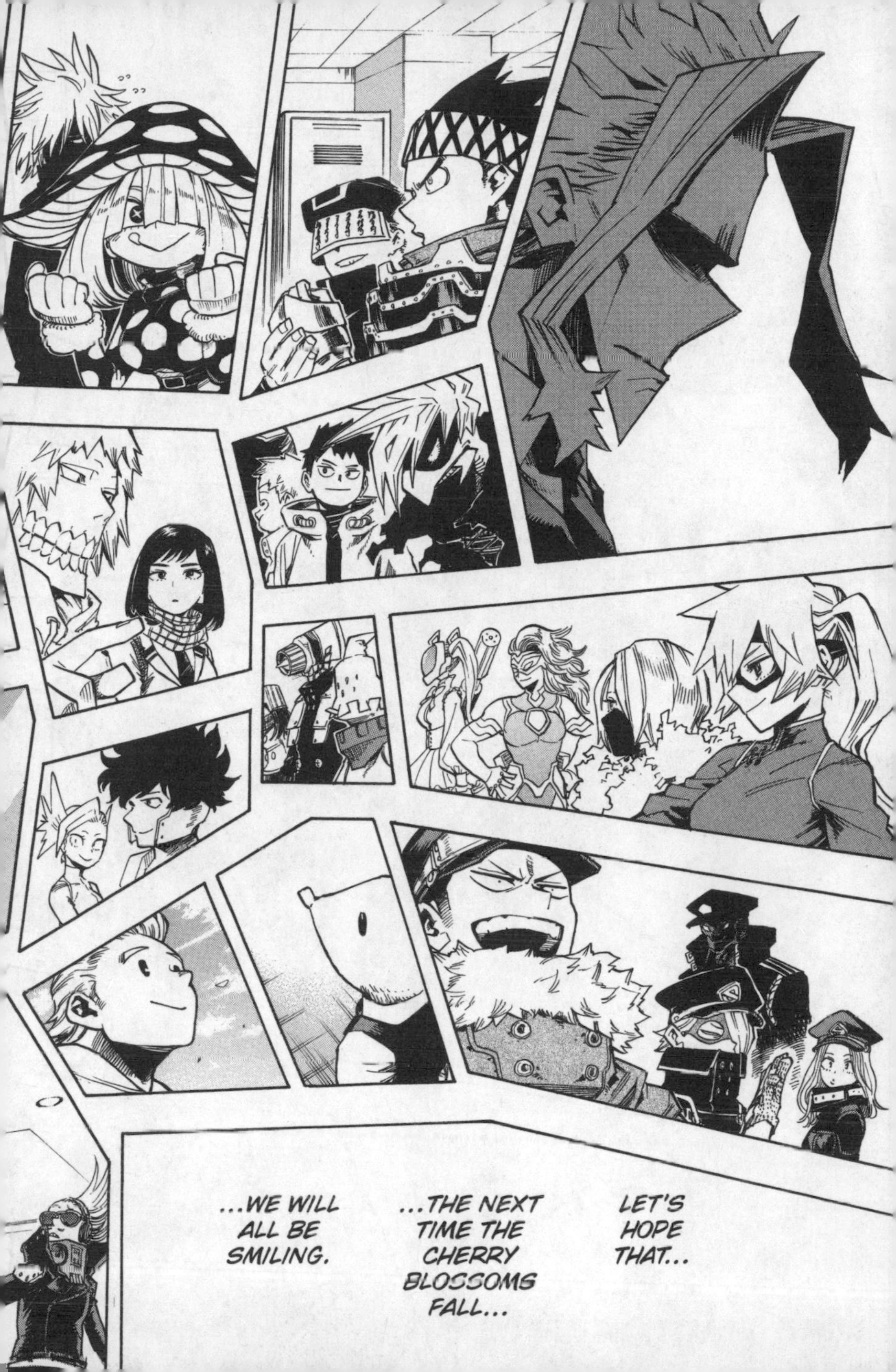
LET'S HOPE THAT...
...THE NEXT TIME THE CHERRY BLOSSOMS FALL...
...WE WILL ALL BE SMILING.

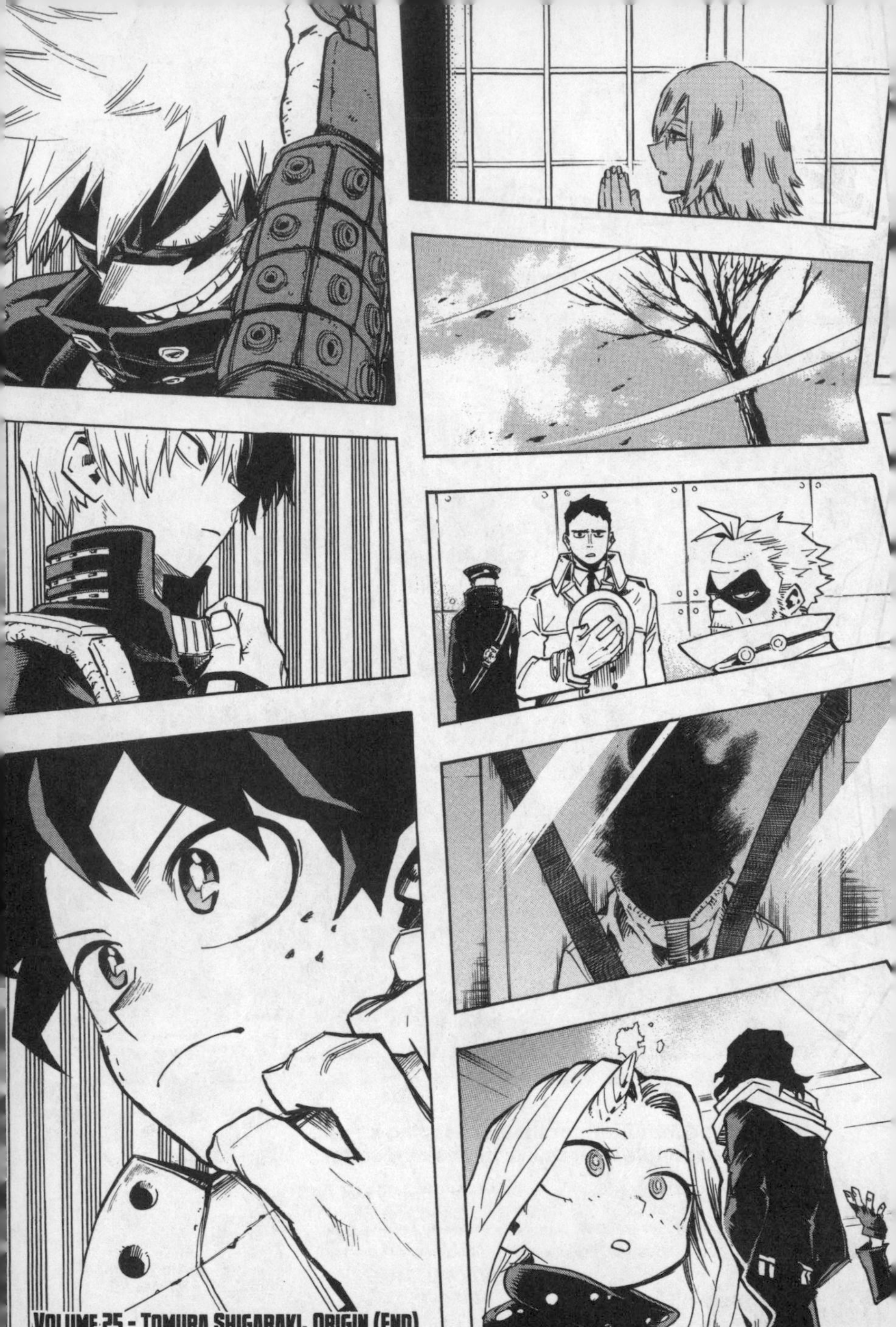

Volume 25 - Tomura Shigaraki: Origin (End)

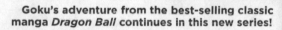

DEMON SLAYER
KIMETSU NO YAIBA

Story and Art by
KOYOHARU GOTOUGE

In Taisho-era Japan, kindhearted Tanjiro Kamado makes a living selling charcoal. But his peaceful life is shattered when a demon slaughters his entire family. His little sister Nezuko is the only survivor, but she has been transformed into a demon herself! Tanjiro sets out on a dangerous journey to find a way to return his sister to normal and destroy the demon who ruined his life.

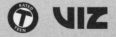

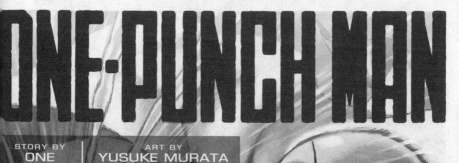
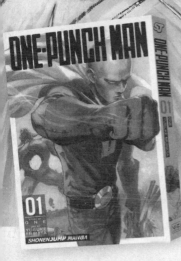

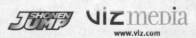

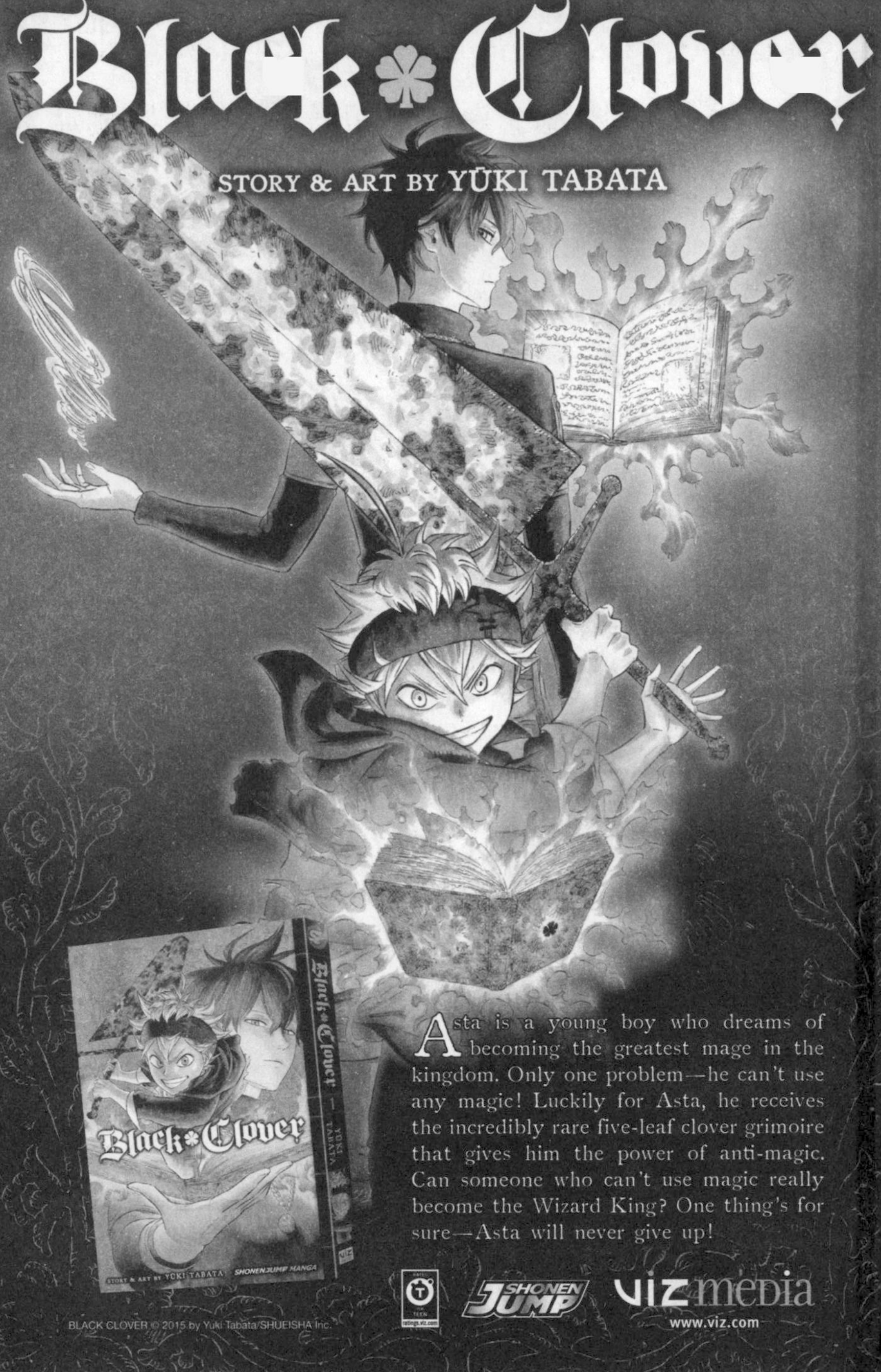
Black Clover
STORY & ART BY YŪKI TABATA
Asta is a young boy who dreams of becoming the greatest mage in the kingdom. Only one problem—he can't use any magic! Luckily for Asta, he receives the incredibly rare five-leaf clover grimoire that gives him the power of anti-magic. Can someone who can't use magic really become the Wizard King? One thing's for sure—Asta will never give up!
Black Clover
YŪKI TABATA
STORY & ART BY YUKI TABATA
SHONEN JUMP MANGA
SHONEN JUMP
VIZ media
www.viz.com
BLACK CLOVER © 2015 by Yuki Tabata/SHUEISHA Inc.

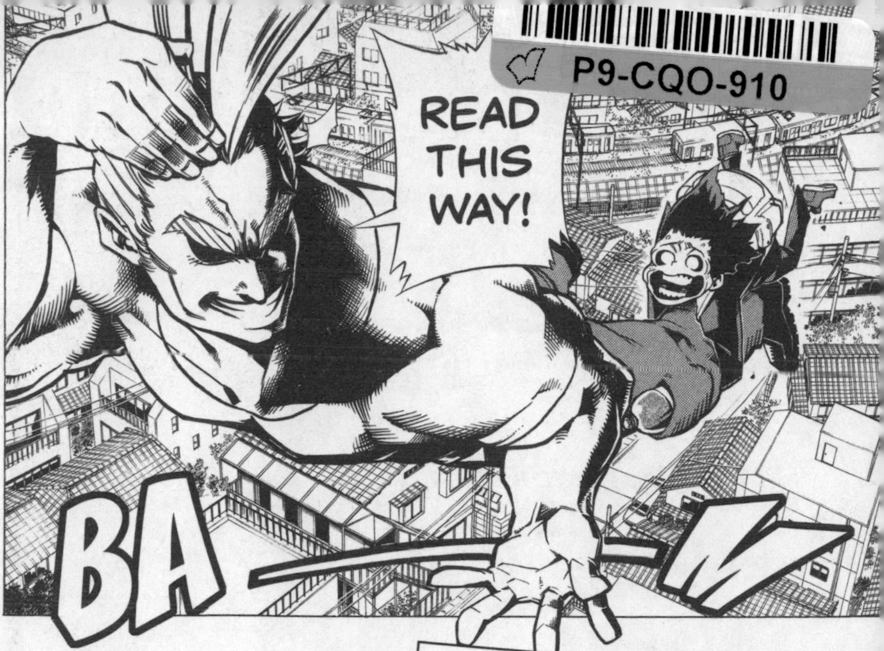
READ THIS WAY!
BA-M

MY HERO ACADEMIA

reads from right to left, starting in the upper-right corner. Japanese is read from right to left, meaning that action, sound effects and word-balloon order are completely reversed from English order.

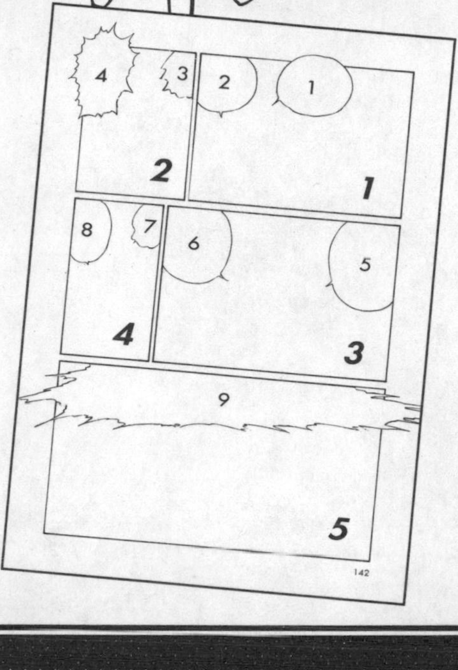
1
1
2
2
3
4
3
5
6
4
7
8
5
9
142